Our 50 States

Mary Evelyn Notgrass McCurdy

NOTGRASS
HISTORY

Dedicated with love to Nate,
my brave woodsman,
and to Clara, Wesley, Peter, and Thomas.
I am very blessed. -MEM

Our 50 States
by Mary Evelyn Notgrass McCurdy
© 2020 Notgrass History.
All rights reserved.

ISBN 978-1-60999-149-4

Cover and interior design by Mary Evelyn Notgrass McCurdy

Cover image: Wasatch Mountains in Utah by Johnny Adolphson / Shutterstock.com

Printed in the United States of America

NOTGRASS
HISTORY
975 Roaring River Road
Gainesboro, TN 38562
1-800-211-8793
www.notgrass.com

Table of Contents

Introduction

Letter to Parents and Students i
Author's Thanks.................................ii
How to Use Our 50 States iii

New England

Unit 1...1
Lessons 1 and 2 - Maine
Lessons 3 and 4 - New Hampshire

Unit 2.......................................19
Lessons 5 and 6 - Vermont
Lessons 7 and 8 - Massachusetts

Unit 3.......................................37
Lessons 9 and 10 - Rhode Island
Lessons 11 and 12 - Connecticut

Mid-Atlantic

Unit 4.......................................55
Lessons 13 and 14 - New York
Lessons 15 and 16 - Pennsylvania

Unit 5.......................................73
Lessons 17 and 18 - New Jersey
Lessons 19 and 20 - Delaware

Unit 6.......................................91
Lessons 21 and 22 - Maryland
Lessons 23 and 24 - Washington, D.C.

South

Unit 7....................................109
Lessons 25 and 26 - Virginia
Lessons 27 and 28 - West Virginia

Unit 8....................................127
Lessons 29 and 30 - Kentucky
Lessons 31 and 32 - Tennessee

Unit 9....................................145
Lessons 33 and 34 - North Carolina
Lessons 35 and 36 - South Carolina

Unit 10..................................163
Lessons 37 and 38 - Georgia
Lessons 39 and 40 - Alabama

Unit 11..................................181
Lessons 41 and 42 - Mississippi
Lessons 43 and 44 - Arkansas

Unit 12..................................199
Lessons 45 and 46 - Louisiana
Lessons 47 and 48 - Florida

Midwest

Unit 13....................................217
Lessons 49 and 50 - Michigan
Lessons 51 and 52 - Ohio

Unit 14....................................235
Lessons 53 and 54 - Indiana
Lessons 55 and 56 - Illinois

Unit 15....................................253
Lessons 57 and 58 - Wisconsin
Lessons 59 and 60 - Minnesota

Unit 16....................................271
Lessons 61 and 62 - Iowa
Lessons 63 and 64 - Missouri

Unit 17....................................289
Lessons 65 and 66 - Kansas
Lessons 67 and 68 - Nebraska

Unit 18....................................307
Lessons 69 and 70 - South Dakota
Lessons 71 and 72 - North Dakota

Rocky Mountain

Unit 19....................................325
Lessons 73 and 74 - Montana
Lessons 75 and 76 - Idaho

Unit 20....................................343
Lessons 77 and 78 - Wyoming
Lessons 79 and 80 - Colorado

Unit 21....................................361
Lessons 81 and 82 - Utah
Lessons 83 and 84 - Nevada

Southwest

Unit 22....................................379
Lessons 85 and 86 - Oklahoma
Lessons 87 and 88 - Texas

Unit 23....................................399
Lessons 89 and 90 - New Mexico
Lessons 91 and 92 - Arizona

Pacific

Unit 24....................................417
Lessons 93 and 94 - California
Lessons 95 and 96 - Oregon

Unit 25....................................435
Lessons 97 and 98 - Washington
Lessons 99 and 100 - Alaska

Hawaii and U.S. Territories

Unit 26....................................453
Lessons 101 and 102 - Hawaii
Lessons 103 and 104 - U.S. Territories

Sources 471
Image Credits 476
Index..486

Dear Parents and Students,

Many years ago, God created the land that became America. God has used ice and wind, floods and droughts, volcanoes and ocean waves to shape this place we call home. You are about to visit many of God's amazing creations through the pages of this book. People have built homes, cities, mounds, monuments, railroads, factories, parks, and bridges on what God has made.

You are about to visit many of those sites through the stories on these pages. You are about to read about many people who have helped to make our country great.

You are about to be inspired to follow their examples and make our country even better—for today and for the future.

Enjoy your journey through *Our 50 States*.

Mary Evelyn Notgrass McCurdy
Gainesboro, Tennessee
July 2020

Parental Supervision

Please review the Family Activities and Hands-On Ideas and discuss with your child what he or she may do alone and what activities need your supervision. The activities include the use of scissors, knives, the oven, the microwave, and the stove. Some children may be allergic to recipe ingredients or craft supplies. Notgrass History cannot accept responsibility for the safety of your child in completing these activities. Thank you for being a conscientious parent who takes responsibility for your child's safety.

Author's Thanks

Thank you, Nate McCurdy, for washing lots of dishes and reading lots of books to our kids and changing lots of diapers and doing lots of other things so that we could develop this curriculum. Thanks for cheering me on. Thank you for creating the beautiful maps for the curriculum. And thank you for asking me to marry you.

Thanks, sweet kids, for your patience as I worked on this project. Clara, you're a great proofreader! Thank you all for helping test out the Family Activity ideas. Wesley, you're so artistic. Peter and Thomas, I'll race you to the sandbox.

Thank you to my parents, Ray and Charlene Notgrass, for homeschooling me and for taking me to 48 states before I became an adult. Thank you for helping me to love Jesus, to love history, to love travel, and to love America. Thanks, Ma, for all your great ideas through the development process. Thank you both for editing the lessons and for your encouragement.

Thank you, Donna Ellenburg, for your wonderful and creative contributions to the Family Activities. Thank you for proofreading and double-checking and finding pictures and all those other details you took care of.

Thank you, Olive Wagar, for helping select the literature titles and helping with research and proofreading. Thank you, Dena Russell, for helping with research, for proofreading, and for your overall development ideas.

Thank you, Titus Anderson, for lending your great musical talent to the audio recordings. Thank you, John Notgrass, for helping with so many technical details. Thank you, Phil Ellenburg, for checking the maps and proofing the lessons. Thank you, Josh Voorhees, for answering everyone's questions about these books. Go, team!

Thank you, Cindy Rhodes, Ron Daise, David and Jamie Cromley, Dean Buchanan Gregorec, Jeffrey Blackburn, Bob Dixson, and Mark Sperry for sharing your stories with me and allowing me to include them in this book.

Thank you, Heavenly Father, for deciding where and when I should live and for putting me right here, right now with these people as a part of my life.

—*Mary Evelyn*

How to Use Our 50 States

Our 50 States is a one-year American geography course designed for students in grades one through four. The curriculum has 26 units with four lessons each. Each unit covers two states (plus Washington, D.C., and the U.S. Territories). We recommend completing one unit most weeks.

The lessons are grouped by region. The curriculum begins in New England and the lessons take students across the country through the Mid-Atlantic, South, Midwest, Rocky Mountain, Southwest, and Pacific regions. It is fine to switch the order of the regions around if you are planning a trip to a certain region or have some other special reason to study certain states at a certain time. The lessons stand alone and do not necessarily have to be completed in a particular order.

Our 50 States is much more than geography. You can also use this curriculum as all or part of your history, literature, creative writing, music, art, and handwriting practice. You may find that eliminating busywork in an entirely separate subject and allowing that subject to be incorporated into this study makes for a less stressful, more engaging, more memorable school year. All of the instructions for what to do each day are included in the blue Activities box at the end of each lesson.

How Does This Curriculum Work?

Parents can read the lessons aloud or students can read the lessons alone. We encourage you to enjoy looking closely at the pictures and talk about them.

This curriculum has two lessons about each state. The first lesson introduces the students to special features in that state, such as key crops, amazing natural wonders, and fascinating historic sites. The second lesson features a song that reflects the history or culture of the state. After you listen to the song, you will enjoy reading a story about a person or place connected to the state you are studying.

The first lesson for each state includes a map of that state with certain cities, sites, and geographic features labeled. These are not necessarily the largest cities or all of the most famous places. They are the sites that the two lessons discuss about that state. As you read the lessons, you will see certain words **in green**. When you come to a **green word**, look at the map at the beginning of the lesson and find that location on the map.

At the end of each lesson is a blue box with activity ideas. Don't think of these as a checklist that you must complete. Look at these as ideas to enhance your study. Let your student's grade, age, abilities, needs, and interests be your guide as you select activities. The activities should challenge your student, but he or she should also feel competent and successful.

Each state has activities to complete in the *Atlas Workbook*, questions to answer in the *Lesson Review*, a simple Hands-On Idea, and a creative writing prompt. The Activities box also includes instructions on when to read each chapter in the literature titles (see more about literature on pages vi-vii). Each unit also includes one Family Activity. These activities include recipes, crafts, and other projects.

Song Selections

The songs included in *Our 50 States* reflect a variety of styles and historic time periods. With the exception of "Deh Wod Been Deh," "It Happened In Sun Valley," "Smokey the Bear," and some original tunes written by Titus Anderson, the songs included in *Our 50 States* are in the public domain. When you come to a song, visit notgrass.com/50songs to listen to a recording of the song while you read along with the lyrics in the book. We were unable to find the historic music for a few of the selections, so Titus Anderson composed tunes for those pieces. A few of the selections were originally published as poems, so Titus composed tunes for those as well.

Family Activities

Each unit includes a Family Activity idea that is connected with one of the lessons in that unit. The instructions are on the last page or pages of each unit. We recommend reading the instructions and gathering the supplies early each week. You can complete the activity on the day it is assigned or on another day that is convenient. Many of these activities are designed with the whole family in mind.

Like all components of *Our 50 States*, the Family Activities are optional. We offer them as extra learning experiences, but do not feel obligated to do them if they do not suit your family's needs or schedule.

Atlas Workbook

After students have read the first lesson for each state, they will complete an illustration in the *Atlas Workbook* that pictures a geographic term mentioned in the lesson. Each of these illustrations is already started for the students to help them build confidence in their drawing skills. After students complete the basic outlines of the illustration, they are free to add their own details and color the illustration.

After they have read the second lesson for a state, students will complete a map activities page for that state in the *Atlas Workbook*. Activities such as coloring illustrations on the map, tracing along rivers, and drawing mountain symbols within a mountain range will help reinforce the geographical, cultural, and historical information the student has learned about that state. Each student studying *Our 50 States* should have his or her own personal *Atlas Workbook*. We suggest using pencils and high-quality colored pencils to complete the activities in the *Atlas Workbook*.

Lesson Review

The *Lesson Review* has five questions about each state and one or two tests for each region (approximately one test every three weeks). The *Lesson Review* is designed primarily for the older students studying this course. It is designed so that students can write their answers directly in the book. It is perfectly fine to use these as discussion questions (especially for younger students), or not to use them at all. It is up to you as the parent to know the best way for your child to retain and enjoy the material. To prepare for the tests, students can look over the review questions for the last three units and also look at the regional map on the inside front cover of *Our 50 States*.

Creative Writing Notebook

If you plan on your child completing the creative writing ideas, we suggest you provide a notebook specifically for that purpose. There are 52 writing prompts in the curriculum, one for each state, plus Washington, D.C., and the U.S. Territories. Each prompt ties into a topic discussed in the story for the state you are studying.

If your child is not ready for creative writing, you can simply discuss the ideas presented in the prompts. You could also have your child draw a picture that illustrates his or her thoughts. A few of the prompts have an alternate activity idea that does not involve writing.

Answer Key and Literature Guide

This booklet for parents contains answers for the review questions and tests in the *Lesson Review*. It also includes a guide for the literature titles.

Literature

Seven suggested literature titles complement the lessons in *Our 50 States*. Each book corresponds to one of the regions in the curriculum. All of the titles are in print and available from Notgrass History and many other sources (with the exception of *Philip of Texas*, which we republished and is not widely available elsewhere).

You can read these titles aloud with your student, which is a fun and memorable way to spend time together. You can have your child read the books independently. You might decide to do a combination, depending on your family's schedule.

Each chapter in each literature title is assigned in the blue Activities box at the end of each lesson. These assignments are merely a suggested guide to help you finish the title while you are studying the corresponding region. You might prefer to read that region's book over a single weekend or on a road trip. The exact time you read each title does not matter, except that we do recommend you read it while you are studying the corresponding region. There are a few lessons without literature assignments when a region has more lessons than there are chapters in the corresponding book.

Each book offers an enjoyable way to learn more about a region, but if reading the literature adds too much pressure to your homeschool schedule, feel free to skip some or all of them.

Rabbit Hill by Robert Lawson (New England, Units 1-3)
The Cabin Faced West by Jean Fritz (Mid-Atlantic, Units 4-6)
Soft Rain by Cornelia Cornelissen (South, Units 7-12)
The Story of George Washington Carver by Eva Moore (Midwest, Units 13-18)
The Trumpet of the Swan by E. B. White (Rocky Mountain, Units 19-21)
Philip of Texas by James Otis (Southwest, Units 22-23)
The Adventures of Paddy the Beaver by Thornton W. Burgess (Pacific, Units 24-26)

 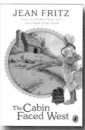     

We at Notgrass History chose these books carefully with great consideration of content. Some of them do have themes or dialogue that we want you to be aware of before you hand it to your child to read. You can find comments about this content in the *Answer Key and Literature Guide*.

For suggestions about additional or replacement literature titles (including some picture books), visit notgrass.com/50links.

How Much Time Will Each Lesson Take?

If you are reading the lessons aloud, each one should take under 15 minutes to read. Answering the questions in the *Lesson Review* should not take more than five or ten minutes. The time it takes for a student to complete the geographic term illustrations in the *Atlas Workbook* will vary greatly depending on the child's attention to detail. The time it takes for a student to complete the map activities in the *Atlas Workbook* will also vary, but 15 minutes should be enough time for most students. Beyond that, the amount of time you invest will depend on the additional activities you choose.

Reading the literature will add some time, but if you follow the reading plan in the blue Activities boxes, you will only read one or two chapters from a literature title each day. If you do all of the suggested activities, we suggest planning on an hour to an hour and a half per lesson on average (not including the Family Activities, which will require additional time). You can use *Our 50 States* four days per week, or spread the lessons and activities over all five days of your school week. The curriculum has a total of 104 lessons divided into 26 units.

What Supplies Will My Student Need?

Students will need a pencil and colored pencils. You will need a smartphone, tablet, or computer to listen to the audio versions of each of the songs. The simple Hands-On Ideas use common items such as play dough, building bricks or blocks, and rocks you might find in your yard. Most Family Activities require additional supplies. You can access a complete supply list at notgrass.com/50links. The individual Family Activity instruction pages at the end of the units also list supplies needed.

How Many Activities Should My Student Complete?

You know best what your student is capable of accomplishing. Some students will benefit most from completing all of the activity ideas. Others will do better completing only some of them. The variety of activities is intended to make it easy for your student to have a positive, rich, and engaging learning experience. You should not feel pressure to complete every assignment.

Helping Struggling Students

For students who struggle with reading or writing, feel free to make adjustments to help them be successful and not become frustrated. You or an older sibling can read the lessons and literature aloud. Struggling students might also benefit from reading aloud to you. You can alter, shorten, or orally complete writing activities and review questions. You can also eliminate them if you feel your student is not ready.

Using Our 50 States with Multiple Ages

Our 50 States is especially designed for first through fourth graders, but other ages can certainly benefit. Younger siblings can listen in on the lessons and literature, look at the pictures, and take part in the Hands-On Ideas and Family Activities. If you have a student who has already completed fourth grade, but you want to keep all your children learning together, you might consider giving your older student some additional assignments, such as copying the Bible verses at the end of the lessons, writing book reports about the literature titles, or researching and writing a report about some of the places or topics presented in the lessons. You can assign each child different activities, depending on his or her age and skill level.

Sample Walk-Through of Unit 1

Here is one way a family might use *Our 50 States* over one homeschool week. Ethan and Hannah Jones have three children. Walter is in 4th grade, Emma is in 2nd grade, and Sam is four years old.

Monday: Hannah and her three children gather on the couch. Hannah opens to Unit 1 and reads aloud "Lesson 1: Maine." Walter and Emma take turns finding the locations written in green on the map at the beginning of the lesson. After they have read the lesson, Walter opens the *Lesson Review* to the questions about Maine. He reads them aloud and they all talk about the answers. Walter writes the answers in the book. Before they go to the table, they scatter around the living room and all pretend to be statues in various positions (which is the Hands-On Idea for the day since the lesson talks about the statue on top of the Maine State House).

At the table, Walter and Emma each open their own *Atlas Workbook*. They both complete the illustration for the geographic term *coast*.

At bedtime Ethan reads aloud the first chapter of *Rabbit Hill* to the family.

Tuesday: In the morning, Walter and Emma help Hannah make blueberry muffins for breakfast, which is the Family Activity for the week. Ethan and Sam do their part of the Family Activity by helping to eat the muffins!

When it is time for school, Hannah and the children gather on the couch again. Hannah pulls up the audio recording of "A Trip to the Grand Banks" on her phone and they all listen to it together as they read along with the lyrics in "Lesson 2: A Song and Story of Maine." Hannah reads aloud the true story about Mary and her summer on Boon Island where her grandfather was a lighthouse keeper. After the lesson, they read the creative writing prompt and have a discussion about what it is like to visit their grandparents every summer.

At the table, Walter and Emma complete the map activities for Maine in their *Atlas Workbooks*. They each pull out their creative writing notebooks and Walter writes three paragraphs about visiting his grandparents. Emma writes three sentences and draws a picture of the tree with a tire swing at their grandparents' house.

Wednesday: The kids all have checkups at the doctor in the morning, so there isn't much time for school. They weren't able to read any of *Rabbit Hill* on Tuesday, so Ethan reads two chapters aloud to the children before they go to bed.

Thursday: Hannah and the children gather and she reads aloud "Lesson 3: New Hampshire." They complete the questions in the *Lesson Review* the same way they did on Monday. While the children are working on their geographic term illustrations in their *Atlas Workbooks*, Hannah gathers some quarters from her purse and the coin jar on the counter. After the children are finished with their illustrations, they study the quarters to see how many different state quarters they can find (which is the Hands-On Idea for the day since the lesson talks about the New Hampshire state quarter).

Friday: Hannah and her children enjoy listening to "New Hampshire Hills" and learning about how workers built a road to the top of Mount Washington in New Hampshire. They also learn that tent companies test their tent designs on the mountain to see if the tents can stand up to the high winds there. Walter and Emma complete the map activities for New Hampshire in their *Atlas Workbooks*. They listen to "New Hampshire Hills" again while they work. In his creative writing notebook, Walter writes the script for a commercial describing his design for a new tent. Emma draws a picture of a new tent design in her notebook. Hannah draws a picture of a tent on a piece of paper for Sam to color.

After supper the Jones family uses sheets, blankets, and dining room chairs to make a tent in the living room. They all get inside and Ethan reads aloud chapter 4 of *Rabbit Hill*.

Respect for All

We at Notgrass History make every effort to write about all people in an honoring and respectful way. We realize that people have different views and preferences when it comes to describing groups such as Native Americans and African Americans. We believe that God has created all people in His own image and that they all have equal value in His sight. We have prayerfully sought to use terminology that honors and respects everyone.

Encouragement for the Journey

Remember that God designed your family and the daily responsibilities you carry. A homeschooling mother who has one child can complete more activities than a homeschooling mother who has seven children and an elderly grandparent living in her home. God will use the efforts of both of these mothers. God does not expect you to do more than you can do. Be kind to yourself. He knows exactly what you and your children need this year. We encourage you to pray about your family's experience using *Our 50 States*. Let it be a tool to help you have a wonderful learning experience with your children.

Remember that out of all the parents in the world to whom He could have given your children, He chose you. He is the one who put your family together. He knows what He is doing. Trust in His choice. God created you. He created your children. Relax and remember that this is the day that the Lord has made. Rejoice and be glad in it (Psalm 118:24)!

We at Notgrass History are here to help you. If you have questions or simply need some encouragement, send us an email (help@notgrass.com) or give us a call (1-800-211-8793).

Portland Headlight, Maine

Unit 1
New England:
Maine and New Hampshire

Fort Fairfield

Penobscot
Acadia National Park
Augusta ★
Rockland
Mount Desert Island
Atlantic Ocean
Westbrook

Boon Island

Climb on the rocks along the coast of Maine and feel the salty spray of the ocean. Pick an island to explore. There are plenty to choose from. Maine has over 4,600! Keep your eyes open as you travel the countryside. You might see a moose. Drink in the beautiful sight of lupines blooming along the roadsides. Find Maine on the map at the beginning of this book. (As you read each lesson, find the locations **written in green** on the green state map at the beginning of the lesson.)

Lupine

Moose

Trees

Almost all of Maine is covered with trees. The Wabanaki people once used the trees of Maine to make tools, build houses, and create birch bark canoes. Europeans who came to the area used the tall, straight trees to make masts for ships.

Maine woods

Maine's first paper mill opened in **Westbrook** in the early 1700s. The mill used old cloth rags to make paper. In the 1800s, people developed a way to make paper using wood. Paper manufacturers grind up the wood and turn it into wet pulp. They spread out the pulp on a mesh screen, where it dries and becomes paper. Since Maine has so many trees, many companies have built paper mills in the state.

Maine paper mill in the 1990s

Potato field in Maine

Potatoes

In the 1940s, Maine grew more potatoes than any other state. Other states now grow more, but potatoes are still an important part of farming in Maine. Almost half of Maine's potatoes become french fries.

Fort Fairfield celebrates potatoes each summer with the Maine Potato Blossom Festival. Would you rather participate in the festival's potato picking race or let people watch you wrestle your friend in a pool of mashed potatoes?

Wild Blueberries

The soil and climate in Maine are perfect for growing wild blueberries. Maine has over 44,000 acres where wild blueberries grow. Since the berries grow wild, they require little maintenance from farmers. Many farms allow people to come and pick their own.

Wild blueberries

Lobsters

People catch more lobsters in Maine than in any other state. In fact, Maine has more lobsters than anywhere else in the world. Every year thousands of people enjoy the Maine Lobster Festival in **Rockland**. When the festival began in 1947, people could buy all the lobster they could eat for $1!

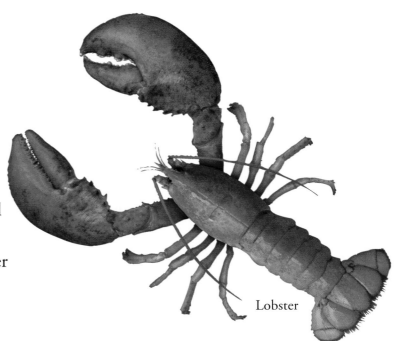

Lobster

Acadia National Park

Mount Desert Island is the largest island off the coast of Maine. The island is part of Acadia National Park. The highest point on the island is Cadillac Mountain. From this point, between October and March, people on Cadillac Mountain are the first ones in the country to see the sunrise. Peregrine falcons, moose, foxes, seals, and many other animals live in Acadia. People call the park the "crown jewel of the North Atlantic coast."

Peregrine falcon

Cadillac Mountain

Capital: Augusta

The Maine State House stands in **Augusta**. Workers completed the original building in 1832. In the early 1900s, the state made the building larger. During that construction project, William Clark Noble heard that there wasn't enough money to pay for a nice statue to go on top of the dome. Mr. Noble couldn't bear the thought of that. He wanted Maine's state house to have the best.

As a boy, William Noble had enjoyed making clay figures using mud from a creek near his Maine home. When he grew up, he became a famous sculptor. Mr. Noble donated his time and talents to design *Lady of Wisdom*, a beautiful statue that now stands on the Maine State House dome.

Lady of Wisdom

Maine State House

Make your ear
attentive to wisdom,
Incline your heart
to understanding.
Proverbs 2:2

Activities

- Illustrate the geographic term for Maine in the *Atlas Workbook* (page 4).

- If you are using the *Lesson Review*, answer the questions for Maine (page 1).

- Read chapter 1 in *Rabbit Hill*. (Parents, please refer to page 15 in the *Answer Key and Literature Guide* for comments about this book.)

- Hands-On Idea: Pretend to be statues. Who or what do your statues represent?

- Family Activity: Make Blueberry Muffins (recipe on page 18).

A Trip to the Grand Banks

Amos Hanson of Penobscot, *Maine, worked as a fisherman all his life. In this song, which he wrote some time before 1890, he celebrates the fishermen of New England who traveled to the Grand Banks of Newfoundland, Canada, to fish each summer. (notgrass.com/50songs, Track 1)*

Early in the spring when the snow is all gone,
The Penobscot boys are anxious their money for to earn;
They'll fit out a fisherman a hundred tons or nigh,
For the Grand Banks of Newfoundland their luck for to try.

Sailing down the river, the weather being fine,
Our families and friends we leave far behind;
We pass the Sable Island as we have done before,
Where the waves dash tremendous on a storm-beaten shore.

We make for the shoals and we make for the rocks,
The hagduls and careys surround us in flocks;
We drop our best anchor where the waves run so high,
On the Grand Banks of Newfoundland for snapeyes to try.

Early in the morning before the break of day,
We jump into our dories and saw, saw away;
The snapeyes steal our bait and we shout and we rave,
And we say if we get home again we'll give up the trade.

Our salt is all wet but one half a pen,
Our colors we will show and the mainsail we will bend;
Wash her down, scrub the decks, and the dories we will stow,
Then it's haul up the anchor, to the westward we go.

Maine coast

Mary on Boon Island

Maine has 65 historic lighthouses along its rugged coast. Workers completed Maine's first lighthouse in 1791. Lighthouses have been an important part of Maine's culture ever since. Today lighthouses have automatic lights, but in their early days dedicated lighthouse keepers worked hard to keep the lights burning.

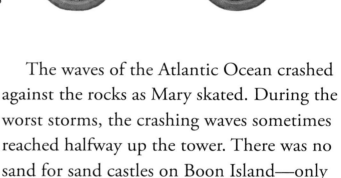

Ka-chunk, ka-chunk, ka-chunk, ka-chunk. Mary's roller skates made a rhythmic sound as she glided down the boardwalk on **Boon Island,** where she had come for the summer. The stone lighthouse that towered above her cast a shadow on her path. Inside that tower, 168 steps spiraled to the top. It was a long, hard climb, but the view was magnificent.

Boon Island

The waves of the Atlantic Ocean crashed against the rocks as Mary skated. During the worst storms, the crashing waves sometimes reached halfway up the tower. There was no sand for sand castles on Boon Island—only rocks. There were no trees—only rocks.

Mary's grandfather, William Williams, and his assistants worked hard to keep the lights burning in the top of the lighthouse. Otherwise, ships might not see the island in time. They might dash to pieces on the rocky shore. It had happened before. Mary's grandfather worked in all kinds of weather to try to keep it from happening again.

Boon Island could be a gloomy place. Mary's grandfather knew that flowers would brighten it up. Every spring he brought boxes and barrels of dirt from the mainland, seven miles away.

Mary helped plant and tend flowers and vegetables in the dirt Grandfather brought. She earned a penny for each caterpillar she picked off the plants. It

Caterpillar

made Mary sad when the winter storms washed all the dirt away, but she always looked forward to new gardens the next summer.

Thrift

At lunchtime, Mary ka-chunked and rolled her way back toward the house for lunch with her grandparents. They enjoyed eating their lunch on the rocks when the weather was nice. They ate lobsters and drank lemonade. Sometimes when they had guests from the mainland, Mary's grandmother made a delicious fish chowder.

Lemons

After lunch, Mary's grandfather took her to check on the lobster traps. Grandfather kept a trap for each of his grandchildren. The money they earned from the lobsters went directly into their bank accounts.

Mary's family had many stories of life on the island. There was the time one January when the temperature dipped to two degrees below zero. Ice became thick on the lighthouse and the other buildings on the island. Ice even blocked up the chimneys, and for a time they could not build a fire to keep warm. "It was the hardest night we ever passed," Grandfather said, "and no one slept on the island the entire night." Even though it was miserable, Grandfather said the sight of the island completely covered with ice was "one of the grandest sights" he had ever seen.

Icicles

8

One November, the food on the island was dwindling. Mary's grandfather didn't know what he and his assistants were going to eat on Thanksgiving. The stormy weather was sure to keep him from being able to spend the holiday with his family who was on the mainland.

The evening before Thanksgiving, Grandfather heard a terrific thud. Something had hit the lighthouse tower! He hurried outside. There on the ground lay eight ducks. The birds had all flown into the tower and fallen to the ground dead. Those ducks became their Thanksgiving dinner. Grandfather and his assistants thanked God for remembering them and sending them a Thanksgiving feast.

Faith was an important part of life for the Williams family. When the family was together on the island, they gathered every evening for a family worship service.

Mary learned about dedication from her grandfather. For 27 years Grandfather Williams was dedicated to his work on Boon Island, saving many lives as he kept the light burning.

O Lord God of hosts,
who is like You, O mighty Lord?
Your faithfulness also surrounds You.
You rule the swelling of the sea;
When its waves rise, You still them.
Psalm 89:8-9

Boon Island Light

Activities

- Complete the map activities for Maine in the *Atlas Workbook* (page 5).

- Read chapter 2 in *Rabbit Hill*.

- Now that you have read what it was like for Mary to visit her grandparents on Boon Island many years ago, think about what it is like when you visit your grandparents or other relatives. What do you eat? What do you play? How is the place where they live different from where you live? If you are keeping a creative writing notebook, write a detailed description of what it is like to visit those relatives.

Lesson 3: New Hampshire

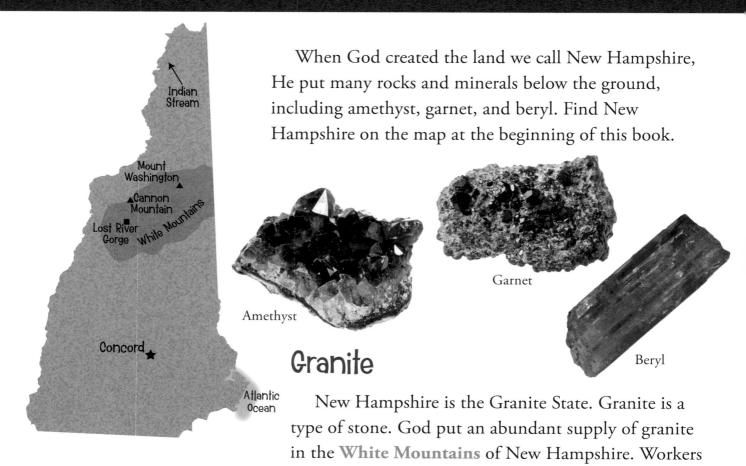

When God created the land we call New Hampshire, He put many rocks and minerals below the ground, including amethyst, garnet, and beryl. Find New Hampshire on the map at the beginning of this book.

Amethyst

Garnet

Beryl

Granite

New Hampshire is the Granite State. Granite is a type of stone. God put an abundant supply of granite in the White Mountains of New Hampshire. Workers at granite quarries cut slabs of granite out of the ground. People use New Hampshire granite to build walls and buildings and to make monuments, benches, and other objects. In the 1890s, workers used 30,000 tons of New Hampshire granite to build a Library of Congress building in Washington, D.C.

White Mountains

Republic of Indian Stream

When the United States was a young nation, we had a disagreement with Canada. Both countries claimed to own a small section of land near **Indian Stream** along our national border. The settlers in the area decided to take care of the issue themselves. In the summer of 1832, around sixty men from the community met in the

Old barn in former Indian Stream

local schoolhouse. They wrote a constitution, created laws, and declared themselves an independent nation: The Republic of Indian Stream. After about ten years, the United States and Canada finally came to an agreement about the land and signed a treaty. The treaty declared the land around Indian Stream to be part of the United States.

Old Man of the Mountain

New Hampshire's **Cannon Mountain** was once home to the Old Man of the Mountain, the rock formation pictured at right. People once came from far and wide to see the Old Man. The outline is on New Hampshire licence plates and on the New Hampshire state quarter. The shape is on road signs throughout the state. Sadly, the formation tumbled down the mountainside in 2003. Even though it is gone, the Old Man of the Mountain will always be part of New Hampshire.

Old Man of the Mountain

State quarter

Lost River Gorge

In 1852 two brothers, Royal and Lyman Jackman, went fishing in New Hampshire's Lost River. Suddenly Lyman disappeared into the ground below! The boy had fallen through a moss-covered hole and accidentally discovered a cave. He landed in a pool of water that came nearly to his waist. The two brothers quickly set out to explore the area and discovered several more caves together.

As the Lost River flows through New Hampshire, it disappears into a gorge that is partially filled with boulders. The river flows along, hidden beneath the rocks, until it emerges again and joins with another river.

Lost River Gorge

Today adventurous visitors can tour the boulder caves along the **Lost River Gorge**. To get through they have to be ready to crawl and scoot and waddle their way along. One of the caves has such a tight spot it's called the Lemon Squeezer.

Concord Coach

Capital: Concord

The city of **Concord** was once famous for making stagecoaches. The Concord Coach Company built fancy, top-of-the-line stagecoaches, such as the one at left. The coaches rumbled down the streets in Concord and across the roads of New England. Some of the coaches even took passengers and mail to the far away western part of the country. Back in the 1800s, a Concord Coach cost more than $1,000. That was a lot of money at a time when many people earned only $1 for a day's work.

12

Mount Washington

Mount Washington in New Hampshire is the tallest mountain in New England. It rises 6,288 feet higher than sea level (which is the level of the ocean). When people built a railroad through the White Mountains in the 1800s, businessmen saw it as a chance to make money. Once the railroad came in, tourists could easily reach the area by train to enjoy the beauty of the White Mountains. Getting those tourists to the top of Mount Washington was quite a job. In the next lesson, you will learn how crews took on the challenge of reaching the top.

> I will lift up my eyes to the mountains;
> From where shall my help come?
> My help comes from the Lord,
> Who made heaven and earth.
> Psalm 121:1-2

Activities

- Illustrate the geographic term for New Hampshire in the *Atlas Workbook* (page 6).
- If you are using the *Lesson Review*, answer the questions for New Hampshire (page 1).
- Read chapter 3 in *Rabbit Hill*.
- Hands-On Idea: Gather up some change at your house and see how many different state quarters you can find.

New Hampshire Hills

Susan F. Colby Colgate was born in New Hampshire in 1817. When she was a child, her father served in the New Hampshire House of Representatives. He later served as governor. Susan became a teacher and a poet. She wrote these words about her beloved state. (notgrass.com/50songs, Track 2)

New Hampshire hills! New Hampshire hills!
Ye homes of rocks and purling rills,
Of fir-trees, huge and high,
Rugged and rough against the sky,
With joy I greet your forms, once more
My native hills, beloved of yore.

New Hampshire hills! New Hampshire hills!
Sweet peace and health your air distills,
As fresh as when the earth was new,
And all the world was good and true;
Emblems ye are of royal state;
Majestic hills, bold, grand and great.

New Hampshire hills! New Hampshire hills!
Your presence every passion stills,
And hushed to peace I long to press
Far up your heights of loveliness,
And stand, the world beneath my feet,
Where earth and heaven enraptured meet.

Swift River

Reaching the Top

General David O. Macomber had ideas. He had grand ideas. He had the grand idea of building a road to take visitors to the top of Mount Washington in New Hampshire. Building the road would be a challenge. It would be expensive, but General Macomber wanted to do it.

By the mid-1800s, tourists traveling through New Hampshire were already visiting Mount Washington. However, they only had two choices for how they could reach the top. They could climb the mountain on foot, or they could ride a horse up the Glen Bridle Path. General Macomber wanted visitors to be able to reach the top more easily.

In 1853 the government of New Hampshire gave General Macomber permission to build a road. The Mount Washington Road Company got to work.

Before they could start building the road, workers had to measure how high the mountain was. Engineers had to figure out the best way to cut into the mountain to make the road. It took a great deal of planning, but finally the building crew got to work.

It was a big job just to get the supplies the crew needed to the work site. They used horses, oxen, and their own strong backs to haul the building supplies from eight miles away.

Work crew camping at Mount Washington

New road

Granite boulder

15

The crew drilled blasting holes into the mountainside by hand. With black powder they blasted away portions of the mountain to make the road flat and smooth. They hauled away tons of blasted rock and gravel.

The road crew worked ten or twelve hours a day, even in cold temperatures and harsh wind. The crew spent their nights in tents and shacks on the mountainside. It took them a year to complete two miles of the road. They still had six miles to go.

General Macomber knew it would be expensive to build the road, but he didn't know just how expensive. Long before the road reached the top, his company ran out of money. Work on the road had to stop. Soon another company took over the project.

Finally, on August 8, 1861, the Mount Washington Carriage Road officially opened for travel. The first vehicle to reach the top that day was a Concord Coach pulled by eight horses. After people started driving cars on the road, the name changed to Mount Washington Auto Road.

In 1869 visitors had another way to travel up Mount Washington with the world's first cog railway. A cog railway is a special kind of railway that is designed for going up steep slopes. Today there are 30 cog railways in the world. Only one of them—a railway in Switzerland—is steeper than the railway that goes up Mount Washington.

Mount Washington Carriage Road

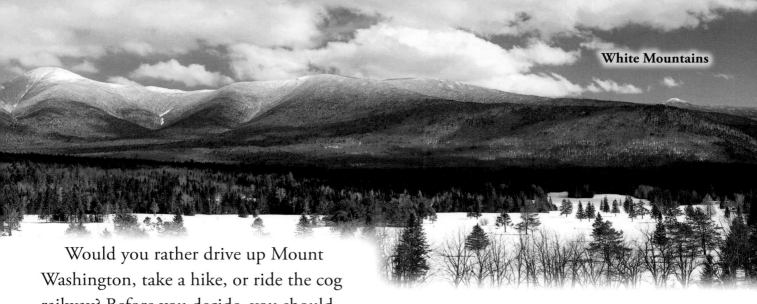

Would you rather drive up Mount Washington, take a hike, or ride the cog railway? Before you decide, you should check the weather forecast. Some say Mount Washington has the worst weather in the world. Sometimes the wind is as powerful as a hurricane. The strongest wind ever recorded anywhere in the world was recorded on Mount Washington in 1934. Some companies that make tents test their designs on Mount Washington. If a tent can stand up to the wind on Mount Washington, it can probably stand up to winds anywhere!

Praise the Lord!
Praise the Lord from the heavens;
Praise Him in the heights!
Psalm 148:1

Mount Washington Auto Road

Activities

- Complete the map activities for New Hampshire in the *Atlas Workbook* (page 7).

- Read chapter 4 in *Rabbit Hill.*

- Companies that manufacture tents test their designs on Mount Washington. Invent a new tent design. What special features are in your tent? Does it come in different colors? Why should people buy it? In your creative writing notebook, write the script for a commercial encouraging people to buy your new type of tent. *or* Build a tent with blankets and other objects in your house (as long as your parents say it's okay).

Family Activity: Blueberry Muffins

Wild blueberries are the official fruit of Maine. Enjoy some blueberry muffins!

Ingredients (makes 12 muffins):
- 2 cups all-purpose flour
- 1 teaspoon baking powder
- ½ teaspoon baking soda
- ¼ teaspoon freshly ground nutmeg
- ½ teaspoon salt
- 1 stick unsalted butter, melted and slightly cooled
- ¾ cup granulated sugar
- 2 large eggs
- 1 teaspoon vanilla extract
- ½ cup buttermilk
- 2 ¼ cups fresh or frozen blueberries
- 1-2 tablespoons turbinado sugar (for optional topping)

Directions:
- Position the oven rack in the middle of the oven. Preheat oven to 375°
- Grease 12 cups of a muffin tin or line with cupcake papers.
- In a large bowl, stir together flour, baking powder, baking soda, nutmeg, and salt.
- In another bowl, whisk the melted butter and sugar together. Whisk in the eggs, one at a time. Combine well. Stir in the vanilla and buttermilk.
- Pour the wet ingredients into the dry ingredients and mix well.
- Fold in the blueberries.
- Spoon the batter into muffin cups. Sprinkle evenly with turbinado sugar, if desired.
- Carefully place the muffin tin in the oven.
- Bake 20-25 minutes, until the tops are golden brown and a toothpick inserted into the center comes out clean.
- Carefully remove from the oven.
- Let the muffins sit until they are cool enough to touch.
- Serve warm or at room temperature.

Be safe with knives and the hot oven. Children must have adult supervision in the kitchen.

Stowe, Vermont

Unit 2
New England:
Vermont and Massachusetts

Derby Line

Lake Champlain

Cabot •

★ Montpelier

Woodstock •

▲ Dorset Mountain

Imagine a pile of pancakes with maple syrup running down the sides. Yum! Maple syrup comes from maple trees. Vermont is full of maple trees. To make the syrup, sugarmakers drill little holes called taps into the trunks of maple trees. The sap drips out of the taps and collects in buckets. Some sugarmakers collect from as many as 60,000 taps! After they collect it, sugarmakers boil the sap to make syrup. Vermont might be a small state, but it produces more maple syrup than any other. Find Vermont on the map at the beginning of this book.

Tapping a maple in Vermont

Cabot Creamery

In 1919 dairy farmers in **Cabot**, Vermont, needed a way to use their extra milk. Ninety-four farmers joined together and started a business. They used the extra milk from their cows to make butter. They sold the butter throughout New England. In 1930 the company began making cheese as well.

Today around 800 dairy farm families from all over the northeast work together to supply the milk for Cabot Creamery. In addition to cheese, the creamery in Cabot makes Greek-style yogurt, cottage cheese, and sour cream. Cabot won the World's Best Cheddar award at the 2006 World Champion Cheese Contest.

Cabot cheese

Near Cabot, Vermont

Capital: Montpelier

Montpelier is our country's smallest state capital. Less than 8,000 people live in the city. (Compare that to Indiana's capital city with over 800,000 people and Arizona's capital with over 1,600,000!)

In 1805 the government of Vermont decided that Montpelier would be the state capital if the citizens of Montpelier could build the state house. The people wanted to help, but not everyone had money to donate. Some donated building materials instead. Some donated vegetables, grain, butter, and cheese. These items could be sold to buy wood, glass, and nails. People donated their time and carpentry skills. Residents agreed for the town to raise taxes to cover the rest of the cost of the building.

Montpelier finished the first state house in 1808. In 1836 the government moved into a new, larger state house. A fire broke out in that state house on a January night in 1857. The people of Montpelier rushed to throw chunks of frozen snow into the burning building. Sadly, they could not put out the fire and it destroyed the state house.

While they waited for a new state house, Vermont's government met in a county courthouse and a local church building. Workers completed a third state house two years later. The government of Vermont has used their third state house ever since. Today's senators sit in the same chairs at the same desks the senators used in 1857.

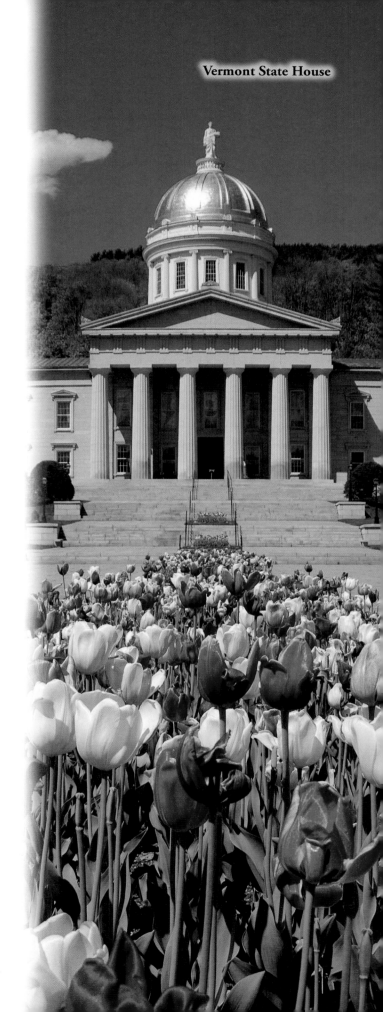

Vermont State House

21

Danby Quarry

Inside the Danby Quarry

Vermont is home to the largest underground marble quarry in the world. Workers have been cutting marble out of the Danby Quarry under **Dorset Mountain** since 1903. Workers also operate an underground factory at the quarry. There they prepare slabs of marble for people to use in building projects around the world.

Vermont Fossils

Lake Champlain lies between Vermont and New York. The lake has abundant fish, attracting fishermen from far and wide. The area around the lake fascinates geologists (scientists who study the earth). They come to the lake to study the fossilized coral reef there. Coral reefs form in the ocean, so apparently Vermont was once under the ocean.

In 1848 railroad workers were laying a track south of Lake Champlain. As they worked along, they dug up part of a fossilized mammoth. The next year, while working on the same railroad, workers discovered the fossilized bones of a beluga whale. It is obvious that long ago, Vermont was a very different place from what it is now!

Lake Champlain

Haskell Free Library and Opera House

Martha Stewart Haskell was Canadian. She married a man from Vermont. In 1901, after her husband's death, Mrs. Haskell decided to build a center for learning and culture in his honor. She and her son built the Haskell Free Public Library and Opera House. They had the building constructed on the border between Vermont and Quebec, Canada. The front door of the building is in Derby Line, Vermont, and the library books are in Rock Island, Quebec! The opera stage is in Canada, but most of the audience sits in the U.S.

Usually when someone in Canada wants to enter the United States, they have to go through an official port of entry. If a Canadian wants to visit the Haskell building, however, they are allowed to simply cross over the border on the sidewalk to get to the front door. The building continues to be a center for learning and culture, just as its founder hoped.

The mind of the prudent
acquires knowledge,
And the ear of the wise
seeks knowledge.
Proverbs 18:15

Haskell Free Library and Opera House

Activities

- Illustrate the geographic term for Vermont in the *Atlas Workbook* (page 8).

- If you are using the *Lesson Review*, answer the questions for Vermont (page 2).

- Read chapter 5 in *Rabbit Hill*.

- Hands-On Idea: Use building bricks or blocks to design a building for the good of your community. Decide what will be the purpose of your building.

- Family Activity: Paint Autumn in New England pictures (instructions on page 36).

Sliding Down the Hill

This sledding song by M. A. Everest was published in Vermont in 1896. (Track 3)

The stars are coming out tonight
And you ought all to know
How the young ones all play on the hill
A-sliding o'er the snow.
Come and go with me tonight
Let the stars shine as they will,
For pleasure now we must not fail
To join our friends on the sliding hill.

Chorus:
Then they go over the snow sitting on a sled,
Down the hill, bumpety-bump, leader on ahead.
Many voices shout, pull up the sled, and turn about.
Ring the bells, blow the horn, sliding down the hill.
Ring the bells, blow the horn, sliding down the hill.

We know that they are young and bright,
We view them now at night,
For they all slide down the hill in fine style
With the stars a-shining bright.
Then may Sue and her good Joe
Join hands and up they go.
With happy songs and right good will
That fills the bill sliding on the snow.

Chorus

They slide in the path and the moon shines out
So beautiful and bright,
And the snow on the ground so brightly shines
Like diamonds in the dark night.
Young and glad and good as well,
With hearts full of love, ring bells,
While music, health, and lots of fun
Have the stars a-sliding down the hill.

Chorus

Vermont countryside

Hitting the Slopes

It's time to bundle up in your warmest clothes. Put on your gloves, and make sure you grab a hat. Step into a pair of skis. Grab two poles and you're off! Feel the fresh mountain air as you glide down over the hard-packed snow. Bend your knees, shift your weight, and watch the trees whizz by!

Skier on a tow rope around 1940

By the 1930s, Americans were discovering the thrill of flying down mountainsides and across hills on skis. Skiing was becoming a pleasure sport, instead of just a useful way to travel in the snow. It was fun, but skiers had a problem. They needed an easy way to get back up to the top once they got down.

Robert and Elizabeth Royce owned an inn near **Woodstock**, Vermont. In 1934 they decided to work on a solution to this skiing problem. They rented a former sheep pasture. They purchased pulleys, a Model T Ford engine, and a rope that was 1,800 feet long. They set up a tow rope with one pulley at the top of the hill and another at the bottom.

The Royces' first ski season with their new tow rope was a success. The engine kept the rope moving between the pulleys—except when it broke down, which happened often. Still, skiers loved it. They paid $1 each for a day of skiing on the slope. Once they reached the bottom, they grabbed onto the tow rope and held on tight as it pulled them back to the top. Now they could ski down again . . . and again!

Chair lift in Vermont

The tow rope idea caught on across New England. Farmers installed them and set up places where visitors could stay on their farms. It was a new way to earn money during the long Vermont winters.

As skiing became more popular, people continued to think of new ways to get skiers back up the hill. One person tried attaching shovel handles to an overhead cable that ran up the mountainside. Someone else rigged up a harness attached to a rope that a horse pulled up the hill.

Over time people developed the chair lift style that skiers use today. One early lift designer got his ideas from a machine he had created to move bales of bananas in Honduras. The machine lifted the bananas off loading docks and loaded them onto boats. With chairs instead of banana hooks, the machine worked great for skiers.

Today millions of people from around the world hit the slopes of Vermont each year to ski—and then catch an easy ride back to the top in a chair lift.

God thunders with His voice wondrously,
Doing great things which we cannot comprehend.
For to the snow He says, "Fall on the earth,"
And to the downpour and the rain, "Be strong."
He seals the hand of every man,
That all men may know His work.
Job 37:5-7

Vintage skis

Activities

- Complete the map activities for Vermont in the *Atlas Workbook* (page 9).

- Read chapter 6 in *Rabbit Hill*.

- Skiers have been using chair lifts for many years. It's time for a new invention. Come up with a new idea for how skiers can get back to the top of the mountain. Use your imagination (your invention doesn't have to be practical or realistic). If you are keeping a creative writing notebook, write a detailed description of your invention.

Lesson 7: Massachusetts

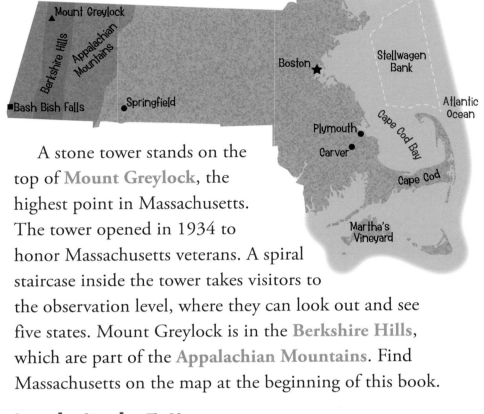

A stone tower stands on the top of **Mount Greylock**, the highest point in Massachusetts. The tower opened in 1934 to honor Massachusetts veterans. A spiral staircase inside the tower takes visitors to the observation level, where they can look out and see five states. Mount Greylock is in the **Berkshire Hills**, which are part of the **Appalachian Mountains**. Find Massachusetts on the map at the beginning of this book.

Mount Greylock

Bash Bish Falls

Bash Bish Falls tumbles down the Berkshire Hills into Bash Bish Brook. (Can you say that ten times fast?) As the water flows down, it hits a large triangular rock. Here the water divides and crashes down both sides of the rock into the brook below. The story goes that the falls and brook got their name from a Mohican woman named Bash Bish.

Bash Bish Falls

Dr. Seuss National Memorial Sculpture Garden

Dr. Seuss and The Cat in the Hat

Have you ever heard of *The Cat in the Hat* or *How the Grinch Stole Christmas* or *Green Eggs and Ham*? Dr. Seuss wrote and illustrated those books, and many more. Dr. Seuss was born in **Springfield**, Massachusetts. Springfield has a delightful sculpture garden with bronze statues of many Dr. Seuss characters. There is also a statue of Dr. Seuss himself.

Capital: Boston

Boston is the capital of Massachusetts and the largest city in New England. This city has been around since 1630, long before the United States even became a country.

Boston Common is the oldest public park in the United States. The Freedom Trail winds through Boston and leads visitors to sites that were important in the early days of our country. The state government has met in the Massachusetts State House in Boston since 1798.

Robert Paget began offering swan boat rides in Boston's Public Garden in 1877. His descendants still offer swan boat rides today. The boat drivers use their feet to pedal the boats along. Large swan figures hide the boats' pedals. The swan boats have become a beloved symbol of Boston.

Swan boats in Boston

29

Plimoth Plantation

Plimoth Plantation in **Plymouth** shows what life was like for the Pilgrims who landed here in 1620. Men, women, and children wearing Pilgrim costumes work in the gardens, tend the livestock, and cook meals over fires. Near the recreated village stands a Wampanoag homesite where visitors learn about the lives of the Pilgrims' neighbors.

Plimouth Plantation

Martha's Vineyard

When English settlers first came to Plymouth, the Wampanoag helped them learn how to survive here. Today some of the descendants of those Wampanoag live on **Martha's Vineyard**, an island off the coast of Massachusetts. Their town of Aquinnah is near the towering clay cliffs on the southern coast of Martha's Vineyard. The Wampanoag work together to preserve their tribe's history and culture through singing, dancing, storytelling, and traditional crafts.

Cottages on Martha's Vineyard

Visitors to Oak Bluffs on Martha's Vineyard love to stroll down the street and see the rows of brightly-colored cottages from the 1800s. Many cottages are decorated with fancy woodwork called gingerbread. The Oak Bluffs community began as a site for summertime camp meetings for Christians.

Cape Cod and Stellwagen Bank

Cape Cod extends east from the mainland of Massachusetts into the Atlantic Ocean around **Cape Cod Bay**. A cape is a narrow strip of land that juts into a body of water.

Cape Cod is near **Stellwagen Bank**, one of the best places in the world to go whale watching. An ocean bank is an area of water that is more shallow than the waters around it. Stellwagen Bank is teeming with life. Porpoises, seals, and dolphins love to play in these waters. Whales come here to feast on creatures such as sand eels. Fishermen come to catch cod, flounder, and tuna. The spectacular beauty and the abundant sea life here remind us of the mighty God who made it all.

You are the God who works wonders;
You have made known Your strength among the peoples.
Psalm 77:14

Cape Cod

Activities

- Illustrate the geographic term for Massachusetts in the *Atlas Workbook* (page 10).

- If you are using the *Lesson Review*, answer the questions for Massachusetts (page 2).

- Read chapter 7 in *Rabbit Hill*.

- Hands-On Idea: If you have any Dr. Seuss books at your house, look closely at the illustrations. Draw your own whimsical picture in the style of Dr. Seuss.

The Popcorn Man

Edward King was a Massachusetts poet. While living in Springfield in the late 1800s he wrote a poem about George S. Page, the town's well-known Popcorn Man. (Track 4)

Hobble, hobble, up and down
Thro' the streets of Springfield Town;
Round the corner, up the street,
Caring naught for cold or heat,
Caring naught for passing jeer
Goes the jolly popcorn man,
Crying loudly as he can
"Sugared, fresh, and salt popcorn!
POPcorn!"

Careful goes he on his way
All the long and weary day;
In his basket huge supply
Of his shapely bundles lie.
Parchen corn in paper bags;
And his courage never flags
While, with voice like dinner horn,
Cries he lustily, "Popcorn!
Sugared, fresh, and salt popcorn!
POPcorn!"

When to lecture or to ball
Crowds approach the City Hall,
By the stairs the old man stands,
With a parcel in his hands
And his basket at his feet,
While these words he doth repeat—
"Here's your corn—your nice popcorn!
Sugared, fresh, and salt popcorn!
POPcorn!"

Morn and eve and eve and morn
Loud the old man cries "Popcorn!"
Long and joyful be his life
Free from care and weary strife.
Courage! old friend! Never fret!
You may be the mayor yet;
Stranger things have chanced before;
Courage! Hobble, work and roar
"Sugared, fresh and salt popcorn!
POPcorn!"

Cranberry Family

James, Jarrod, and Patrick Rhodes grew up surrounded by cranberries. Their parents, Matthew and Cindy, have owned cranberry bogs for as long as the boys can remember. The ground in a bog is wet and muddy. Bogs are a great place for growing cranberries. They are also a great place for kids to catch turtles, tadpoles, and frogs. A cranberry farm was a great place for the boys to grow up. Their cousins liked to join in the fun, too. James, Jarrod, and Patrick loved to ride with their dad as he drove the tractor around the bogs. Some days, when they were very young, their mom planted cranberries while carrying one of the boys in a carrier on her back.

Patrick using the dry method to harvest in 2007

As James, Jarrod, and Patrick grew up, they learned how to care for cranberries. They learned that sometimes their parents had to stay up all night to protect the berries from frost. If it got too cold, their parents had to turn on sprinklers to protect the plants. They learned that one frost can ruin a whole crop.

The Rhodes boys learned how to harvest cranberries using the dry method with a machine that looks like a lawn mower. They watched their dad walk behind the machine as it combed the berries into bags. They learned to manage the machine themselves. They also learned how to harvest cranberries using the wet picking method. As their parents flooded the bogs with water, the boys watched a machine knock the cranberries off the vines. They watched as one by one all the little red berries floated to the top of the water. They saw the floating berries get pumped from the bogs into a waiting truck.

Cranberries floating on top of a bog

33

Now James, Jarrod, and Patrick Rhodes are grown up. They are the fourth generation in their family to work as cranberry farmers. They work with their parents at Edgewood Bogs, their family's cranberry operation in **Carver**, Massachusetts.

Edgewood Bogs after a frosty night

During harvest time, the Rhodes hire around 50 people to help bring in the crop. They even hire a helicopter to lift huge bins full of cranberries off the bogs. Sometimes members of the family get to go for a ride in the helicopter. Employees and customers enjoy taking a turn in the helicopter, too. Everyone loves to see the spectacular view of the cranberry bogs from the air. Edgewood Bogs produces between four and five million pounds of cranberries every year!

Some people think cranberries are just to eat at Thanksgiving, but the Rhodes family doesn't agree. Over 4,000 grocery stores across the country carry their Cape Cod Select frozen cranberries. The Rhodes want people to be able to enjoy cranberries all year long.

Cindy Rhodes loves to cook with cranberries. She puts cranberries in bread and oatmeal. Her cranberry turkey chili won a first place award in a contest on the nearby island of Martha's Vineyard. In the Rhodes family, cranberries go with pasta, shrimp, and even Brussels sprouts. Their cranberry squares are a delicious dessert. In the Rhodes family, cranberries make their way into a breakfast smoothie almost every morning.

Edgewood Bogs full of cranberries

Edgewood Bogs is all about cranberries. It is also all about family. Cindy Rhodes says that, "Family is about love and respect for one another. It is also about supporting each other when times call for it. Farming can be a lot of fun, but it can also be very stressful when something goes wrong in the field or in the processing plant. Watching my boys work together and also with non-family employees to solve problems brings me special joy. I also love to see their excitement during harvest season as they work twelve-hour days, seven days per week, to get the crop in!"

Behold, how good and how pleasant it is for brothers to dwell together in unity!
Psalm 133:1

Activities

- Complete the map activities for Massachusetts in the *Atlas Workbook* (page 11).

- Read chapter 8 in *Rabbit Hill*.

- Imagine that you are riding in a helicopter over a cranberry bog. Look closely at the pictures in this lesson. Notice little details. If you are keeping a creative writing notebook, write a description of what you might see from a helicopter window. How do you feel being in the helicopter? Do you see any animals? What are the people below doing? If you are not keeping a notebook, pretend a couch or a couple of chairs is your helicopter. Climb in with a family member and describe the view of the cranberry bog below.

Autumn in New England is especially beautiful. Every autumn, leaf peepers come to New England to drive through the countryside and enjoy the spectacular colors. ("Leaf peepers" is just a fun term for people who like to peep at leaves.) Follow these instructions to create a beautiful painting of autumn in New England.

Supplies:
- cardstock or other heavy paper
- pencil
- acrylic paints (blue, white, red, yellow, orange, green)
- paper plate
- artist sponge and/or wide circular paintbrush with coarse bristles
- water for cleaning the sponge or paintbrush
- paper towels for drying the sponge or paintbrush

Directions:
- Use a pencil to draw a faint line across your paper about 1/3 of the way up from the bottom. Now draw faint hills above the line.
- Squirt some blue paint on the paper plate. Paint the sky blue and let it dry.
- After the blue is dry, squirt some white paint on the paper plate. Use a clean and dry sponge or paintbrush to dab wispy clouds in the sky.
- Squirt some red, yellow, and orange paint on the paper plate. Do not mix the colors. Use a clean and dry sponge or paintbrush to lightly dab small amounts of autumn colors on the hills. You do not need to clean your brush or sponge between colors. Dab the colors here and there on the hills to cover them with autumn trees.
- Squirt some green paint on the paper plate. Use a clean paintbrush to apply the green to your painting using short, upward strokes to look like grass.

Hartford, Connecticut

Unit 3
New England:
Rhode Island and Connecticut

Lesson 9: Rhode Island

The carousel in **Watch Hill**, Rhode Island, built in 1867, is one of the oldest you will find anywhere. The horses are only attached at the top, which makes them appear to fly as the carousel spins around. In the 1800s, a real horse hitched to the carousel walked in circles to make it turn. Find Rhode Island, the smallest state of all, on the map at the beginning of this book.

Watch Hill Flying Horse Carousel

A Place for All

Roger Williams established the colony of Rhode Island in 1636. At that time, the people in some colonies did not want members of certain religious groups to live in their colonies. Roger Williams decided that Rhode Island would welcome people of all religions. Many people who were persecuted in other places moved to Rhode Island. Quakers, Baptists, Jews, and other groups came to live and worship in peace.

Rhode Island coast

Touro Synagogue stands in Newport. A synagogue is a building where Jews gather for worship and learning. Workers completed the Touro Synagogue in 1763. It is the oldest synagogue in the United States.

Salt Marshes

Salt marshes lie along the Rhode Island shoreline. A marsh is an area of low land that stays wet all or most of the time. Fish, shellfish, birds, and mammals find food, lay their eggs, and raise their young in the marshes of Rhode Island.

Marshes are an important ecosystem. An ecosystem is a system in a particular area where certain plants, animals, weather, and landscapes work together. Salt marshes naturally filter pollution out of water before the water reaches the ocean. They also absorb water during floods. This helps prevent flooding of nearby homes and businesses.

Outside and inside of Tuoro Synagogue

Salt marsh in Newport

Capital: Providence

Roger Williams established **Providence** in 1636 on land he purchased from the Narragansett people. He chose the name Providence because he was thankful for God's merciful providence to him. Roger Williams wanted the city to be a shelter for people in distress. It is one of the oldest cities in the United States.

Illustration of Narragansetts with Roger Williams

The Ocean State

Rhode Island is the Ocean State. No matter where a person is in Rhode Island, he is not more than 30 minutes from the coast. Rhode Island might be small, but it has plenty of sandy beaches.

Narragansett Bay is the largest estuary in New England. An estuary is an area where rivers and streams meet the ocean. In an estuary, fresh water from rivers or streams mixes with the salt water of the ocean. God created some animals and plants to live only in fresh water. He designed others to live only in salt water. The animals and plants He created for estuaries thrive on a mixture of these waters.

Beavertail Lighthouse at the entrance to Narragansett Bay

Rhode Island Mansions

In the late 1800s and early 1900s, several wealthy families built summer homes in Newport. They called these homes "cottages," though they were really quite large. The Breakers is the most famous house in Rhode Island. The Vanderbilt family had it built in the late 1800s.

The Breakers

The Breakers features shimmering crystal chandeliers and shiny blue marble. It contains 70 rooms. The ceiling in the pantry is two stories high so it could hold all the Vanderbilts' dishes. French workers built part of The Breakers in Paris, France. When they finished that part of the house, they took it apart, shipped it across the ocean, and put it back together in Rhode Island.

Marble House

People build great things, but we must remember that they are small compared to the greatness of God.

Bless the Lord, O my soul!
O Lord my God, You are very great;
You are clothed with splendor and majesty.
Psalm 104:1

Rosecliff

Activities

- Illustrate the geographic term for Rhode Island in the *Atlas Workbook* (pages 12).
- If you are using the *Lesson Review*, answer the questions for Rhode Island (page 3).
- Read chapter 9 in *Rabbit Hill*.
- Hands-On Idea: Use building bricks or blocks to build a grand mansion. Build gardens and fountains around the outside.

Fisher's Cradle Song

M. V. Freese and L. M. Monroe published this lullaby in Rhode Island in 1893. (Track 5)

Soft the waves come rolling,
Winds are sobbing, sobbing low,
Hear the fog bell tolling,
Gently, gently, gently row.
Close thine eyes, my darling,
'Ere we reach the land,
Sink to sleep, my starling,
Rocked by ocean's hand.

Bright the lights are gleaming
Far along the sandy shore,
Red the rays are streaming
From the distant lighthouse tower.
Little eyes are closing
In the moonlight ray.
Baby is reposing
In the dreamland bay.

Roll, waves, steadily roll;
Toll, bell, solemnly toll.
Sing a soothing lullaby,
Sing it softly, tenderly,
While my baby sleeps,
While my baby sleeps.

Grandfather's Chickens

A dozen hens scratched at the ground around David's feet. A rooster crowed nearby. David Patten loved to be up early. He gazed off across the water. In the distance he could see the Vanderbilts' new home, The Breakers. He could see other grand homes in Newport, owned by other grand and important families.

David turned around and looked at his grandfather's farmhouse. He smiled. His grandfather, Isaac Wilbour, was grand and important, too. Isaac Wilbour had the biggest poultry farm in the whole country! Magazine reporters from big cities came to Grandfather's farm in **Little Compton**, Rhode Island. They wrote articles about Grandfather's chicken business. Farmers having chickens was nothing new, but Americans were fascinated with the new idea of a farmer actually earning a living from chickens and geese.

David watched one of Grandfather's hired hands come up from the cookhouse in the feed wagon. He was a Portuguese immigrant, as were most of the farmhands. David jumped on the wagon. He knew the morning rounds would take two hours, but he didn't mind that. He loved this part of the day.

The horse pulled the feed wagon up to the first white hen house. Nobody had to drive the horse. She knew just when and where to stop.

Near Little Compton

43

The hired hand jumped out. From the largest bin on the wagon he scooped out a shovelful of dough. He had mixed up the dough the night before. He dumped the dough in the chickens' feed trough. He threw in some oyster shells. When the chickens had oyster shells to eat, their eggs were stronger. The Portuguese man filled the chickens' water keg from the barrel on the wagon. When he was finished, the horse knew to pull the wagon on to the next hen house. One hen house down, seventy-four more to go.

All day the chickens wandered about the farm. David loved to watch and listen to three or four thousand chickens busily scratching and clucking their day away. Every night, the horse pulled the feed wagon back around to each hen house. David and the hired hand gave the chickens their ration of corn and gathered the day's eggs. Each day they gathered an average of 5,000 eggs! Grandfather's chickens laid close to two million eggs a year.

Once a week, David got to ride on the egg wagon with Clarence, the farm foreman. This wagon, with its yellow wheels and bright red sides, pulled up to one nearby farm after another. Clarence paid the farmers for their eggs. Clarence and Grandfather took these eggs, plus all the eggs from their own farm, to market in Providence. Merchants carried the best eggs on to Boston.

Rhode Island Reds

The chickens around Little Compton were famous. Before David was born, one of Grandfather's neighbors had bred his own chickens with chickens that came on a ship all the way from Asia. Grandfather liked his neighbor's chickens. He bought some and bred them with his own chickens. Grandfather's flock became healthier and stronger. They laid large brown eggs. They were good meat birds, too.

One day someone told Grandfather he should come up with a name for this new breed of chickens. Grandfather replied, "Why, wouldn't Rhode Island Reds do?"

When he was a boy, David watched some men on Grandfather's farm load 50 Rhode Island Reds into crates. The birds went to David's uncle in Iowa. Before long, other farmers in Iowa had Rhode Island Reds pecking around their farms, too. Grandfather's new chicken breed kept spreading.

In 1954 the Rhode Island legislature voted to make the Rhode Island Red the state bird of Rhode Island. Today Rhode Island Reds cluck and scratch on farms across America and around the world.

. . . O Lord, it is You who made the heaven and the earth and the sea, and all that is in them.
Acts 4:24

Crate

Rhode Island Red monument in Little Compton

Activities

- Complete the map activities for Rhode Island in the *Atlas Workbook* (page 13).
- Read chapter 10 in *Rabbit Hill*.
- Ask an adult in your family to share a memory they have of visiting their grandparents when they were young. If you are keeping a creative writing notebook, write down their story in your own words.

Lesson 11: Connecticut

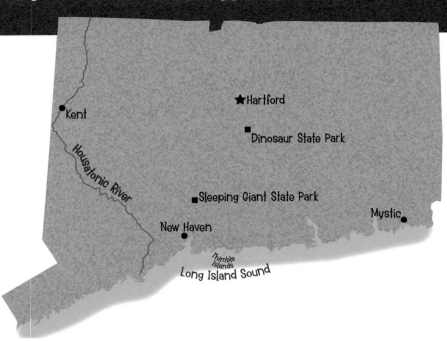

The water of **Long Island Sound** separates Connecticut and New York. A sound is a narrow part of an ocean or sea with land on both sides. Jellyfish, sea turtles, and sharks swim in these waters. Some ocean creatures lay their eggs in the sound and on the sandy beaches that surround it. Find Connecticut on the map at the beginning of this book.

Long Island Sound

The *Charles W. Morgan*

Mystic Seaport Museum

The Mystic River is one of the many rivers that flow into Long Island Sound. The Mystic Seaport Museum stands at the river's edge in **Mystic**, Connecticut. Here visitors experience what life was like in a New England fishing village in the 1800s. They watch workers build wooden ships the old-fashioned way. The museum is home to an 1841 wooden whaling ship, the *Charles W. Morgan*. This ship once hunted whales around the world.

Thimble Islands

Hundreds of small islands lie clustered off the coast of Connecticut. The Mattabasek people who once lived in this area called them *Kuttomquosh*, which means "the beautiful sea rocks." Today they are known as the Thimble Islands.

Some of the Thimble Islands are large enough for several houses; others are just a small rocky place you can only see during low tide. Tides are the rising and falling of a body of water. In most coastal places, there are two high tides and two low tides each day. When the tide is high, the water comes up. When the tide is low, the water goes down. The moon's gravity makes the tides rise and fall.

Thimble Islands

Sleeping Giant State Park

Would you like to go for a walk on a sleeping giant? Connecticut's sleeping giant is a natural land form that looks like, well, a sleeping giant! In the early 1900s, people started blowing this giant to bits. The owner of the giant's head leased his land to a company that quarried rocks out of the ground. People who lived nearby complained about all the blasting from the quarry. They also complained that the giant was going to lose his shape.

Sleeping Giant

Mountain Laurel

People worked together and organized the Sleeping Giant Park Association and **Sleeping Giant State Park**. Members of the association still volunteer to help keep the trails in good shape. Thanks to the work of many people, visitors continue to enjoy walking on Connecticut's sleeping giant.

Mountain laurel, the state flower of Connecticut, grows abundantly around the state park. Captain John Smith wrote about these flowers when he explored New England in the 1600s.

Dinosaur State Park

Imagine footprints up to 16 inches long. Imagine footprints up to four and a half feet apart. Imagine dinosaurs walking across Connecticut!

In 1966 a construction worker used a bulldozer to turn over a slab of sandstone. Underneath it he saw a large footprint with three toes. Soon people discovered more footprints. They decided to put a stop to the construction project. They turned the area

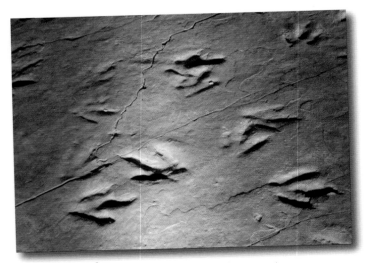
Dinosaur footprints at Dinosaur State Park

into **Dinosaur State Park**. Today 500 tracks are on display in the park. The footprints are protected from the weather so that people can continue marveling at this part of God's creation for years to come.

Capital: Hartford

For many years, Connecticut had two capital cities. Citizens took care of some government business in **Hartford**, and other business in **New Haven**. Each city had its own state house. The Old State House in Hartford has been around since 1796. It is the oldest state house in the country. In addition to seeing where the senate and house of representatives once met, visitors can see a two-headed calf!

Connecticut State Capitol

Joseph Steward opened a portrait gallery in the state house in 1797. Not many people visited his gallery, so he created a museum to try to draw larger crowds. It worked. Steward's Museum of Natural and Other Curiosities certainly made people curious. Visitors paid 20 cents each to come inside and see a variety of curious items, including a stuffed two-headed calf. Steward's museum closed in the mid-1800s. In the 1990s, the director of the Old State House worked hard to recreate it. Now visitors to the Old State House can see a museum similar to the one that was here 200 years ago.

In 1873 the people of Connecticut voted to make Hartford their one and only capital city. They built a new capitol building, which is where the state senators and representatives meet today.

The Bible teaches us to pray for our government leaders.

First of all, then, I urge that entreaties and prayers, petitions and thanksgivings, be made on behalf of all men, for kings and all who are in authority, so that we may lead a tranquil and quiet life in all godliness and dignity.
1 Timothy 2:1-2

Activities

- Illustrate the geographic term for Connecticut in the *Atlas Workbook* (pages 14).

- If you are using the *Lesson Review*, answer the questions for Connecticut (page 3).

- Read chapter 11 in *Rabbit Hill*.

- Hands-On Idea: Lay out blankets or pillows on the floor to represent the Thimble Islands. Pick one island to live on. Perhaps other family members can live on other islands. How will you travel from one to another?

- Family Activity: Go on a Shape Walk (instructions on page 54).

The Connecticut Peddler

Peddlers once traveled across the countryside selling a variety of items to farm families along the way. Imagine a peddler coming up your road singing this song. The "tracts upon popular sins" were brochures about common sins and how to overcome them. (Track 6)

I'm a peddler, I'm a peddler,
I'm a peddler from Connecticut,
I'm a peddler, I'm a peddler,
And don't you want to buy?

Many goods have I in store,
So listen while I name them o'er,
So many goods you never saw before,
So very many goods you never saw before,
So listen while I name them o'er,

Here are pins,
Papers and needles and pins,
Tracts upon popular sins,
Any of which I will sell you.

And here are the seeds of asparagus,
Lettuce, beets, onions, and peppergrass
From the Limited Sodety,
Seeds of all kinds and variety.

Da, da, da, tiddle-dum, tiddle-dum,
Rum, turn tiddle-dum, tiddle-dee,
Rinktum, te-tiddle-dee, rinktum te-tiddle-dee
Tiddle-dum, tiddle-dum, faddle whee.

Peddler

Connecticut countryside

A Good Neighbor

Crayola crayons box from the early 1900s

Little George Laurence Nelson loved to hold a pencil in his hand. He loved to watch animals take shape on the paper in front of him. He loved to look at his mother's beautiful face and sketch her features. He drew other people, too, but mostly he drew his mother.

George's parents were both artists. They met in Paris, France, while studying art. They moved to New York and became an art team. They painted. They designed fashions. They created calendars. The Nelson family loved art.

When George Nelson was ten years old, he started writing and illustrating his own magazine. In 1904 George was excited to use a new drawing tool—crayons! Crayola Crayons were a brand new invention. The company held a drawing contest, and George won first prize for his drawing of a cow. His prize was a pair of skates.

George studied art and became an art teacher. He also had a wonderful voice and learned to play five instruments. After his mother died, he and his father moved together to **Kent**, Connecticut, on the **Housatonic River**. They organized a summer art school, the Nelson Outdoor Painting Class.

Housatonic River

Painting of Helen by George Laurence Nelson

Self-portrait by George Laurence Nelson

In 1915 Helen Redgrave came to interview George Nelson. Instead of interviewing him, she sat while Mr. Nelson painted her portrait. He thought that she was the most beautiful girl in the world. They married the next year.

George Nelson spent the rest of his life in Kent. A minister in Kent once described him as having a shy smile, a twinkling eye, and a warm handshake. Even though he was famous, he was gentle and humble. The minister said he was a good neighbor with many friends. He said that Mr. Nelson was "always interested in the welfare of his house, his district, his community."

Like George Nelson, each of us has the opportunity to take an interest in the place where we live. We can each be a good neighbor in our own community.

Each of us is to please his neighbor
for his good, to his edification.
Romans 15:2

Activities

- Complete the map activities for Connecticut in the *Atlas Workbook* (page 15).

- Read chapter 12 in *Rabbit Hill*.

- Who is someone you know who is interested in the welfare of their community as George Nelson was? If you are keeping a creative writing notebook, describe that person and what he or she does.

- If you are using the *Lesson Review*, take the New England Test (page 29). (Note: If you want to study for the test, look over the questions in the *Lesson Review* for Units 1-3 and look at the New England region on the map at the beginning of this book. This is the best method to prepare for all tests in *Our 50 States*.)

Family Activity: Shape Walk

God's world is full of fun and interesting shapes, such as the Sleeping Giant in Connecticut. Go on a shape walk with your family. Take a walk around your yard or around your neighborhood. Look for fun shapes in the forks of trees, in the clouds, in the lay of the land, and in your neighbor's flower bed. You might like to see if you can find shapes of all the letters of the alphabet. You could look for simple shapes, such as squares, rectangles, and diamonds. You could let your imaginations run wild and find shapes that remind you of dinosaurs or unicorns. You might like to take photographs or draw pictures of what you find and create a book. You might rather simply go for a walk and enjoy the search. Either way, have fun.

Letchworth State Park, New York

Unit 4
Mid-Atlantic:
New York and Pennsylvania

55

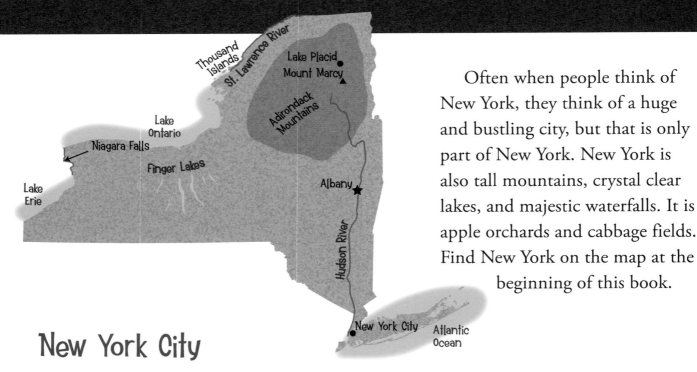

Often when people think of New York, they think of a huge and bustling city, but that is only part of New York. New York is also tall mountains, crystal clear lakes, and majestic waterfalls. It is apple orchards and cabbage fields. Find New York on the map at the beginning of this book.

New York City

The Statue of Liberty has held up her torch over New York City since the 1880s. For many years, she welcomed immigrants arriving in New York City by ship from Europe. Today visitors from around the world climb up into her crown for a view of New York City.

New York City is the largest city in America. Over eight million people call this place home. Millions more visit every year to ride the subway, see a Broadway play, and celebrate New Year's Eve in Times Square. People call New York the City that Never Sleeps.

The Statue of Liberty in New York City

Hudson River

Hudson River Valley

An important river flows through the state of New York from the **Adirondack Mountains** to New York City. The Mohicans called it *Muhheakunnuk*, which means "great waters constantly in motion." English explorer Henry Hudson explored this river valley in 1609. He hoped to find a route that would take him all the way to the Pacific Ocean. At that time, no one knew how big North America really is.

Henry Hudson and his crew sailed 150 miles up the river valley before they turned around and headed back to the Atlantic. The river that Henry Hudson explored is now called the **Hudson River**. Today companies ship a variety of cargo on the river, including scrap metal, grain, and cocoa beans.

Capital: Albany

Hundreds of workers spent 32 years in the late 1800s building New York's capitol in **Albany**. It was an expensive project. Can you guess how much it cost just to build the Million Dollar Staircase? The building's intricate carvings are the work of over 500 stonecutters. Some of the carvings show faces people recognize, such as George Washington and Abraham Lincoln. Other stone figures show the faces of some of the stonecutters' relatives and friends.

Million Dollar Staircase

Lake Placid

Lake Placid hosted the Winter Olympic Games in 1932 and again in 1980. Hockey players and figure skaters from around the world competed against each other at Lake Placid's ice rink. Visitors today can take a ride on a bobsled and see the slopes where Olympic athletes skied. The top of the ski jump tower offers a stunning view of **Mount Marcy**, the highest point in New York State. Athletes come to Lake Placid to train so they will be ready to compete in future Olympic Games.

Ski jump at Lake Placid

Thousand Islands

Have you ever heard of Thousand Island dressing? Maybe you have seen it on a salad bar. Maybe there is a bottle in your fridge. This dressing is named for the **Thousand Islands** region in the **St. Lawrence River** that flows between New York and Canada. There are more than 1,700 islands in this region.

The St. Lawrence River is part of the St. Lawrence Seaway. This busy seaway allows ships to travel from the Atlantic Ocean to cities on the Great Lakes, and then back again. This route lets ships bring their cargo to and from the middle of America and Canada without using trains or trucks. Workers have constructed locks along the seaway, which make the water deep enough for large ocean ships. A lock raises and lowers water levels between huge gates so that ships can pass through safely.

Thousand Islands

Finger Lakes

Eleven long, skinny lakes stretch through the hills of central New York creating the **Finger Lakes** region. The soil and climate among these hills are just right for growing grapes. Snowshoeing, snowmobiling, skiing, and ice fishing are popular sports here in the winter. Ice fishermen cut holes in the frozen lakes and lower their fishing lines into the water below. Some ice fishermen bring a small shack or shanty onto the ice so they can be warm while they fish.

Niagara Falls

Niagara Falls (American and Bridal Veil Falls)

Niagara Falls is on the border between the United States and Canada. Niagara Falls is actually made up of three waterfalls: American Falls, Bridal Veil Falls, and Horseshoe Falls. The highest point on the falls is over 176 feet. A series of locks on the St. Lawrence Seaway allows ships to go around Niagara Falls on their way to the Great Lakes.

The powerful flow of water over Niagara Falls reminds us of the awesome power of the One who created it.

Once God has spoken; twice I have heard this:
That power belongs to God.
Psalm 62:11

Activities

- Illustrate the geographic term for New York in the *Atlas Workbook* (page 16).

- If you are using the *Lesson Review*, answer the questions for New York (page 4).

- Read chapter 1 in *The Cabin Faced West*. (Parents, please refer to page 15 in the *Answer Key and Literature Guide* for comments about this book.)

- Hands-On Idea: Notice all the winter sports mentioned in this lesson: skiing, bobsledding, hockey, figure skating, snowshoeing, snowmobiling, ice fishing. Even if there's no snow where you are, pretend to compete in some of those sports.

Old Roger the Tin-Maker Man

This song by C. C. Haskins and W. B. Richardson was published in New York in 1867. Tin-makers make dishes, lanterns, and other items out of tin, which is a type of metal. New York was once called New Amsterdam. A garret is a small attic room. (Track 7)

'Twas jolly Old Roger the tin-maker man,
Who lived in a garret in New Amsterdam,
And showered down blessings like rain in the spring,
On maidens and matrons, of him I will sing.

Chorus:
His mallet and hammer the whole day long,
Rang out a tin chorus to old Roger's song.
Oh, never was yet a boy or a man,
Who better could mend a kettle or pan,
A bucket or skimmer or dipper or can,
Than happy old Roger, the tinker man.
Che-whang, che-whang,
che-whang, che-whang
Te-rattle, te-rattle,
te-rattle, te-rattle, te-bang.

Now you who have tinware or kettles to mend,
Just take them to jolly Old Roger, my friend;
You'll find him as clever and happy old man,
As ever yet soldered a kettle or pan.

Chorus

Tin

A Kite String

Charles Ellet Jr.

It was 1847. Charles Ellet Jr. looked down at the Whirlpool Rapids near Niagara Falls. The water twisted and turned and rushed and splashed as he pondered his problem. It was his job to build a bridge from the United States to Canada right at this spot. But how could he get the bridge started? The walls of the Niagara River gorge towered high above the water. He needed to get a cable from one side of the gorge to the other, but how? The water here was too swift for a boat to carry the cable across. He just needed a little cable going from one side to the other to get the project going. Maybe just a single wire or a rope would do. He thought about attaching a rope to some fireworks and shooting it from one side to the other, but he wasn't so sure that was a good idea. How could he connect the two sides? Just a string would do!

Someone gave Charles Ellet an idea. He could offer a ten dollar reward to any boy who could fly a kite from one side of the gorge to the other. Several local boys were ready to join in the contest, including Homan Walsh.

Whirlpool Rapids

Homan Walsh was a teenager. He and his parents had come to the United States from Ireland when Homan was a small boy. Now they lived in the town of Niagara Falls, New York. When Homan heard about the contest, he built a six-sided kite to enter. He covered his kite with fabric to make it stronger.

The contest opened in January of 1848. Homan traveled downriver and took a ferry to the Canadian side. With the wind blowing from west to east, all the boys needed to be on that side of the river. Carrying his kite, Homan hiked two miles to the future site of the bridge. It was cold. Very cold! Homan and other boys flew their kites for hours, but no one could quite get his kite to reach the other side. Finally, Homan's kite tumbled down into the American side of the gorge and broke. Homan wanted to cross back to the American side to get his kite, but it was too cold. The nearby ferry couldn't take him because there was too much ice in the river. Homan stayed with friends in Canada for eight days. Finally the weather warmed up enough for the ferry to take him back across. Homan found his kite, fixed it, and went back to Canada. He was ready to fly it again.

The kite-flying contest

This time it worked. Homan flew his kite all the way across the gorge. He won the contest and the ten dollars.

Workers attached a stronger line to the end of Homan's kite string on the American side. Then they carefully pulled on the kite string from the Canadian side, which also pulled the stronger line across the river. Once the stronger line was in place, they attached a thick rope to it and pulled it back across the river. Now they had a thick rope going across the gorge. They attached a metal cable to the rope and pulled it across. From that metal cable the crew built a suspension bridge strong enough for trains and carriages to cross—and it all began with a kite string!

Homan Walsh as an adult

The earth is the Lord's, and all it contains,
The world, and those who dwell in it.
Psalm 24:1

Niagara Falls Suspension Bridge

Activities

- Complete the map activities for New York in the *Atlas Workbook* (page 17).
- Read chapter 2 in *The Cabin Faced West*.
- Imagine how Homan Walsh might have felt when his kite string broke. How do you think he felt when he tried again and had success? In your creative writing notebook, write a journal entry about the experience from Homan's perspective. *or* Act out the story of Homan's adventure with his kite.

Lesson 15: Pennsylvania

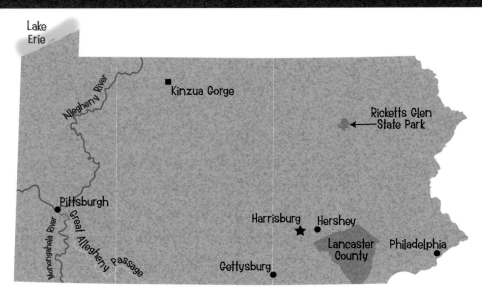

Black bears, elk, foxes, and deer ramble through the woods of Pennsylvania. More than half of the state is forest land. Find Pennsylvania on the map at the beginning of this book.

Kinzua Gorge

Fox in Pennsylvania

Trains once carried oil, coal, and lumber across Pennsylvania's **Kinzua Gorge**. A tornado damaged the railroad bridge in 2003, but the section that remains is strong and secure. It is now a skywalk for visitors to Kinzua Gorge State Park. From the deck at the end of the skywalk you can see for miles. People who are brave enough can look down through the glass floor of the deck to see the steel towers that hold up the bridge. This bridge was once the highest and longest in the world.

Kinzua Gorge Skywalk

Pittsburgh

Pittsburgh

The **Allegheny River** and the **Monongahela River** meet to form the Ohio River at **Pittsburgh**. In America's early days, many pioneers passed through this area as they moved west. Pittsburgh earned the nickname Gateway to the West.

At one time, the city of Pittsburgh manufactured half of the steel made in America. The city earned a new nickname, Steel City. Pittsburgh's professional football team is called the Steelers.

People also call Pittsburgh the City of Bridges. With 446 bridges, you can understand why. That is more bridges than any other city in the world.

The Great Allegheny Passage

Bridge on the Great Allegheny Passage

Bikers on the **Great Allegheny Passage** travel across the Eastern Continental Divide, which runs along the tops of the Appalachian Mountains. All the water in the creeks and rivers to the west of the Eastern Continental Divide eventually flows into the Gulf of Mexico. All the water to the east of the Divide eventually reaches the Atlantic Ocean.

65

Capital: Harrisburg

The architect who designed the capitol building in **Harrisburg** wanted it to be a "palace of art." President Theodore Roosevelt attended the building's dedication ceremony in 1906. He declared, "This is the handsomest building I ever saw." The capitol is indeed a palace of art, from the shimmering green glaze on the dome roof tiles to the enormous murals and marble staircases inside.

Almost 400 mosaic scenes decorate the floor of the capitol. The designs show animals, plants, and scenes from Pennsylvania life, including a skunk, a spinning wheel, a cow, and a housefly.

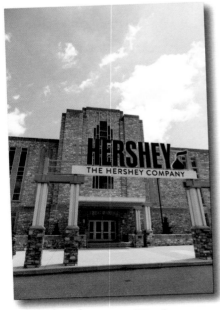
Hershey factory in Hershey

Hershey

In the early 1900s, Milton Hershey built a chocolate factory in Pennsylvania. He built an entire community around the factory for his employees and their families. They had their own post office, store, bank, and school. He opened his factory for tours in 1915. People came to visit **Hershey** by the thousands.

Hershey, Pennsylvania, is still the headquarters for The Hershey Company. Today the company operates several factories around the world. Two are in Hershey. One manufactures Reese's candy products. The other makes over 70 million chocolate kisses every day.

Lancaster County

Many Amish families live in **Lancaster County**. The Amish live a plain and simple lifestyle. Visitors to Lancaster County share the road with horses and buggies.

Philadelphia

This is the city where America was born. In **Philadelphia**'s Independence Hall, men signed the Declaration of Independence in 1776. That document declared America to be an independent country. Today visitors can step inside Independence Hall and imagine being there with John Adams, John Hancock, and Thomas Jefferson. Philadelphia was the capital city of our new nation for ten years while workers built Washington, D.C.

The word *Philadelphia* is a Greek word that means "brotherly love." Philadelphia is known as the City of Brotherly Love.

> And this commandment we have from Him,
> that the one who loves God
> should love his brother also.
> 1 John 4:21

Amish buggy in Lancaster County

Independence Hall

Activities

- Illustrate the geographic term for Pennsylvania in the *Atlas Workbook* (page 18).
- If you are using the *Lesson Review*, answer the questions for Pennsylvania (page 4).
- Read chapter 3 in *The Cabin Faced West*.
- Hands-On Idea: Go on a bike ride and imagine you are on the Great Allegheny Passage crossing over the Eastern Continental Divide.
- Family Activity: Make Capitol Mosaics (instructions on page 72).

The Bear in the Hill

Samuel Preston Bayard was born in Pennsylvania in 1908. He spent many years collecting folk songs throughout his home state. This song is from his collection. (Track 8)

There's a bear in yon hill, and he is a brave fellow,
He's plenty in store, and lives at his ease.
All he wants is a wife, and he's travelled all over,
To find a companion his fancy to please.

As he was a-pattin', a-pattin, and a-blatin'
One day up the river he chanced for to meet—
As he was a-pattin', he met with a possum,
And kind, loving compliments had to her there.

"O dearest possum, where air you a-goin'?
It is a cold and blustery day.
If you'll go with me, oh, how I will love you!
I'll take you to my den, love, and there you may stay."

With all these kind compliments, possum lie grinning,
And then returned to her love and did say:
"Go to my uncle on the banks of the river,
And if he is willing, with you I'll agree."

So the bear and the possum they patted together
Till they retch' the bank of the river side.
He says, "Uncle Raccoon, I've been courting your possum,
And if you are willing, I'll make her my bride."

The match was struck up, all things were made ready,
This couple was joined in the very same day.
The wildcats and ground hogs were chosen for waiters,
The priest was a panther, I've heard people say.

Colonel Ricketts and His Park

Cannon on Gettysburg battlefield

The battle at **Gettysburg**, Pennsylvania, was one of the hardest and most important battles of the Civil War. There were many heroes on the battlefield that day. One of the heroes was Captain Robert Bruce Ricketts of the Union Army.

Robert Ricketts was preparing to become a lawyer when the Civil War began in 1861. At 22 years old he left his dreams to fight for the Union. He fought with courage. He bravely led many troops in one battle after another. By the time the war ended, Robert Ricketts had become a colonel.

Colonel Ricketts got married three years after the end of the Civil War. The next year, when Colonel Ricketts was 30 years old, he bought a large piece of land from his father. He also bought a hotel called Stone House, which his father and uncle had built.

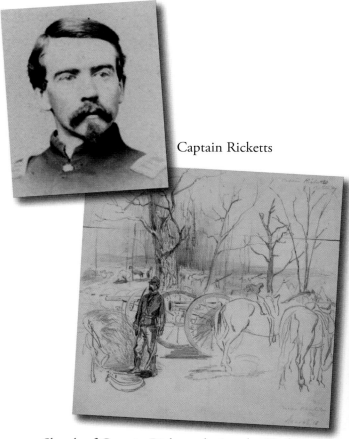

Captain Ricketts

Sketch of Captain Ricketts during the Civil War

Adams Falls on Kitchen Creek

Colonel Ricketts eventually purchased tens of thousands of acres in this northeastern corner of Pennsylvania. Visitors to his land enjoyed the beauty of Lake Ganoga. *Ganoga* is a Seneca word that means "water on the mountain." Ganoga is the highest lake east of the Rocky Mountains.

Colonel Ricketts' land included 21 waterfalls along Kitchen Creek. He built trails through the woods so his visitors could enjoy the beauty of these falls. The colonel used native tribal words to name some of the waterfalls. He named others after special friends and members of his family.

Many years after the Civil War, Colonel Ricketts became a member of the Pennsylvania Gettysburg Monument Commission. This organization set up war memorials on the Gettysburg battlefield. The monuments still stand in Gettysburg to honor the soldiers who fought there.

Monuments at Gettysburg

Ricketts Glen State Park

Colonel Ricketts had many friends. One of his dearest friends was John Green. John Green had been enslaved before the Civil War. During the war, he was forced to serve with a Confederate officer. Union troops captured him during a battle. Colonel Ricketts was put in charge of this new prisoner. The two became friends. John Green stayed with the Ricketts family for the rest of his life, but he was not their slave. The Ricketts treated him as a member of their family. Mr. Green loved to study history, science, and poetry. He was an excellent cook. The people of the Lake Ganoga community loved him dearly. Colonel Ricketts paid for John Green to attend school so that he could become a minister.

Colonel Robert Bruce Ricketts had a gentle soul and a special love of nature. After he died, his descendants sold some of his land to the state of Pennsylvania. It became Ricketts Glen State Park.

But the fruit of the Spirit is love, joy, peace, patience, kindness, goodness, faithfulness, gentleness, self-control; against such things there is no law.
Galatians 5:22-23

Activities

- Complete the map activities for Pennsylvania in the *Atlas Workbook* (page 19).
- Read chapter 4 in *The Cabin Faced West*.
- Imagine that you own a piece of land with 21 waterfalls on it. What would you name them all? If you are keeping a creative writing notebook, make a list of your ideas.

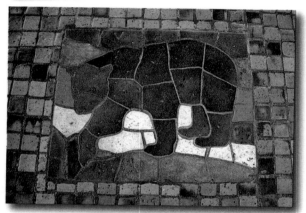

Supplies:

- orange, white, black, brown, and green construction paper
- glue
- scissors
- printed pattern

1. The mosaics pictured at left are on the floor of the Pennsylvania State Capitol. Visit notgrass. com/50links to choose and print a mosaic pattern for this activity.

2. Cut small pieces of construction paper in the colors you will need for your design. Cut a variety of shapes and sizes. The pieces you cut do not need to fit into the outlined areas exactly. You can use several small pieces that overlap each other to fill in an area. For all of the designs, cut squares of orange construction paper (approximately 1") for the borders.

3. Apply glue to one area of your pattern. Lay pieces of the appropriate color of construction paper in that area until it is filled in. It's okay if some small areas of white still show.

4. Continue this process until all the areas of your pattern are filled in with construction paper.

5. Glue a border of orange squares around the design.

72

The Greenbank Mill in Marshallton, New Jersey

New Jersey produce

New Jersey is the Garden State. Back in 1876, a New Jersey man named Abraham Browning spoke at a celebration. He used the term "Garden State." He said New Jersey was like a large barrel, filled with good things to eat. He said that people from Pennsylvania grab from one end of the barrel and people from New York grab from the other. The nickname stuck. "The Garden State" is printed on signs and license plates across New Jersey. Find New Jersey on the map at the beginning of this book.

Rutan Hill

Rutan Hill in New Jersey has a surprising history. Today it looks like a simple grassy hill. However, it appears that long ago, the hill was quite different. The land around Rutan Hill contains many igneous rocks. It takes something very hot to make these rocks. Geologists believe that Rutan Hill is an extinct volcano. An extinct volcano is one that doesn't erupt anymore. It's hard to imagine fire and lava spewing out of this grassy hill. It certainly shows that things on our planet do not always stay the same.

Rutan Hill

74

Lenape women

Delaware River

Delaware River

The **Delaware River** forms the border between New Jersey and Delaware. This part of the country was once home to the Lenape. Englishman George Fox traveled through this area in 1672. George Fox and his companions hired Lenape guides to lead them on their journey. The Lenape carried them across the Delaware River in their canoes. They welcomed the English people into their homes. George Fox wrote, "I came at last and lay at one Indian king's house and he and his queen received me lovingly and his attendants also and laid me a mat to lie upon." George Fox was careful to respect the Lenape people and their customs while he was in their territory.

Delaware Bay

The Delaware River flows into **Delaware Bay**. Every spring thousands of horseshoe crabs crawl out of the bay's water

Horseshoe crabs in New Jersey

to lay their eggs on the sandy beach. At the same time, close to one million migrating birds stop at the bay to rest on their journeys. The birds need to fatten up to continue their long flights. Some will travel all the way to the Arctic for the summer. The horseshoe crab eggs are a tasty treat. Since a female horseshoe crab can lay up to 100,000 eggs each spring, there are plenty of eggs at Delaware Bay. Some of the birds who arrive at Delaware Bay come from as far away as the southern tip of South America. They will fly around 10,000 miles before their journey is over.

Capital: Trenton

The government of New Jersey has met in the same state house in **Trenton** since 1792. In the 1990s, the dome of the State House was starting to crumble. It needed a $12 million repair job. New Jersey children raised about $40,000 in a fundraiser called Dimes for the Dome. The money they raised helped pay for the glistening gold leaf that now covers the restored dome.

Capitol dome

Sleds in Moorestown

Flexible Flyer

In 1889 Samuel Leeds Allen of **Moorestown**, New Jersey, had an idea. Mr. Allen owned a company that made farm equipment. Not many people in the northeast need to buy farm equipment in the winter. Mr. Allen invented the Flexible Flyer sled. Manufacturing the sleds gave his workers something to do in the winter when they weren't making farm equipment. Today the library in Moorestown houses the Flexible Flyer Sled Museum. The longest sled in the museum is eight and half feet long!

Barnegat Lighthouse

Barnegat Lighthouse stands on **Long Beach Island**. This barrier island is about eighteen miles long. A barrier island is a long, narrow island that lies beside the mainland. A barrier island protects the mainland from the ocean's stormy winds and powerful waves.

Local people call Barnegat Lighthouse "Old Barney." From the top of Old Barney, visitors can see the island's maritime forest. The trees and other plants that grow in this type of forest withstand strong winds, flooding, and the salty spray of the ocean. Their roots help hold the sandy soil in place as ocean waves crash against the island.

Salt water taffy in Atlantic City

Atlantic City

When the boardwalk opened in **Atlantic City**, New Jersey, in 1870, it was the first of its kind in the country. A boardwalk is a raised wooden sidewalk on the beach.

Have you ever played Monopoly? Most of the places on the game board are in Atlantic City, including Indiana Avenue, Park Place, and of course Boardwalk.

If you're up for something sticky, stop in a candy shop on the boardwalk for a famous Atlantic City treat: salt water taffy. The story goes that in 1883, ocean waves splashed over a local candy seller's stand. When someone bought a piece of his taffy the next day, the man told her it was salt water taffy. The new treat was a hit. Candy shops have been selling salt water taffy on the boardwalk in Atlantic City ever since.

On the boardwalk in Atlantic City

Praise the Lord! Praise the Lord, O my soul!
Who made heaven and earth, the sea and all that is in them;
Who keeps faith forever.
Psalm 146:1, 6

Activities

- Illustrate the geographic term for New Jersey in the *Atlas Workbook* (page 20).

- If you are using the *Lesson Review*, answer the questions for New Jersey (page 5).

- Read chapter 5 in *The Cabin Faced West*.

- Hands-On Idea: Look at a Monopoly board and notice the street names. Ask an adult to find a map of Atlantic City online. How many Monopoly street names can you find on the map?

Lesson 18: A Song and Story of New Jersey

Ode to Cape May

This poem by Dr. Theophilus T. Price was published in a book about the history of Cape May, New Jersey, in 1897. (Track 9)

Dear land of my nativity!
And scene of childhood's play,
I fondly sing my love to thee
In humble, fervent lay.
Let others roam who have a mind;
With thee I'd rather stay,
For many ties there are that bind
My heart to thee, Cape May.

Chorus:
Cape May! Cape May!
My thoughts to thee will stray
With fond delight, in memories bright,
When I am far away.

The sunny skies look down serene
Where warbling woodlands lay;
And fertile fields stretch out between
The ocean and the bay.
The health on every breeze is borne
That o'er thee takes its way;
And plenty pours her teeming horn
Into thy lap, Cape May.

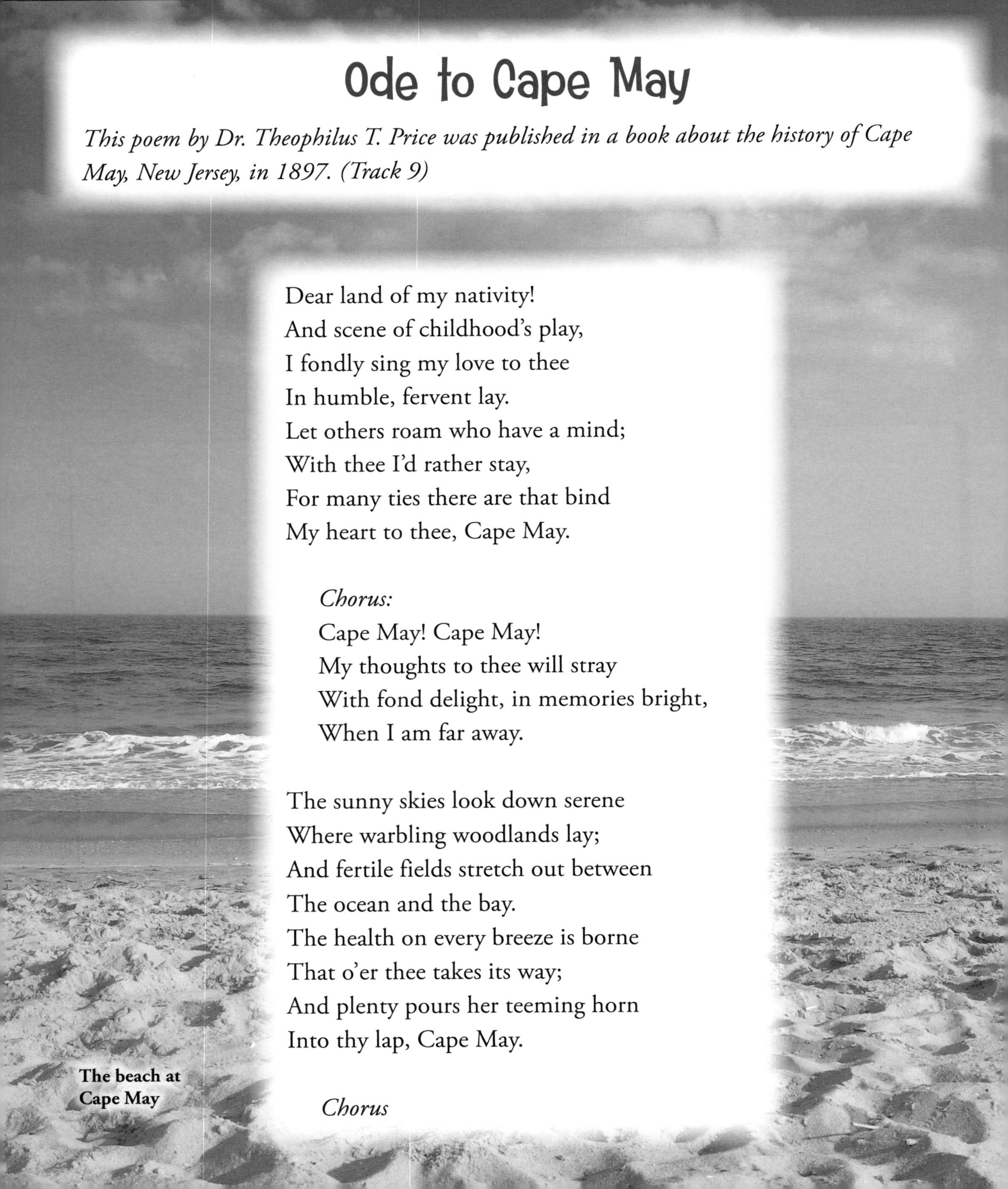

The beach at Cape May

Chorus

A President's Picture

The Cape May peninsula lies at the very southern tip of New Jersey. A peninsula is an area of land that is surrounded by water on three sides. People consider Cape May to be America's oldest seaside resort.

It was Sunday, August 24, 1890. President Benjamin Harrison, his wife, and their niece rode away from Cold Spring Church on the **Cape May** peninsula. They had worshiped there together that morning. The Harrisons were spending their summer here, away from the stifling heat of Washington, D.C. Several other presidents chose to spend part of their summers in New Jersey as well.

As they rode along in their coach, the Harrisons thought about a photograph they had seen of an older couple who lived nearby. The photo showed "Uncle Dan" and "Aunt Judy" Kelly in front of their vine-covered seaside cottage. The photograph had charmed the Harrisons. They wanted to see the cottage and the couple for themselves.

Historic homes on Cape May

Their coachman knew the Cape May peninsula well. He drove them right to the cottage and stopped at the garden gate. President Harrison climbed down and entered the yard. Aunt Judy had been asleep inside, but she awoke when she heard the coach drive up. She went outside.

President Harrison with his family

Garden on Cape May

President Harrison was thirsty, and asked Aunt Judy for a drink of water. Aunt Judy lowered an old wooden bucket into their well, and drew it back up. She watched her visitor closely as he drank the fresh, cool water.

President Harrison told her, "I have a photograph of you and your husband."

"What might your name be?" asked Aunt Judy.

"I am General Harrison," he replied.

"The saints be praised," Aunt Judy cried. "I have lived to see a president and talk to him. Daniel! Daniel! Come out here, old man. Sure as the president has come to see us!"

Uncle Dan could not get around well anymore, but he managed to come outside. He dropped his hat. He stood speechless as he stared at the president of the United States, standing in his own yard.

Aunt Judy turned back to President Harrison. "If you have my picture," she said, "can't I have one of yourn?"

"I have no picture of myself with me," the president answered. But then he had an idea. With a twinkle in his eye, he reached into his pocket. He pulled out something and handed it to Aunt Judy. "But this is the picture of another president."

Aunt Judy clasped the gift tightly with one hand. With her other she shook hands with the president of the United States. President Harrison turned back to the coach. He tipped his hat and bid the couple farewell as he and his wife and their niece rode away.

Aunt Judy then looked down at the president's gift. To her surprise and delight she held in her hand a picture of Andrew Jackson—on a five dollar bill.*

. . . You shall love your neighbor as yourself. . . .
Mark 12:31

Activities

- Complete the map activities for New Jersey in the *Atlas Workbook* (page 21).
- Read chapter 6 in *The Cabin Faced West*.
- Imagine that the president is coming for a vacation to your town and you get to be the tour guide. What sites around town should the president see? Will the president have dinner with your family, or will you go to a restaurant? What will everyone eat? In your creative writing notebook, write a story about the president's visit to your town. **or** Have someone in your family pretend to be the president as you pretend to be the tour guide around your house, pointing out special places and things you like to do.

Today Andrew Jackson's portrait is on the $20 bill, but in 1890 it was on the $5 bill.

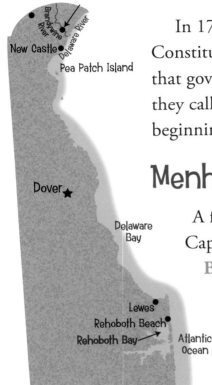

In 1787 Delaware was the first state to ratify (or approve) the Constitution of the United States. The Constitution is the set of laws that governs our country. Delaware is proud that they were first, so they call themselves the First State. Find Delaware on the map at the beginning of this book.

Menhaden Fish

A ferry allows people to travel between Lewes, Delaware, and Cape May, New Jersey. The ferry crosses the waters of Delaware Bay. Lewes was once the largest seafood port in the whole country. Factories stood all along the edge of the water. The factories processed the fish caught in these waters. The fish helped the people earn good money, but they sure made the town a smelly place. The most important fish in the industry was menhaden. Pilots in small planes flew over the water to look for schools (or groups) of menhaden. When a pilot spotted a school, he used a radio to let the fishermen know where to go. Menhaden fishing was so popular that in the 1960s, the Delaware Bay started to run out of them. These days the government has set limits on how many menhaden people can catch. Many other types of fish, as well as birds and other animals, eat the nutritious menhaden. Some people call menhaden the most important fish in the sea.

Two cormorants fight over a menhaden

Pea Patch Island

Pea Patch Island sits in the middle of the Delaware River. The story goes that a long time ago, there was just a shoal where this island is now. A shoal is an area of shallow water. Shoals can cause a ship to wreck. Supposedly, that's just what happened here. A ship wrecked and lost its cargo—a cargo of pea plants that were beginning to sprout. The pea plants took root in the sandbar. All those plants started catching dirt and sand floating down the Delaware River. As the pile of dirt and sand grew, it formed an island!

The U.S. government built a fort on Pea Patch Island. During the Civil War, the Union Army kept thousands of Confederate prisoners in the fort. Now Fort Delaware is a living history museum. The fort has a moat around it and a drawbridge. It almost looks like a castle.

Delaware Memorial Bridge

Delaware Memorial Bridge

The Delaware Memorial Bridge is actually two bridges. Workers completed a bridge between New Castle, Delaware, and Pennsville, New Jersey, in 1951. People soon realized that one bridge was not enough for all the traffic. Workers then built a second bridge almost exactly like the first bridge right next to it. The Delaware Memorial Bridge is a toll bridge. This means that drivers have to pay to cross it. The money helps pay for taking care of the bridge. Around 80,000 vehicles cross the twin bridges every day.

The du Pont Family

In 1800 the French du Pont family moved to Delaware. Two years later, E. I. du Pont built a mill beside Delaware's Brandywine River near **Wilmington**. The mill made gunpowder. The du Pont family became very wealthy. Today the company E. I. du Pont founded manufactures a wide variety of products, including fertilizers, special fabrics, water filters, building materials, and probiotics. The Hagley Museum and Library is now located on the site of the original mill. Visitors can see a restored du Pont gunpowder mill from the 1800s.

E. I. du Pont

Descendants of the du Pont family built the Winterthur mansion nearby. This du Pont home has 175 rooms. Members of the du Pont family lived in the home from 1839 until 1969. Members of the family opened their home as a museum in 1951. Today the museum has over 90,000 works of art, including paintings, glass, furniture, and needlework. The oldest piece of art is from 1630.

Winterthur

Capital: Dover

In 1847 a slave auction took place on the steps of the Old State House in **Dover**, Delaware. Samuel Burris was up for auction. He had been a free black man, but authorities caught him helping enslaved people escape to freedom. His punishment was to be sold and become enslaved himself.

Samuel Burris

Old State House

Old State House courtroom

At the auction, Isaac Flint purchased Samuel Burris for $500. After they rode away from the crowd, Isaac Flint told Samuel Burris a secret. Instead of taking him to a life of slavery, he was taking him north to freedom. Samuel Burris was overjoyed. Instead of becoming enslaved, he was able to join his wife and children and live in freedom in Pennsylvania.

Today Delaware's Old State House is a museum. Sometimes people use the Old State House for special ceremonies. In 2015 Delaware Governor Jack Markell stood in the Old State House courtroom—the same room where Samuel Burris had received his sentence exactly 168 years earlier. At the ceremony, Governor Markell issued an official pardon for Samuel Burris. The pardon was Delaware's way of saying, "Our government was wrong to say Samuel Burris was guilty of a crime." Several descendants of Samuel Burris attended the ceremony in honor of their ancestor.

Sometimes admitting we were wrong is hard to do, but the Bible teaches that it is right. The Bible also teaches us to forgive.

Be kind to one another, tender-hearted,
forgiving each other, just as God in Christ also has forgiven you.
Ephesians 4:32

Activities

- Illustrate the geographic term for Delaware in the *Atlas Workbook* (page 22).

- If you are using the *Lesson Review*, answer the questions for Delaware (page 5).

- Read chapter 7 in *The Cabin Faced West*.

- Hands-On Idea: The du Pont family collected historic American art. Look around your house and talk about special family heirlooms and artwork you have.

- Family Activity: Make Strawberry Shortcake (instructions on page 90).

Lesson 20: A Song and Story of Delaware

Our Delaware

This song by George B. Hynson and Will M. S. Brown is the state song of Delaware. (Track 10)

Oh, the hills of dear New Castle,
And the smiling vales between,
When the corn is all in tassel,
And the meadowlands are green;
Where the cattle crop the clover,
And its breath is in the air,
While the sun is shining over
Our beloved Delaware.

Chorus:
Oh, our Delaware!
Our beloved Delaware!
For the sun is shining over
Our beloved Delaware,
Oh, our Delaware
Our beloved Delaware!
Here's the loyal son that pledges
Faith to good old Delaware.

Where the wheatfields break and billow,
In the peaceful land of Kent,
Where the toiler seeks his pillow,
With the blessings of content;
Where the bloom that tints the peaches,
Cheeks of merry maidens share,
And the woodland chorus preaches
A rejoicing Delaware.

Chorus

Dear old Sussex visions linger,
Of the holly and the pine,
Of Henlopens Jeweled finger,
Flashing out across the brine;
Of the gardens and the hedges,
And the welcome waiting there,
For the loyal son that pledges
Faith to good old Delaware.

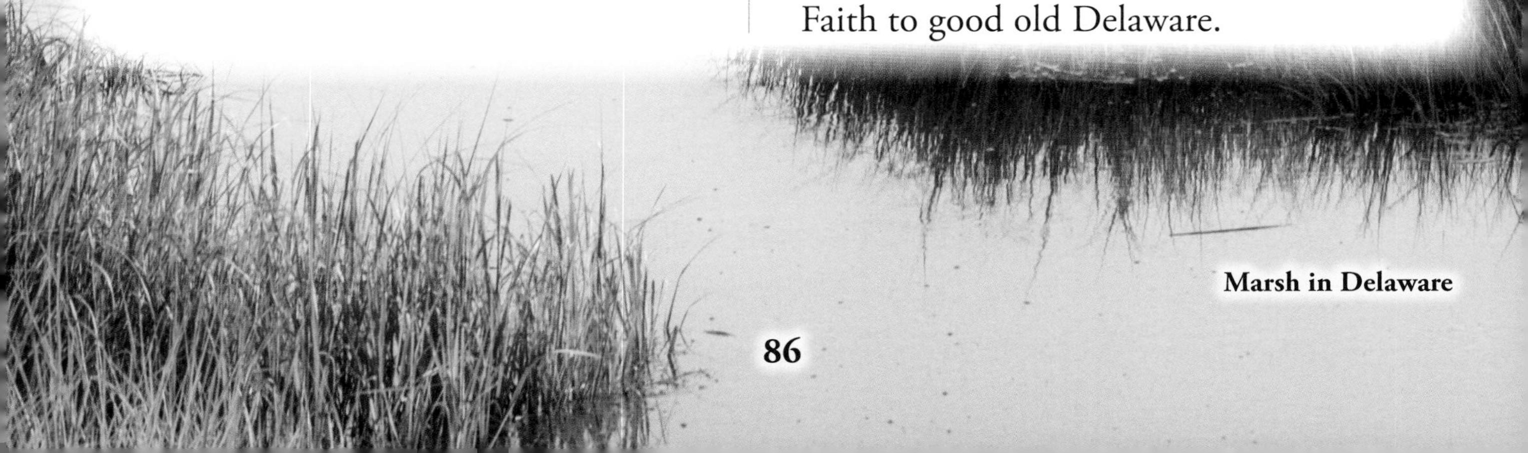

Marsh in Delaware

The Minister's Idea

Rehoboth Beach is one of Delaware's most popular destinations. It is the largest beach resort in the state. People come to enjoy sandy beaches, visit shops and restaurants, and get dizzy on fun rides. How does a tourist attraction like this ever get started?

Robert Todd was worn out. He needed a break from his duties as minister in **Wilmington**, Delaware. Mr. Todd traveled to Ocean Grove, New Jersey. After a relaxing stay at the beach, he felt refreshed and energized. He shared with his church how much his trip had helped him. Mr. Todd longed for his church members to experience what he had experienced at the sea. He had an idea. Why not establish a place for Christians to go to the beach together?

Purple sandpiper on Rehoboth Beach

Seagull on Rehoboth Beach

Robert Todd looked at land in New Jersey, but it was too expensive. He kept looking. He found just what he wanted near Delaware's **Rehoboth Bay**. Here quiet woods, peaceful ponds, and the majesty of the ocean waves all came together. A group of men formed the Rehoboth Beach Camp Meeting Association in 1873. The group purchased land and divided it into lots. They made a plan for streets. They wanted visitors to have "plenty of room, air, and sunshine."

Rehoboth Beach

87

Rehoboth Bay

People eagerly bought land at **Rehoboth Beach**. Each lot cost between $75 and $150. People built simple wooden houses on their lots. They called their simple houses "tents." The association built a place to hold yearly camp meetings when people would come together for days at a time. They listened to ministers, sang, and just enjoyed spending time with other Christians.

The camp meetings didn't last very long, but Rehoboth Beach became a popular vacation spot. Today a historical marker stands in the town to honor its Christ-centered beginning.

Robert Todd himself was sunny like the seaside. He had a special sparkle about him. He loved the Bible and had a fun sense of humor. He enjoyed sharing stories of funny things that happened in churches.

Historic illustrations of Rehoboth Beach from the 1930s-1940s

One of Mr. Todd's stories was about a fellow minister named William Barnes. William Barnes was once praying at a church service in Milton, Delaware, near Rehoboth Beach. All of a sudden, a wasp flew down the minister's collar. He stopped his prayer to go after the wasp. The minister took off his coat, then his vest. He took off

Rehoboth Beach

his large necktie and then his collar. During this time, the wasp went farther down— inside his shirt! The minister knew only one thing to do. Still standing up in front of the congregation, he took that shirt off. He shook out the wasp and crushed it on the floor with his foot. Then he casually dressed himself again and calmly finished the prayer where he had left off. He thanked God for delivering him from that nasty wasp.

One church member after another shook with laughter. They tried to keep their laughter in, but they just couldn't. When another wasp flew near the head of the minister during his sermon, they couldn't help but laugh again.

A joyful heart is good medicine,
But a broken spirit dries up the bones.
Proverbs 17:22

Rehoboth Beach

Activities

- Complete the map activities for Delaware in the *Atlas Workbook* (page 23).
- Read chapter 8 and "A Postscript from the Author" in *The Cabin Faced West*.
- If you could choose any place to go for a relaxing vacation, what type of place would it be? In the mountains? At the beach? In your creative writing notebook, write a description of the spot. **or** Pretend that you are having a camp meeting at Rehoboth Beach.

Family Activity: Strawberry Shortcake

Strawberries are the official fruit of Delaware. Enjoy some strawberry shortcake.

Ingredients (6 servings)

For the strawberries:
- 1 ½ pounds strawberries (green tops removed and fruit cut in half or in quarters if large)
- 3 tablespoons sugar

For the shortcake:
- 2 cups all-purpose flour
- 2 tablespoons sugar
- 2 teaspoons baking powder
- ¾ teaspoon salt
- ¼ teaspoon baking soda
- 1 ½ cups heavy whipping cream

For the whipped cream:
- 1 ½ cups heavy whipping cream, chilled
- 3 tablespoons sugar
- 1 ½ teaspoons vanilla extract
- 1 teaspoon finely grated lemon zest (optional)

Directions
- Gently mix strawberries with 3 tablespoons sugar. Cover bowl and refrigerate for at least 30 minutes.
- Position a rack in the middle of the oven. Preheat oven to 400°.
- Sift together flour, sugar, baking powder, baking soda, and salt into a medium bowl.
- Add heavy cream to flour mixture and mix until combined. Don't overmix.
- Pour mixture into a greased 8" square pan.
- Carefully place the pan in the oven.
- Bake until golden brown, 18 to 20 minutes.
- Remove from the oven.
- Remove the cake from the pan and place on a rack to cool slightly.
- Cut the cake into 6 pieces and slice each piece horizontally.
- Just before you serve your strawberry shortcake, beat together the whipped cream ingredients until soft peaks form (about 1 ½ - 2 minutes).
- Spoon some of the strawberries onto each shortcake bottom. Top with whipped cream and then the shortcake top. Spoon more strawberries over top.

Be safe with knives and the hot oven. Children must have adult supervision in the kitchen.

Jefferson Memorial in Washington, D.C.

Unit 6
Mid-Atlantic:
Maryland and Washington, D.C.

91

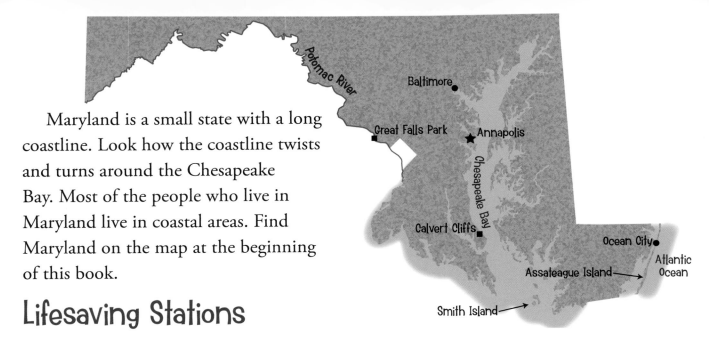

Maryland is a small state with a long coastline. Look how the coastline twists and turns around the Chesapeake Bay. Most of the people who live in Maryland live in coastal areas. Find Maryland on the map at the beginning of this book.

Lifesaving Stations

In the late 1800s, the United States government operated 25 lifesaving stations along the Atlantic Coast. Each station had a keeper and up to eight surfmen. Their job was to watch out for ships that were in trouble. If a ship got into trouble, the surfmen rushed to rescue anyone who needed help. The U.S. Lifesaving Station Museum in **Ocean City**, Maryland, tells the story of these lifesaving stations and the brave people who worked at them.

U.S. Lifesaving Station Museum

Assateague Island

There are not many places in the United States where you can see wild horses, but **Assateague Island** is one place you can. Part of Assateague Island belongs to Maryland and part of it belongs to Virginia. Each state has its own herd of wild horses on the island.

Wild horse on Assateague

Wild horses on Assateague

No one knows for sure how these horses reached Assateague. They might be descendants of horses that survived a shipwreck long ago and came ashore on the island. They might be the descendants of horses that belonged to early settlers on the mainland.

Chesapeake Bay

The states of Maryland and Virginia surround Chesapeake Bay. This estuary is the largest in the United States. Do you remember what an estuary is? It's where fresh water from rivers and streams meets the salty water of the ocean. Around 51 billion gallons of fresh river water flow into the bay each day. Much of the Chesapeake Bay is shallow and perfect for wading.

Fossils from Calvert Cliffs

Fossil hunters love to visit Calvert Cliffs on the western side of Chesapeake Bay. Fossilized whales, sharks, and birds lie hidden in the rocks. Some of these animals were as big as a small airplane!

Chesapeake Bay

Smith Island

Everything arrives by boat for the Maryland residents who live on **Smith Island**. Groceries, clothes, mail—everything! There are not many cars on Smith Island. Visitors can rent a golf cart or a bike to get around.

Many Smith Island families earn their living catching crabs. Their fathers and grandfathers and great-grandfathers did the same. Smith Island is famous for its fried crab cakes. It is also famous for Smith Island cake, the official dessert of Maryland. To make the cake, people bake several very thin cake layers. They stack the layers with icing between each one. Some people make Smith Island cakes with eight cake layers. Others use ten or twelve layers. Some even go as high as sixteen!

Crab traps near Smith Island

Smith Island cake

State House dome

Capital: Annapolis

The colonial governor of Maryland laid the cornerstone for the Maryland State House in **Annapolis** in 1772. The first dome that stood on top of the building quickly began to leak. People complained about the dome's ugly appearance. The government hired Joseph Clark, a local architect, to build a new one. The wooden pieces of Joseph Clark's dome fit together tightly, like a puzzle. He did not use any metal nails to hold the dome together. Instead he used wooden pegs. The dome is reinforced with iron straps. It has stood over the city since 1788. The dome is featured on the back of the Maryland state quarter.

94

Maryland quarter

Baltimore

Baltimore's Inner Harbor on Chesapeake Bay has been an important part of the city since the 1700s. A harbor is a sheltered place where ships and boats can dock. People once bustled about this harbor building ships and making sails. In the late 1900s, the city

World War II submarine

leaders of Baltimore decided to turn the harbor into a place for tourists. The harbor offers museums, restaurants, musical performances, and a collection of historic ships. Visitors can explore an authentic Civil War warship and a World War II submarine.

Great Falls Park

Great Falls Park

Great Falls Park is quite different from the busy harbor and crowded streets of Baltimore, but it is still a noisy place. Here the **Potomac River** crashes over rocks as it flows toward Chesapeake Bay. This is the same river that flows past Washington, D.C. The Potomac River marks the border between Maryland and Virginia.

O sing to the Lord a new song, for He has done wonderful things . . . .
Let the rivers clap their hands, let the mountains sing together for joy.
Psalm 98:1, 8

Activities

- Illustrate the geographic term for Maryland in the *Atlas Workbook* (page 24).

- If you are using the *Lesson Review*, answer the questions for Maryland (page 6).

- Hands-On Idea: Use play dough to make a Smith Island cake. Can you make it sixteen layers high?

Lesson 22: A Song and Story of Maryland

Hail Ye Happy Spirits

Harriet Tubman was born into slavery in Maryland in the early 1800s. She escaped from slavery in 1849. She returned to Maryland several times to help other enslaved people also escape. Enslaved people and those helping them often sang to communicate secret messages. This is one of the songs Harriet Tubman sang. (Track 11)

Hail, oh hail, ye happy spirits,
Death no more shall make you fear,
Grief nor sorrow, pain nor anguish,
Shall no more distress you there.

Around Him are ten thousand angels,
Always ready to obey command;
They are always hovering 'round you,
Till you reach the heavenly land.

Jesus, Jesus will go with you,
He will lead you to his throne;
He who died, has gone before you,
Through the wine-press all alone.

He whose thunders shake creation,
He who bids the planets roll;
He who rides upon the tempest,
And whose scepter sways the whole.

Dark and thorny is the pathway,
Where the pilgrim makes his ways;
But beyond this vale of sorrow,
Lie the fields of endless days.

Maryland countryside

Harriet Tubman

Beside the Potomac

James Deane pulled at another pesky weed in the watermelon patch. It was another typical day on the Mason plantation where he was enslaved in Maryland. He had been in the cornfield at sunup with other enslaved children.

Suddenly, James heard the distant sound of someone blowing a loud call through an old conch shell. James met the eyes of another enslaved child. They smiled at each other. They knew they had something to look forward to now.

Reconstructed slave cabin near the Potomac River

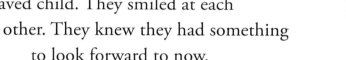

Conch shell

After the sun went down, James and his family gathered back at their log cabin. They ate the cornbread and fat hog meat James' mother had prepared. When everyone was finished, the family headed for the bank of the nearby Potomac River. They heard someone blow on the conch shell again. They all knew the signal meant to gather at the river.

One by one, and family by family, the number of people on the riverbank grew. Someone had brought his homemade fiddle. He began to play. James' two sisters began to dance and James joined them. Soon the riverbank was alive with music and dancing. As the moon broke through the clouds, someone started singing a song with gusto. Everyone joined in. Their voices carried across the Potomac River. A group of enslaved people on the Virginia shore heard them and sang back.

Potomac River

It was a beautiful night. When James and his family got back to their cabin, they were exhausted. James was glad it was Saturday. Even though he would have to help feed the animals the next day, he wouldn't have to work in the fields.

Prayer card

On Sunday morning, James and his family joined the others in the slave gallery at the local church. White people and black people joined their voices, but they didn't sit in the same pews. As the congregation recited the Lord's Prayer together, James didn't miss a beat. He knew every word.

For Sunday dinner, James and his family ate crabs—a special treat. In the afternoon, James played marbles with his friends. They played London Bridge. In the evening, after everyone had eaten, they gathered again to sing and tell stories. James loved the stories, no matter how many times he had heard them before. This time everyone gathered by the Deane cabin. They would go back to the riverbank another day.

Marbles

The next morning James was back in the cornfield. The corn was just coming up, but already James looked forward to shucking time. All the enslaved people from other nearby plantations would come to the barn. A fiddler would play all day as they shucked. They would eat roast pig and apple sauce. When the work was finished, they would dance. Oh, how they would dance! The dancing and music would keep going until the sun came up the next morning.

Corn

James knew that enslaved people on other plantations sometimes got whipped. Sometimes they got sold. James never experienced those things on the Mason plantation, but he was still enslaved. Life was hard, but James learned from his family and community to smile and laugh and sometimes dance in the midst of it all.

Now may our Lord Jesus Christ Himself and God our Father,
who has loved us and given us eternal comfort and good hope by grace,
comfort and strengthen your hearts in every good work and word.
2 Thessalonians 2:16-17

Enslaved people making music on a southern plantation

Activities

- Complete the map activities for Maryland in the *Atlas Workbook* (page 25).
- Talk with your family about a hard time you have gone through together when the Lord Jesus Christ and God the Father comforted and strengthened your hearts. If you are keeping a creative writing notebook, write about that hard time.

Lesson 23: Washington, D.C.

Washington, D.C., is the capital of the United States. D.C. stands for District of Columbia. The city is named for George Washington, our first president. The district is named after Christopher Columbus, the Italian explorer who sailed to the New World in 1492. The land in the district once belonged to Maryland. Washington, D.C., is its own district and is not part of any state. Its monuments and museums remind us of our past and help us to be thankful for our freedom. Find Washington, D.C., on the map at the beginning of this book.

Planning Our Capital

The American colonies declared their independence from Britain in 1776. They declared themselves to be their own country, but they had to figure out how to set up their government. They had to write laws and decide who would be the country's leader. They had to decide where the capital city of their new country would be.

George Washington, our nation's first president, chose a spot beside the **Potomac River** near his own home of Mount Vernon. Pierre Charles L'Enfant, a French immigrant who fought in the Revolutionary War, designed the city.

Early plan for Washington, D.C.

The White House

While George Washington was serving as president, workers began building a presidential home in Washington. It took several years to plan and build, so George Washington never lived in the house himself. John Adams, our second president, moved into the house in 1800.

The White House

Workers have added to the president's house, called the White House, several times. Today it has 132 rooms, 35 bathrooms, 28 fireplaces, 8 staircases, and 3 elevators. It takes 570 gallons of white paint to repaint the outside!

The U.S. Capitol

U.S. Capitol

Each state has two senators who serve in the U.S. Senate. Each state also has representatives who serve in the U.S. House of Representatives. Senators and representatives meet in the U.S. Capitol to make laws for our country.

The National Mall

When Pierre Charles L'Enfant designed Washington, D.C., he made plans for a Grand Avenue. Today we call this part of the city the National Mall. The National Mall stretches from the banks of the Potomac River to the U.S. Capitol. The places featured on the following pages are some of the sites on the National Mall.

Lincoln Memorial

The Lincoln Memorial beside the Potomac River honors Abraham Lincoln who led our country during the Civil War. Look at the back of a penny and notice the tiny statue of President Lincoln pictured inside the memorial. The real statue is much larger! The original plan was to make the statue ten feet tall, but people were concerned that would not be impressive enough. They decided to make the statue 19 feet tall. If the statue could stand up, it would be 28 feet tall.

Lincoln Memorial

Washington Monument

The Washington Monument stands 555 feet tall and is the tallest building in Washington, D.C. Workers completed it in 1884 as a memorial to George Washington. Around the monument are fifty American flags, which represent our fifty states.

World War II Memorial

In 2004 over 150,000 people came to the National Mall for the dedication of the World War II Memorial. The memorial honors members of the military who served during the war from 1941 until 1945. It also honors Americans on the home front who worked in factories building planes and tanks, raised food in their own gardens so there would be enough for soldiers, and helped America win the war in countless other ways.

World War II Memorial with the Washington Monument in the background

Korean War Memorial

Nineteen statues showing members of the U.S. military honor the brave Americans who served during the Korean War from 1950 until 1953. They are arranged among strips of stone on the ground that represent the rice paddies of Korea where they fought.

Korean War Memorial

Vietnam Veterans Memorial

Etched onto the walls of the Vietnam Veterans Memorial are 58,318 names of the men and women who died serving our country during that conflict from 1955 until 1975.

The war memorials on the National Mall are full of sadness, but they are also full of courage and strength. Millions of Americans have sacrificed to keep our country strong. It is right to honor them. It is good to remember our country's past so that we can learn from it and be stronger in the future.

In the Bible, God gave the Israelites instructions to remember their past and to pass on the story of their people to future generations so they would always remember the goodness of the Lord.

Vietnam Veterans Memorial

Only give heed to yourself
and keep your soul diligently,
so that you do not forget the things
which your eyes have seen
and they do not depart from your heart
all the days of your life;
but make them known to your
sons and your grandsons.
Deuteronomy 4:9

Activities

- Illustrate the geographic term for Washington, D.C., in the *Atlas Workbook* (page 26).
- If you are using the *Lesson Review*, answer the questions for Washington, D.C. (page 6).
- Hands-On Idea: Use building bricks or blocks to create a memorial.
- Family Activity: Work together to Thank a Veteran (instructions on page 108).

Hail to the Chief

Since the early 1800s, the Marine Band has played this melody to announce the arrival of the president at official gatherings and special events. The words, written later by Albert Gamse, are rarely sung. (Track 12)

Hail to the Chief we have chosen for the nation,
Hail to the Chief! We salute him, one and all.
Hail to the Chief, as we pledge cooperation
In proud fulfillment of a great, noble call.

Yours is the aim to make this grand country grander,
This you will do, that is our strong, firm belief.
Hail to the one we selected as commander,
Hail to the President! Hail to the Chief!

Washington Monument

White House Pets

Many presidential pets of all types have lived at the White House through the years. When Donald Trump became president in 2017, he was the first president in over 100 years to have no pet at the White House.

Fala with photographers at the White House in 1942

Fala

Americans adored President Franklin Roosevelt's dog Fala. Thousands of people wrote the dog letters and he had his own secretary to answer his mail. Fala entertained famous guests who came to the White House by doing tricks for them. They laughed when the dog curled his lip into a smile. When White House staff prepared President Roosevelt's breakfast tray each morning, they always included a bone for Fala. Fala often traveled with the president by train, car, and boat.

Rebecca

In 1926 someone from Mississippi gave the family of President Calvin Coolidge the gift of a raccoon. The Mississippian suggested the family have the raccoon for their Thanksgiving dinner. Instead, they named the coon Rebecca and kept her as a pet. Rebecca had her own little wooden house on the grounds of the White House. She

traveled with the family and joined them for special celebrations inside the White House. One of her favorite things to do was play with a bar of soap in the bathtub. When it was time for the Coolidges to leave the White House, they said goodbye to Rebecca and sent her to live at a nearby zoo. When Rebecca no longer needed her little wooden house at the White House, Billy Possum moved in.

Calvin Coolidge's wife Grace with Rebecca in 1927

Baa, Baa, Black Sheep

When World War I started, Americans everywhere had to change the way they did things. It takes many people to take care of the grounds around the White House, but those people needed to work in factories and become soldiers. During the war, President Woodrow Wilson and his family kept a flock of sheep at the White House to help take care of the grass. This allowed more people to help with war effort. The wool from the sheep raised thousands of dollars for the Red Cross, an organization that helps people in need.

Sheep in front of the White House in 1919

Neigh and Hiss

Theodore Roosevelt's family kept many animals at the White House, including Jonathan Edwards the bear, Josiah the badger, Eli Yale the blue macaw, a hyena, a barn owl, and a pony named Algonquin. Once two of the Roosevelt boys snuck Algonquin into the White House and up the elevator to the room where their brother was sick in bed. Algonquin was fascinated by his reflection in the elevator mirror. The pony got startled, slipped, and landed on the floor with a thud. The thud was loud enough to let others in the house know that *something* was happening upstairs!

Once the president's son Quentin bought four snakes from a neighborhood pet store. He was excited to show them to his father. President Roosevelt was in a meeting when Quentin got back to the White House, but that didn't stop him. He burst into his father's office and dropped the snakes on the table. The senators and others at the meeting scrambled to get out of the way. The snakes had to go back to the pet shop.

Quentin on Algonquin at the White House in 1905

Meow

President Abraham Lincoln had also allowed his children to keep a variety of pets at the White House. President Lincoln bought two goats, Nanny and Nanko, for his son Tad. Once Tad hitched the goats to a kitchen chair and rode the chair like a sled. The goats pulled him through the fancy East Room in the White House where his mother was hosting a gathering.

East Room of the White House in 1898

President Lincoln's wife once said that her husband's hobby was cats. Once during the Civil War, President Lincoln traveled to Virginia. While there he noticed three kittens alone in a telegraph hut. He cuddled the motherless kittens in his lap. Before he left, President Lincoln made sure that someone was going to feed the kittens and find homes for them.

Elephants? Not Quite.

When James Buchanan was president, he received a letter from King Mongkut of Siam (now Thailand). King Mongkut said he had heard that the United States had no elephants. The king offered to send several pairs of elephants to America so they could be let loose in our forests and jungles and become large herds. There was one little problem, though. America doesn't have any jungles. While the United States appreciated the king's kind and generous offer, we had to turn him down and let him keep his elephants.

You alone are the Lord. You have made the heavens, the heaven of heavens with all their host, the earth and all that is on it, the seas and all that is in them. You give life to all of them and the heavenly host bows down before You.
Nehemiah 9:6

Activities

- Complete the map activities for Washington, D.C., in the *Atlas Workbook* (page 27).
- Imagine that you are growing up at the White House and your parents tell you to pick out any pet you want. What will you pick? What will you name it? If you are keeping a creative writing notebook, write about your White House pet.
- If you are using the *Lesson Review*, take the Mid-Atlantic Test (page 31).

Family Activity: Thank a Veteran

Work together as a family to thank a veteran you know for his or her service to our country. Make patriotic thank you cards or a poster for the veteran. If the veteran you are thanking lives nearby, deliver your cards or poster in person, along with a plate of cookies or some other treat. Tell the veteran that you recently learned about veteran memorials in Washington, D.C. If the veteran is comfortable with it, ask questions about his or her time in the service, such as:

- How long did you serve?
- Where did you serve?
- What was basic training like?
- What were some of your duties?

The veteran might enjoy showing your family some pictures, a uniform, or other special military keepsakes.

If the veteran you are thanking lives far away, mail your cards to him or her. You might be able to arrange a phone or video call to ask the veteran questions about his or her time in the service.

Harper's Ferry, West Virginia

Unit 7
South:
Virginia and West Virginia

Lesson 25: Virginia

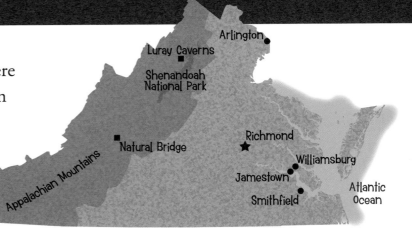

Eight of our country's presidents were born in Virginia—more presidents than were born in any other state. Find Virginia on the map at the beginning of this book.

Jamestown

In 1607 a group of 104 men and boys came to North America from England to establish a new settlement. They chose a spot in what is now Virginia. No native tribes lived there, although the area they chose was Powhatan hunting land. They called their new settlement Jamestown in honor of King James I of England. Jamestown became the first permanent English settlement in America.

Replica of a ship that brought settlers to Jamestown

Williamsburg

Settlers established Williamsburg in 1699. Visitors to Williamsburg today step back in time and experience life in America's colonial times. The colonial times began when settlers established Jamestown in 1607. It ended in 1776 when America declared their independence from Great Britain.

Playing fifes and drums in Williamsburg

Carriage ride in Williamsburg

Smithfield

Native people taught the settlers who established **Smithfield** how to gather salt from the ocean water. They showed them how to use the salt to preserve meat so that it would last longer. Settlers used this knowledge to help them develop a method for preserving ham from their hogs. They shipped their hams to Europe and people loved them. Smithfield ham became famous. Today Smithfield, Virginia, is the Ham Capital of the World. The city is home to Smithfield Foods, the largest pork-producing company in the world.

Hog

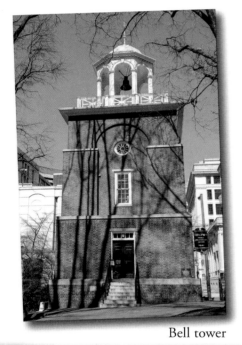

Bell tower

Capital: Richmond

Thomas Jefferson designed the state capitol of Virginia in **Richmond** before he became president. He got the idea for the building's design from an ancient Roman temple he saw in France.

A bell tower stands near the capitol. During the early 1800s, the Virginia Public Guard used this tower as a guardhouse. Members of this guard protected the area the way police officers do today. They used the bell tower to warn the people of Richmond in case of fire or other emergency. Today the bell rings when it is time for the Virginia General Assembly to meet in the nearby capitol.

Virginia Capitol

Arlington National Cemetery

Arlington, Virginia, lies on the banks of the Potomac River, just across from Washington, D.C. This city is home to Arlington National Cemetery. Thousands of men and women who served in our nation's military are buried here. The first soldiers buried here died during the Civil War.

Arlington National Cemetery

Luray Caverns

The largest musical instrument in the world lies below the ground in **Luray Caverns** in northern Virginia. Deep in the ground sits an organ connected by wires to stalactites all over the cave. When a musician plays a key on the organ, it causes a rubber mallet to gently strike one of the stalactites. The stalactites produce different tones depending on their size. The sound of the Great Stalacpipe Organ is gentle and soothing as it echoes off the cavern walls.

Great Stalacpipe Organ in Luray Caverns

Shenandoah National Park

When European settlers first came to North America, they found abundant wildlife. Countless bears wandered through Virginia's Shenandoah Valley. As more people moved in, more bears moved out. Settlers killed many of the bears; and by the 1940s, only about ten bears lived in the new Shenandoah National Park. People have worked hard to help the bears thrive again. Today hundreds of bears roam through the park.

Shenandoah National Park lies in the Blue Ridge Mountains, which are part of the Appalachian Mountains. A trail through the Appalachian Mountains stretches all the way from Georgia to Maine. People who hike the Appalachian Trail pass through Shenandoah National Park. Many people enjoy taking a day hike on a portion of the trail. Some adventurous people hike the entire trail straight through. Do you think you could make it the whole way? The trail is over 2,000 miles long. It takes around six months of hard hiking to make it from one end to the other!

Before the mountains were born or You gave birth to the earth and the world,
Even from everlasting to everlasting, You are God.
Psalm 90:2

Shenandoah National Park

Activities

- Illustrate the geographic term for Virginia in the *Atlas Workbook* (page 28).

- If you are using the *Lesson Review*, answer the questions for Virginia (page 7).

- Read the chapter titled "A Sad Letter" in *Soft Rain*. (Parents, please refer to page 16 in the *Answer Key and Literature Guide* for comments about this book.)

- Hands-On Idea: The Great Stalacpipe Organ is a unique instrument. Look around your house and find things to make your own unique instruments.

Lesson 26: A Story and Song of Virginia

The Barnyard

When early settlers came to America from Europe, they brought with them many folk songs. Songs such as this one from England spread throughout Virginia and the rest of the United States and became part of American culture as well. (Track 13)

I had a cat and the cat pleased me,
I fed my cat under yonder tree.
Cat goes fiddle-dee-dee!

I had a hen and the hen pleased me,
I fed my hen under yonder tree.
Hen goes shimmy-shack, shimmy-shack,
Cat goes fiddle-dee-dee!

I had a sheep and the sheep pleased me,
I fed my sheep under yonder tree.
Sheep goes baa-baa,
Hen goes shimmy-shack, shimmy-shack,
Cat goes fiddle-dee-dee!

I had a horse and the horse pleased me,
I fed my horse under yonder tree.
Horse goes neigh-neigh
Sheep goes baa-baa,
Hen goes shimmy-shack, shimmy-shack,
Cat goes fiddle-dee-dee!

I had a goose and the goose pleased me,
I fed my goose under yonder tree.
Goose goes splishy-splashy,
Horse goes neigh-neigh
Sheep goes baa-baa,
Hen goes shimmy-shack, shimmy-shack,
Cat goes fiddle-dee-dee!

I had a girl and the girl pleased me,
I fed my girl under yonder tree,
Girl goes honey-honey,
Goose goes splishy-splashy,
Horse goes neigh-neigh
Sheep goes baa-baa,
Hen goes shimmy-shack, shimmy-shack,
Cat goes fiddle-dee-dee!

I had a man and the man pleased me,
I fed my man under yonder tree,
Man goes money-money,
Girl goes honey-honey,
Goose goes splishy-splashy,
Horse goes neigh-neigh
Sheep goes baa-baa,
Hen goes shimmy-shack, shimmy-shack,
Cat goes fiddle-dee-dee!
Cat goes fiddle-dee-dee!

Virginia farmland

Natural Bridge

March 5, 1927, was a cold day. Snow lay on the ground and icicles hung from the rocks that surround Cedar Creek. A group of men and women gathered on nearby Pulpit Rock in their coats and hats. The sun warmed their backs. High above they could see Virginia's **Natural Bridge**, which crosses Cedar Creek almost 200 feet above the water. They watched Dr. Chester Reeds step into a large wooden basket, built especially for this moment. The basket was attached to a rope, which went through a pulley at the top of the bridge. The other end of the rope was tied securely to a fencepost. Dr. Reeds was a geologist. His mission was to study the Natural Bridge up close and take photographs of its features.

As Dr. Reeds stood waiting, he clutched the handle of a large black camera as it rested on the side of the wooden basket.

Dr. Reeds ready for his descent

A crowd watching on Pulpit Rock

A group of men stood with him on the top of the Natural Bridge. Several of the men clutched the rope to make sure it didn't slip. The rope was wound around a wooden log attached to a metal crank. A man grasped the crank, ready to turn it carefully.

When all was set, the man at the crank began to turn. As he turned the crank, the rope slowly lowered the basket with Dr. Reeds in it toward the rushing creek below. The spectators on Pulpit Rock watched eagerly. As the rope lowered the basket from the bridge, it began to spin. It kept spinning . . . and spinning!

Dr. Reeds in his basket

Natural Bridge

Dr. Reeds got so dizzy it was hard to take the photos he wanted. Gradually he was able to hold the camera steady and capture some pictures. He photographed the bridge, the creek below, and the rock walls that support the bridge on each side. Dr. Reeds used his pictures to illustrate a book that he wrote about the bridge. He called the bridge "the most striking curiosity of its kind in America." His writing and photographs helped people better understand what he called "one of the great wonders of the world."

Dr. Reeds' book

George Washington visited the Natural Bridge around 150 years before Dr. Reeds was there. When George Washington was a young man, he worked as a surveyor, taking measurements of land in Virginia. On one wall of the bridge, visitors today can still see the initials "G.W." carved into the face of the rock, along with an official surveyor's cross. People have found two stones near the bridge also marked by a surveyor long ago. One of them also has the initials "G.W."

Thomas Jefferson purchased the Natural Bridge and several acres of land around it in 1774. He visited the bridge several times, always marveling at its beauty and grandeur. While he was serving as president in 1802, Thomas Jefferson visited the bridge again and created the first map showing it and the surrounding land.

A writer once called Virginia's Natural Bridge "God's greatest miracle in stone." It does indeed declare to all the world the power and majesty of our God.

Splendid and majestic is His work,
And His righteousness endures forever.
Psalm 111:3

Activities

- Complete the map activities for Virginia in the *Atlas Workbook* (page 29).

- Read the chapter titled "The Little People" in *Soft Rain*.

- Imagine that you are a bird watching Dr. Reeds descend in his basket. What do you think this human is doing? What is the black box he is holding that keeps making clicking noises? Why is there a crowd of other humans watching him? If you are keeping a creative writing notebook, write "Thoughts about Dr. Reeds" from the perspective of a bird.

Lesson 27: West Virginia

West Virginia was once part of the state of Virginia. It became a separate state during the Civil War. The northern portion of West Virginia is called the panhandle. In some places, the panhandle is only four miles wide. Find West Virginia on the map at the beginning of this book.

Map labels: Wheeling, Ohio River, Fairmont, Harrison County, Canaan Valley, Seneca Rocks, Spruce Knob, Kanawha River, Gauley River, Charleston, New River Gorge Bridge, New River

Spruce Knob

The highest point in West Virginia is **Spruce Knob**. A knob is a prominent rounded hill (*prominent* means that it stands out). Spruce Knob is named for the spruce trees that grow there. The wind blows so hard on Spruce Knob that some of the spruce trees only grow branches on one side!

Seneca Rocks

Spruce trees on Spruce Knob

Rock climbers love to take on the challenge of climbing **Seneca Rocks**. These jagged rock formations tower 900 feet into the sky not far from Spruce Knob.

Two views of Seneca Rocks

118

In the 1940s, when the United States was fighting in World War II, the Army brought a group of soldiers to Seneca Rocks for rock climbing training. The Army was preparing the soldiers to fight against our enemies in Europe.

The soldiers finished their training and traveled across the Atlantic Ocean to fight in Italy where the mountains are similar to Seneca Rocks. They successfully took over places in the mountains that the enemy controlled. The soldiers' courage and their good training in West Virginia helped to defeat the enemy.

World War II soldiers at Seneca Rocks

Canaan Valley

David Hunter Strother explored the **Canaan Valley** of West Virginia in the 1850s. (It is pronounced ke-nayne by the locals.) Strother wrote that the area was hard to explore. He said not many people had even entered the valley—even the most adventurous. He wrote, "The settlers on its borders speak of it with a sort of dread." He described the valley as being "filled with bears, panthers, impassable laurel brakes, and dangerous precipices." The laurel grew so thick that people could walk on the plants like on a carpet. A forest fire burned through the valley in 1865 and cleared away the tangled growth. After the fire, people began to settle in the valley. Today the Canaan Valley is a favorite spot for outdoor adventure.

Canaan Valley

119

Capital: Charleston

West Virginia capitol

For several years, West Virginia's capital city bounced back and forth. At first it was in **Wheeling**. Seven years later, in 1870, workers loaded official government paperwork and other items onto a steamship. They traveled on the Ohio River, then on the Kanawha River, and finally arrived in **Charleston**, the new capital. Five years later, the government decided to move the capital back to Wheeling. Workers loaded up everything again and took it all back.

In 1877 the people of West Virginia voted on where they wanted the permanent state capital to be. They chose Charleston. Once again workers loaded up steamships and headed back down the Ohio River to the Kanawha River, and finally to Charleston. This time the capital stayed put.

Workers completed West Virginia's current capitol building in 1932. Two stone tablets stand at the base of the capitol dome. Each is inscribed with a passage from the Bible. One reads: "Wisdom is the principal thing. Therefore, get wisdom. And with all of thy getting, get understanding." The other inscription says: "Happy is the man that findeth wisdom and getteth understanding."

Coal Mining

John Peter Salley discovered coal in what is now West Virginia in 1742. In the 1800s, people began using coal to heat their homes, power steamboats, and operate factories. Coal mining became an important part of life in West Virginia. Some coal mines in West Virginia have closed because people do not use as much coal today as they used to. However, coal mining is still an important part of the state's culture and economy.

West Virginia coal miners in 1938

Coal miner statue at the West Virginia capitol

New River Gorge Bridge

To build the New River Gorge Bridge, workers first built a tower on each side of the gorge. They stretched cables between the towers. They ran trolleys along the cables. The trolleys carried the steel pieces of the bridge so workers could put them in place. The New River Gorge Bridge opened in 1977. It stretches over 3,000 feet from one end to the other. The West Virginia state quarter features an image of the bridge.

One day each year is Bridge Day at the New River Gorge Bridge. On that day, people are not allowed to drive their cars on the bridge. Instead, the bridge is open for walking. Those with adventurous spirits jump off the bridge—with parachutes, of course! People also head off the bridge on a zipline and by rapelling. Which one would you like to try?

Thus says the Lord,
your Redeemer,
and the one who formed you
from the womb,
"I, the Lord, am the
maker of all things,
Stretching out the heavens
by Myself
And spreading out
the earth all alone."
Isaiah 44:24

Parachuting and rappelling off the New River Gorge Bridge
(The tiny dots in the sky are people rappelling.)

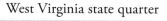

West Virginia state quarter

Activities

- Illustrate the geographic term for West Virginia in the *Atlas Workbook* (page 30).

- If you are using the *Lesson Review*, answer the questions for West Virginia (page 7).

- Read the chapter titled "Green Fern" in *Soft Rain*.

- Hands-On Idea: Think about the words on the stone tablets in the West Virginia capitol. Go outside and use sidewalk chalk to write "Get Wisdom" and "Get Understanding" on the ground. Decorate around the words.

- Family Activity: Make Pepperoni Rolls (instructions on page 126).

The Coal Loading Machine

In this song, coal miners wonder if the new coal loading machines are going to put them out of work. To say a person's "pocketbook is growing lean" means he doesn't have much money. In the song, one miner has the idea to work extra hard so that they can outdo the machine. (Track 14)

Chorus:
Tell me, what will a coal miner do?
Tell me, what will a coal miner do?
When he goes down in the mine,
Joy loaders he will find.
Tell me, what will a coal miner do?

Miners' poor pocketbooks are growing lean,
Miners' poor pocketbooks are growing lean,
They can't make a dollar at all,
Here is where we place the fault:
Place it all on that coal loading machine.

Chorus

Now boys, I think I have a scheme,
And I'm sure that it's neither rude nor mean.
We will pick our bone and refuse,
Then we'll know our coal is clean,
Then we'll outdo that coal loading machine.

Chorus

Modern coal conveyor

122

Luther Goes to School

The mountains of West Virginia made it hard for early settlers to even think of sending their children to school. They lived in a wild land. Life was dangerous. Fathers needed their boys to know how to shoot a gun. They needed their sons to help to clear a forest. Mothers needed their daughters to know how to help in the garden and take care of the home. Many parents were much more interested in those things than in reading and writing. Still, some of the early settlers had been to school themselves. They longed for their children to have at least a little schooling.

Gradually people began to establish schools among the mountains. Parents paid for their children to attend. Parents who didn't have enough money sometimes paid with items they had raised on their farm.

1800s cabin in West Virginia

Luther Haymond was born in 1809 in Harrison County in the part of Virginia that is now West Virginia. He attended one of the area's early schools as a child. He later wrote, "The school houses were generally old abandoned log cabins, the furniture consisted of slabs with holes bored in each end and pins driven in them for legs. . . . The master made all the pens out of goose quills." One of Luther's classmates was a grown woman who came to school with her children. The mother wanted to learn to read so that she could read the Bible.

Luther Haymond's early education helped to prepare him for a life of service. He worked as a surveyor, helping to mark out new roads. His work helped the people of West Virginia travel more easily through their Mountain State. He served in the state legislature and as a colonel during the Civil War. He was the treasurer of Harrison County, which means he handled the money for his community. He also worked as a bank officer. He did not retire from the bank until he was 86 years old.

When Luther Haymond died at the age of 99, the local newspaper published an article about him. The article described him as Harrison County's "oldest and grandest resident." The article also called him a "wonderful old man of exemplary character, unblemished career and patriotic citizenship."

Now for this very reason also, applying all diligence, in your faith supply moral excellence,
and in your moral excellence, knowledge, and in your knowledge, self-control,
and in your self-control, perseverance, and in your perseverance, godliness,
and in your godliness, brotherly kindness, and in your brotherly kindness, love.
2 Peter 1:5-7

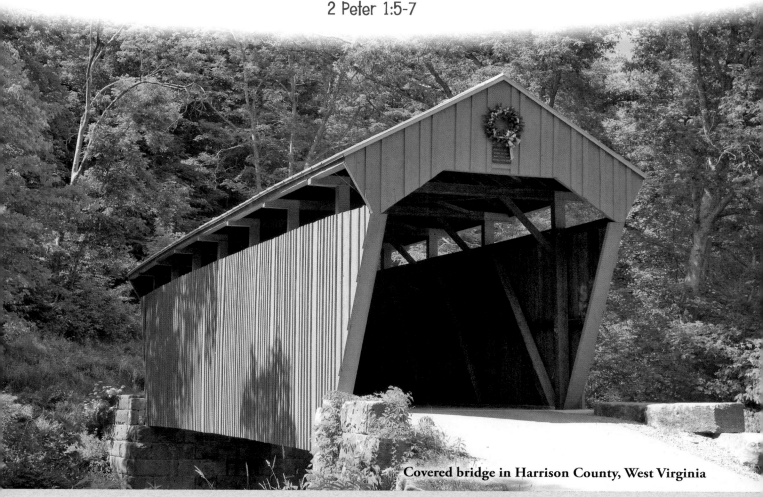

Covered bridge in Harrison County, West Virginia

Activities

- Complete the map activities for *West Virginia* in the Atlas Workbook (page 31).
- Read the chapter titled "Planting *Selu*" in *Soft Rain*.
- Luther Haymond wrote a description of his school. Where do you do most of your schoolwork? At a table or a desk? On the couch or the floor? If you are keeping a creative writing notebook, write a description of where you do most of your schoolwork. You might like to draw a picture of it as well.

Family Activity: Pepperoni Rolls

Giuseppe Argiro moved from Italy to West Virginia in 1920 to work in a coal mine. Italian coal miners often took bread and pepperoni to the mines for lunch. In 1927 Giuseppe Argiro opened a bakery in **Fairmont** where he created the famous pepperoni roll—bread and pepperoni rolled into an easy on-the-go meal. His bakery is still in operation today, and still making pepperoni rolls, the official food of West Virginia.

Be safe with knives and the hot oven. Children must have adult supervision.

Ingredients (makes 16 rolls):
- 1 cup warm water (100°)
- ½ teaspoon sugar
- 1 (.25 oz) package active dry yeast
- 5 cups all-purpose flour
- ¾ cup sugar
- 2 teaspoons salt
- 2 eggs, beaten
- ½ cup butter (melted)
- ¼ cup grated parmesan cheese
- 8 oz pkg sliced pepperoni
- 10 slices mozzarella cheese (cut in half)

Directions:
- In a small bowl, dissolve ½ teaspoon sugar in 1 cup warm water.
- Sprinkle yeast over the sugar-water mixture and let stand for 5 minutes.
- In a large bowl mix flour, ¾ cup sugar, and 2 teaspoons salt.
- Use a rubber spatula to mix the yeast mixture, beaten eggs, and melted butter into the flour mixture.
- When the dough has pulled together, turn it out onto a floured surface and knead until smooth and elastic, 7-9 minutes.
- Lightly oil a large bowl. Place the dough into the bowl and turn the dough around to coat the dough ball with oil. Cover with a light cloth and let rise in a warm place until doubled in size, about 1½ hours.
- Preheat oven to 350°.
- Grease a baking sheet.
- Punch down the dough. Divide dough into 16 equal pieces.
- Use your fingertips to flatten each piece into a rectangle about 4" x 5".
- Sprinkle parmesan cheese on each rectangle. Leave at least ¼" around the sides.
- Place 6 slices of pepperoni on each dough square, slightly overlapping the slices. Leave at least ¼" around the sides.
- Place a half slice of mozzarella on top of the pepperoni slices.
- Roll tightly, tuck in the ends, and pinch the edges with your fingertips to make sure all of the edges are sealed.
- Place the rolls on the prepared baking sheet.
- Place baking sheet on the center rack of your preheated oven.
- Bake 14-16 minutes. The bottoms should be lightly browned and the tops lightly golden.

Horse farm in Kentucky

Unit 8
South:
Kentucky and Tennessee

Lesson 29: Kentucky

Horses, strong and sleek, munch and nibble the bluegrass in Kentucky, the Bluegrass State. Bluegrass is green like other grass until it grows tall. Then it produces blue seed heads that give fields a blueish tint. The limestone under Kentucky makes the grass extra nutritious for the horses.

Horse Capital of the World

The city of **Lexington** is the Horse Capital of the World. Hundreds of horse farms surround the city. Many people in Kentucky earn money from horses. They raise horses to sell. They participate in horse shows and horse races. Some people pay millions of dollars for the perfect Kentucky horse.

The most famous horse race in the United States is the Kentucky Derby. Kentuckians have held this race at Churchill Downs every year since 1875. Churchill Downs is a racetrack in Louisville.

Kentucky horse farm

Outside Churchill Downs

Louisville

Louisville is Kentucky's largest city. Beneath the city lies Mega Cavern. A cavern is a large cave. This man-made cavern used to be a limestone mine. The mine closed many years ago. Now Mega Cavern is a storage facility and an underground adventure playground where people walk, bike, ride trams, and take zipline rides. Much of the Louisville Zoo sits on top of the Mega Cavern, but don't worry. The lion cage doesn't go that deep!

Capital: Frankfort

After Kentucky became a state, the government had to choose a capital city. Andrew Holmes lived in Frankfort. He offered to donate land and stone for a capitol building. He said he would provide ten boxes of glass, locks, hinges, and 1,500 pounds of nails. Andrew Holmes said the government could use his sawmill, carriage, wagon, and two good

Kentucky State Capitol

horses. He said they could cut down any trees they needed from his land. Eight other men offered to donate three thousand dollars each if the government chose Frankfort.

The government could not refuse this generous offer and decided that Frankfort would be the capital city. The state of Kentucky has had four capitol buildings. The state legislature has met in the current building since 1910.

Kentucky Bend

Look closely at the map of Kentucky and find the Kentucky Bend. It's the tiny bubble that stands alone on the far western end of the state. The Bend borders Tennessee on the south. The Mississippi River cuts it off from the rest of Kentucky.

Barges on the
Mississippi River
at the Kentucky Bend

Tennessee and Kentucky argued for years over who really owned the land. Some people who lived on the Bend wanted to be Kentuckians. Others wanted to be part of Tennessee. A church built a building on the state line. Every Sunday church members loyal to Kentucky sat on one side and the members loyal to Tennessee sat on the other.

Tennessee finally gave up trying to claim the area as its own. Hundreds of people once lived on the Bend, but today only a handful remain.

Mammoth Cave

Mammoth Cave

A mining company created Mega Cavern, but God created an abundance of caves throughout Kentucky. When God put limestone under Kentucky, He created a caving wonderland. When surface water seeps below the ground, it erodes (or wears away) the limestone. This creates caves. Kentucky's **Mammoth Cave** is the largest known cave system in the world. People have mapped out over 400 miles of the cave, and there is still more left to discover.

Kentucky Fried Chicken

During the 1930s, Colonel Harland Sanders owned a gas station in **North Corbin**, Kentucky. He sold meals to people traveling through the area. At first he served the meals from his own dining table. He only had room for six people to eat at a time. Soon he opened a restaurant with room to serve 142 customers at a time.

Colonel Sanders developed a recipe for fried chicken that people loved. He scratched his secret recipe on the back of the door in his kitchen. He soon started a restaurant chain. His Kentucky Fried Chicken (KFC) restaurants opened in cities across the country and around the world. Today you can find them in about 140 different countries.

KFC in China

Cumberland Falls

Niagara Falls in New York is the largest waterfall in the United States. People call **Cumberland Falls** in Kentucky the Little Niagara and the Niagara of the South. When the moon is full and the sky is clear, visitors to Cumberland Falls see something very special. As the water crashes over the falls, mist rises up from the water. When the light of a full moon shines into the mist just right, a moonbow appears. Cumberland Falls is the only place on our side of the world where moonbows appear regularly.

In the Bible, the prophet Ezekiel described a vision he saw of the glory of the Lord. He compared it to the beauty of a rainbow.

As the appearance of the rainbow in the clouds on a rainy day,
so was the appearance of the surrounding radiance.
Such was the appearance of the likeness of the glory of the Lord. . . .
Ezekiel 1:28

Cumberland Falls

Activities

- Illustrate the geographic term for Kentucky in the *Atlas Workbook* (page 32).
- If you are using the *Lesson Review*, answer the questions for Kentucky (page 8).
- Read the chapter titled "The Doll" in *Soft Rain*.
- Hands-On Idea: Pretend you own a restaurant. Perhaps some of your family members will be your customers. What secret recipe does your restaurant offer?

Lesson 30: A Song and Story of Kentucky

My Old Kentucky Home

Stephen Foster wrote the original version of this song in 1852. It became the official state song of Kentucky in 1928. Each year at the Kentucky Derby, thousands of fans sing the song together as the horses parade by before the race. (Track 15)

The sun shines bright on my old Kentucky home,
'Tis summer, the flowers are gay;
The corn-top's ripe and the meadow's in the bloom
While the birds make music all the day.

Chorus:
Weep no more my lady.
Oh! Weep no more today!
We will sing one song
For my old Kentucky home
For my old Kentucky home, far away.

The young folks roll on the little cabin floor
All merry, all happy, and bright;
By 'n' by hard times comes a-knocking at the door
Then my old Kentucky home, Good-night!

Chorus

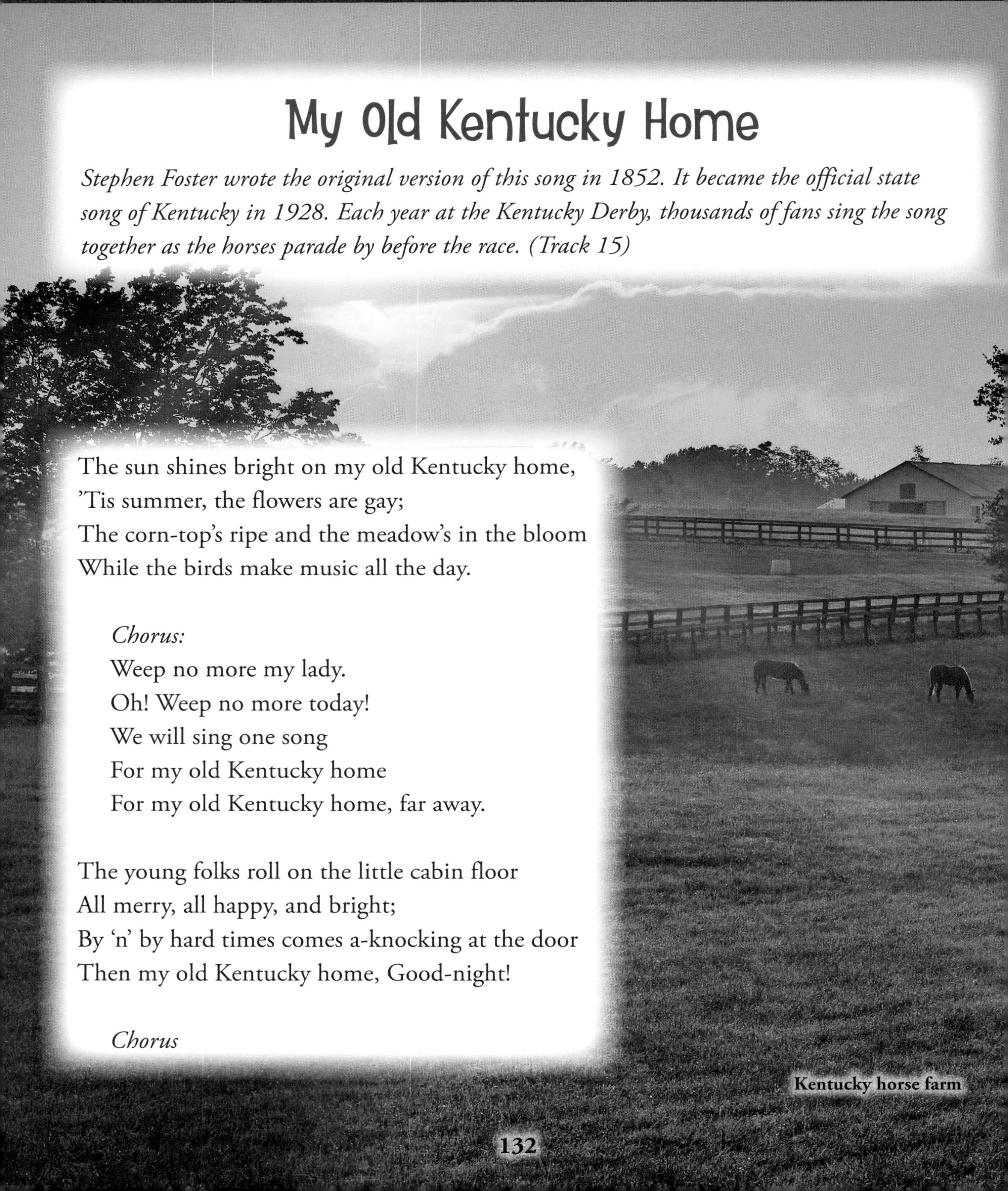

Kentucky horse farm

Pack Horse Librarians

*The **Appalachian Mountains** run through the eastern part of Kentucky. Long ago the mountains kept the families who lived there isolated from the outside world. Many mountain families lived in poverty. During the 1930s, hardworking Kentucky women stepped up to change lives in the mountains—on horseback.*

Nan Milan mounted Sunny Jim, the trusty horse she had ridden so many times before. She prepared to travel again up a lonely mountain path. She joked that Sunny Jim had shorter legs on one side than the other. That's how he kept from sliding down the steep mountainsides. Her bags were loaded with things to read. People from wealthier communities had donated books, old magazines, and Sunday school material. Nan Milan distributed the reading material among the mountain homes. She usually visited each place twice a month. Each time she brought new items to read and picked up what she had left the time before. In this way, the books and magazines circulated among the mountain families.

Pack horse librarian

Appalachian Mountains

Nan Milan was a pack horse librarian. The United States government paid Nan and the other librarians to ride horses and mules along rugged trails. These librarians distributed reading materials to families and communities nestled among the Appalachians. They knew the books could make a big difference in the lives of the mountaineers, by lifting their spirits and perhaps even helping to lift them out of poverty.

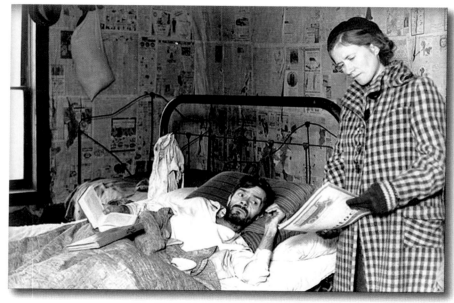

Pack horse librarian visiting a bedridden man

Sometimes the librarians' winter routes took them through icy mountain streams. Sometimes they rode 120 miles in a week. There wasn't much that could stop these librarians from getting books to the people they served.

Sometimes the children in a mountain family were the only ones who could read. Their parents had never been to school. Children read aloud to their parents from the books the librarians brought. They liked books with pictures the best.

Pack horse librarians

134

When the books wore out, the librarians knew they were too precious to throw away. They took stories and pictures from the books that were falling apart and pasted them into scrapbooks. People also made scrapbooks with recipes and quilt patterns to share among neighboring communities.

The pack horse librarians served thousands of families. At first some of the mountaineers didn't like the idea of strangers bringing in strange ideas. Some librarians earned the people's trust by reading aloud to them from the Bible. Many of the mountain people had heard of Noah and Moses and Jesus, but to have someone read about these people from a printed page was something new. They realized that if the librarians were bringing Bible stories, maybe the other things they brought were okay after all.

Whatever you do in word or deed, do all in the name of the Lord Jesus,
giving thanks through Him to God the Father.
Colossians 3:17

Pack horse librarian at a mountain cabin

Activities

- Complete the map activities for Kentucky in the *Atlas Workbook* (page 33).
- Read the chapter titled "To the Stockade" in *Soft Rain*.
- Imagine that you are a child living in the Appalachian Mountains of Kentucky in the 1930s. You are so excited about the books the pack horse librarian brings to your family. In your creative writing notebook, write about one of her visits. What does she look like? What color is her horse? What does she bring you to read? *or* Act out a visit from a pack horse librarian with others in your family.
- Family Activity: Make a Pack Horse Scrapbook (instructions on page 144).

Lesson 31: Tennessee

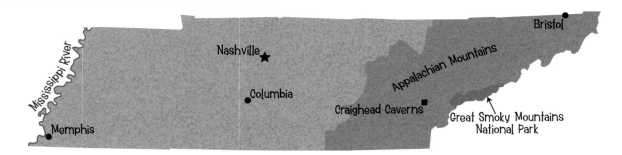

After a large number of Tennesseeans volunteered to be soldiers when the U.S. fought the War of 1812, Tennessee became the Volunteer State. That is why the University of Tennessee's football team is the Vols. Find Tennessee on the map at the beginning of this book.

Great Smoky Mountains

The United States has sixty-two national parks. More people visit **Great Smoky Mountains National Park** than any other. The Great Smoky Mountains are part of the Appalachian Mountains. They lie along the border between North Carolina and Tennessee. These mountains are also called the Smokies. The mountains don't really smoke, but they do sometimes have a blue-colored haze or mist on their peaks. The Cherokee people who first settled among these mountains called them *Shaconage*, which means "place of blue smoke."

Do you ever catch fireflies or lightning bugs in the summertime? The synchronous fireflies in the Smokies put on an impressive light show every summer. *Synchronous* means they light up in sync, or at the same time. For about two weeks, the male fireflies light up the mountains as they flash their lights at the same time, instead of randomly as most fireflies do. Only our God knows exactly why these fireflies do this. Even though we don't understand why, we can certainly marvel at our Creator's amazing design.

Great Smoky Mountains

Bristol

In the early 1900s, most musicians recorded their music in big cities such as Atlanta and New York City. In 1927 music recorder Ralph Peer brought recording equipment to **Bristol**, Tennessee, to record old time mountain music in a mountain region. The recordings he captured of the Carter family and Jimmie Rodgers became popular all over the country. In 1998 the United States Congress officially named Bristol, Tennessee, as the Birthplace of Country Music.

The Carter family

Lost Sea

Lost Sea

In 1905 Ben Sands squeezed through a tiny opening in **Craighead Caverns** in southeast Tennessee. He ended up in a huge cave room. The room had water in it, but he couldn't tell how much. He picked up a ball of mud and threw it hard. He heard it splash. He picked up more mud and threw it in a different direction. It splashed as well. He kept throwing mud and kept hearing more splashes. Could it be that the entire cave room was filled with water? Yes. Ben Sands had discovered the largest underground lake in America, now called the Lost Sea.

Capital: Nashville

Nashville, the capital of Tennessee, is nicknamed Music City. Many country and gospel musicians have recorded songs in the recording studios along Nashville's Music Row. Nashville's Grand Ole Opry is the longest-running radio show in the history of America. Country music stars have performed on this show since 1925.

Nashville

Goo Goo Clusters

Howell Campbell Sr. loved sweets. He was particular about his sweets, though, and wanted them to taste just right. He started the Standard Candy Company in Nashville in 1901. A few years later he and his factory supervisor came up with a new candy recipe. Up until that time, most people sold either chocolate candy, caramel candy, or taffy candy. Howard Campbell wanted to combine different types of candies into a completely new kind of candy bar. The result was the Goo Goo Cluster—a delicious blend of caramel, marshmallow nougat, peanuts, and milk chocolate. The company advertised the treat as "A Nourishing Lunch for a Nickel." (Do you think your mom would consider a candy bar a "nourishing lunch"?) For many years the Standard Candy Company sponsored the Grand Ole Opry radio show. Performers advertised the company's famous candy by saying, "Go get a Goo Goo . . . it's goooood!"

Today the Standard Candy Company factory in Nashville can produce 20,000 Goo Goos in a single hour!

Mule Capital of the World

A mule is an animal whose father is a donkey and whose mother is a horse. Farmers have bred mules since ancient times. Mules are strong. They are similar to horses, but they are able to work longer. They also eat less than horses and are often more gentle.

Before farmers had tractors, they used mules to plow their fields. During the 1840s, **Columbia**, Tennessee, began to host Breeder's Day every April. Area farmers and breeders brought their livestock to this event to buy, sell, and trade.

People do not use mules as much as they used to, but Columbia still celebrates the animal every April. Breeder's Day eventually became Mule Day. The event now includes a parade and fun contests, including a contest to see which team of mules can pull the heaviest load. Columbia is the Mule Capital of the World.

Memphis

Many farmers in west Tennessee grow cotton. Farmers once brought their cotton to Memphis to sell it to cotton traders. The traders sold the cotton to manufacturers around the world. Boats and barges carried the cotton away from Memphis on the Mississippi River. Memphis was the Cotton Capital of the World.

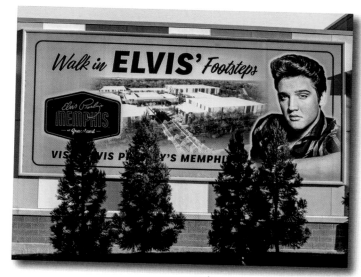
Elvis sign in Memphis

Today people call Memphis the Home of the Blues and the Birthplace of Rock 'n' Roll. The blues and rock 'n' roll are two styles of music. Elvis Presley was a famous rock 'n' roll star who lived in Memphis. His Graceland home in Memphis is the second most visited home in the United States. Only the White House is more popular!

From Bristol in the east to Memphis in the west, Tennessee is truly a musical state. Our Father in heaven loves to hear music that honors and glorifies His name.

Be exalted, O Lord, in Your strength;
We will sing and praise Your power.
Psalm 21:13

Memphis and the Mississippi River

Activities

- Illustrate the geographic term for Tennessee in the *Atlas Workbook* (page 34).

- If you are using the *Lesson Review*, answer the questions for Tennessee (page 8).

- Read the chapter titled "In the Pen" in *Soft Rain*.

- Hands-On Idea: Put on a simple Grand Ole Opry radio show with your family.

Wabash Cannonball

This folk song is about a train called the Wabash Cannonball. It mentions Daddy Cleton, but it is unclear who Daddy Cleton was. This is one of the many tunes the Carter family played. (Track 16)

**Tennessee
railroad bridge**

Out from the wide Pacific to the broad Atlantic shore,
She climbs the flowery mountains, o'er hills and by the shore.
Although she's tall and handsome and she's known quite well by all,
She's a regular combination of the Wabash Cannonball.
Oh, the eastern states are dandy, so the western people say:
Chicago, Rock Island, St. Louis by the way.
To the lakes of Minnesota, where the rippling waters fall,
No changes to be taken on the Wabash Cannonball.

Chorus:
Oh, listen to the jingle, the rumble, and the roar,
As she glides along the woodlands, over hills and by the shore.
She climbs the flowery mountains, hear the merry hobo squall,
She glides along the woodlands, the Wabash Cannonball.

Oh, here's old Daddy Cleton, let his name forever be,
And long be he remembered in the courts of Tennessee,
For he is a good old rounder, till the curtain round him fall,
He'll be carried back to victory on the Wabash Cannonball.
I have rode the I.C. Limited, also the Royal Blue
Across the eastern countries, on mail car number two.
I have rode those highball trains from coast to coast, that's all,
But I have found no equal to the Wabash Cannonball.

Chorus

The Hermitage

Ella and Her Music

Ella Sheppard was three years old. She lived on The Hermitage, a plantation near Nashville, Tennessee, where her mother Sarah was enslaved. Ella's father was a free man, but since her mother was enslaved, Ella was enslaved, too. Former President Andrew Jackson had owned The Hermitage until he died just a few years before Ella was born. Now the President's adopted son owned the plantation.

Cabin of an enslaved family at The Hermitage

One day Sarah Sheppard found out that her master was selling her to a new owner. She was heartbroken at the thought of being forced to leave her little girl behind. She didn't want her daughter to grow up enslaved without a mother. A wise older enslaved woman gave Sarah hope when she told her, "God's got a great work for this baby to do. She's going to stand before kings and queens."

141

Cincinnati, Ohio, in 1855

Sarah Sheppard's master sold her in 1854. Ella's father was able to buy his little girl's freedom. Ella moved with her father to a new home in Cincinnati, Ohio.

People around Ella noticed the girl's talent for music. Her father bought a piano for her. At that time, most music teachers would not give lessons to African Americans. A music teacher in Cincinnati agreed to give Ella lessons, but only if the lessons stayed a secret. Ella had to enter the teacher's house by the back door. She could only come when it was dark so that others wouldn't see her.

America's Civil War began when Ella was about ten years old. During the war, President Abraham Lincoln declared that all slaves in the South were free. After the war was over, Ella traveled to Nashville where she was reunited with her mother. Ella spent three months with her mother and then went back to her home in Cincinnati.

The next year, when Ella was fifteen, her father died suddenly. Ella had to work hard to earn a living. She took in washing and ironing. She gave music lessons to a few students, but they didn't pay her very much. She soon moved back to Tennessee and became a teacher.

After Ella saved up enough money, she decided to go to college. She enrolled at Fisk College, a new school for black students in Nashville. (The school is now a university). Ella continued to give music lessons. She also became the music teacher at the college. She was the school's first black teacher.

Fisk University

Fisk Jubilee Singers around 1872 (Ella is fourth from the right)

Ella Sheppard began playing the piano and singing with the college choir. This musical group became the Fisk Jubilee Singers. They sang in concerts across America. The group could sing fine classical pieces, but the songs their audiences loved most were traditional African American spirituals, such as "Swing Low, Sweet Chariot" and "Steal Away to Jesus."

The Fisk Jubilee Singers became popular. Their concerts often had standing room only. Their success helped Nashville become known as a musical city.

Ella Sheppard and the other singers traveled to Europe, and the words spoken to Ella's mother years before came true. The enslaved woman had told Sarah Sheppard that her daughter would stand before kings and queens. While on tour, the Fisk Jubilee Singers sang before European royalty, including Queen Victoria of England.

Therefore I will give thanks to You among the nations, O Lord,
And I will sing praises to Your name.
Psalm 18:49

Activities

- Complete the map activities for Tennessee in the *Atlas Workbook* (page 35).

- Read the chapter titled "The Coughing Disease" in *Soft Rain*.

- In your creative writing notebook, write a journal entry from the perspective of one of the Fisk Jubilee Singers who has just performed for a king or queen. What was it like? How did you feel?

Family Activity: Pack Horse Scrapbook

Supplies:
- heavy paper
- catalogs, magazines, newspapers (that are approved by a parent)
- old pictures printed from a computer (optional)
- scissors
- glue
- pencils, crayons, markers
- stapler or hole punch and string (for binding)

The pack horse librarians made scrapbooks to share articles, stories, poems, recipes, quilt patterns, and more with people in the Appalachian Mountains of Kentucky. Make your own pack horse scrapbook. Cut pictures, articles, and recipes out of magazines and catalogs (as long as no one minds if you cut them up!). With parental supervision you can also print old pictures off a computer to include. You can handwrite your own recipes, stories, and poems as well. You can draw pictures. Be creative and include things you think might interest your friends and neighbors, just as the pack horse librarians did. Glue your items onto heavy paper. Bind the pages together using staples or by punching holes and binding them together with string.

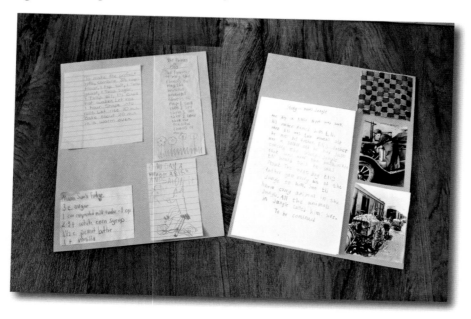

Lake Jocassee, South Carolina

Unit 9
South:
North Carolina and South Carolina

Lesson 33: North Carolina

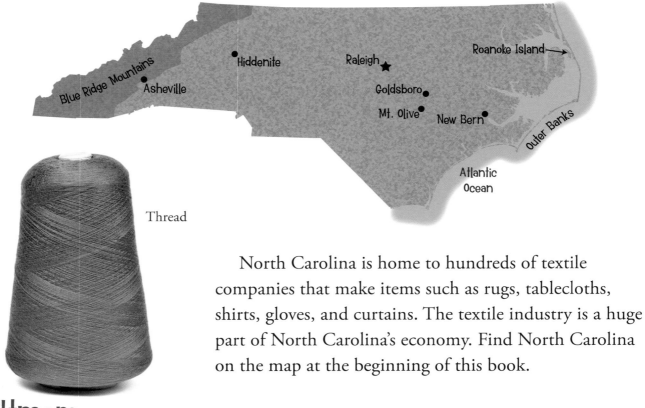

Thread

North Carolina is home to hundreds of textile companies that make items such as rugs, tablecloths, shirts, gloves, and curtains. The textile industry is a huge part of North Carolina's economy. Find North Carolina on the map at the beginning of this book.

Biltmore

In the late 1800s, George Vanderbilt chose **Asheville**, North Carolina, as the site for his grand mansion—the Biltmore. Nestled among the **Blue Ridge Mountains**, the Biltmore is the largest privately-owned home in the United States. The house has 35 bedrooms, 43 bathrooms, an indoor pool, and a bowling alley!

Biltmore

Hiddenite

One day in the late 1800s, young George Warren was plowing a field on his family's farm near the Blue Ridge Mountains. George gathered a few of the rocks the plow turned up and used them in his slingshot. Some of the rocks had an interesting green color. They seemed too special to shoot in a slingshot, so he took them home to show his parents. When a neighbor saw the rocks, he suggested the Warrens show them to a mineralogist (a person who studies minerals).

George's rocks turned out to be a rare type of precious gem. The gem was named hiddenite after mineralogist William Earl Hidden. Hiddenite is similar to an emerald. People have found hiddenite in a few other countries, but Alexander County, North Carolina, is the only place where people have found hiddenite in the United States. Today visitors to **Hiddenite**, North Carolina, can search for their own precious gems at Emerald Hollow Mine.

Alexander County, North Carolina

Hiddenite

Capital: Raleigh

In 1792 the state of North Carolina purchased 1,000 acres of land from a plantation owner to build their capital city: **Raleigh**. Workers completed a brick state house two years later. The building served the needs of the state government and also served as a place for public meetings, balls, and religious gatherings.

After the first state house burned down, work began on a second one. Mules hauled the stone to the building site, pulling railroad cars along a wooden track. When workers completed the new building in 1840, North Carolinians celebrated for three days with speeches, balls, and parades.

North Carolina State Capitol

Sweet Potatoes

Sweet potatoes

Farmers grow more sweet potatoes in North Carolina than in any other state. Hundreds of farmers plant thousands of acres and harvest billions of sweet potatoes each year. The plants grow well in the sandy soil of the state's coastal plain region.

Pepsi

In 1893 North Carolina pharmacist Caleb Bradham perfected a recipe for a new drink by mixing sugar, water, caramel, lemon oil, nutmeg, and other ingredients. He sold it to customers who came to his pharmacy. They called it Brad's Drink and loved it. After selling Brad's Drink for five years, Mr. Bradham gave it a new name: Pepsi-Cola.

Soon other stores in other places wanted to sell Pepsi-Cola to their customers. Caleb Bradham established the Pepsi-Cola Company. By 1910 Pepsi-Cola was available in 24 states. PepsiCo now sells a variety of drinks and other products in over 200 countries around the world. In **New Bern**, North Carolina, you can still visit the drug store where Caleb Bradham started it all.

Old Pepsi-Cola bottles

Bradham's Pharmacy

Outer Banks

The **Outer Banks** are a string of barrier islands that begin at the southern border of Virginia and stretch 120 miles south down the coast of North Carolina.

Roanoke Island is part of the Outer Banks. In 1587 Sir Walter Raleigh brought around 115 English men, women, and children to Roanoke to establish a new settlement. Some time after they arrived, the group disappeared. No one knows for sure what happened to them. They are known as the Lost Colony of Roanoke. North Carolina's capital is named after Sir Walter Raleigh.

Millions of tourists visit the Outer Banks every year, reaching the islands by bridge or ferry. They visit Kitty Hawk, the sight of the world's first successful airplane flight by the Wright Brothers in 1903. They learn about the pirates who once lived on the islands. They enjoy the beaches and climb inside the lighthouse towers to enjoy the view of God's glorious creation.

> But as for me, the nearness of God is my good;
> I have made the Lord God my refuge,
> That I may tell of all Your works.
> Psalm 73:28

Bodie Island Lighthouse

Activities

- Illustrate the geographic term for North Carolina in the *Atlas Workbook* (page 36).
- If you are using the *Lesson Review*, answer the questions for North Carolina (page 9).
- Read the chapter titled "Rain Comes" in *Soft Rain*.
- Hands-On Idea: Use building bricks or blocks to build a lighthouse.

Great-Granddad

This song comes from the Appalachian Mountains of North Carolina. (Track 17)

Great-Granddad was a busy man.
He cooked his grub in a frying pan;
He picked his teeth with a huntin' knife,
He wore the same suit all his life.

Twenty-one children came to bless
The old man's home in the wilderness;
Doubt this statement if you can,
Great-Granddad was a busy man.

He raised them rough, but he raised them strong;
When their feet took hold on the road to wrong,
He straightened them out with the old ramrod,
And filled them full of the fear of God.

They grew strong in heart and hand,
A firm foundation of our land;
They made the best citizens we ever had,
We need more men like Great-Granddad.

Granddad died at eighty-nine,
Twenty-one boys he left behind;
Times are changed but you never can tell,
You might yet do half as well.

Historic North Carolina farm

Cucumbers and Patriotism

Cucumber

Shikrey Baddour arrived in New York City in 1894, a 19-year-old immigrant from Lebanon in the Middle East. Baddour settled in Tennessee. When the United States fought the Spanish-American War a few years later, Shikrey Baddour joined the Army of his new homeland. In 1914 Mr. Baddour moved to North Carolina.

Pickles

In the 1920s, Shikrey Baddour noticed a problem in his area, and he wanted to find a solution. Local farmers had more cucumbers than they could sell. Mr. Baddour did not want their crops to go to waste. He decided to buy up the cucumbers and put them in brine, a mixture of vinegar and water. He thought he would sell his brined cucumbers to pickle companies, but his idea didn't work. Mr. Baddour couldn't find any pickle companies that wanted to buy his product.

Shikrey Baddour was in a pickle. Several businessmen got together to take care of the pickle problem. They established the Mt. Olive Pickle Company in **Mt. Olive**, North Carolina, to pack and sell their own pickles. Mr. Baddour became the company salesman. The company grew until it became the top pickle company in the Southeast. Today the company's facility has enough room to store 40,000,000 pounds of cucumbers!

Shikrey Baddour's life in America was about much more than pickles. President Woodrow Wilson asked Mr. Baddour to work with an organization called the Near East Relief Commission. This group raised millions of dollars to help the Armenian people who were being persecuted in Europe. Mr. Baddour also worked with organizations that helped immigrants who had come to America.

After Shikrey Baddour died in 1938, he was described as "a man of sterling character, great ability, cheerful and generous in disposition, and loyal to his friends. He was a leader among men." People appreciated Mr. Baddour's unselfish service to others.

The Baddour family (Shikrey is in the middle of the back row)

Shikrey Baddour's legacy of serving has continued on through his descendants. His son served on the **Goldsboro** City Council for 16 years. His grandson was elected to the North Carolina House of Representatives. His great-grandson became a superior court judge.

Shikrey Baddour was patriotic. People highly respected him. He helped others to become better citizens of the country that had become his own.

So, as those who have been chosen of God, holy and beloved,
put on a heart of compassion, kindness, humility, gentleness and patience.
Colossians 3:12

Activities

- Complete the map activities for North Carolina in the *Atlas Workbook* (page 37).
- Read the chapter titled "The Young Chief" in *Soft Rain*.
- If you were going to open a food factory, what would you produce? How would you package your product? What would be the name of your company? If you are keeping a creative writing notebook, write the name of your company and a description of what you make. If you would like, you could also draw your logo design in your notebook.
- Family Activity: Conduct an Immigrant Interview (instructions on page 162).

The palmetto is the state tree of South Carolina. It is featured on the state flag and on the state quarter. Find South Carolina on the map at the beginning of this book.

South Carolina state quarter

Greenville
Columbia
Congaree National Park
Myrtle Beach
Charleston
Wadmalaw Island
St. Helena Island
Atlantic Ocean

Greenville

A concrete bridge once took travelers over the Reedy River in downtown **Greenville**. The bridge got people where they needed to go, but it hid one of Greenville's most beautiful features—a waterfall right downtown. In the 1980s, people decided the waterfall should be part of a park. Workers removed the huge bridge and created the gorgeous Falls Park that people enjoy today. People can now walk across the river on a new curved suspension bridge, built especially so that pedestrians can enjoy the view.

Greenville is home to many big businesses. Michelin is a French company that makes tires. The company's North American headquarters are in Greenville. Michelin has several tire factories in South Carolina. At a facility near Greenville, workers make tires for earthmoving equipment. The tires are up to thirteen feet tall!

Falls Park, Greenville

Capital: Columbia

On the grounds of the South Carolina State House in **Columbia** stands a palmetto tree statue made out of iron, copper, and brass. Christopher Werner created the metal tree in the mid-1800s. He installed it on the state house grounds—without permission. He hoped the government would like it and would pay him for it. The government finally decided to pay Mr. Werner for the monument in 1856. They decided the tree would honor South Carolina soldiers who had died in the Mexican War a few years earlier. They had Christopher Werner create metal plaques with the soldiers' names. Mr. Werner spelled many of the names wrong and had to do the plaques over again. He didn't spell all the names right on the second plaques either. The government only paid him about half of what he said the monument was worth, but no one had asked him to create the monument in the first place!

A storm blew the palmetto monument to the ground in 1875. A tornado damaged it again in 1939. Each time workers carefully restored it and the tree still stands as a symbol of South Carolina and a monument to brave soldiers who served our country.

Palmetto monument

Congaree National Park

Trees grow big in South Carolina's **Congaree National Park**. The park has more champion trees than any other area in the country. A champion tree is a tree that is judged to be the largest of its species, based on its height, trunk size, and the spread of its branches (called a crown spread). Some of the loblolly pine trees here are as tall as a 17-story building!

Loblolly pine in Congaree National Park

A terrible storm hit Biloxi in 1916. The fierce winds blew a pelican into the glass in the lighthouse tower. In the middle of the night, with the wind howling and with shattered glass around them, Maria and Miranda Younghans managed to replace the glass temporarily so they could keep the lights burning. They knew the importance of the light to any ships that might be struggling through the storm.

When Maria Younghans retired in 1919, Miranda Younghans took over as the official lighthouse keeper. She served for ten years. During her time as keeper, electricians installed electricity in the lighthouse.

In 2005 a powerful hurricane slammed against the Gulf Coast. Hurricane Katrina destroyed thousands of buildings. The water rose over 21 feet inside the Biloxi Lighthouse, but the tower remained standing. After the storm, an American flag draped over the lighthouse railing became a symbol of hope for the hurting people of Mississippi.

The light of the Biloxi Lighthouse has shone brightly for generations. It has guided countless ships to safety. Sailors have looked to the light and known they were safe.

The light of Jesus shines much brighter and guides us through the darkest storms. We can look to His light, and know that we are safe—forever.

Biloxi Lighthouse
after Hurricane Katrina

Then Jesus again spoke to them, saying,
"I am the Light of the world;
he who follows Me will not walk in the darkness,
but will have the Light of life."
John 8:12

Activities

- Complete the map activities for Mississippi in the *Atlas Workbook* (page 45).

- In your creative writing notebook, write a description of the Biloxi Lighthouse as pictured on the opposite page. Include descriptions of the plants and sky. *or* Pretend that you are a lighthouse keeper during a storm.

Myrtle Beach

Myrtle Beach

It's hard to believe that almost no one lived on South Carolina's Myrtle Beach until the 1900s. A business built a hotel on the beach in 1901. People could buy an oceanfront lot for just $25. People called the growing community "New Town." A newspaper held a contest to come up with a new official name. The winning entry was

Charleston

Myrtle Beach, named after the wax myrtle trees that grow along the shore. Today Myrtle Beach has over 400 hotels for the many travelers who come to enjoy the city.

Charleston

Charleston lies in South Carolina's Lowcountry. It is one of America's oldest cities. During the 1700s, it became a bustling seaport. Merchant ships once traveled from Charleston to England carrying items such as deer skins, rice, cotton, and indigo, a plant used to dye fabric.

Charleston Tea Garden

Most of the world's tea grows in Asia, Africa, and South America. The Charleston Tea Garden is the one and only tea garden in North America. Located on Wadmalaw Island south of Charleston, the garden has hundreds of thousands of tea bushes. The land was once a potato farm. People began growing tea there in the 1960s, but the plants are descended from tea bushes that have been growing in South Carolina since 1888.

Charleston Tea Garden

Gullah Culture

Gullah people live in the coastal areas and sea islands of North Carolina, South Carolina, Georgia, and Florida. These people are descendants of enslaved men and women who came from West Africa. Other names for this people group are Geechee and Gullah Geechee.

Weaving a sweetgrass basket

The Gullah Geechee have strong traditions that reflect their African roots. They speak their own language, also called Gullah, Geechee, or Gullah Geechee. Many Gullah words and expressions come from West African languages. Traditional Gullah foods are similar to the foods people prepare in West Africa, such as shrimp and grits and fried okra. Through the years the Gullah Geechee have passed down their handcraft traditions, such as wood carving and basket sewing (or weaving) with sweetgrass. The Gullah people also have strong musical traditions they pass on from one generation to the next.

When the apostle Paul wrote a letter to the Ephesians, he told them to be filled with the Spirit,

speaking to one another in psalms and hymns and spiritual songs,
singing and making melody with your heart to the Lord.
Ephesians 5:19

Gullah sweetgrass baskets

Activities

- Illustrate the geographic term for South Carolina in the *Atlas Workbook* (page 38).
- If you are using the *Lesson Review*, answer the questions for South Carolina (page 9).
- Read the chapter titled "Rattlesnake Springs" in *Soft Rain*.
- Hands-On Idea: Use play dough to make a palmetto monument.

De Wod Been Deh

Ron Daise of St. Helena Island, South Carolina, wrote this song in Gullah based on John 1:1 and Luke 11:18. (Track 18) Lyrics and Music © 2011 Ronald Daise. Used with permission.

Chorus:

Fo God mek de wol,	*(Before God made the world,)*
De Wod been deh.	*(The Word was there.)*
De Wod been deh wid God!	*(The Word was there with God!)*
Chullun, fo God mek de wol,	*(Children, before God made the world,)*
De Wod been deh.	*(The Word was there.)*
De Wod been deh wid God!	*(The Word was there with God!)*

Dey bless fa true, dem wa know God!	*(They are blessed, those who know God!)*
God mek a way fa e chullun!	*(God makes a way for His children!)*
God da de Wod! So yeddy, den keep de Wod,	*(God is the Word! So listen to, then keep the Word,)*
An den watch God mek a way fa e chullun!	*(And watch God make a way for His children!)*
Dey full op wid peace, dem wa know God!	*(They are filled with peace, those who know God!)*
God mek a way fa e chullun!	*(God makes a way for His children!)*
God da de Wod! So yeddy, den keep de Wod,	*(God is the Word! So listen to, then keep the Word,)*
An den watch God mek a way fa e chullun!	*(And watch God make a way for His children!)*

Chorus

Dey lob dey enemy, dem wa know God!	*(They love their enemies, those who know God!)*
God mek a way fa e chullun!	*(God makes a way for His children!)*
God da de Wod! So yeddy, den keep de Wod,	*(God is the Word! So listen to, then keep the Word,)*
An den watch God mek a way fa e chullun!	*(And watch God make a way for His children!)*
Dey git op when dey fall, dem wa know God!	*(They arise when they fall, those who know God!)*
God mek a way fa e chullun!	*(God makes a way for His children!)*
God da de Wod! So yeddy, den keep de Wod,	*(God is the Word! So listen to, then keep the Word,)*
An den watch God mek a way fa e chullun!	*(And watch God make a way for His children!)*

Chorus

St. Helena Island

Remember to Stay Close to God

On November 1, 1913, Gertrude Grant cradled her newborn baby in her arms. This was her seventh child. She loved her baby, but her heart was heavy. Her husband Ezekiel would never see the child. Ezekiel had passed away just weeks before. Before he died, he told Gertrude that if the baby was a boy, he wanted her to name him Ezekiel. The baby now in Gertrude's arms was a girl. She named the baby Kathleen, but they called her Zeke in honor of her father.

Kathleen (right) and friends

As a child, Kathleen learned about Jesus and became a part of a local church. She attended the Penn School on St. Helena Island. The school had been established before the Civil War as an experiment to see if formerly enslaved people could be educated. It was very successful in showing the world that black people could indeed learn just as well as anyone else.

After she graduated, Kathleen began teaching in one-room schoolhouses on the island. In 1936 she married Henry Daise, who had also graduated from the Penn School. Henry and Kathleen had nine children. Kathleen stopped teaching to take care of their growing family.

St. Helena Island

Henry and Kathleen were devoted parents. They prayed with their children and taught them to follow God. Their life on St. Helena Island was full of love, music, and faith. Sometimes they had island adventures, such as when a hurricane hit St. Helena in 1959. When the children peeked out the window during the storm, they saw chickens flying by in the wind!

Henry Daise died when their youngest son, Ron, was nine years old. Kathleen Daise went back to teaching at the Penn Center Day Care to support the family. Sometimes she skipped meals, just to make sure her children had enough. She continued to guide her children in God's way. She taught them to seek first His kingdom and His righteousness. Her favorite words of wisdom were, "Remember to stay close to God!"

Henry and Kathleen's son Ron was the last to leave home when he left the island to attend college. Ron had grown up speaking Gullah, but he also spoke English. Others at college could hear a difference in the way Ron talked. Ron has always been proud of his heritage, but it took some time for him to identify his Sea Island speech and heritage as "Gullah." His family had not described themselves that way while he was growing up. Today Ron completely celebrates being Gullah Geechee.

Kathleen with two of her children

The Daise family

Kathleen with children at the Penn Center Day Care

St. Helena Island

160

After Ron Daise married his wife Natalie, the two put together a show which they performed on stage whenever they could. They loved sharing Gullah songs and stories with their audiences. Through their stage production, God opened a door for them to be the stars of "Gullah Gullah Island," a children's television series produced in the 1990s.

Ron, his wife Natalie, and his mother Kathleen all participated in the Sea Island Translation Team and Literacy Project, which translated the New Testament into Gullah. In 2011 Mr. Daise helped create an audio version of the translation. He read the words of Jesus for the recording of the Gospel of John. His understanding of the Bible and his knowledge of the Gullah language helped him to perform his part well. For the project, he also wrote and performed songs that conveyed the rhythms and language of the spirituals he had heard since childhood, including "De Wod Been Deh."

Ron and Natalie with their children, Sara and Simeon

Ron Daise has embraced his Gullah heritage. He believes that all people need to understand and embrace the heritage that is their own. In doing so, they can better enrich the lives of those around them. Ron has also embraced the heritage of faith he learned from his parents. He encourages others to trust God and to let God direct their paths.

Trust in the Lord with all your heart and do not lean on your own understanding.
In all your ways acknowledge Him, and He will make your paths straight.
Proverbs 3:5-6

Activities

- Complete the map activities for South Carolina in the *Atlas Workbook* (page 39).

- Read the chapter titled "Rivers, Valleys, and Mountains" in *Soft Rain*.

- What are some important parts of your family's culture? Think about holiday traditions, how you worship together, and bedtime routines. If you are keeping a creative writing notebook, write about your family's culture.

- If you are using the *Lesson Review*, take the South (Part 1) test (page 33).

Family Activity: Immigrant Interview

Does your family know any immigrants—people who were born in a different country, but now make their home in America? If you or your parents are immigrants yourselves, do you know someone whose homeland is different from yours? If you know an immigrant who lives close to you, invite them to your house for an interview. You might like to have them join you for a meal or for dessert. Tell them ahead of time that you want to ask them questions about their immigrant story. Before they arrive, write out some questions you would like to ask. You can use the suggestions below to help you get started on ideas. Be sure to listen politely as they give their answers. Show interest in their story. If you do not know an immigrant who lives nearby, perhaps you can set up a time to have a video call with an immigrant you know who lives far away. If you do not know a first-generation immigrant, perhaps you can talk to someone whose parent or grandparent immigrated to the United States.

- In what country were you born?
- What are some games you played when you were growing up?
- What are some special foods your family ate?
- What holiday traditions did you have?
- How old were you when you came to America?
- What things in America seemed strange at first?
- What are some things you enjoyed right away?
- What are some things you miss about your home country?

Alligator in Okefenokee Swamp, Georgia

Unit 10
South:
Georgia and Alabama

163

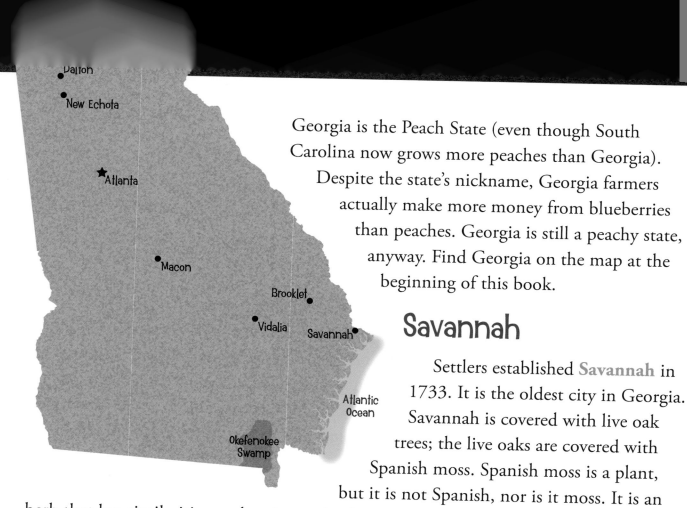

Dalton

New Echota

★ Atlanta

Macon

Brooklet

Vidalia

Savannah

Atlantic
Ocean

Okefenokee
Swamp

Georgia is the Peach State (even though South Carolina now grows more peaches than Georgia). Despite the state's nickname, Georgia farmers actually make more money from blueberries than peaches. Georgia is still a peachy state, anyway. Find Georgia on the map at the beginning of this book.

Savannah

Settlers established Savannah in 1733. It is the oldest city in Georgia. Savannah is covered with live oak trees; the live oaks are covered with Spanish moss. Spanish moss is a plant, but it is not Spanish, nor is it moss. It is an herb that has similarities to the pineapple plant. Spanish moss grows in humid climates where the air is warm and moist. Native peoples once wove Spanish moss into cloth for bedding and mats. They also twisted it together to make rope. Birds, bats, reptiles, and amphibians all use the plant for shelter. Watch out, though. Chiggers also like to make their homes in Spanish moss. You'll be itching for days if you mess with them!

Spanish Moss hanging in Forsyth Park in Savannah

Okefenokee Swamp

The Okefenokee Swamp in southern Georgia is home to snakes, bears, otters, and alligators. Swamps are wet, low-lying land. Oscar the Alligator already lived in the Okefenokee when the area became a park in 1946. Oscar lived until 2007. He was around one hundred years old! Most of the alligators that live in the park today are Oscar's descendants.

Vidalia

Sweet-tasting Vidalia onions are a popular crop in Georgia. True Vidalia onions only grow in Georgia. They are named after the town of Vidalia, which hosts an onion festival every year. Would you like to enter the onion eating contest?

Vidalia onion

YKK in Macon

If you look closely on the clothes in your house, you will probably find several zippers that are printed with the letters YKK. YKK is a Japanese company that has factories all over the world. The company makes a variety of closures, including zippers, snaps, and buttons. The factory in Macon makes around five million zipper sliders every day.

YKK zipper

165

Capital: Atlanta

Like many states, Georgia has not always had the same capital city. Atlanta is Georgia's fifth. Georgia's capitol building stands where the Atlanta city hall once stood. When workers tore down the city hall, they saved the bricks. They reused over 500,000 of them when they built the capitol.

In 1996 Atlanta hosted the Summer Olympic Games. That year over 10,000 athletes from almost 200 different countries traveled through Atlanta's airport, which is the busiest airport in the world.

New Echota

New Echota, Georgia, was once the capital of the Cherokee nation. Thousands of Cherokee once farmed the land and fished in the rivers of northern Georgia and other southern states. White settlers wanted the Cherokees' land, especially after they found out there was gold in the hills of Georgia. In 1838 the United States government forced Cherokee people to leave their homes in Georgia, Alabama, Tennessee, and North Carolina and travel to Oklahoma. Many Cherokee died on the journey, which is known today as the Trail of Tears.

Cherokee print shop in New Echota

Cherokee supreme court building in New Echota

Carpet Capital of the World

In 1895 Catherine Evans Whitener of **Dalton**, Georgia, made a tufted bedspread to give her brother as a wedding gift. Catherine was 15 years old. Other people liked her bedspread and wanted one for themselves. Catherine made another tufted bedspread and sold it for $2.50. Before long there were men, women, and children all over Dalton making tufted (or chenille) bedspreads, pillows, and other items. They hung their items outside as advertisements. People driving by stopped to admire and to buy their handwork. Dalton became the Bedspread Capital of the World.

Catherine Evans Whitener years later

After several years, people figured out how to make the tufted bedspreads by machine. Then they began creating mats and rugs using the same process. As people continued to figure out new ways to make new products, Dalton went from being the Bedspread Capital of the World to the Carpet Capital of the World. Today most of the world's carpet is made in and around Dalton, Georgia.

When God created people, He created us with the ability to create. We please Him when we use our creativity for His glory.

Making bedspreads in Dalton

For we are His workmanship,
created in Christ Jesus for good works,
which God prepared beforehand
so that we would walk in them.
Ephesians 2:10

Activities

- Illustrate the geographic term for Georgia in the *Atlas Workbook* (page 40).
- If you are using the *Lesson Review*, answer the questions for Georgia (page 10).
- Read the chapter titled "The Barn" in *Soft Rain*.
- Hands-On Idea: See if you can find ten zippers in your house with the letters YKK.

Goober Peas

Before the Civil War, many people thought peanuts were only good enough for animals and for people who couldn't afford better things to eat. During the Civil War, peanuts helped Southerners survive when other food was scarce. This song became popular among soldiers during the Civil War. Goober peas is another term for peanuts. Today Georgia raises more peanuts than any other state. (Track 19)

Sittin' by the roadside on a summer's day,
Chattin' with my messmates, passin' time away,
Lying in the shadow underneath the trees,
Oh, they're so delicious, eating goober peas!

Chorus:
Peas, peas, peas, peas, eating goober peas!
Oh, they're so delicious, eating goober peas!

When a horseman passes, the soldiers have a rule,
To cry out at their loudest, "Mister, here's your mule."
But another pleasure, enchantinger than these,
Is wearing out your grinders eating goober peas!   *Chorus*

Just before the battle, the general hears a row,
He says, "The Yanks are coming, I hear the rifles now."
He turns around in wonder, and what do you think he sees?
The Georgia Militia, eating goober peas!   *Chorus*

I think my song has lasted almost long enough,
The subject's interesting but rhymes are mighty rough,
I wish this war was over when free from rags and fleas,
We'd kiss our wives and sweethearts and gobble goober peas!   *Chorus*

Peanut Farmer

When David Cromley's great-great-great-grandparents left South Carolina and settled on a farm in Georgia, they did not know that 150 years later their descendants would still be planting and harvesting on that same land. David Cromley, their great-great-great-grandson, is proud to be doing just that.

Along with his family, David Cromley operates Nellwood Farms in **Brooklet**, Georgia. The Cromleys' land lies in Georgia's coastal plain region, about sixty miles from the coast of the Atlantic Ocean. The weather and soil in this part of Georgia are just right for growing peanuts. When the Cromleys' ancestors first settled here, they wrote back to their relatives in South Carolina to tell them there wasn't a single rock in the sandy soil.

Nellwood Farms

David Cromley and the others at Nellwood Farms plant their peanuts in April or May, depending on the weather. They are always sure to start with good quality seeds. Peanut plants grow vines and leaves above the ground, while the peanuts themselves grow below the ground.

In September it's time to dig up the peanuts with a tractor and peanut plow. Once the peanuts are dug, they spend some time lying in the field to dry out. After a few days, tractors and peanut pickers gather the peanuts from the vines. The peanuts leave Nellwood Farms and head to a buying point. At the buying point, people grade and sort the peanuts according to quality. Then they head off to a warehouse. From there the peanuts travel to a facility where more machines remove the shells. Finally the peanuts are ready to travel to factories where they can become something delicious to eat, such as peanut butter.

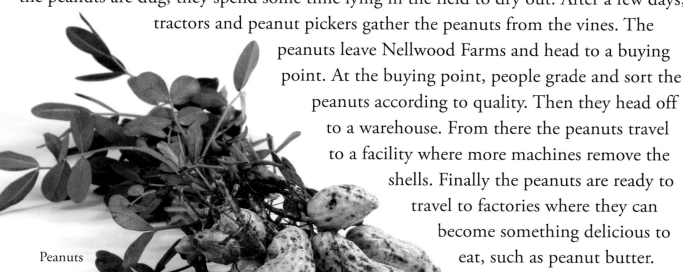
Peanuts

Nellwood Farms

In addition to growing peanuts, the Cromley family raises cotton and beef cattle at Nellwood Farms. If they grow peanuts in a field one year, they grow cotton in that field for the next two years. This helps keep the right balance of nutrients in the soil to help the plants grow well.

Farmers work hard, but the harvest always depends on many things that are out of their control. Sometimes there is too much rain. Some years there is not enough.

David with his wife Jamie and daughter Libby

Sometimes a hurricane hits the coast. Through it all, David Cromley knows that God is in control. Knowing that gives him great comfort.

When David was a little boy, he loved to help his dad on the farm. If he got tired during the day, he had the perfect place to take a nap—right in the cab of his dad's tractor. Once when he and his older siblings went with their dad to check on the crops, their truck got stuck in the mud. The kids all got out to help push. David's siblings played a dirty trick on him—a very dirty trick. They told him to stand behind the tire while they all pushed. The tire splattered mud all over David, from head to toe!

"My parents both have a very strong faith in Jesus Christ," David said, "and I'm thankful that they raised my siblings and me to trust in Him for everything. I have seen fruit in their lives from as early as I can remember. They have had love, joy, peace, patience, kindness, goodness, faithfulness, gentleness, and self-control through the good times and bad."

David's wife Jamie grew up in Atlanta, but she loves farm life. When she isn't teaching at the nearby university, she enjoys working on the farm, tending their garden, and taking their daughter Libby to visit Daddy on the tractor. The days can be long for a farming family, but the Cromleys are grateful for the opportunity to raise crops and care for the land God has given them.

David and Libby checking on the peanut crop

David Cromley loves that farming gives him plenty of time to be outside, enjoying God's creation with his family. He enjoys pointing out to his daughter the miracles of a tiny seed beginning to sprout and a newborn calf wobbling through the field. He is a farmer at heart, but farming is not the most important thing in his life. "My faith in Christ," he said, "defines who I am more than me saying that I am a farmer."

Do not worry then, saying, "What will we eat?" or "What will we drink?" or "What will we wear for clothing?" For the Gentiles eagerly seek all these things; for your heavenly Father knows that you need all these things. But seek first His kingdom and His righteousness, and all these things will be added to you.
Matthew 6:31-33

Activities

- Complete the map activities for Georgia in the *Atlas Workbook* (page 41).
- Read the chapter titled "A New Leader" in *Soft Rain*.
- Spend some time outside looking for small wonders in God's creation. If you are keeping a creative writing notebook, write a detailed description of one of God's creations you find.

Alabama is the Heart of Dixie. Dixie is a name for the southern part of the United States. Alabama has hot summers and mild winters. The state receives a great deal of rain every year. This makes for a humid climate. Snails love humidity. Close to half of all the snails in the United States live in Alabama. Find Alabama on the map at the beginning of this book.

Snail

Dismals Canyon

Moss and ferns cover Dismals Canyon in northwest Alabama. Huge trees tower up from the canyon floor. In 2006 people found a rare giant salamander in the canyon. The salamander is about two feet long. The canyon is also home to the amazing dismalites, tiny insects that glow with a bright blue light. These insects only live in Australia, New Zealand, and Alabama.

Muscle Shoals

The Tennessee River flows through northern Alabama. When native people and early European settlers first traveled along this river, they encountered a dangerous stretch of water. The river dropped significantly, which caused swift rapids. Jagged rocks near the surface of the water created shoals.

Dismals Canyon

172

People called the area Muscle Shoals. Some say the name came from the mussels found in Muscle Shoals. Mussels are similar to clams and oysters. Other people think the area's name came from the fact that you had to use a lot of muscle to get a boat safely through the rapids.

Mussels

People don't have to worry about navigating through Muscle Shoals anymore. Workers built dams along the Tennessee River in the mid-1900s. The dams made the Tennessee River deeper where it had been shallow and also made the rapids disappear. Boats can now travel the river safely.

Wilson Dam on the Tennessee River in Alabama

Rocket City

Huntsville is Alabama's Rocket City. In the 1950s, scientists there developed rockets that launched our country's first satellite into outer space. They developed the rockets that sent American astronauts into space in the 1960s. Today scientists at the Marshall Space Flight Center in Huntsville continue researching and developing spacecraft.

At the U.S. Space and Rocket Center in Huntsville, guests can see a huge collection of real rockets and other artifacts from the space program. Special machines called simulators allow people to feel what it is like to be an astronaut in space.

U.S. Space and Rocket Center

Fire Hydrant Capital of the World

Fire hydrants stand along city streets around the world. If you look closely, you will see "Mueller Albertville" on many of them. Those hydrants came from the Mueller factory in **Albertville**, Alabama, the Fire Hydrant Capital of the World. Workers at the factory here can produce as many as 700 fire hydrants in a single day. They have made over four million since the factory began operating in 1976.

Mueller fire hydrant

Capital: Montgomery

In the early 1800s, Andrew Dexter wanted **Montgomery** to be Alabama's capital city. Dexter owned land in Montgomery, including Goat Hill. Dexter thought the hill would be just right for the state capitol building, and he offered the hill to the state for free. Since

Alabama Capitol

Montgomery was in the middle of the state and had a good system of railroads, and since Dexter had offered a free building site there, the state government chose the city to become the capital. Workers finished the capitol building on Goat Hill in 1851. It's been a long time since goats grazed on the hill, but people still call the site Goat Hill today. You can even buy a souvenir in the capitol's Goat Hill Museum Store.

A statue of Rosa Parks stands near a fountain in Montgomery. In 1955 Rosa Parks, a black woman, was arrested because she did not let a white man have her seat on a Montgomery city bus. After her arrest, many African Americans in Montgomery refused to ride the city buses for over a year. Their actions helped America see the need to treat people the same, no matter the color of their skin.

Rosa Parks statue

174

Great Blue Heron on the Alabama coast

Alabama Coast

Most of southern Alabama borders Florida, but a small part of the state touches the Gulf of Mexico. The Alabama coast is home to many creatures, including herons, sea turtles, and Alabama beach mice. The sand dunes on the Alabama coast are the only place in the world where these mice live. Alabama beach mice are good at staying hidden, and people rarely see them. If you take an early morning walk on the beach, though, you are likely to see tiny mouse footprints in the sand.

Magnolia Springs

The town of **Magnolia Springs** has a mail route like no other in the country. Some residents of this riverside town have mailboxes that face the water instead of the street.

Mailman delivering mail in Magnolia Springs

They receive their mail by boat all year round. The mail carrier loads up his boat with letters and packages and spends about four hours each day on the water, traveling from one mailbox to the next. He sees snakes and bobcats and alligators on his route, but he doesn't usually have any mail for them.

The Lord reigns, let the earth rejoice;
Let the many islands be glad.
Psalm 97:1

Activities

- Illustrate the geographic term for Alabama in the *Atlas Workbook* (page 42).
- If you are using the *Lesson Review*, answer the questions for Alabama (page 10).
- Read the chapter titled "The Mississippi River" in *Soft Rain*.
- Hands-On Idea: Use building bricks, blocks, or play dough to make a rocket.
- Family Activity: Make Biscuits and Gravy (instructions on page 180).

Tombigbee River

This song by S. S. Steele and A. F. Winnemore was published in 1847. The Tombigbee River begins in Mississippi and flows through Alabama. (Track 20)

On Tombigbee River so bright I was born
In a hut made of husks of the tall yellow corn.
And there I first met with my Julia so true,
And I rowed her about in my Gum Tree Canoe.

> *Chorus:*
> Singing row away, row o'er the waters so blue,
> Like a feather we'll float in my Gum Tree Canoe.

All day in the field the soft cotton I hoe,
I think of my Julia and sing as I go.
Oh, I catch her a bird with a wing of true blue,
And at night sail her 'round in my Gum Tree Canoe.

> *Chorus*

With my hands on the banjo and toe on the oar,
I sing to the sound of the river's soft roar.
While the stars they look down on my Julia so true
And dance in her eyes in my Gum Tree Canoe.

> *Chorus*

One night the stream bore us so far away
That we couldn't come back, so we thought we'd just stay.
Oh, we spied a tall ship with a flag of true blue,
And it took us in tow in our Gum Tree Canoe.

> *Chorus*

Tombigbee River

Father of Veterans Day

Raymond Weeks grew up in **Birmingham**, Alabama. During World War II, Mr. Weeks joined the Navy. He served his country well. After the war was over, he returned home to Birmingham.

Birmingham in 1935

For several years, the United States had celebrated a national holiday on November 11 to remember the end of World War I. This holiday, called Armistice Day, was a special time to honor the soldiers who served in that war. An armistice is an official agreement to end a war. After World War II, Raymond Weeks felt the country should have a holiday to honor all veterans, not just those who served during World War I. He wanted the government to change Armistice Day to Veterans Day.

The Pentagon in Washington, D.C.

In 1947 Raymond Weeks traveled to the Pentagon, the headquarters of the U.S. Department of Defense, in Washington, D.C. Mr. Weeks met with General Dwight Eisenhower, the Army Chief of Staff, to share with him his idea about Veterans Day. General Eisenhower liked the idea and gave his approval for a National Veterans Day celebration in Birmingham.

Even though Birmingham celebrated Veterans Day, the holiday was still officially called Armistice Day. Raymond Weeks did not let his dream die. He sent petitions and letters to Congress. General Eisenhower became president in 1953. Mr. Weeks traveled back to Washington to discuss his idea for Veterans Day with President Eisenhower again. The President was enthusiastic. In 1954 he signed a new law designating November 11 as Veterans Day.

Members of the Alabama Air National Guard in the 2015 Veterans Day parade in Birmingham

Raymond Weeks continued to lead the Veterans Day parade in Birmingham every year until his death in 1985. The tradition of a large Veterans Day celebration in Birmingham continues today. People remember Raymond Weeks and honor him as the Father of Veterans Day.

President Ronald Reagan and Raymond Weeks

In 1982, three years before he died, Raymond Weeks traveled to Washington again. This time his wife and his daughters went, too. They were all invited to the White House for a special presentation. President Ronald Reagan awarded Raymond Weeks the Presidential Citizens Medal. Presidents give this award to people "who have performed exemplary deeds of service for their country or their fellow citizens."

In a speech at the ceremony, President Reagan said, ". . . Mr. Weeks has exemplified the finest traditions of American voluntarism by his unselfish service to his country. As director of the National Veterans Day Celebration in Birmingham for the past 36 years, Raymond Weeks, a World War II veteran himself, has devoted his life to serving others, his community, the American veteran, and his nation. He was the driving force behind the congressional action which in 1954 established this special holiday as a day to honor all American veterans.

"It's a pleasure for me to present Mr. Weeks the Presidential Citizens Medal," the President continued, "given to those who have made outstanding contributions to their country. And, Mr. Weeks, in honoring you, we honor the ideals that we hope to live up to. Your country is mighty grateful for what you've done."

And do not neglect doing good and sharing,
for with such sacrifices God is pleased.
Hebrews 13:16

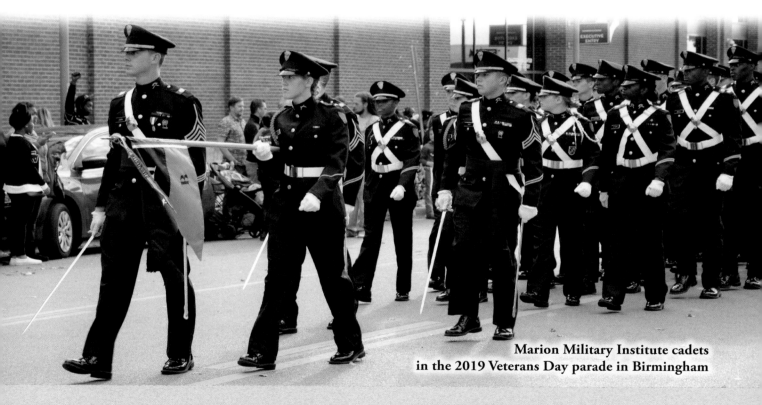

Marion Military Institute cadets in the 2019 Veterans Day parade in Birmingham

Activities

- Complete the map activities for Alabama in the *Atlas Workbook* (page 43).
- Read the chapter titled "White Children" in *Soft Rain*.
- Have you ever watched a patriotic parade? Have you ever seen a flag flying at half-mast? Have you ever been to an event that honored veterans? If you are keeping a creative writing notebook, write about one of those experiences.

Family Activity: Biscuits and Gravy

Long ago, when people didn't have butter for their biscuits, they added gravy instead. Biscuits and gravy became a classic southern combo and is now popular across the country.

Biscuits

Ingredients (makes about 20 biscuits):
- 4 cups self rising flour, plus more for work surface
- 2 tablespoons baking powder
- 1 teaspoon baking soda
- 3 sticks salted butter, cold, cut into ½" pieces
- 2 large eggs
- 1 ½ cups buttermilk
- 2 tablespoons melted butter for tops

Directions:
- In a large bowl whisk together flour, baking powder, and baking soda.
- Using a pastry blender or your fingers, mix cold butter into the flour mixture. You should have fairly even-sized tiny balls when you're finished.
- Using a wooden spoon, stir 2 beaten eggs into the flour and butter mixture until combined.
- Stir in 1 ½ cups of buttermilk until dough comes together. It will be sticky.
- If it seems dry, add more buttermilk, a tablespoon at a time, mixing after each addition.
- Cover the bowl and refrigerate for at least 30 minutes.
- Position a rack in the middle of the oven and preheat to 400°.
- Grease a baking sheet or line it with parchment paper.
- Scrape the dough onto a floured work surface. Using floured hands, press the dough into a ½" thickness, about 14" across.
- Use a floured 2 ¾" biscuit cutter (or drinking glass) to cut out 20 biscuits.
- Place biscuits onto your prepared baking sheet (they should be touching).
- In a small bowl, melt 2 tablespoons of butter. Let cool slightly and brush onto the biscuit tops.
- Bake until golden brown, 15-20 minutes.
- Let cool slightly before removing from the pan.

Gravy

Ingredients:
- 1 lb. breakfast sausage
- ⅓ cup all-purpose flour
- 4 cups milk
- ½ teaspoons seasoned salt
- 2 teaspoons black pepper

Directions:
- In a large pan, brown the sausage over medium-high heat.
- Reduce the heat to medium-low.
- Stir flour into sausage a little at a time until all of the flour is wet.
- Cook sausage-flour mixture for 2 to 3 minutes.
- Slowly add the milk, stirring constantly.
- Cook the gravy until it thickens, stirring frequently.
- Stir in the salt and pepper.
- Serve warm over biscuits.

Be safe with knives and the hot stove and oven. Children must have adult supervision in the kitchen.

Cotton bales in a Mississippi cotton field

Unit 11
South:
Mississippi and Arkansas

181

Magnolia trees grow tall and grand in Mississippi. The magnolia is the state tree and the blossom is the state flower of Mississippi—the Magnolia State. Magnolia blossoms can grow as large as twelve inches across. Find Mississippi on the map at the beginning of this book.

Magnolia

Oxford

The founders of one Mississippi town hoped that one day people would decide to build a university there. They thought it would help to name their town **Oxford** after a town by that name in England which is home to a famous university. The plan worked. Oxford, Mississippi, became the home of the University of Mississippi. Today the city loves to celebrate their connection with England. In Oxford, Mississippi, you can ride on a double decker bus, just like the buses in Oxford, England. The buses are real English buses that came to Mississippi on ships from England.

Oxford

Mississippi Delta

Belzoni

Yazoo River

Mississippi River

Vicksburg

Jackson

Natchez

Biloxi Pascagoula

Cat Island

Gulf of Mexico

Double decker buses in front of the courthouse in Oxford

Mississippi Delta

The **Mississippi River** forms the western border of the state of Mississippi. The Anishinabe people called this river *Messipi*, which means "Big River." They also called it *Mee-zee-see-bee*, or "Father of Waters."

A delta is a flat wetland area where a river empties into another body of water. The area where the **Yazoo River** empties into the Mississippi River forms the **Mississippi Delta**. The Mississippi Delta lies along the western edge of the state. The soil in the delta is rich. Farming is an important part of life there. Cotton is the most valuable crop. Catfish are important, too. Mississippi raises more catfish in ponds than any other state. The delta town of **Belzoni** is the Catfish Capital of the World. Over 30 statues of catfish decorate Belzoni. People have painted the statues to look like a musician, Uncle Sam, Little Red Riding Hood, and other characters.

Musician catfish

Capital: Jackson

Deep under the streets of Mississippi's capital city of **Jackson** sits an extinct volcano. No other big city in the country can claim that! Thankfully, the volcano is about three thousand feet under the ground and scientists do not expect it ever to erupt again.

Mississippi Capitol

Vicksburg

The Mississippi River is an important way to transport goods from one place to another. Before trucks and trains carried cargo across the country, the river was even more important than it is now.

The city of **Vicksburg** is beside the Mississippi River. During the Civil War, the South fought to keep control of Vicksburg so they could continue to carry soldiers and supplies on the river. In 1864 the North fought to take over Vicksburg to hurt the South. In the end, the North won the Battle of Vicksburg. Today the battlefield is part of the Vicksburg National Military Park.

Natchez

Natchez, Mississippi, was once an important ceremonial center for the Natchez people. French settlers conquered the Natchez in the 1700s. They sold some of them as slaves and the rest escaped and joined other tribes. French settlers established the town of Natchez on a bluff overlooking the Mississippi River. Visitors to Natchez today enjoy touring grand old southern mansions built before the Civil War.

Mansion in Natchez

Ingalls Shipbuilding

At a shipyard in **Pascagoula**, Mississippi, thousands of men and women work together as engineers, painters, electricians, designers, insulators, pipefitters, and welders. These skilled workers at Ingalls Shipbuilding build ships for the U.S. Navy, Marines, and

Coast Guard. The company began building ships in 1938. Their facility in Pascagoula covers 800 acres. It takes a great deal of space to build ships that are up to 844 feet long. (That's about as long as three football fields put together. That is one big ship!)

Ingalls Shipbuilding

Cat Island

Six barrier islands lie in the Gulf of Mexico off the southern coast of Mississippi. When early French explorers came to the area, they saw animals they didn't recognize on one of the islands. They assumed the animals were cats and named the island **Cat Island**. It turns out the animals were raccoons, but the name Cat Island stuck.

During World War II, the U.S. army trained hundreds of dogs on Cat Island to help in the war effort. The Army chose Cat Island since it was similar to islands where the

dogs would serve in the Pacific Ocean. Soldiers trained the dogs to be guards and scouts and to carry messages. The dogs served well and helped to defeat the enemy. After the war, many of the dogs were able to go back home to the patriotic families who had donated their pets to serve in the war.

Marines and dogs in World War II

Hospitality

To be hospitable means to be friendly and welcoming. Mississippi has a long tradition of being hospitable and has earned the nickname Hospitality State. The Bible teaches Christians to be hospitable as we welcome others with generous and servant hearts.

Let love be without hypocrisy. Abhor what is evil; cling to what is good.
Be devoted to one another in brotherly love; give preference to one another in honor . . .
contributing to the needs of the saints, practicing hospitality.
Romans 12:9-10, 13

Cat Island

Activities

- Illustrate the geographic term for Mississippi in the *Atlas Workbook* (page 44).
- If you are using the *Lesson Review*, answer the questions for Mississippi (page 11).
- Read the chapter titled "The Last Apple" in *Soft Rain*.
- Hands-On Idea: Pretend that you are a dog trainer on Cat Island during World War II.

Lesson 42: A Song and Story of Mississippi

Be True, Be True Blues

Musicians express their emotions through music. Mississippi Delta blues music has sad tones. The words often express sorrow and loss. The roots of blues music run deep in the Mississippi Delta where enslaved people once worked the cotton fields. The blues style of music came from their songs. Several famous blues musicians grew up in the Mississippi Delta, including Charley Patton. Patton recorded this blues song with Henry Sims in 1929. (Track 21)

Be true, be true, don't lose your life.
Be true, be true, don't lose your life.
You may go away to some distant place.
Be true, be true, don't lose your life.

All I want is to find a good way.
All I want is to find a good way.
You may go, you may know, you may seek,
    you may go.
Be true, be true, don't lose your life.

I'm going, I'm going to some lonesome place.
I'm going, I'm going to some lonesome place.
I'm going, I'm going, to lose my life.
I'm going, I'm going to a lonesome place.

I've been travelin', travelin' all my life.
I've been travelin', travelin' all my life.
I've been travelin' ways all my life.
I've been travelin' all my life.

So be, be true, don't lose your life.
Be true, be true, don't lose your life.
All I want is to find a good way.
Be true, be true, don't lose your life.

Biloxi Lighthouse

Mary Reynolds, Maria Younghans, and Miranda Younghans were all brave. They were all strong. They all knew the importance of their work. They were all keepers of the Biloxi Lighthouse. The service of these three women kept the lighthouse operating faithfully for 74 years.

In 1847 the United States government decided to build a lighthouse in **Biloxi** to guide the oyster and shrimp boats in the Gulf of Mexico. A company in Baltimore, Maryland, made the iron sections of the lighthouse and then shipped them to Mississippi. Once in Biloxi, a crew bolted the sections together. They laid a lining of bricks on the inside of the tower to make it stronger.

Two hurricanes in 1860 washed away part of the sand under the lighthouse foundation. The lighthouse began leaning two feet to the side. An engineer suggested workers dig out some of the sand from the other side in hopes that the lighthouse would straighten itself out. It took a great deal of digging, but his idea worked.

Biloxi Lighthouse

Biloxi Public Pier across from the lighthouse

Marcellus Howard was the first keeper of the Biloxi Lighthouse. After his service, Mary Reynolds came to keep the light. She was not married, but she cared for several orphaned children. Every night she faithfully kept the oil in the lighthouse lamps burning bright.

Mary Reynolds left the lighthouse in 1866 and the Younghans family moved in. Perry Younghans served as lighthouse keeper for one year, but died in 1867. His wife Maria, who was just 25, continued to live at the lighthouse with their young daughter, Miranda. Maria Younghans kept the lighthouse for 53 years. A newspaper described her as a "plucky woman." Through heat and cold and stormy winds, she was faithful to her work.

Biloxi Lighthouse

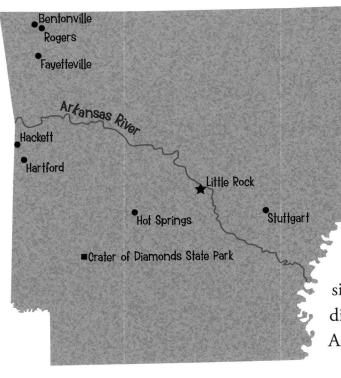

The Quapaw people once lived in the area that became the state of Arkansas. French explorers who came through the area called them "Oo-ka-na-sa," the name that a nearby tribe used for them. The explorers wrote down the names of various native nations as they sounded to their French ears. Oo-ka-na-sa became Arkansas. In French the *s* on the end of the word "Arkansas" was silent. European people spelled the word many different ways through the years, including Arkensa, Arkancas, Akansa, and Arkansaw.

Soon after Arkansas became a state, their two U.S. senators disagreed on how to pronounce the state's name. One said "AR-kan-SAW," while the other said "Ar-KAN-SAS." In 1881 the state government passed a law declaring that the correct pronunciation is "AR-kan-SAW." They felt this was the best historic pronunciation and better honored the original inhabitants for whom the state is named.

Find Arkansas on the map at the beginning of this book (but don't pronounce the final *s*!).

Bentonville

In 1950 Sam Walton opened Walton's 5&10 in **Bentonville**, Arkansas. Customers could find a wide variety of items in the store that cost five or ten cents. Sam Walton's store was a success. He and his brother Bud soon opened more locations in Arkansas and Missouri.

Sam Walton's original store in Bentonville

Walmart Home Office

In 1962 Sam Walton opened a new store in **Rogers**, Arkansas. Using the first three letters of his last name, he called it Wal-Mart. He continued to open more Wal-Mart stores in more states. Today his company operates stores (now called Walmart) in all 50 states and in 26 other countries. The company's headquarters are in Bentonville and the original Walton's 5&10 building houses The Walmart Museum.

Stuttgart

Arkansas grows more rice than any other state. The world's largest rice milling company is Riceland in **Stuttgart**. The company packages their rice in one-pound bags, one-ton bags, and many sizes in between. Riceland rice travels in trucks across the country and in container ships around the world.

Every year Stuttgart hosts the World's Champion Duck Calling Contest. Usually the participants in the contest use duck call instruments to make their duck sounds. In 1936 and 1942, however, the winners used only their mouths. All over the world, people win prize money in many different types of contests. In Stuttgart, Arkansas, people win money if they can sound like a duck.

Arkansas rice field

Razorbacks

Arkansas farmers have to deal with a big pest that loves to uproot what they have planted. Arkansas is full of wild hogs that destroy yards and fields. Farmers sometimes install huge traps which can catch 30 or 40 of these pesky animals at a time. Another name for a wild hog is a razorback. The name refers to the tall hair that runs down the animal's backbone.

Wild hog (razorback)

In the early 1900s, students at the University of Arkansas in Fayetteville began calling their football team the Razorbacks. In 1909 the school's football coach made the nickname more popular. He said that his team "played like a wild band of razorbacks." The following year, students at the school changed their school mascot from the Cardinals to the Razorbacks. The new mascot must have certainly sounded more intimidating to their opposing teams.

Capital: Little Rock

When a French explorer sailed up the Arkansas River in 1722, he saw a rocky outcropping on the riverbank. He called it La Petite Roche, which means "The Little Rock" in French.

Arkansas Capitol

The settlement of Little Rock began in 1820 with a small cabin beside the Arkansas River. The population of the community grew to be around 30 people that year. Today the city is home to around 200,000.

The state capitol building in Little Rock is built to look like the U.S. Capitol building in Washington, D.C. The buildings look so similar that some movies have been filmed in Little Rock to look like they take place in Washington, D.C.

Steaming water from a hot spring in Hot Springs

Hot Springs

For hundreds of years, people have come to bathe in the waters of central Arkansas. Springs here run deep in the heart of the earth where the rocks are hot. The hot rocks heat the water. For centuries people have believed that bathing in the water from the hot springs would improve their health.

In the 1800s, people set up canvas tents as bathhouses. People later built simple wooden structures; but these often collapsed, rotted, or burned down.

In the late 1800s and early 1900s, businessmen built the grand and elegant bathhouses that now stand along Bathhouse Row in **Hot Springs**. One of the bathhouses offered guests five different sizes of tubs so that guests of all heights could be comfortable.

Bathhouses in Hot Springs

Crater of Diamonds State Park

Usually state parks don't want anyone to take flowers or rocks or anything from the park home with them. They want everyone to leave everything for others to enjoy. **Crater of Diamonds State Park** in Murfreesboro, Arkansas, is different. The park encourages visitors to hunt through a plowed field and take home whatever diamonds they might find. Over the years, people have found over 30,000 diamonds in this park, including the largest diamond ever found in the United States.

When God placed every one of diamonds in Arkansas, He knew who would find each one.

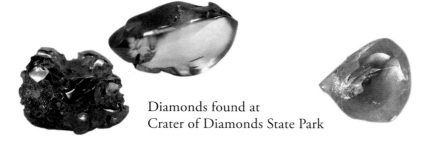

Diamonds found at
Crater of Diamonds State Park

In the beginning
God created
the heavens and the earth.
Genesis 1:1

Activities

- Illustrate the geographic term for Arkansas in the *Atlas Workbook* (page 46).
- If you are using the *Lesson Review*, answer the questions for Arkansas (page 11).
- Hands-On Idea: If you can't make it to Stuttgart, Arkansas, this year, host a World's Champion Animal Sounds Contest with your family.

Making Music for Jesus

Hackett, Arkansas

Eugene Monroe (E. M.) Bartlett sat in a classroom with other fifth-grade boys and girls in **Hackett**, Arkansas. He felt awkward. He was embarrassed. He thought that surely the other students were giggling behind his back because he was so much taller than the rest of the fifth-grade class. His classmates were only ten and eleven years old. E. M. Bartlett was 26.

When E. M. was a child, he had to drop out of school at a young age. He wasn't able to return until he was 26, but he was determined to get an education. He wasn't going to let anything stand in the way. E. M. Bartlett, who was born in 1885, went on to earn four college degrees from four different schools.

E. M. Bartlett loved music. He loved using music to praise his heavenly Father. He wanted to share his love of music with others.

In 1918 Mr. Bartlett partnered with other music lovers to organize the Hartford Music Company in **Hartford**, Arkansas. Three years later the company opened the Hartford Musical Institute. The school offered three-week sessions, during which time students studied harmony, voice, piano, stringed instruments, piano tuning, and other skills. Students participated in two-hour singing sessions at least five days a week. The students also gathered each day for worship and prayer.

Hartford, Arkansas

Hartford Musical Institute in the early 1920s (E. M. Bartlett is seated on the far left in the front row.)

Most of the students were from the South, but some came from other parts of the country. Many of the students stayed with local families while they attended the school. Seventy-five students attended the Hartford Musical Institute its first year. Eleven years later, the school taught nearly 400.

In addition to training music students, the Hartford Music Company published songbooks full of original hymns. Mr. Bartlett wrote many of the hymns himself. The books also contained many hymns that students wrote. The Hartford Music Company wanted to give songwriters a way to share their skills with others. They also wanted to give the songwriters a way to earn money by publishing their songs. For several years, the company published two different songbooks each year. People across the country used the songbooks in singing schools. The singing schools were community gatherings where people spent hours learning to blend their voices as they sang together.

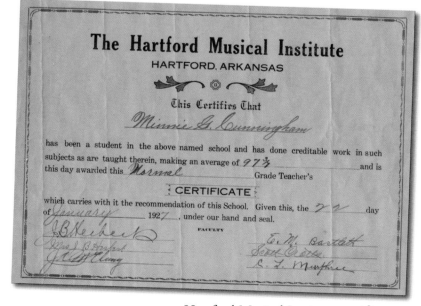

Hartford Musical Institute certificate

Display of Hartford Music Company songbooks

The company's first songbook, *Living Songs of Truth*, contained 177 songs that were "suitable for all religious occasions." The company printed 15,000 copies of the book and sold them for 35 cents each. E. M. Bartlett wrote ten of the songs in this first volume. During the 1930s, the Hartford Music Company sold up to 100,000 songbooks each year.

E. M. Bartlett was a jolly man who devoted his life to sharing Jesus through music. He inspired and encouraged many musicians and helped them grow in their musical skills. His love of music and of his Savior reached thousands of people. During his lifetime, he wrote almost 500 hymns.

At a large group singing in Oklahoma in 1939, E. M. Bartlett marvelled at the tenor voice of another attendee, Erasmus Hummingbird. Mr. Bartlett met privately with the young native man and taught him a new song he had written. That same day, Erasmus performed the new song at the singing. The tenor voice of Erasmus rang out loud and clear as people heard for the first time the now-famous words, "O victory in Jesus, my Savior forever."

> . . . thanks be to God, who gives us the victory
> through our Lord Jesus Christ.
> 1 Corinthians 15:57

O Victory in Jesus

E. M. Bartlett, who helped train hundreds of musicians in Hartford, Arkansas, wrote this hymn. In the song, ere *means "before." (Track 22)*

I heard an old, old story,
How a Savior came from glory,
How He gave His life on Calvary
To save a wretch like me;
I heard about His groaning,
Of His precious blood's atoning,
Then I repented of my sins
And won the victory.

Chorus:
O victory in Jesus,
My Savior, forever.
He sought me and bought me
With His redeeming blood;
He loved me ere I knew Him
And all my love is due Him,
He plunged me to victory,
Beneath the cleansing flood.

I heard about His healing,
Of His cleansing pow'r revealing.
How He made the lame to walk again
And caused the blind to see;
And then I cried, "Dear Jesus,
Come and heal my broken spirit,"
And somehow Jesus came and bro't
To me the victory.

Chorus

I heard about a mansion
He has built for me in glory.
And I heard about the streets of gold
Beyond the crystal sea;
About the angels singing,
And the old redemption story,
And some sweet day I'll sing up there
The song of victory.

Chorus

Ouachita National Forest, Arkansas

Activities

- Complete the map activities for Arkansas in the *Atlas Workbook* (page 47).

- If you are keeping a creative writing notebook, write a poem about Jesus. Set the poem to music using your own tune or a tune you already know.

- Family Activity: Have an Old Fashioned Singing (instructions on page 198).

Family Activity: Old Fashioned Singing

Invite some people to come to your house, to a park, or to another location for an Old Fashioned Singing. If you are able to borrow several songbooks from a church, you can use them for the singing. If not, choose several old hymns that are in the public domain and have an adult print several copies from a computer. You could also send out digital copies of public domain songs to your guests so they can look at them on their phone or other personal device. Have fun lifting up your voices and praising God together.

Great white egret in Atchafalaya Basin, a swamp in Louisiana

Unit 12
South:
Louisiana and Florida

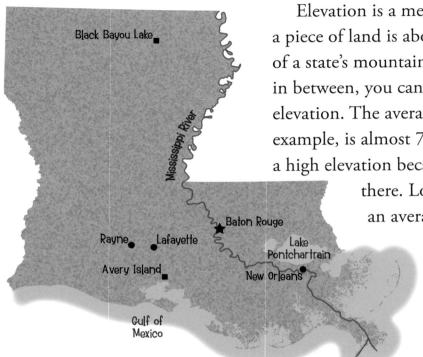

Black Bayou Lake

Mississippi River

Baton Rouge

Rayne   Lafayette

Avery Island

Lake Pontchartrain

New Orleans

Gulf of Mexico

Elevation is a measurement that tells how high a piece of land is above sea level. If you measure all of a state's mountains and valleys and all the land in between, you can figure out the state's average elevation. The average elevation of Colorado, for example, is almost 7,000 feet above sea level. It has a high elevation because there are many mountains there. Louisiana, on the other hand, has an average elevation of just 100 feet.

That's a big difference! Find Louisiana on the map at the beginning of this book.

Alligator snapping turtle

Black Bayou Lake

Louisiana is full of bayous. A bayou is a swampy area in a river or lake where the water is still. A creek that moves along slowly can also be called a bayou. Cypress and tupelo trees thrive in swampy bayou ground.

Black Bayou Lake makes the perfect home for snakes and alligators. Alligator snapping turtles also live in the bayou. Look at the picture above and you can see why people also call them dinosaur turtles. Many kinds of frogs live in the bayou. Their calls are so loud after a spring rain that you just might want to cover your ears!

Black Bayou Lake

Mural in Rayne

Frog Capital of the World

Black Bayou Lake is not the only place in Louisiana that teems with frogs. The city of **Rayne** calls itself the Frog Capital of the World. They hold a Frog Festival every year. Would you rather enter a frog in the frog jumping contest, or participate in the frog leg eating contest at the festival?

Cajun Country

Jambalaya

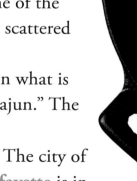

In the early 1600s, thousands of French-speaking Catholics left Europe and traveled across the Atlantic Ocean. They established the colony of Acadia in what is now Nova Scotia, Canada. In 1754 a British officer demanded that the Acadians reject their Catholic faith and let the British rule them. The Acadians refused. As punishment the British forced them to leave their homes. The British army burned their crops and their villages. Some of the Acadians died. Many of them fled on ships and scattered to different countries.

Over time, thousands of Acadians resettled in what is now Louisiana. The term "Acadian" became "Cajun." The Cajun culture is still strong in Louisiana.

The city of **Lafayette** is in the heart of Louisiana's Cajun Country. Lafayette keeps the Cajun culture alive with the music they play, the French phrases they speak, and the foods they eat. One famous Cajun dish is jambalaya—a mixture of rice, meat, vegetables, and spices.

Jambalaya Cajun Band in Lafayette

Outside and inside of the Old State Capitol

Capital: Baton Rouge

A stained glass cathedral dome tops Louisiana's Old State Capitol in **Baton Rouge**. This castle-like building stands high on a bluff and overlooks the **Mississippi River**. It served the state until 1932, when the new capitol building opened. The new building has 34 floors and is the tallest state capitol in the country.

Louisiana State Capitol

New Orleans

The Creole people of Louisiana are a mixture of French, Spanish, and African. Many Creoles live in **New Orleans** near the **Gulf of Mexico**. After Louisiana became a state, New Orleans had two distinct sections: white people settled mainly in the American Quarter and Creoles settled mainly in the French Quarter. Many Creole traditions continue in New Orleans through their famous recipes, colorful architecture, and music. New Orleans is the birthplace of its own musical style: jazz.

Jazz musicians performing in the French Quarter of New Orleans

Lake Pontchartrain

Would you like to know a little secret? The body of water called **Lake Pontchartrain** in southern Louisiana isn't really a lake at all. It is an estuary, where rivers, streams, and bayous meet water from the Gulf of Mexico. Early inhabitants called it *Okwata*, or "wide water." In 1699 a Frenchman renamed it to honor Count de Pontchartrain, a government official in France.

One of the longest bridges in the world connects the north and south shores of Lake Pontchartrain. It takes about an hour to cross the Lake Pontchartrain Causeway, which is almost 24 miles long.

Two hurricanes hit the coast of Louisiana in 2005: Hurricane Katrina and Hurricane Rita. The hurricanes nearly destroyed the historic New Canal Lighthouse beside Lake Pontchartrain. The Lake Pontchartrain Basin Foundation used wood from the damaged lighthouse to rebuild the lighthouse that stands by the water today.

Be strong
and let your heart take courage,
All you who hope in the Lord.
Psalm 31:24

Lake Pontchartrain Causeway

Damaged New Canal Lighthouse in 2005

New Canal Lighthouse rebuilt

Activities

- Illustrate the geographic term for Louisiana in the *Atlas Workbook* (page 48).

- If you are using the *Lesson Review*, answer the questions for Louisiana (page 12).

- Hands-On Idea: Get some of your family members together and pretend that you are the frogs at the Rayne Frog Festival. Who can jump the farthest?

Spicy Sauce and Spirituals

Edmund McIlhenny

Edmund McIlhenny knew what it was like to be successful. He had made a fortune in the New Orleans banking business before the Civil War. Now the Civil War was over, and Edmund McIlhenny was learning what it was like to be jobless. He and his wife's family had fled to Texas for safety during the war. Now it was time to go back to Louisiana and see what was left of their former lives.

Edmund McIlhenny's wife Mary also knew what it was like to be successful. Her father, Judge Avery, had been an accomplished judge and plantation owner before the war. When they all got back to the Avery homeplace on **Avery Island**, they tried to put the pieces of life back together.

In the midst of the destruction, Edmund McIlhenny found pleasure in gardening. Someone gave him some hot pepper seeds, which he planted on Avery Island. Before the Civil War, enslaved men and women had worked the Avery plantation. Now as free persons they helped Edmund McIlhenny pick, mash, and combine his peppers with salt and vinegar. Mr. McIlhenny let the mixture sit for several weeks and was delighted with the result. His new sauce certainly added pizazz to the bland food available after the war.

Edmund McIlhenny thought others might like his sauce, too. He was right. In 1868 he sold 658 bottles for one dollar each, which at the time was a great deal of money. He called his sauce TABASCO.

Pepper plants

The McIlhenny family still owns the business Edmund McIlhenny started. Today the recipe for TABASCO Sauce is essentially the same as it was in 1868 (though now it ages in barrels for up to three years). McIlhenny Company still grows the peppers and bottles the sauce right on Avery Island. They mine their own salt from the enormous underground salt dome that lies under Avery Island. From this island, little glass bottles filled with spicy hot TABASCO Sauce go out to restaurants and grocery stores around the world.

Edmund and Mary's son, John McIlhenny, joined the military and served in Texas and Cuba. He also served the people of Louisiana as a state representative and state senator. He later worked in Washington, D.C., for three U.S. presidents.

Another of Edmund and Mary McIlhenny's sons, Edward, was born on Avery Island in 1872. As an adult, he led the family business for 51 years. The business was important to him, but other things were important to him as well. He was an explorer who led an Arctic expedition. He established a refuge for snowy egrets on Avery Island. Without his efforts, the snowy egret might be extinct today.

Snowy Egret on Avery Island

In addition to these activities, Edward McIlhenny became very interested in studying the African American spirituals he heard growing up. As a child he befriended many of the formerly enslaved people who still lived on Avery Island. Some of his earliest childhood memories were singing with them in their little church and watching the baptisms in the nearby pond. He learned many of their spirituals by heart. He spent many nights sitting beside a campfire with his friend John, a deacon in the church. Together they sang one spiritual after another.

Baptism in a pond on Avery Island

Church on Avery Island

Edward McIlhenny

While Edward McIlhenny was leading the family business, he collected 120 African American spirituals and published them in a book. He wanted to preserve this music, which he described as "beautiful and inspiring."

"Let one hear them sung as I have, time after time," Edward McIlhenny wrote, "in the quiet of some little country church, so small that often not more than half of those attending could get inside, or in the fervor and excitement of camp-meetings, or baptizing, or under some moss hung live-oak grove with only the moon and stars for light, and hear the plaintive crooning echo of their voices come floating back from the mist banks rising in the forests; if one is not then soon entranced by, and eager to hear more of their music, that one has no music in his soul."

Sing to the Lord, bless His name;
proclaim good tidings of His salvation from day to day.
Tell of His glory among the nations,
His wonderful deeds among all the peoples.
Psalm 96:2-3

I Want to Go to Heaven All Dressed In White

Alberta Bradford and Becky Elzy were both enslaved on Avery Island before the Civil War. These two women helped Edward McIlhenny collect the songs he included in his book. This is one of the songs they sang. (Track 23)

Alberta Bradford

Becky Elzy

Jesus, I wanna pray right,
Oh, Jesus, when I pray, I wanna pray right.
Jesus, when I pray, I wanna pray right,
I wanna go to Heaven all dressed in white.

Jesus, I wanna sing right,
Oh, Jesus, when I sing, I wanna sing right.
Jesus, when I sing, I wanna sing right,
I wanna go to Heaven all dressed in white.

Jesus, I wanna mourn right,
Oh, Jesus, when I mourn, I wanna mourn right.
Jesus, when I mourn, I wanna mourn right,
I wanna go to Heaven all dressed in white.

Jesus, I wanna die right,
Oh, Jesus, when I die, I wanna die right.
Jesus, when I die, I wanna die right,
I wanna go to Heaven all dressed in white.

Avery Island, Louisiana

Activities

- Complete the map activities for Louisiana in the *Atlas Workbook* (page 49).
- Listen again to "I Want to Go to Heaven All Dressed in White" (Track 23). Close your eyes and imagine an enslaved person singing the song. Are you picturing a child or an adult? What work is the person doing? If you are keeping a creative writing notebook, write a description of the enslaved person you imagined singing this song.

Lesson 47: Florida

Alligators live in every county in Florida from the state's panhandle to the southern tip. (Notice the panhandle shape in the map at right.) Florida's largest alligator on record was over 14 feet long! Have you ever eaten gator meat? Floridians enjoy gator in chili, in burgers, grilled, smoked, and fried. Find Florida on the map at the beginning of this book.

Pensacola • Britton Hill

Tallahassee ★

Suwannee River

St. Augustine •
Anastasia Island

Manatee Springs State Park ■

Kennedy Space Center ■

Cape Canaveral

Atlantic Ocean

Gulf of Mexico

Lake Okeechobee • Indiantown

Miami •

Everglades National Park

Florida Keys

Alligator

St. Augustine

Castillo de San Marcos

Spanish settlers established **St. Augustine** in 1565. During the 1600s, the Spanish built Castillo de San Marcos to defend their city. It is the oldest standing stone fort in the country. The Spanish built the fort using coquina from nearby **Anastasia Island**. Coquina is a type of stone made from shells that have been pressed together underground. Some of the walls of the fort are nine feet thick. Other sections are 18 feet thick. These strong walls have kept the fort standing for hundreds of years, despite being hit by cannon fire and hurricanes.

Spanish settlers planted orange trees around St. Augustine. Today there are many orange groves across the state. Most Florida oranges become orange juice. Orange juice is the official state drink of Florida.

Florida orange grove

Capital: Tallahassee

When the Spanish explorers came to Florida in the 1500s, they conquered lands that belonged to the native nations who already lived there. The British took Florida from the Spanish in the 1700s. A few years later, Spain took the land back.

Old State Capitol in Tallahassee

In 1821 the United States and Spain made an agreement that Florida would become part of the United States. At that time, the area was divided into East Florida and West Florida. **Pensacola** was the western capital and St. Augustine was the eastern capital. Without good roads it took government officials between 28 and 59 days to travel between the two cities. They decided they needed a new capital between the two original ones. In 1824 they decided on the site of an abandoned Apalachee settlement: **Tallahassee**. That is where the capital has been ever since.

Britton Hill

Britton Hill

When you look at the picture of Britton Hill at left, you might ask, "Where is the hill?" The small monument on the right side of the picture marks the highest point in the state of Florida. Out of all the high points in all the states in our country, Florida's **Britton Hill** is the lowest. It rises just 345 feet above sea level. When you compare that to the highest point in Alaska, which is 20,320 feet above sea level, Britton Hill seems quite low indeed.

Florida might not have mountains for climbing, but it has plenty of beaches for playing. God has placed a variety of sand on the beaches of Florida. Some beaches have sand so white it almost looks like sugar. In some places, bits of shells and fossils mix with the sand to make the beaches gray, orange, or almost black.

Florida white sand

Manatee Springs State Park

During the winter months, manatees look for places to get warm. Some manatees swim from the Gulf of Mexico into the **Suwannee River** on the western side of Florida. At **Manatee Springs State Park**, an underwater spring warms the river, making it just right for the manatees. Visitors to the park can even take a dip in the water themselves to swim with the manatees.

Manatee in Florida

Cape Canaveral and the Kennedy Space Center

3 . . . 2 . . . 1 . . . Lift off! Thousands of rockets have launched into space from the Florida coast. The first rocket to launch from **Cape Canaveral** went up in 1950. The first launch from the nearby **Kennedy Space Center** happened in 1967. That launch was one of the loudest sounds humans have ever created. The force of it made windows rattle three miles away. Two years later, in 1969, the Apollo 11 space mission carried astronauts from Florida to the moon.

Space Shuttle launch from the Kennedy Space Center in 1993

Everglades National Park

When **Lake Okeechobee** overflows during the rainy season, water runs out of the lake into a slow-moving marshy river. The water creeps along through swamps filled with cypress and mangrove trees and through wet prairies. Long-legged birds wade in the water, hunting for fish. Snakes slither around rocks and trees while panthers stalk through the swaying grasses. Alligators and crocodiles bask in the sun. This is **Everglades National Park**. The native people from southern Florida called the area *Pahayokee*, which means "grassy waters."

Rosetta spoonbill in the Everglades

210

In 1947 Marjory Stoneman Douglas wrote a book about the Everglades. She called the environment a "river of grass." Her writing helped others appreciate the beauty of the Everglades. She helped people understand the importance of preserving this part of the world for generations to come.

The Florida Keys

Off the southern tip of Florida lie the **Florida Keys**. This string of islands stretches over 100 miles into the Gulf of Mexico. During the 1930s, construction crews built a highway to connect the islands. The highway includes 42 bridges. One of them is seven miles long.

Scuba divers love to explore the barrier reef that lies off the coast of Florida and runs through the Keys. A barrier reef is an ocean ecosystem, home to coral and many other types of ocean life. The Florida Reef is one of the largest coral reefs in the world.

O Lord, how many are Your works!
In wisdom You have made them all;
The earth is full of Your possessions.
There is the sea, great and broad,
In which are swarms without number,
Animals both small and great.
Psalm 104:24-25

Highway through the Florida Keys

Activities

- Illustrate the geographic term for Florida in the *Atlas Workbook* (page 50).
- If you are using the *Lesson Review*, answer the questions for Florida (page 12).
- Hands-On Idea: Use building bricks, blocks, or play dough to build the Florida Keys and the highway that connects them.

Lesson 48: A Song and Story of Florida

Mama, Papa, y el Niño

The island nation of Cuba lies in the Gulf of Mexico, not far from the Florida Keys. Many Cubans have immigrated to the United States and live in Florida. Between 1937 and 1942 the United States government recorded people across the United States telling stories and singing traditional songs. Six-year-old Rachelita Sanchez of Key West, Florida, took part in the project by singing a Cuban song about visiting a banana grove. (Track 24)

Mama, Papa, y el niño
Se fueron al plantanar,
Los peros le cayeron,
Jau, jau, jau!

Mama, Papa, and the child,
Have gone to the banana grove,
The dogs chased after,
Bow, wow, wow!

Banana tree

Remember Where You Come From

In April of 1923, a group of Seminole women built a birth chickee in the Big Forest near **Indiantown**, Florida. The chickee had open sides and a thatched roof made of palmetto leaves. On April 27, inside the chickee built especially for this moment, Ada Tiger gave birth to a baby girl: Betty Mae. Ada Tiger was a Seminole. The baby's father was French. According to the Seminole culture, a baby that was only part Seminole must die. This mother, however, did not let anyone kill her baby girl. Two years later, Ada Tiger gave birth to a baby boy, Howard.

Modern chickee

Ada Tiger took good care of her children. She taught Betty how to create traditional Seminole crafts, such as baskets, dolls, and beadwork. Betty's mother was a midwife. Sometimes she took Betty along when it was time to deliver a baby. Ada Tiger owned hundreds of cows, as well as chickens and pigs. Betty and Howard's father was not allowed to live among the Seminoles.

When Betty was five years old, a mob of angry Seminoles came to the Tiger family's home. They wanted to kill Betty and Howard because their father was French, but Uncle Jimmie scared away the mob in time. He wasn't about to let anyone hurt his great-niece and great-nephew. Uncle Jimmie was a Christian. He used to be an angry and hateful man like the men in the mob, but Jesus had changed him.

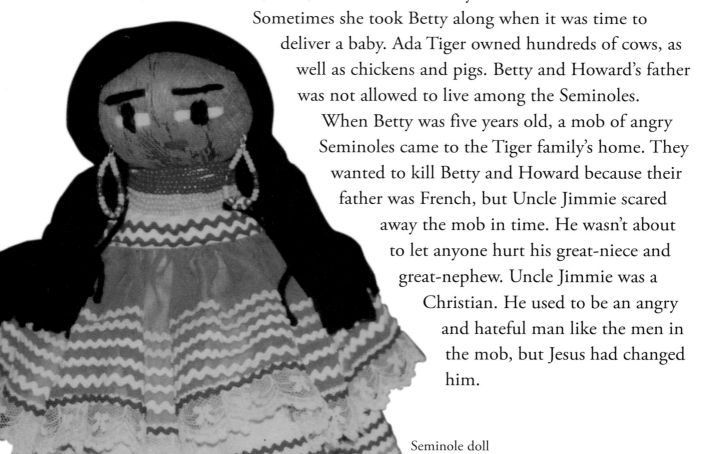

Seminole doll

The family soon left Indiantown and moved where they could live in peace. Ada Tiger was able to sell some of the family's livestock before they left, but money was tight in their new home. They did not always have enough to eat. Betty's family earned money working in the fields of white farmers.

When Betty was a child, a traveling preacher from Oklahoma came to teach the Seminoles in Florida about Jesus. When Betty heard the preacher's words, they touched her heart. Betty gave her life to Jesus and clung to Him her whole life.

Betty desperately wanted to go to school, but she was Seminole. The school for white

Near Indiantown, Florida

children wouldn't let her attend because she wasn't white. She couldn't go to the school for black children because she wasn't black. There was no school in Florida where she could learn. When Betty was 14, her family sent her to a Cherokee boarding school in North Carolina. In 1945 Betty became the first Seminole to graduate from high school.

Betty Mae Jumper with Princess

After high school, Betty moved to Oklahoma to study nursing. After a year, she moved back to Florida and worked at a hospital in **Miami**. She also made medical visits among Seminole families and helped establish a health program for native people in Florida.

In 1946 Betty married Moses Jumper Jr. He earned money entertaining tourists—by wrestling alligators! Sometimes, when her husband wasn't able to go to work, Betty stepped into the alligator pit in his place! Betty Jumper also spent time with a panther named Princess. She was a brave woman.

Betty Jumper had a heart to serve. She worked to make life better for her people. She helped establish a government for the Seminole tribe. Since she spoke English and two Seminole languages, she often served as a translator. She established tribal newspapers. In 1967 her people elected her to serve as their chief. She was the first elected female chief of any native tribe in the country. President Richard Nixon chose her to serve on the National Council on Indian Opportunity to help the United States government know how to help native people across America.

Betty Jumper believed strongly in preserving the culture and stories of her people. She collected many traditional Seminole tales into a book, *Legends of the Seminoles*. "Be proud of your heritage," she advised. "Remember where you come from."

Honor your father and your mother, that your days may be prolonged in the land which the Lord your God gives you.
Exodus 20:12

Betty Mae Jumper (standing, center) with the first Tribal Council of the Seminole Tribe of Florida around 1958

Betty Mae Jumper (second from left) with other Seminole women in traditional dress in 1998

Betty Mae Jumper speaking to children in a chickee

Activities

- Complete the map activities for Florida in the *Atlas Workbook* (page 51).
- If you were going to wrestle or train a wild animal, what animal would you choose? If you are keeping a creative writing notebook, write about the animal. How would you wrestle it or what would you train it to do?
- Family Activity: Make a Chickee Treat (instructions on page 216).
- If you are using the *Lesson Review*, take the South (Part 2) Test (page 35).

Family Activity: Chickee Treat

Supplies:
- chocolate candy melts
- 4 graham crackers
- 6 large pretzel dipping sticks
- 28 small pretzel sticks
- square cereal with ridges

Directions:
- Melt candy melts in the microwave (follow package directions) or by using a double boiler on the stovetop.
- For the roof, spread a thin layer of melted candy onto one full-size graham cracker. Place cereal squares onto the thin layer of melted candy to make a "thatched roof." Repeat this process on a second graham cracker. Candy mixture will set quickly, so you might have to remelt it.
- Using a spoon, spread a line of melted candy along one long edge of each graham cracker roof piece. Put the two candy-coated edges together with the cereal sides facing out to make an L-shape. Hold together for a couple of minutes to allow the candy to set.
- For the floor, lay the two remaining graham crackers down side by side, long sides together. Dip one "cypress post" pretzel dipping stick into the melted candy. Place the candy end of the pretzel in one corner approximately ½" from the edge of the graham cracker floor. Hold the pretzel in place until it stands on its own. Repeat this process with the remaining 5 dipping sticks as pictured.
- Once your pretzels are in place and able to stand on their own, cover the floor with pretzel sticks.
- To add the side rails to your chickee, place a dot of melted candy on each end of a pretzel stick and a dot on the two posts where you will be attaching your rail. Hold each stick in place until dry. Repeat this process 3 more times so that you have 2 rails on each side of your chickee.
- Using a spoon, place a dot of melted candy on the top of each pretzel rod. Carefully place your thatched roof onto the cypress posts and your chickee is done!

Old Mackinac Point Lighthouse, Michigan

Unit 13
Midwest:
Michigan and Ohio

Lesson 49: Michigan

Michiganders call the Upper Peninsula of their state the U.P. People who live in the U.P. are Yoopers. The U.P. receives a large amount of snow each winter. The Yoopers in **Mohawk**, Michigan, keep track of their snowfall records with the gauge pictured at left. In the winter of 1978-1979, they received over 390 inches of snow! Find Michigan on the map at the beginning of this book.

Snow gauge in Mohawk

Frozen waterfall in Pictured Rocks

Pictured Rocks National Lakeshore

The dazzling waterfalls of the **Pictured Rocks National Lakeshore** become solid ice in cold weather. Some rock climbers brave the weather to climb up these icy falls. People also explore the park's sea caves, lakes, bogs, marshes, and cedar swamplands.

This park gets its name from the colorful cliffs that rise out of Lake Superior. When minerals such as iron and copper ooze out of cracks in the ground and run down the face of the cliffs, they create colorful stripes on the rocks.

Pictured Rocks National Lakeshore

Isle Royale National Park

An archipelago is a group of islands. The Isle Royale archipelago in Lake Superior has around 450 islands. Compared to other national parks, not many people visit **Isle Royale National Park**. Some national parks have more visitors in a single day than this park has in a whole year. There are no bridges to these islands. Visitors arrive by boat or by seaplane. Scuba divers come to Isle Royale to explore the remains of shipwrecks that lie deep in the waters of Lake Superior. Kayakers explore coves hidden among the islands. A cove is a small, sheltered bay. Campers sometimes spot a moose or a wolf roaming the islands.

Seaplane in Isle Royale

Soo Locks

Look at the names of all five of the Great Lakes on the map at the beginning of this book. The city of **Sault** (pronounced Soo) **Sainte Marie** lies on the St. Mary's River, which connects Lake Superior with Lake Huron. It is Michigan's oldest city. The rapids here once made it impossible for large ships to travel between Lake Superior and Lake Huron. Rapids are areas of a river where the water is shallow and flows quickly. In the mid-1800s workers began constructing the Soo Locks. The locks raise and lower ships, allowing them to pass around the rapids. Workers have improved and expanded these locks through the years. Many ships travel on the Great Lakes, transporting goods from one port city to another. Soo Locks are the busiest locks in the world.

Soo Locks

Mackinac Island

Mackinac Island

Mackinac (pronounced Mackinaw) **Island** attracts people to Michigan from around the world. Visitors reach the island by taking a ferry or a small plane. Once on the island, people can choose to walk, ride a bike, or take a horse-drawn carriage to get around. No one is allowed to have a car on Mackinac. There are a handful of emergency vehicles on the island, plus a few snowplows to get them through the winter, but that's about it. People like to take it slow on Mackinac. The island is famous for its fudge shops. You can watch the fudge-makers at work making huge slabs of fudge in their kitchens. Would you rather sample peanut butter, mint chocolate chip, or maple cherry?

Mackinac Island fudge

Silver Lake Sand Dunes

Michigan's **Silver Lake Sand Dunes** separate Lake Michigan from Silver Lake. These dunes are a giant playground. People love to walk and climb, tumble and run, and drive off-road vehicles across these dunes all day long.

Silver Lake Sand Dunes

Capital: Lansing

The state capitol building in **Lansing** has some construction secrets. Workers built this capitol in the 1870s. At that time, the government didn't have enough money to buy all the best materials. People had to get creative. They used cheap pine lumber and painted it to look like expensive walnut. The columns in the building are made of iron and painted to look like fancy marble. The result is a beautiful masterpiece. The glass floor under the dome makes a glass ceiling on the floor below.

Glass floor in the Michigan State Capitol

Ford automobile factory in Detroit

Detroit

In the 1900s, many people moved to **Detroit** from other parts of Michigan and from other parts of the country. They came for the jobs available at Detroit's many automobile factories. Detroit became Motor City.

Making automobiles requires many people doing many different jobs, all working together. In a similar way, the Bible teaches us that each person in a church has an important job to do. The church is a body—different parts all working together as one.

But now God has placed the members, each one of them,
in the body, just as He desired.
1 Corinthians 12:18

Activities

- Illustrate the geographic term for Michigan in the *Atlas Workbook* (page 52).
- If you are using the *Lesson Review*, answer the questions for Michigan (page 13).
- Read chapter 1 in *The Story of George Washington Carver*. (Parents, please refer to page 17 in the *Answer Key and Literature Guide* for comments about this book.)
- Hands-On Idea: If you have a sandbox, make some dunes in it.
- Family Activity: Make a Great Lakes Lighthouse (instructions on page 234).

Lesson 50: A Song and Story of Michigan

Red Iron Ore

This ballad (a song that tells a story) tells about sailors working on the Great Lakes in the 1800s. The E. C. Roberts *is the name of their ship. "Death's Door" refers to a dangerous spot on Lake Michigan. Escanaba is a Michigan town where the sailors loaded iron ore into their ship. (Track 25)*

Come, all you bold sailors that follow the lakes
On an iron ore vessel, your living to make;
I shipped in Chicago, bid adieu to the shore,
Bound away to Escanaba for red iron ore.
Derry Down, Down, Down, Derry Down.

In the month of September, the seventeenth day,
Two dollars and a quarter is all they would pay,
And on Monday morning from Bridgeport did take
The *E. C. Roberts* out in the lake.
Derry Down, Down, Down, Derry Down.

The wind from the southard sprang up a fresh breeze,
And away through Lake Michigan the *Roberts* did sneeze,
Down through Lake Michigan the *Roberts* did roar,
And on Friday morning we passed through death's door.
Derry Down, Down, Down, Derry Down.

Now my song it is ended, I hope you won't laugh,
Our dunnage is packed and all hands are paid off;
Here is health to the *Roberts*, she's staunch, strong and true,
Not forgotten the bold boys that comprise her crew.
Derry Down, Down, Down, Derry Down.

Escanaba, Michigan

Building More than Cars

Dean Buchanan was nervous. It was her first day of work at the Willow Run factory in **Ypsilanti**, Michigan, near Detroit. During World War II, workers at this factory made B-24 bombers. After World War II, workers at the factory began building cars.

Building bombers at Willow Run during World War II

Building cars at Willow Run in 1950

In 1978, 22-year-old Dean Buchanan got a job on the assembly line at Willow Run. She had never seen the inside of such an enormous factory. She was scared and nervous about her new job.

After Dean arrived at Willow Run on her first day, another employee drove her through the factory in a golf cart. He drove her to her assigned position on the assembly line. Someone showed her exactly how to do her new job. He showed her how to spread tar in the window channel on the top of the car doors. Someone else down the line would attach rubber seals to the tar. The rubber seals were for the car's windows. Each car was complex. There were so many different parts that all had to be put in place just right. Each person had to know exactly how to do his or her job. They all worked together to assemble each car, piece by piece. They each had less than a minute to do their part.

Dean Buchanan

The cars rolled slowly along through the factory on a conveyor belt in an endless line. Dean walked along beside each car until her job was done. Then she walked back to her starting point on the line. Another car was already there, ready for her to do her job again.

As Dean worked, she noticed another young woman working about ten feet down the line. The young woman looked at Dean with twinkling eyes. She gave her a warm and friendly smile. Her smile made some of Dean's fear melt away. The young woman later introduced herself as Georgia McCurdy.

Georgia McCurdy

Georgia's job on the line was to install a sun visor on the driver's side of each car. As each car rolled along on the conveyor belt, Georgia grabbed a sun visor from the table beside her. She picked up a matching bracket and three screws. In less than a minute, she had the visor screwed into place.

Hour after hour, Georgia screwed in visors. Hour after hour, Dean spread tar. Georgia was exhausted, but she still managed to smile. She could tell that Dean was nervous about her new job. Georgia invited Dean to eat with her on their break. They became friends right away. They talked about their hobbies and about their families.

Rick and Georgia with their sons, Nate and Matt, in 1981

Georgia told Dean about her husband Rick. Rick worked the night shift at a different automobile factory where he helped to manage the inventory.

Dean was a Christian. She loved to talk to her new friend about Jesus. Georgia had not grown up in a Christian family, but when she was a child she often went to church with her neighbor. After Georgia grew up and married, though, she stopped going to church.

Dean's life overflowed with the hope and joy of Jesus. Georgia wanted to have Jesus in her own life, too. Dean studied the Bible with Georgia and Rick. Georgia decided to be baptized. She went to church with Dean for a while, but then she stopped going. Then, one Sunday morning, Georgia knew what she needed to do. She went back to church. She walked in and found Dean already sitting on a pew. Georgia sat down on the pew behind her friend. She put her hand on Dean's shoulder. "I'm back," Georgia said, "and I'm never leaving again." Georgia kept her word.

Georgia's husband Rick became a Christian, too. Before long, Georgia quit her job at the factory. She wanted to be at home to take care of their children. Georgia was glad to leave her job at the factory, but she was always thankful for it. God had used that assembly line to build more than cars. He had used it to build a love for Jesus in Georgia's heart—a love that she spread to her family and to everyone around her.

Jesus said:

If anyone serves Me, he must follow Me; and where I am, there My servant will be also; if anyone serves Me, the Father will honor him.
John 12:26

Georgia with her children, Nate, Liz, Rebecca, and Matt

The McCurdy family in 2012 and 2018

Activities

- Complete the map activities for Michigan in the *Atlas Workbook* (page 53).
- Read chapter 2 in *The Story of George Washington Carver*.
- Think about people you know who have helped you learn about Jesus. Think about parents and grandparents, ministers and teachers, relatives and friends. If you are keeping a creative writing notebook, write down their names.

Author's note: Georgia McCurdy (1955-2019) was my dear mother-in-law. We miss her greatly, but are honored to carry on her legacy of faith.

Lesson 51: Ohio

Ohio is the Buckeye State. Ohio buckeye trees are common in the state. The nuts that grow on these trees look like the eye of a buck (a male deer). Ohioans have called themselves Buckeyes since at least 1840. Find Ohio on the map at the beginning of this book.

Buckeyes

Marblehead Lighthouse

The top of **Marblehead Lighthouse** offers a glorious view of **Lake Erie**. On clear days, visitors can see the city of Cleveland, fifty miles away. This lighthouse has lit the waters of Lake Erie since 1822. It is the oldest continuously operating lighthouse on the Great Lakes.

Marblehead Lighthouse

Cleveland

A land company founded **Cleveland** in 1796. They divided their city into 220 lots. The company invited people to buy lots for homes and businesses. They charged 50 dollars per lot, but that price was too high. By 1800 only three men lived in Cleveland.

The city grew slowly until the mid-1800s. Better roads and railroads finally made it easier to get to and from Cleveland. Thousands of people began moving to Cleveland to work in new steel mills and other factories.

Cleveland

Ashtabula County

Nineteen covered bridges stand in **Ashtabula County**. It was once common to build a roof over a bridge to protect it from the rain and snow. Two of the county's covered bridges date back to 1867. Every year in October, Ashtabula County celebrates their local history with a Covered Bridge Festival. The money raised at the festival helps the county maintain the bridges so that people can continue to enjoy them.

Covered bridge across the Ashtabula River

Cuyahoga Valley National Park

Brandywine Falls in **Cuyahoga Valley National Park** once powered a sawmill, a grist mill, and a woolen mill. The flowing water turned the wheels in the mills that sawed lumber, ground grain, and processed wool. The mills are gone now, but visitors can still enjoy the beauty and majesty of the falls. Along the Brandywine Gorge Trail, vernal pools reflect the clear blue sky overhead. Vernal pools are pools that fill with water in the rainy season and dry up during other parts of the year. The vernal pools here are the perfect spots for frogs and salamanders to lay their eggs.

Brandywine Falls

Capital: Columbus

Workers began constructing the Ohio Statehouse in **Columbus** in 1839. After they finished digging the basement and laying the foundation, work stopped. Some people did not want Columbus to be the state capital. They wanted the government to choose a different city. While people discussed the question, workers filled in the basement they had dug. For eight years, animals munched the grass that grew over the filled-in basement. Finally the government decided that Columbus would remain the capital. Workers dug the basement again, and continued building up from the foundation.

On the day the statehouse officially opened, people came from all over Ohio to join the celebration. As they celebrated at the capitol, the visitors ate 1,600 loaves of bread, 15 barrels of crackers, 900 pounds of butter, four barrels of crushed sugar, 24 barrels of milk, 300 turkeys, 125 hams, and 1,000 gallons of oysters!

Ohio Statehouse

Cincinnati

Old-fashioned steamboat
on the Ohio River in Cincinnati

The bustling city of **Cincinnati** lies on the northern bank of the **Ohio River**. Early settlers established businesses building and repairing steamboats on the river. They built hotels and restaurants for the many travelers who journeyed on the river. Farmers shipped their crops from Cincinnati down the Ohio to the Mississippi River. So many farmers brought their cows and pigs to Cincinnati for processing that the city earned the nickname Porkopolis.

Birthplace of Aviation

Ohio is proud of its aviation (or flying) heritage. Ohio license plates declare that the state is the "Birthplace of Aviation." Wilbur and Orville Wright, the brothers who invented the first successful airplane, grew up in **Dayton**, Ohio. Neil Armstrong, the first man to walk on the moon, was born and raised in **Wapakoneta**, Ohio.

Today around 30,000 men and women work at Wright-Patterson Air Force Base near Dayton. Workers there test aircraft and develop new inventions in aviation.

People created in the image of God have accomplished amazing things as they have explored His universe.

Neil Armstrong

The heavens are telling of the glory of God;
And their expanse is declaring the work of His hands.
Psalm 19:1

Activities

- Illustrate the geographic term for Ohio in the *Atlas Workbook* (page 54).
- If you are using the *Lesson Review*, answer the questions for Ohio (page 13).
- Read chapter 3 in *The Story of George Washington Carver*.
- Hands-On Idea: What do you have that can fly? A kite? A paper airplane? Fly it!

Lesson 52: A Song and Story of Ohio

Beautiful Isle of Somewhere

Jessie Brown Pounds was born in Ohio in 1861. She was homeschooled as a child. When she was 15, she began writing for local newspapers. As an adult, she wrote many books and songs. She is the author of over 400 hymns. This hymn from 1897 is one of her most famous. It speaks of heaven as the "Beautiful Isle of Somewhere." President William McKinley was also from Ohio. This hymn was one of his favorites. Four women from Ohio sang it at President McKinley's funeral in 1901. (Track 26)

Somewhere the sun is shining,
Somewhere the songbirds dwell;
Hush, then, thy sad repining,
God lives, and all is well.

Chorus:
Somewhere, somewhere,
Beautiful Isle of Somewhere!
Land of the true, where we live anew,
Beautiful Isle of Somewhere!

Somewhere the day is longer,
Somewhere the task is done;
Somewhere the heart is stronger,
Somewhere the prize is won.

Chorus

Somewhere the load is lifted,
Close by an open gate;
Somewhere the clouds are rifted,
Somewhere the angels wait.

Chorus

A Boy and a Cave

Robert Noffsinger was a 17-year-old farmhand in 1897. He worked for Abraham Reams in **West Liberty**, Ohio. As he went about his farm duties, Robert wondered about a low spot on the Reams farm. Why did rainwater disappear so quickly from that area? One day Robert decided to investigate. He dug into the dirt a little bit, and then a little bit more. There was limestone under the soil. He kept digging and found a fissure in the rock. A fissure is a crack or split in a rock that makes a long, narrow opening. Robert was curious and adventurous. He decided to climb down inside. He discovered a wondrous maze of underground passageways. He saw stalagmites and stalactites—impressive formations of calcium salts that form inside caves. Robert climbed back out and told Abraham Reams about his discovery.

Ohio Caverns

Within just a few weeks, Abraham Reams started making money on the cave. He welcomed visitors to his farm for 25 years. They paid their admission and climbed down into the spectacular cave system. Sadly, not everyone treated the cave with respect. Some people broke off stalactites and stalagmites and took them home. Some visitors covered the cave walls with graffiti.

In 1922 Abraham Reams sold his property to the Smith brothers from Dayton, Ohio. Allen and Ira Smith knew the cave was a treasure. They knew they needed to protect it.

They worked with a crew for three years to carefully dig out small rocks and mud from the cave system. They opened up three miles of tunnels. In 1925 they opened Ohio Caverns to the public.

Vintage postcard of Ohio Caverns entrance

The Smith family still owns Ohio Caverns. Visitors from all over the world come to enjoy the colorful wonders God placed there. One of the cave's most impressive features is the Crystal King, a stalactite that measures five feet long!

God has placed many buried treasures under the earth. They all declare His glory and show His power and might.

For the Lord is a great God
And a great King above all gods,
In whose hand
are the depths of the earth,
The peaks of the mountains
are His also.
The sea is His,
for it was He who made it,
And His hands formed the dry land.
Psalm 95:3-5

Crystal King

Activities

- Complete the map activities for Ohio in the *Atlas Workbook* (page 55).
- Read chapter 4 in *The Story of George Washington Carver*.
- Imagine that you discover a hidden treasure where your family lives. In your creative writing notebook, write about your imaginary discovery. *or* Act out the story you imagine about your discovery.

Family Activity: Great Lakes Lighthouse

Make a miniature version of the Grand Haven South Pierhead Inner Light on Lake Michigan.

Supplies:

- scissors or knife
- one piece of red craft foam
- empty round chip can
- empty disposable plastic water bottle
- red craft paint
- paint brush
- glue dots (not essential, but they make the project much simpler)
- toothpicks
- small battery-operated votive candle
- red yarn

Directions:

- Adult: Carefully cut the water bottle approximately 4 ½" from the top.
- Paint the top of the water bottle with red paint. Set aside to dry.
- Paint 6 toothpicks with red paint and set aside to dry.
- Wrap the craft foam around the chip can to see how long it needs to be to cover it. Cut the foam to size.
- Place glue dots all along the outside edge of the craft foam.
- Lay the chip can on one edge of the foam, carefully lining up the bottom edge of the can with the foam. Wrap the foam all the way around the chip can. The bottom of the can is now the top of your lighthouse.
- Place 6 glue dots, evenly spaced, around the top of the lighthouse, approximately ½" from the top.
- Place a toothpick on each glue dot.
- Cut a 1" strip of craft foam that will fit around the top of the lighthouse.
- Lay the strip flat. Place a glue dot on each end of the strip and 5-6 down the middle.
- Wrap the strip around top edge of the container to cover the bottom of the toothpicks.
- Cut a piece of red yarn about 15" long. Carefully wrap the yarn around one toothpick, leaving one end hanging down several inches. Wrap the other end of the yarn once around the next toothpick and on around until the railing goes all the way around the lighthouse. Tie the two yarn ends together and trim off any extra.
- Turn on the votive candle and place it in the center of the top of the lighthouse. Place the water bottle over the lantern. Place it where all passing ships will see its light!

234

Door Prairie Barn in La Porte, Indiana

Unit 14
Midwest:
Indiana and Illinois

Indiana is famous for one of the oldest snacks in the world: popcorn! Every year farmers in Indiana raise hundreds of millions of pounds of popcorn. There is even a community in Indiana named **Popcorn**. Find Indiana on the map at the beginning of this book.

Capital: Indianapolis

In the center of Indiana's capital city of **Indianapolis** stands the Soldiers and Sailors Monument. Indiana dedicated this monument in 1902 to honor their veterans who had served in the military. Visitors can climb 330 steps to the observation deck at the top of the monument for a bird's-eye view of the city.

Several men worked together to create the monument and the many statues that decorate it. Rudolf Schwarz came to Indianapolis from Austria to carve some of the figures. His lifelike statues had marvelous detail. They looked like real Civil War soldiers—almost.

Soldiers and Sailors Monument

Many years after the monument was finished, a veteran looked at the statues and commented that they looked more European than American. He said that Civil War soldiers would not have had beards like the ones on the statues. So, several years after the monument's dedication, Rudolf Schwarz picked up a chisel again and chipped away at the beards on his statues. He felt like a barber as he removed their beards to make them look more American.

Soldiers and Sailors Monument detail

Indianapolis Motor Speedway

Across town from the monument is the Indianapolis Motor Speedway. Hundreds of thousands of racing fans come to this racetrack every year. They watch cars zoom around the track in the Indy 500 race. Racing fans have come here since the track opened in 1909. The first race held here was a hot air balloon race. The balloons lifted off from the track and took to the skies. The winner landed in Alabama.

Indiana Dunes National Park

In the north, Indiana borders Lake Michigan for 45 miles. Along that shoreline is **Indiana Dunes National Park**. Park rangers guide visitors to Pinhook Bog. This special habitat is home to a huge variety of plants and animals. Part of the bog has a thick layer of sphagnum moss. God gave this moss special healing properties. People once harvested it to treat wounds.

Pinhook Bog

Colonel Leiber statue at
Turkey Run State Park

McCormick's Creek State Park

Persimmons

Colonel Richard Lieber

During the early 1900s, Colonel Richard Lieber worked hard to establish state parks in Indiana. Thanks to his work, visitors can enjoy places such as **Turkey Run State Park**.

Colonel Lieber also helped establish nearby **McCormick's Creek State Park**. God put a special type of limestone under the ground in this area. It is some of the strongest limestone in the world. Builders have used it for hundreds of years. It has become foundations and walls for many famous buildings. The statehouse in Indianapolis, the Empire State Building in New York City, and the Pentagon in Washington, D.C, are all made of Indiana limestone. A trail in the park leads to an old limestone quarry where workers once cut this limestone out of the earth.

Persimmons

Every year in the fall, you can find the people of **Mitchell**, Indiana, harvesting persimmons. These little orange fruits grow well in southern Indiana. The fruit is the sweetest after it has fallen off the tree. Some say persimmons taste like pumpkin. People mash up the ripe persimmons and use the pulp to make persimmon pudding. Locals compete against each other in a persimmon pudding contest at the Persimmon Festival in Mitchell each September. The festival offers persimmon ice cream, too.

West Baden Springs and French Lick

Early Americans discovered mineral spring water in Orange County, Indiana. In spite of its terrible taste and terrible smell, the water made them feel better. In the 1800s, people began traveling here from miles around. They drank the mineral water and also bathed in it. People built hotels so the travelers would have a place to stay. It became a fancy resort for wealthy people. The hotel in West Baden Springs was magnificent. Another grand hotel welcomed visitors in nearby French Lick.

As the years passed, drinking mineral water became less popular. When the country went through the Great Depression in the 1930s, people didn't have as much money to stay in fancy hotels. Eventually the West Baden Springs hotel closed down. It stood empty for years. Finally it started to fall apart. People got together and decided to save it. They worked hard to fix it up. Today travelers can enjoy the beauty of this grand building once again.

People have come to Orange County hoping the waters would nourish and heal their bodies. Jesus offers living water to nourish and heal our souls. He said:

He who believes in Me, as the Scripture said,
"From his innermost being will flow rivers of living water."
John 7:38

West Baden Springs Hotel

Activities

- Illustrate the geographic term for Indiana in the *Atlas Workbook* (page 56).

- If you are using the *Lesson Review*, answer the questions for Indiana (page 14).

- Read chapter 5 in *The Story of George Washington Carver*.

- Hands-On Idea: Use building bricks or blocks to build a grand hotel.

- Family Activity: Make Popcorn Balls (recipe on page 252).

Indiana

Sarah T. Bolton was born in 1814. She grew up in a log cabin on an Indiana farm. A newspaper first published one of her poems when she was 13. For the next several years, one of her writings appeared in a newspaper almost every week. Some of her poems were set to music, including this one about her home state. The first verse compares Indiana to famous places around the world. (Track 27)

Though many laud Italia's clime,
And call Helvetia's land sublime,
Tell Gallia's praise in prose and rhyme,
   And worship old Hispania;
The winds of Heaven never fanned,
The circling sunlight never spanned
The borders of a better land
   Than our own Indiana.

Encrowned with forests grand and old,
Enthroned on mineral wealth untold.
Coining her soil to yellow gold,
Through labor's great arcana.
She fosters commerce, science, art,
With willing hand and generous heart,
And sends to many a foreign mart,
   Riches of Indiana.

Her gentle mothers, pure and good,
In stately homes or cabins rude,
Are types of noble womanhood;
   Her girls are sweet and cannie;
Her sons, among the bravest, brave,
Call no man master, no man slave--
Holding the heritage God gave
   In fee to Indiana.

But even while our hearts rejoice
In the dear home-land of our choice,
We should, with one united voice,
   Give thanks, and sing Hosanna
To Him whose love and bounteous grace
Gave to the people of our race
A freehold, an abiding place,
   In glorious Indiana.

Indiana farm field

West Baden Springs Hotel

Preserving the Past

In the late 1800s, the hotel in West Baden Springs glittered and sparkled. Many wealthy guests came to the hotel to bathe in the mineral waters. They enjoyed the entertainment at the local opera house. They visited the pony track and the baseball field. They ate fancy meals. Many people came to enjoy all the comforts the hotel had to offer, but not everyone was welcome.

At this time in history, African Americans were not allowed to stay in the West Baden Springs Hotel. Lee Sinclair, the owner of the hotel, hired black men and women to carry the suitcases, wash the sheets, clean the floors, cook the food, and look after the children of the white guests. The hotel couldn't operate without these African American workers, but because of the color of their skin, they were not allowed to stay in the hotel as guests.

Inside the West Baden Springs Hotel

Church members outside the First Baptist Church

First Baptist Church in need of restoration

Restoration begins on First Baptist Church

Sinclair realized the black community of West Baden Springs and French Lick should have a place of worship. He sold a piece of land to a group of black citizens for $1. On it they built a lovely white church building. The building became a center for worship and also for other social gatherings. It was an important part of life for the African Americans in West Baden Springs. The church reached out to those in need—no matter the color of their skin.

Over time, as the hotels became less popular, many black workers lost their jobs. Many moved away to find work in other places. Church membership dwindled. Eventually a white congregation began meeting in the First Baptist Church building. It dwindled in size, too. Finally the local historical society bought the building for $1. A few years later the historical society gave the building to the town of West Baden Springs.

Year after year, the building sat empty. Just like the hotel, it started to fall apart. Finally people decided the building was too important to let fall down. They decided to save it. A pastor in the nearby town of Bloomington heard about the building. He heard about the bad shape it was in. He decided to do something about it. He asked the members of his congregation to help him fix it up. It was going to take a lot of work, but they were ready to help. They got out their hammers and nails and they got busy.

Twice a week, week after week, volunteers made the hour-long drive to West Baden Springs to work on the building. People from the West Baden Springs community appreciated the volunteers coming. They dropped by to bring them snacks and donated money for building supplies. The project continued for years, one board and one can of paint at a time, to preserve a piece of history.

People cared about the First Baptist Church building in West Baden Springs. They cared enough to fix it up so it didn't fall down. They didn't only care about the peeling paint and the rotten boards. They cared about the people who once met inside the building. They cared about preserving their story—a story of working hard and loving God and serving others, even when others weren't treating them right.

Beloved, if God so loved us,
we also ought to love one another.
1 John 4:11

Installing a new ceiling

New floor

First Baptist Church restored

Activities

- Complete the map activities for Indiana in the *Atlas Workbook* (page 57).
- Read chapter 6 in *The Story of George Washington Carver*.
- Imagine that you work at the hotel in West Baden Springs in the late 1800s. Look back at the second paragraph in the story and read about the jobs you might have done. In your creative writing notebook, write a journal entry about your day working at the hotel. *or* Ask some of your family members to pretend to be guests at the hotel while you pretend to be one of the workers.

Three out of every four acres of land in Illinois are farmland. Farmers raise corn, soybeans, pumpkins, and pigs. Illinois ships its farm products to other places by truck and by train. Some of the grain farmers raise here travels down the **Mississippi River** to the Gulf of Mexico on huge flat-bottomed boats called barges. From there the grain travels to other countries. Find Illinois on the map at the beginning of this book.

Barge on the Mississippi River

Shawnee National Forest

God created deep canyons, bubbling springs, and surprising rock formations at **Shawnee National Forest**. This forest is in the southern tip of Illinois. It lies between the Ohio and Mississippi Rivers. The formation pictured here is called Camel Rock. Can you see the camel?

Camel Rock

The largest mound at Cahokia

Cahokia Mounds

North of Shawnee National Forest is **Cahokia Mounds**. Thousands of native people once lived on these lands. Historians believe that around the year 1100, Cahokia was one of the largest cities in the world. The native people who lived here built huge mounds as part of their city. Imagine how hard it must have been to create these massive mounds of earth—without any bulldozers or tractors.

Replica of tablet found at Cahokia

The Squirrels of Olney

The small town of **Olney** is famous for its white (albino) squirrels. Residents discovered these chattering creatures around 1900. The people of Olney have loved their special squirrels ever since. Local laws and squirrel crossing signs help to protect these little critters. Be careful as you travel through town. If you happen to hurt one of these furry white residents, you might have to pay a fine of $750!

Squirrel in Olney

Caterpillar 797 mining truck compared to a pickup

Caterpillar

Peoria is home to the Caterpillar Visitors Center. Caterpillar (or Cat for short) makes equipment for big jobs. People use Cat machines in mines, on construction sites, and on farms. People on Caterpillar equipment have built dams in the United States, made roads in India, explored Antarctica, and dug an underwater tunnel that connects England and France. This company operates factories all over the world.

Caterpillar makes their 797 mining trucks at a factory in **Decatur**. These trucks haul sand, copper, coal, and iron ore at mines around the globe. The 797 is huge. Its tires are 14 feet tall. The 797 display model at the visitors center in Peoria doesn't haul minerals from a mine. Instead, the massive truck bed holds 62 theater seats. Visitors have a seat inside to watch a video on a big screen. In one of those seats it's easy to start feeling like you are driving the giant truck yourself.

Chicago

Chicago is the largest city in Illinois. It is the third largest city in the country. Chicago sits on the shores of Lake Michigan. The wind from the lake gives the city its nickname: Windy City.

The Cloud Gate sculpture in Chicago's Millennium Park offers a fun view of the skyline. It is easy to see why this sculpture (pictured here) is nicknamed The Bean.

The Bean in Chicago

Capital: Springfield

Illinois is the Land of Lincoln. Abraham Lincoln spent much of his life in the state before he became president. He moved to **Springfield** in 1837 when he was 28 years old. Springfield is full of Lincoln sites and statues. You can see the pew in the church building where Abraham Lincoln and his family sat together to worship God. You can visit his home and lawyer's office.

Every year thousands of people rub the nose on the statue of Abraham Lincoln's head at his tomb in Springfield. The constant rubbing has given President Lincoln's nose quite a shine.

Statue of Abraham Lincoln at his tomb

The Illinois Prairie

Before anyone thought of building a skyscraper in Chicago or a mining truck in Decatur, native people hunted buffalo and elk on the Illinois prairie. Prairie chickens pecked and scratched in the dirt. Foxes, coyotes, and deer bounded across the vast open land. Illinois does not have as much prairie land as it once did, but it is still the Prairie State.

Prairie chicken

The grass withers, the flower fades, but the word of our God stands forever.
Isaiah 40:8

Activities

- Illustrate the geographic term for Illinois in the *Atlas Workbook* (page 58).
- If you are using the *Lesson Review*, answer the questions for Illinois (page 14).
- Read chapter 7 in *The Story of George Washington Carver*.
- Hands-On Idea: Look at the picture of Camel Rock on page 244. Go outside and look for rocks that have interesting shapes. You could also use rocks to create an interesting shape yourself.

Lesson 56: A Song and Story of Illinois

Prairie Summer Song

This poem by an unknown author celebrates summertime on the Illinois prairie. It was published in 1859. (Track 28)

Ah! the summer is coming,
Shout! for the flowers are up:
Over the prairies humming,
The wild bee finds his cup.

Close by lake and river
The broad flag spreads his leaves;
And the bird-song like a shiver
Of music round us heaves.

See, the shadows are flying
Over the long green grass;
How the white clouds are lying
Soft in each rounded mass!

O, the beautiful prairies!
Purple, and gold, and white:
Surely the realms of fairies
Never were half so bright.

Illinois prairie

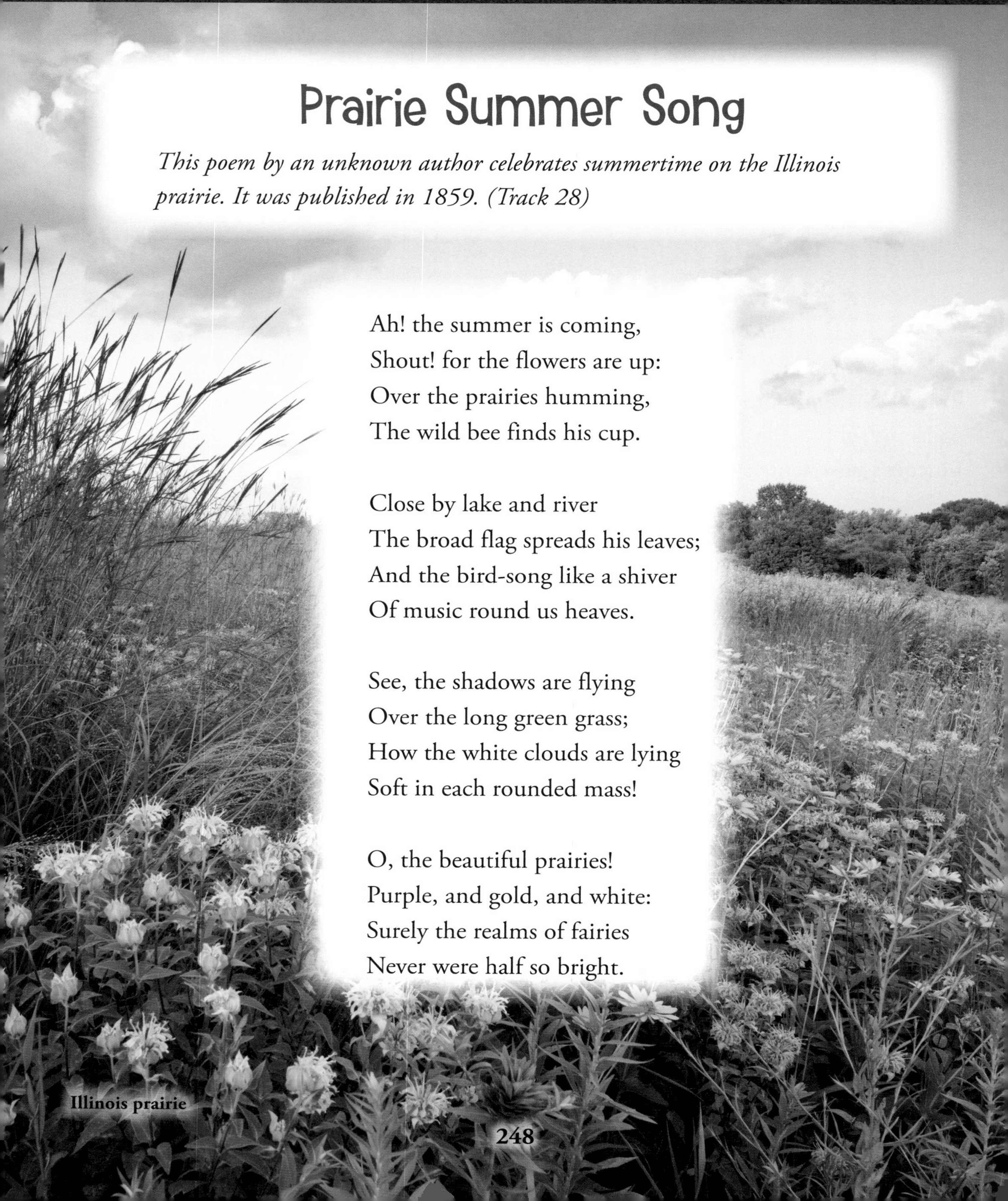

Boy Pioneer

F. M. Perryman

F. M. Perryman was born in 1836. He grew up in a little cabin beside Mitchell Creek in western Illinois. His parents taught him and his siblings to honor God. They taught them to love their country, their home, and their neighbors.

F. M. Perryman worked hard throughout his childhood. He shook wild plums out of trees for the hogs to eat. He carried water and helped make soap. He made leather and cloth. He found places on the prairie to cut hay. He helped in the fields.

F. M. and other pioneer children worked together when it was time to plant corn. Some of them dropped the corn in the ground; others used hoes to cover the corn with dirt. "Sometimes," Mr. Perryman later remembered, "when the girls were not in the field, they would go and shoot a mess of squirrels and make a big pot pie for their brothers' dinner."

Hogs

F. M. Perryman had a happy childhood. He had a deep respect for the pioneers who lived around him. They were brave. Sometimes they killed 20 or 30 rattlesnakes in a day. When Mr. Perryman grew older he thanked God "that such men and women have lived in the world to make our pathway brighter, and make the world better."

Rattlesnake

When Mr. Perryman was a boy, the area around Mitchell Creek did not have a good school. Once a stranger came to the area and offered to teach the local children. He opened a school, but Mr. Perryman said the man "did not know much more than a goat."

Young F. M. got his education in other ways. He wrote, "At that time there was a poor chance for a boy to get an education; but we love to think of those days, because nature in all her beauties was so near like the hand of God had formed it; the skill of man had changed it so little, and it was our school and our delight to roam over the wide unbroken prairies, where the lark was singing in his native home. Where the wildflowers, of all colors, were more beautiful than Solomon in all his glory. These scenes inspired a feeling in a boy's heart of awe and reverence for the God of nature . . . . and his eyes would fill with tears and from the depths of his boyish heart he would give glory to God . . . ."

Jacob's ladder

Corn field

F. M. Perryman was proud to be from Illinois. In 1907 he wrote a book about his childhood on the prairie. "The man who lives in Illinois and don't enjoy life," he wrote, "is a man who does not know a good thing when he has it."

Mr. Perryman called his home state "the best State in the best Government under the sun. Illinois," he continued, "is where things grow; the corn, the wheat, the hay, the oats, the fruit, the vegetables, the horses, the cattle, the hogs; the eggs don't grow on bushes in Illinois, but they come as near to it as they do in any other State. And not only these things, which have been mentioned, grow in Illinois, but brains grow in Illinois too; and if they are about to be bothered to find a man who is smart enough for President, tell them not to be uneasy, that Illinois can furnish five hundred, if that many were needed. Yes, Illinois is where things grow."

For as the earth brings forth its sprouts,
And as a garden causes the things sown in it
to spring up,
So the Lord God will cause righteousness and praise
To spring up before all the nations.
Isaiah 61:11

Meadowlark

Activities

- Complete the map activities for Illinois in the *Atlas Workbook* (page 59).
- Read chapter 8 in *The Story of George Washington Carver*.
- F. M. Perryman wrote about memories from his childhood. What is a special memory you have of something that happened to you when you were younger? If you are keeping a creative writing notebook, write a detailed description of your special memory. Think about details such as the weather, who was there, and how you felt.

Family Activity: Popcorn Balls

Ingredients (makes 6 balls):
- 6 cups popped popcorn
- 3 tablespoons butter
- 8 oz marshmallows

Directions:
- Melt the butter in a large pot over medium heat.
- Add marshmallows to the melted butter and stir until marshmallows have melted.
- Remove from heat.
- With a plastic or wooden spoon, gently stir popped popcorn into the butter/marshmallow mixture.
- Transfer the mixture to a large bowl.
- Let sit until the mixture is cool enough to touch.
- Butter up your hands and form the mixture into six balls.
- Place on wax or parchment paper to cool completely before serving.

Be safe with the hot stove. Children must have adult supervision in the kitchen.

Wisconsin Dells

Unit 15
Midwest:
Wisconsin and Minnesota

Lesson 57: Wisconsin

Lake Winnebago is the largest lake in Wisconsin. When the lake freezes in the winter, the ice can be up to 30 inches thick. Many people drive their cars across the lake. Find Wisconsin on the map at the beginning of this book.

Apostle Islands

Off the northern coast of Wisconsin lie the **Apostle Islands**. Apostle Islands National Lakeshore includes 21 islands in Lake Superior. God has used the crashing waves of the lake to create stone arches and spectacular sea caves that run deep into the cliffs. In the winter, ice formations cover the cliffs. The main village of the Ojibwe nation was once on Madeline Island. It is largest of the Apostle Islands. Many Ojibwe and people of other native nations still live in Wisconsin.

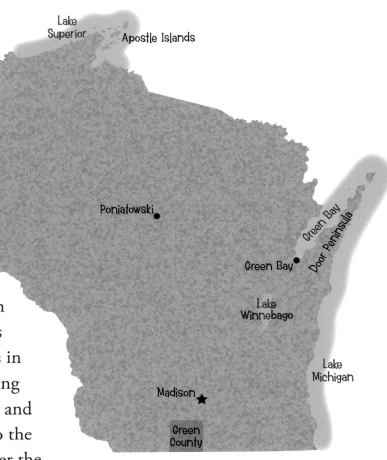

Lake Superior
Apostle Islands
Poniatowski
Green Bay
Door Peninsula
Green Bay
Lake Winnebago
Lake Michigan
Madison
Green County

Among the Apostle Islands

254

Latitude and Longitude

Poniatowski lies in the heart of Wisconsin. This tiny community has a special place on the map. A drive through local farm fields brings visitors to a geographical marker. When you stand at this marker you are in the center of the northern half of the Western Hemisphere. You are exactly halfway between the Equator and the North Pole.

People used lines of latitude and meridians of longitude to figure out where to put this marker. Lines of latitude and longitude are imaginary lines. These man-made lines help us measure distances. They help people create accurate maps. They help navigation apps get us where we need to go. This spot in Wisconsin is right where the 45th line of latitude crosses the 90th meridian of longitude.

Badger

Capital: Madison

A brilliant gold statue stands on top of the Wisconsin state capitol in **Madison**. Her name is *Wisconsin*. She has a surprising feature on her head. Look closely at the picture of *Wisconsin* at left. Do you see it? She has a golden badger on her head! The badger is the state animal of Wisconsin.

Madison is the only U.S. capitol built on an isthmus. An isthmus is a narrow strip of land between two bodies of water. In the photo below you can see the capitol dome rising up from the Madison Isthmus between Lake Mendota and Lake Monona.

Wisconsin

Madison Isthmus

Green Bay

North of Lake Winnebago lies **Green Bay**. This bay is part of Lake Michigan. The city of **Green Bay** is beside the waters of Green Bay. This is the oldest city in Wisconsin. For over 100 years it has been home to the Green Bay Packers football team. The Packers play their home games in Lambeau Field. This stadium seats 81,441 people.

Lambeau Field

Cherries

Stretching north from the city of Green Bay is the **Door Peninsula**. The waters of Green Bay are on one side of the peninsula. Lake Michigan itself is on the other. The land and climate here are perfect for growing cherries. The area produces around ten million pounds of cherries every year.

Machines harvest most of the cherries. A machine can harvest the cherries on ten trees in just one minute. Many years ago, all the cherries on Door Peninsula had to be harvested by hand.

Door County Cherry Orchard

In the 1940s and 1950s, the owners of Horseshoe Bay Farms held Cherry Camps for teenage boys. The boys had to pick seven and a half buckets of cherries every day to earn their food and lodging. If they wanted to, they could earn money by picking more cherries.

Working in a cherry orchard was a wonderful experience for the boys. After they finished picking cherries for the day, they enjoyed swimming and playing sports. Every night they had cherry pie for dessert.

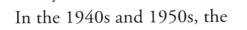

Cherries

Wisconsin Cheese

Wisconsin is America's Dairyland. It produces over three billion pounds of cheese a year—more than any other state. Do you have a favorite kind of cheese? In Wisconsin you can choose from over 600 varieties.

A group of 108 immigrants from Switzerland settled in **Green County**, Wisconsin, in 1845. More Swiss immigrants followed later. Switzerland is famous for making cheese. Some of the Swiss immigrants who moved to Green County brought along their skills for making Swiss cheese.

Green County is proud of its Swiss heritage. Every other year, the area hosts a Cheese Days festival. People dress up in traditional Swiss costumes for the event. Visitors listen to performers play Swiss music. They learn about historic and modern farming, and they eat cheese!

Dairy cow

Swiss cheese

Give thanks to the Lord, for He is good, for His lovingkindness is everlasting.
Who gives food to all flesh, for His lovingkindness is everlasting.
Psalm 136: 1, 25

Activities

- Illustrate the geographic term for Wisconsin in the *Atlas Workbook* (page 60).
- If you are using the *Lesson Review*, answer the questions for Wisconsin (page 15).
- Read chapter 9 in *The Story of George Washington Carver*.
- Hands-On Idea: Grab a football and pretend you play for the Green Bay Packers.

The Dairies of Wisconsin

This song was performed at a meeting of the Wisconsin Dairymen's Association in 1885. The second verse refers to margarine, which is a butter substitute. "Purveyors" are people who sell something, such as butter and cheese. (Track 29)

We sing you a song of Wisconsin's chief glory,
The fruit of the dairy, so rich and so great,
Which renders Wisconsin so famous in story,
Her butter and cheese are the pride of the State.
The vales of Wisconsin are sprinkled with flowers;
What beauties in nature are rivals of these?
Where the cows of the dairy in summer's bright hours,
Are laying up treasures of butter and cheese.

    The sweet golden butter, the creamery butter,
    The premium butter, the cream of the cheese.

The fruit of the churn is the crown of our table,
Our Governor tells us "the cow is the queen;"
Her horn is exalted, for now she is able
To kick up her heels at the vile margarine.
All hail to Wisconsin, her hills and her waters,
So ample the lover of nature to please;
And last, but not least, are the dairymen's daughters,
The lovely purveyors of butter and cheese.

    The sweet golden butter, the creamery butter,
    The premium butter, the cream of the cheese.

Casper Jaggi, Cheesemaker

Clank-clank. Ca-clank. Clank. From sunrise to sunset, cow bells clanked on the mountainsides of Canton Bern, Switzerland. The year was 1900. Six-year-old Casper Jaggi was again in the mountains with his father and their cows. They spent every summer here.

Day after day, Casper and his father worked together. Casper was learning how to make Swiss cheese. His father made sure Casper did everything just right. He wanted his son to learn the art of cheesemaking well.

In 1913, when Casper was 20 years old, he moved to the United States. He settled in southwestern Wisconsin, where two of his older brothers already lived.

Casper Jaggi tried to become a farmer, but he didn't like farming. He missed making cheese. For several years, he worked in different cheese factories. Then in 1941, he bought his own factory. In the 1950s, Casper Jaggi's factory was the biggest Swiss cheese factory in Wisconsin.

Swiss cowbell

Wisconsin dairy farm

Casper Jaggi with wheels of Swiss cheese

Mr. Jaggi sold some of his cheese in a shop beside his factory. Some of his cheese traveled by train to other states. A railroad track ran right up to the factory. Workers loaded huge wheels of his famous Swiss cheese into the railcars. Each wheel weighed about 200 pounds.

Casper Jaggi married Frieda, who had also moved to Wisconsin from Switzerland. Casper and Frieda adopted a little boy named Fritz. Mr. Jaggi taught young Fritz how to make cheese, just as his father had taught him in Switzerland. The Jaggis also adopted a daughter, Annabelle.

Frieda Jaggi in a cheese factory

Casper Jaggi worked hard. He made sure his factory stayed clean. He always received a perfect score when a government inspector stopped by to grade his factory. He never knew when inspectors might come, but he was always ready for them.

Mr. Jaggi cared about people. He was kind to his employees. He bought the milk he used to make cheese from 145 local farmers. Sometimes he helped those farmers cut hay or chop wood.

The work at the cheese factory never ended. Cows must be milked every day—even on weekends and holidays. Casper Jaggi was a busy man. When he did have a little time off, the Jaggi family enjoyed visiting their relatives who lived nearby. Mr. Jaggi also enjoyed bowling and playing the accordion.

Mr. Jaggi always remembered his father's instruction. "If you can't do a job right, don't do it at all." Casper Jaggi did his job right.

Milk can

Do you see a man
skilled in his work?
He will stand before kings;
He will not stand
before obscure men.
Proverbs 22:29

Casper Jaggi's cheese factory

Activities

- Complete the map activities for Wisconsin in the *Atlas Workbook* (page 61).
- Read the chapter 10 in *The Story of George Washington Carver*.
- Casper Jaggi remembered lessons his father taught him when he was young. Ask a parent to tell you something they learned from one of their parents when they were young. If you are keeping a creative writing notebook, write down the teaching your parent shared.

Northwest Angle

Boundary Waters Canoe Area Wilderness

White Earth Reservation

Split Rock Lighthouse

Lake Superior

Mississippi River

Monticello

Minneapolis

St. Paul

Le Sueur

Rochester

Minnesota has over 11,000 lakes. Over 1,000 of them lie in the **Boundary Waters Canoe Area Wilderness**. Find Minnesota on the map at the beginning of this book.

Boundary Waters Canoe Area Wilderness

Capital: St. Paul

Archaeologists believe that the native Hopewell people once lived beside the Mississippi River in the area that is now **St. Paul**. The Dakota people later lived here. During the 1700s, Great Britain, France, and Spain all wanted to control this part of North America.

In 1838 Frenchman Pierre Parrant established a settlement called Pig's Eye Landing (the man's nickname was Pig's Eye). When a Catholic priest came to the area a few years later, he didn't like the name. He renamed it St. Paul after the apostle.

When Minnesota became a state, St. Paul became the state capital. Just think. The capital could have been called Pig's Eye!

Minnesota State Capitol

Mill City

Mill City Museum

Up the river from St. Paul is the city of **Minneapolis**. These cities are so close together they are called the Twin Cities. Over half of all the people in Minnesota live in the Twin Cities area. The Mill City Museum in Minneapolis tells about an important part of this city's heritage.

The museum is housed in a building once called the Washburn A Mill. It was the largest flour mill in the world. Trains brought in loads of wheat. The rushing waters of Saint Anthony Falls on the Mississippi River powered the mill, which turned the wheat into flour. At one time, the Washburn A Mill ground enough flour to make twelve million loaves of bread every day. The mill no longer operates, but the museum is a great place to learn about the flour industry. This industry gave Minneapolis the nickname Mill City.

Swan City

In the town of **Monticello**, a power plant produces warm runoff water that flows into the Mississippi River. This makes the river water warmer here than it is in other places. Warmer water means Monticello is a good place for water birds to spend the winter.

Trumpeter swans were once common in Minnesota. They were common throughout the United States and Canada. Over the years, people hunted too many of the swans. They almost became extinct.

Trumpeter swan

Trumpeter swans in Monticello

During the winter of 1988, Sheila Lawrence noticed a pair of trumpeter swans near her home in Monticello. Mrs. Lawrence enjoyed feeding corn to her trumpeter swan guests. Throughout the winter, she continued to toss out corn on the snowy ground. Winter after winter, more trumpeter swans came. Eventually she spent hours every day feeding the swans. People called Sheila Lawrence the Swan Lady. Finally she and her husband created an automatic swan feeder.

The number of trumpeter swans who winter in Monticello has continued to grow. The city is now home to over 2,000. Monticello has earned the nickname Swan City. The government now protects trumpeter swans, and their numbers are making a comeback.

North Shore

Split Rock Lighthouse stands on Minnesota's North Shore. The lighthouse began shining on Lake Superior in 1910. It guided ships away from the lake's dangerous rocky shoreline. For several years, lighthouse keepers could only reach the lighthouse by boat. Workers completed a highway around Lake Superior in 1924. This made life a little easier for the lighthouse keepers and their families. The highway also made it easier for tourists to visit this beautiful spot.

Northwest Angle

Take a close look at the map of Minnesota on page 262. Notice the little area of land to the north that is not connected to the rest of the state. This is the **Northwest Angle**.

Split Rock Lighthouse

The United States and Great Britain signed a peace treaty in 1783 after the Revolutionary War. Since Canada was part of the British Empire, the treaty included details on where the border

Young's Bay Resort in Angle Inlet

between the U.S. and Canada would be. The problem was that the map they used to work out this treaty had a mistake. Because of the mistake, the Northwest Angle ended up in the United States.

The tiny community of Angle Inlet is on the Northwest Angle. Only a few dozen people live here year-round. Many visitors come to fish for walleye. The few children in the community go to Minnesota's last one-room schoolhouse.

Walleye

White Earth Reservation

Minnesota has eleven reservations for native nations. The **White Earth Reservation** is the largest. It is home to the Chippewa. These Chippewa use traditional methods to harvest the wild rice that grows on their reservation. Harvesters paddle out in canoes and gather the wild rice by hand as their people have done for generations.

While the earth remains, seedtime and harvest,
And cold and heat, and summer and winter,
And day and night shall not cease.
Genesis 8:22

Wild rice

Activities

- Illustrate the geographic term for Minnesota in the *Atlas Workbook* (page 62).

- If you are using the *Lesson Review*, answer the questions for Minnesota (page 15).

- Read chapter 11 in *The Story of George Washington Carver*.

- Hands-On Idea: Look closely at a map of the United States and notice the shapes of the different states.

- Family Activity: Make a Bird Feeder (instructions on page 270).

Lesson 60: A Song and Story of Minnesota

The Lumberman's Alphabet

During the 1800s, lumbermen came to Minnesota to work in the abundant forests. 1905 was the busiest year for the Minnesota lumber industry. At that time people called the lumbermen "shanty boys." A "jobber" was a man who bought and sold lumber. Lumbermen across the United States and Canada enjoyed singing this song as they worked. (Track 30)

A is for axes you very well know;
B is the boys who can swing them also.
C is for chopping we first do begin;
D is for danger we oftentimes are in.

E is the echo that through the woods rang,
And F is the foreman, the boss of our gang.
G is the grindstone that swiftly does move;
And H is the handle, so slick and so smooth.

Chorus:
So merry, so merry, so merry are we
No mortal on earth is as happy as we.
Sing hi derry, ho derry, hi derry down,
Use a shanty boy right and nothing goes wrong.

Kettle River in Minnesota

Well, I is the iron to mark all the pine,
And J is the jobber who's never on time.
K is keen edges our axes do keep,
And L is the lice that keep us from sleep.

M is the moss that we stuff in our camp,
And N is the needle that mends our old pants.
O is the owl that hoots in the night;
P is the pine that we fell in daylight.

Chorus

Well, Q is the quarreling we never allow,
And R is the river in which our logs plow.
S is the sleds so stout and so strong,
T is the teams that do haul them along.

U is the uses we put our teams to,
And V is the valley we drive the logs through;
W the woods which we leave in the spring,
And X, Y, Z, that's all I'm going to sing.

Chorus

A House in Le Sueur

The Mayo House

In 1859 Dr. William Mayo began building a house on North Main Street in **Le Sueur**, Minnesota. He wasn't a very talented carpenter. His brother helped him, but they didn't quite get the foundation straight. They didn't manage to get all the rafters to come together in the right places either. Still, the house kept out the rain. It gave Dr. Mayo's wife Louise a kitchen for cooking. It gave their children a place to sleep. It helped them all stay warm during the Minnesota blizzards—at least, warm enough.

Stethoscope

William Mayo had been trained as a doctor, but in Le Sueur he tried a variety of jobs, hoping to find one that suited him better. He finally decided to settle back into being a doctor. His first patient was a horse. When the horse got well, Dr. Mayo's neighbors were impressed. He earned their trust as a doctor for people. An upstairs room in the family's house became Dr. Mayo's office.

In 1862 members of the Sioux tribe in Minnesota were angry about the unfair way the U.S. government treated them. A group of Sioux attacked white settlers in the southern part of the state. Dr. Mayo went to help care for the wounded settlers. Several families fled to Le Sueur to escape the fighting. Dr. Mayo's wife Louise invited eleven of these families to stay with her. Some stayed in their barn. The rest stayed in the Mayo family's little white house.

The Mayo family moved to **Rochester**, Minnesota, in 1864. Dr. Mayo continued to work as a doctor. William and Louise had three daughters and two sons. When their sons Will and Charlie grew up, they became doctors like their father.

The three Mayo doctors helped to establish a new hospital in Rochester. This hospital came to be called the Mayo Clinic. The Mayo Clinic continues to be one of the most respected hospitals in the world.

A few years after the Mayo family moved to Rochester, the Cosgrove family moved into their little white house on North Main Street in Le Sueur. Carson Cosgrove founded a canning company in Le Sueur in 1903. It became the Green Giant Company and provided jobs for thousands of Minnesotans. Look for the Jolly Green

William Mayo (center) with his sons Will (left) and Charlie (right)

Giant logo in your grocery store. The canning factory in Le Sueur closed in 1995. The company now operates factories in other cities, but you can still find some old Green Giant signs in Le Sueur.

Today the little white house on North Main Street in Le Sueur is open for tours. The house honors two families who both had a big impact in Minnesota, and who both called that little white house "home."

By wisdom a house is built,
And by understanding it is established.
Proverbs 24:3

Activities

- Complete the map activities for Minnesota in the *Atlas Workbook* (page 63).
- Read chapter 12 in *The Story of George Washington Carver*.
- Sometimes a house stays in the same family for several generations. Sometimes many different families live in a house one after the other. Talk about when your family moved into your house. Do you know anything about the people who lived in your house before you did? If you are keeping a creative writing notebook, think of an imaginary house. Write a description of the house and at least three families who have lived there. How long did each family live in the house? What were their occupations?
- If you are using the *Lesson Review*, take the Midwest (Part 1) Test (page 31).

Family Activity: Bird Feeder

You might not have any trumpeter swans in your backyard, but you probably have some other birds who would like a treat!

Supplies:
- egg carton
- twine or yarn
- scissors
- tape
- bird seed

Instructions:
- Carefully cut off the top of the egg carton.
- Cut the top and bottom of the egg cartoon to your desired size.
- Carefully poke a small hole in each of the four outside corners of the top and bottom pieces, as seen in the photos at right.

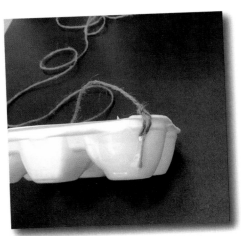

- Cut four pieces of twine to desired length.
- Thread the four pieces of twine through the four corner holes of the bottom piece. Tie each one in a double knot.
- Tape the loose ends of the twine to the outside of the cartoon.
- Tie a knot several inches up on each piece of twine.
- Thread the twine through the four corner holes of the top piece. (Make sure your knots are large enough so that they do not go through the corner holes in the top piece.)

- Fill your feeder with bird seed and tie it to a tree branch.

Be safe with scissors! Children must have adult supervision.

Iowa farmland

Unit 16
Midwest:
Iowa and Missouri

Lesson 61: Iowa

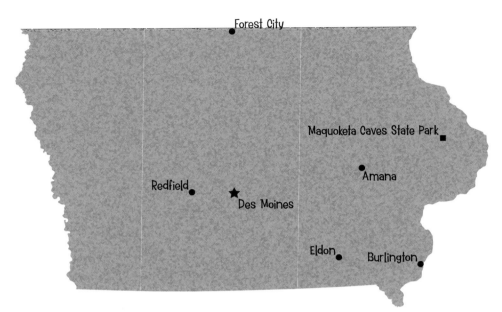

Iowa farms raise more pigs and their chickens lay more eggs than any other state. Most years they grow more corn and soybeans than any other state, too. Find Iowa on the map at the beginning of this book.

Farming

Volunteers at Heritage Park in **Forest City**, Iowa, work hard to preserve America's rural heritage. The word *rural* has to do with life in the country and away from big cities. While there are many cities and towns in Iowa, a large number of people there live a rural farming lifestyle. Heritage Park is a place that honors this part of Iowa's story.

Raccoon Forks Farm in **Redfield** offers a place for adults with special needs to work. People do most of the work on this farm by hand. Workers use small garden tools and wagons to plant and harvest most of the crops. They farm organically, which means they don't use chemicals to make the plants grow or to keep the weeds down.

Iowa pig farm

Mural inside the Iowa State Capitol

Capital: Des Moines

Inside the capitol building in **Des Moines** is an enormous mural that Edward Blashfield completed in 1906. It is 40 feet wide and 14 feet tall. Mr. Blashfield's painting features pioneers traveling west in a covered wagon to establish farms in Iowa.

Above the mural are six mosaics. Three of the mosaics represent the three branches of government: Executive, Legislative, and Judiciary. The other three represent three things the government provides: Defense, Charities, and Education. The group in charge of decorating the capitol chose artist Frederick Dielman to create these mosaics. Mr. Dielman traveled to Italy in the early 1900s. There he hired Italian artists to help him. They used small pieces of colored glass tiles to create the beautiful pictures. The mosaics traveled from Italy to Iowa, where people have enjoyed them in the state capitol ever since.

Outside and inside the Iowa State Capitol

Amana

Immigrants from Germany settled in the **Amana** colonies in Iowa in 1855. They lived a communal lifestyle. That means they shared everything they had with each other. No one owned anything as his own. The immigrants earned money through farming. They also sold wool from their sheep and traditional German handcrafts. These communities no longer have a communal lifestyle, but their German heritage is still strong.

Inside an Amana kitchen in 1907

Maquoketa Caves State Park

How adventurous are you when it comes to caving? **Maquoketa Caves State Park** has a cave with stairs leading down to it and a sidewalk through it. Lights inside the cave keep it well lit. The park has another cave where people have to crawl on their hands and knees and get dirty to go through. Which cave would you choose?

People have found pottery and stone tools in these caves left by native people who lived in the area long ago. Sadly, you won't see many stalactites or stalagmites in these caves. Years ago visitors broke these off and took them home as souvenirs.

Maqoketa Caves State Park

American Gothic

Many people visit **Eldon**, Iowa, to take a picture in front of a little white house. Have you ever seen this painting called *American Gothic*? The artist, Grant Wood, was from Iowa. He visited Eldon in 1930. A little house with an interesting upstairs window caught his eye. He decided to stop and sketch it on an envelope so he would remember what it looked like. Later he created a painting with the house in the background. He painted a farmer and the farmer's daughter standing in front of the house. His painting won an award in Chicago. It quickly became one of the most famous paintings of all time.

Today there is a visitors center next to the house where you can borrow a pitchfork and costumes so that you can make your own *American Gothic* picture. Say cheese! Actually, if you want to look like the farmers in *American Gothic*, you shouldn't smile after all. You can smile when you look at the picture and see how silly you look.

A joyful heart makes a cheerful face,
But when the heart is sad,
the spirit is broken.
Proverbs 15:13

American Gothic house

American Gothic

Activities

- Illustrate the geographic term for Iowa in the *Atlas Workbook* (page 64).
- If you are using the *Lesson Review,* answer the questions for Iowa (page 16).
- Read chapter 13 in *The Story of George Washington Carver.*
- Hands-On Idea: Take some *American Gothic* pictures of people in your family.

A Load of Hay

Prairie Gold, *a collection of works by authors and artists from Iowa published in 1917, included this poem by James B. Weaver. It tells of a businessman on his way to work in a busy city. His chauffeur (or driver) is driving him in his auto (or car). They almost run into a cart carrying a load of hay. His chauffeur is mad, but the hay reminds the author of when he was young, growing up on an Iowa farm. (Track 31)*

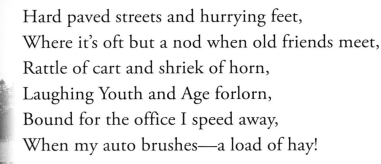

Hard paved streets and hurrying feet,
Where it's oft but a nod when old friends meet,
Rattle of cart and shriek of horn,
Laughing Youth and Age forlorn,
Bound for the office I speed away,
When my auto brushes—a load of hay!

Chauffeur shouts, I scarcely hear,
For things I loved as a boy seem near:
Scent of meadows at early morn,
Miles of waving fields of corn,
Lowing cattle and colts at play—
Far have I drifted another way!

Hark, the bell as it calls the noon!
Boys at their chores, hear them whistle a tune!
Barn doors creaking on rusty locks,
Rattle of corn in the old feed-box,
Answering nicker at toss of hay—
Old sweet sounds of a far-off day.

There, my driver stops with a jerk;
Then far aloft to the scene of my work;
But all day long midst the city's roar
My heart is the heart of a boy once more,
My feet in old-time fields astray,
Lured—by the scent from a load of hay!

Snake Alley

Snake Alley

Burlington, Iowa, is nestled among hills. This provides a beautiful setting, but it also brings challenges. Before the invention of cars, people who lived on top of the hills had a hard time getting to the businesses in the valley and then back home. Surely there was an easier way to get around their city.

In 1894 three German men who lived in Burlington had an idea. One of the men was an architect and a landscape engineer. Another was an engineer for the city. The third was a paving contractor who had paved the first brick street in Burlington. The three men worked together. They came up with a design for a new roadway that would twist and curve down a Burlington hillside.

The construction project was complicated. The men had to figure out the exact angles of the curves so the road would be safe to travel. They had to think hard about what materials would be best to use. They decided to pave the road with limestone and blue clay bricks. Workers laid the bricks up on their ends instead of flat. This made the road less slippery. Residents soon started calling the new road Snake Alley. The road is only the length of one city block (or about as long as a football field), but it has five half-curves and two quarter-curves!

Snake Alley bricks

The Burlington Fire Department had been established over 50 years before workers built Snake Alley. At first the department didn't do very well putting out fires. It was hard to put out a fire when all you had to haul water were small leather buckets. In 1851 the city bought a fire pump. Firefighters used the fire pump to pump water out of a cistern or a creek to put out fires. This worked better than

Firefighters pulling a pump in the 1800s

the leather buckets, but firefighters had a hard time pulling the pump up and down the hills of Burlington. In 1872 the city of Burlington finally agreed to pay for the fire department to buy horses to pull their fire pump.

Not all horses were fit for the job. The fire department needed to test each horse. They wanted to make sure their animals were able to pull the fire pump wherever they needed to go. Snake Alley became the perfect test course.

Horses hitched to a fire pump in 1880

Snake Alley Criterium

Firefighters harnessed the horses to the fire pump and timed them as they raced up Snake Alley. The fastest and strongest horses got the job. The people of Burlington loved to gather to watch the horses race.

The fire department doesn't need horses to pull their fire pump anymore. People still gather at Snake Alley to watch races, though. Every year on Memorial Day weekend, people race up this crooked road on bicycles during the Snake Alley Criterium. They ride over the same bricks on which the horses raced many years ago. The route for the bike race makes a loop through Burlington. The cyclists racing in the highest skill category have to pedal up Snake Alley 25 times!

The Bible teaches us that we should live our lives as if we are in a race. We should never let sin get in our way. We should keep our eyes on Jesus. He will help us reach the finish line.

Let us also lay aside every encumbrance and the sin which so easily entangles us, and let us run with endurance the race that is set before us, fixing our eyes on Jesus, the author and perfecter of faith, who for the joy set before Him endured the cross, despising the shame, and has sat down at the right hand of the throne of God.
Hebrews 12:1-2

Activities

- Complete the map activities for Iowa in the *Atlas Workbook* (page 65).
- Read chapter 14 in *The Story of George Washington Carver*.
- Imagine that you are a child in Burlington, Iowa, watching the fire department test out a new team of horses. What do the horses look like? Do they make it up Snake Alley? In your creative writing notebook, write a journal entry about your experience watching the horses being tested. *or* Act it out!

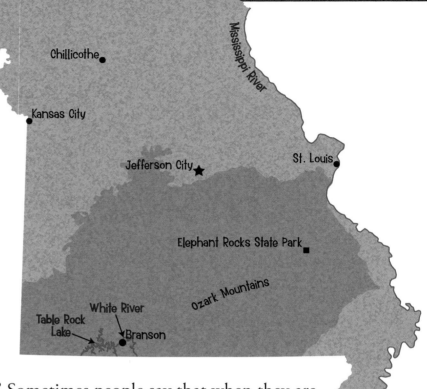

Before white settlers crossed the Mississippi River into what is now Missouri, the Missouri tribe lived here. *Missouri* means "town of the large canoes." Find Missouri on the map at the beginning of this book.

Sliced Bread

Perhaps you have heard people say, "That's the greatest thing since sliced bread!" Sometimes people say that when they are using a handy new invention. Sliced bread was once a handy new invention itself.

The town of **Chillicothe**, Missouri, is the Home of Sliced Bread. The Chillicothe Baking Company installed a fancy new machine in 1928 that could slice a whole loaf of bread at once. It was amazing! The people of Chillicothe were excited about the new invention. Buying sliced bread quickly became popular at bakeries across the country.

For generations, the people of Chillicothe forgot that their town was the home of sliced bread. Then in 2001, a local resident came across an old newspaper article from 1928. It reminded the town of a piece of their history they had forgotten. People can't miss that history now. A large mural on the side of a downtown building features a picture of—what else?—sliced bread!

Mural in Chillicothe

St. Louis

For many years the city of **St. Louis** was a jumping-off point for settlers moving into the wilderness of the West. Today the Gateway Arch stands in St. Louis as a memorial to our nation's early European explorers and settlers. It is the tallest historic monument in the country. Visitors can take a ride to the top for a spectacular view of the Mississippi River on one side and the city of St. Louis on the other.

Gateway Arch

Elephant Rocks

Children and adults have fun climbing around at **Elephant Rocks State Park**. The rocks are huge. Missouri's Elephant Rocks form a tor. A *tor* is a mass of rocks that lies in the open on the top of a hill. This is one of the many playgrounds God created that people enjoy.

Elephant Rocks

Missouri Bootheel

Before Missouri became a state, John Hardeman Walker purchased a large amount of land near the Mississippi River. As people began making plans for Missouri to become a state, Walker wanted his land to be included. He talked to government officials in Missouri and in Washington, D.C. He convinced them that the land he owned should be part of the new state. Look at the map at left and notice the interesting shape jutting out of the southern border. That was Walker's land. People call that part of the state the Bootheel. Cotton grows well in the Missouri Bootheel.

Cotton

Table Rock Lake

The Ozarks

The **Ozark Mountains** cover much of southern Missouri and northern Arkansas. This mountainous region also extends into Oklahoma. In 1958 workers completed a dam on the **White River**, which flows through the Ozarks. The dam created **Table Rock Lake** where people enjoy fishing and water sports. The dam also produces electricity for the area.

Branson's Famous Baldknobbers

In 1959 the four Mabe brothers began performing a show for Ozark visitors. They called themselves the Baldknobbers. They played mountain music, complete with instruments made from a washtub, a washboard, and the jawbone of a mule! Their show was a hit. It began a tradition of entertainment in Branson, Missouri, that is still going strong.

Capital: Jefferson City

Inside the state capitol in Jefferson City, visitors stroll through the Hall of Famous Missourians. It is a way the people of Missouri honor their heritage. The statues in the hall help people remember and appreciate Missourians who have made the world a better place. The hall features many statues, including George Washington Carver, the man who was born into slavery and grew up to develop 300 ways to use peanuts; Harry Truman, who served as one of our country's presidents; Laura Ingalls Wilder, the author of the Little House book series; Sacajawea, the Shoshone woman who helped Lewis and Clark on their famous exploration of the West; and Emmett Kelly, a famous clown from Missouri who helped cheer people up during the Great Depression of the 1930s.

Missouri State Capitol in Jefferson City

Render to all what is due them:
tax to whom tax is due; custom to whom custom;
fear to whom fear; honor to whom honor.
Romans 13:7

Activities

- Illustrate the geographic term for Missouri in the *Atlas Workbook* (page 66).

- If you are using the *Lesson Review*, answer the questions for Missouri (page 16).

- Read chapter 15 in *The Story of George Washington Carver*.

- Hands-On Idea: Use play dough to create a statue of someone who is important in your life.

- Family Activity: Make St. Louis Gooey Butter Cake (instructions on page 288).

Muskrat Song

Muskrats are common in wetlands across the United States. Max Hunter spent 20 years collecting traditional folk songs in Missouri's Ozark Mountains. A Missourian sang this song for him in 1960. (Track 32)

Muskrat, muskrat, what makes your tail so slick?
Been livin' in the water all my life,
It's a wonder I ain't sick, I ain't sick,
I ain't sick, I ain't sick, I ain't sick.

Jaybird, jaybird, what makes you fly so high?
Been eating these acorns all my life,
It's wonder I don't die, I don't die,
I don't die, I don't die, I don't die.

Groundhog, groundhog what makes your back so brown?
It's a wonder I don't suffocate
Just a livin' in the ground, in the ground,
In the ground, in the ground, in the ground.

Tom cat, tom cat, what makes your tail so long?
Well, the way those boys been pulling my tail
It's a wonder I ain't gone, I ain't gone,
I ain't gone, I ain't gone, I ain't gone.

Muskrat in Missouri

J. C. Hall
and His Mark on a City

J. C. Hall as a boy

J. C. Hall with his brother Rollie and sister Marie

J. C. Hall arrived in Kansas City, Missouri, in 1910. He was 18 years old. He didn't have much money, but he had two boxes of postcards to sell. He visited a variety of businesses around town. He hoped they would buy some of his postcards to sell in their stores. Soon he traveled to nearby towns to sell postcards in other places. J. C.'s

J. C. Hall

postcard business grew. His brother soon joined him in his work. In addition to their postcards they began selling stationery, books, and gifts.

In 1915 a fire destroyed their inventory, but it didn't destroy their determination. They pressed on and their business grew. They bought their own printing press and started making their own greeting cards later that year. In 1916 they opened a store on Petticoat Lane in a fashionable part of Kansas City. The next year they began producing and selling their own new invention: wrapping paper.

The Hall brothers gave their business a new name: Hallmark. Their headquarters were in Kansas City, but they advertised their greeting cards far and wide. Soon people all across America and around the world bought and sold Hallmark greeting cards.

Artists at work in an early Hallmark design studio

Vintage Hallmark cards

By the 1960s, the part of Kansas City where the Hallmark office was located was in bad shape. Many of the buildings were falling apart. J. C. Hall and his son Donald decided to do something about it. They worked hard to organize an urban revitalization project. *Urban* means something that has to do with a city. To

Crown Center Square Fountain

revitalize something means to give it new life. The Halls turned a crumbling part of Kansas City into Crown Center. Crown Center became a thriving place for people to live, shop, and work. The Crown Center Square Fountain performs a dancing water show. Music plays as jets shoot water 60 feet up into the air in special formations and patterns. Over 200 other fountains decorate parks and courtyards from one end of Kansas City to the other, giving it the nickname City of Fountains.

J. C. Hall

J. C. Hall believed in God. He believed in excellence and in creating quality products for his customers. He believed in being a good employer. He cared about people and he cared about his hometown. Every year from 1910 until he died in 1982, he donated a portion of his profits to help the people of Kansas City. He left his mark on this city and on the world.

Owe nothing to anyone except to love one another;
for he who loves his neighbor has fulfilled the law.
Romans 13:8

Activities

- Complete the map activities for Missouri in the *Atlas Workbook* (page 67).
- Read chapter 16 in *The Story of George Washington Carver*.
- Imagine that you work for Hallmark. Make a card for a relative or friend with a fun illustration and your own little poem. Mail it to him or her to brighten their day. If you are keeping a creative writing notebook, write your poem in your notebook as well.

Family Activity: St. Louis Gooey Butter Cake

No one knows for sure who invented this delicious treat. Some say a German-American baker in St. Louis made a mistake while mixing up a cake in the 1930s. The result was a sweet gooey accident that people loved. No matter who invented it, the cake is a St. Louis favorite. You'll find versions of it in bakeries all over the city, where people enjoy it any time of day—even for breakfast.

Ingredients (9 servings):

For the crust:
- 6 tablespoons butter, melted
- ½ cup sugar
- ½ cup brown sugar, packed
- 2 eggs
- ¾ teaspoon salt
- 1 ½ cups all purpose flour
- 2 teaspoons baking powder

For the filling:
- 8 oz cream cheese, softened
- 6 tablespoons brown sugar
- 2 eggs
- 1 tablespoon vanilla
- 3 ½ cups powdered sugar, plus extra to sprinkle over top

Directions:
- Preheat the oven to 350°.
- Line a 9"x9" baking dish with parchment paper.
- In a large mixing bowl cream together butter, sugar, brown sugar, and eggs.
- In a medium bowl combine salt, flour and baking powder.
- Stir the flour mixture into the butter mixture.
- Pour mixture into the prepared baking dish.
- In the bowl you used for the butter mixture, stir together softened cream cheese, brown sugar, eggs, vanilla, and powdered sugar.
- Pour cream cheese mixture in the pan over the cake mixture.
- Bake 55-60 minutes.
- Allow to cool.
- Cut cake into 9 squares. Sprinkle with powdered sugar and serve.

Be safe with the hot stove and oven. Children must have adult supervision in the kitchen.

Nebraska sandhills

Unit 17
Midwest:
Kansas and Nebraska

Lesson 65: Kansas

Kansas is the Sunflower State. When you drive through Kansas in sunflower season, you pass acres and acres of shining golden flowers. Young flower heads turn to follow the sun as it travels across the sky. People use

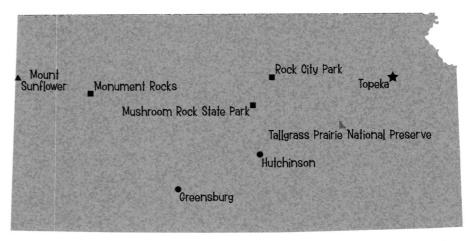

many of the seeds from Kansas sunflowers to make sunflower oil. Traders ship many of the seeds to Spain. Find Kansas on the map at the beginning of this book.

Kansas sunflowers

Capital: Topeka

It's not often that visitors can go to the very top of a capitol dome. In **Topeka**, Kansas, they can. After an elevator ride to the fifth floor, visitors climb 296 steps until they are right under the dome's roof. They walk outside onto an observation deck for a spectacular view of Topeka. The dome behind them is covered with enough copper to make over two million pennies.

Kansas State Capitol

Tallgrass Prairie

Tallgrass prairie once covered around 170 million acres of North America. As people built cities and plowed land for crops, most of the tallgrass prairie disappeared. The largest section that remains is in **Tallgrass Prairie National Preserve** in the Flint Hills of Kansas. Even though it might appear simple, the tallgrass prairie has a complex ecosystem. Between 40 and 60 different types of grasses grow here. Some of the grass grows up to six feet tall. Animals large and small—including weasels, bobcats, mice, and deer—are all important to the health of the tallgrass prairie ecosystem.

Tallgrass Prairie National Preserve

Salt

In 1887 Ben Blanchard found saltwater in his well near **Hutchinson**, Kansas. He didn't know then that he had discovered one of the largest deposits of rock salt in the world. People have been mining salt in Hutchinson ever since. Part of the salt deposit here is 400 feet thick. Today the Hutchinson Salt Company is able to mine four tons of salt every three minutes. The salt from this mine is not for humans to eat, but people use it for a variety of things, such as melting snow on winter roads and feeding animals.

Inside an early Kansas salt mine

At the Strataca Underground Salt Museum, visitors get to go inside a working salt mine. They put on a hard hat and travel 650 feet below ground where they are surrounded by walls and a ceiling made entirely of salt. Everyone gets to take home a souvenir chunk of rock salt to remember their trip to the depths of the earth.

Mushroom Rock State Park

Rock Formations

The formations in **Mushroom Rock State Park** are made of sandstone. The sandstone on top has a natural type of cement mixed with it, which makes it very hard. These are called *concretions*. Much of the sandstone under the concretions has eroded away, leaving mushroom-shaped rocks. The concretions in nearby **Rock City Park** look like soccer balls for giants! Farther west in Kansas, God has filled the **Monument Rocks** (also called Chalk Pyramids) with fossils of turtles, sharks, reptiles, clams, and other creatures.

Rock City Park

Monument Rocks (Chalk Pyramids)

Mount Sunflower

The land of eastern Kansas has rolling hills. As you travel west, the land gradually becomes flat until it looks like a giant pancake. Even though the land is flat in western Kansas, it is actually higher than the hills in the east. The highest point in Kansas is **Mount Sunflower**, pictured below. A mountain? That's what it's called! If you ever climb it, just be careful not to fall off.

Shout for joy, O heavens! And rejoice, O earth! Break forth into joyful shouting, O mountains! For the Lord has comforted His people and will have compassion on His afflicted.
Isaiah 49:13

Activities

- Illustrate the geographic term for Kansas in the *Atlas Workbook* (page 68).

- If you are using the *Lesson Review*, answer the questions for Kansas (page 17).

- Read chapter 17 in *The Story of George Washington Carver*.

- Hands-On Idea: Use wet sand or play dough to make some Kansas concretions.

Home On the Range

Dr. Brewster Higley wrote the original version of this song in 1872. It quickly became a cowboy classic and is the official state song of Kansas. (Track 33)

Oh, give me a home where the buffalo roam,
Where the deer and the antelope play,
Where seldom is heard a discouraging word
And the skies are not cloudy all day.

Chorus:
Home, home on the range,
Where the deer and the antelope play;
Where seldom is heard a discouraging word
And the skies are not cloudy all day.

Where the air is so pure, the zephyrs so free,
The breezes so balmy and light,
That I would not exchange my home on the range
For all of the cities so bright.

Chorus

How often at night when the heavens are bright
With the light from the glittering stars
Have I stood here amazed and asked as I gazed
If their glory exceeds that of ours.

Chorus

Buffalo in Kansas

Joy No Matter What

Cassie Blackburn was used to prairie winds. She was used to storms. She was used to the tornado siren going off, warning all residents of Greensburg, Kansas, to take cover. She knew that Greensburg was in Tornado Alley—an area of the United States that is more likely to have a tornado than other areas.

Lori, Cassie, and Jeffrey Blackburn in 2007

On May 4, 2007, the tornado siren sounded once again. Seventeen-year-old Cassie and her parents headed to their basement bathroom. It was the safest place in their house. They had done this many times before. Cassie carried her tornado bag with her. Her parents had taught her how to pack her bag any time there was a tornado warning. She packed some clothes, maybe some extra shoes, and a few other items. They had never needed their tornado bags before, but this night was going to be different.

As Cassie huddled in the basement with her parents and their cat, the sounds of the storm grew louder. They couldn't even hear each other over the noise. Finally, it was over. The tornado was gone, but it had destroyed almost all of the buildings in Greensburg, including the Blackburns' house.

After the storm, the Blackburns wandered into the street. They wondered where they should go. Gradually their neighbors joined them. There was so much to do, but where should they start? The Blackburns saw a neighbor who worked at the grocery store. He was barefoot, so Cassie gave him an extra pair of flip-flops she had in her tornado bag. The man's wife needed a dry shirt. Their little boy didn't have on a shirt at all. Cassie's dad shared two T-shirts from his tornado bag with them. One family helping another—Greensburg was about to do a lot of that.

Cassie's school after the tornado

Greensburg water tower after the tornado

Jeffrey Blackburn, Cassie's dad, was a pastor. The tornado destroyed the Blackburn's church building, but it did not destroy their church. It did not destroy their faith, either. They clung to God. Two days after the tornado hit, members of their church met together in a school in a nearby town. Cassie's dad shared a lesson from Psalm 91. "I will say of the Lord, 'He is my refuge and my fortress, my God, in whom I trust.'"

Just a few days after the tornado, Greensburg set up a large tent. The tent became the center of the community. People met under the tent to plan how to rebuild their town. Since the tornado destroyed all the church buildings, all the churches met together under the tent every Sunday. Church leaders took turns leading the worship services. Bob Dixson, who later became the mayor of Greensburg, said, "We hugged together, cried together, laughed together, planned together, and worshipped together under the tent. The tent was a place of healing for many."

Town Meeting in the tent in Greensburg after the tornado

For many months, people from across Kansas and around the country came to Greensburg to help. They cleared away rubble from the streets. They picked up debris the tornado had carried into the surrounding farm fields. They prepared meals. They made repairs. They rebuilt. They helped any way they could.

The people of Greensburg decided to rebuild their town sustainably. That means they used earth-friendly building materials. The new buildings use less energy, which makes them better for the environment. The residents thought through everything carefully. They worked hard to make their town even better than it had been before.

One Greensburg landmark that survived the tornado is the Big Well. In 1887 and 1888, men used shovels and picks, barrels and pulleys to create the largest hand-dug well in the world. It is 32 feet across and 109 feet deep. Workers lined the well with stones all the way down. Today people visit the Big Well Museum to learn about Greensburg. They learn about the well and about the tornado. They learn how the community worked together and grew stronger in the midst of hardship. They can even walk down a spiral staircase to the bottom of the well.

Inside the Big Well

In 2017 Cassie's dad wrote a book about the Greensburg tornado: *Light at the End of the Funnel*. He wrote that going through the tornado made him believe even more strongly that God lives inside him. He knows that God's plan is for his own good and for God's glory. Like the apostle Paul, he has learned that it really is possible to have joy—no matter what.

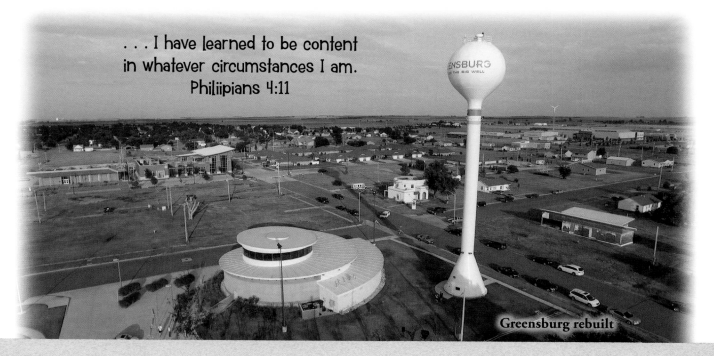
. . . I have learned to be content in whatever circumstances I am. Philiipians 4:11

Greensburg rebuilt

Activities

- Complete the map activities for Kansas in the *Atlas Workbook* (page 69).
- Read chapter 18 in *The Story of George Washington Carver*.
- Think about a time someone in your community has done something kind for your family. Perhaps they brought you a meal or helped with a repair at your house. If you are keeping a creative writing notebook, write about that time.

Lesson 67: Nebraska

A footbridge stretches across the **Missouri River** between Council Bluffs, Iowa, and **Omaha**, Nebraska. A line in the middle of the bridge marks where Iowa and Nebraska come together. Find Iowa on the map at the beginning of this book.

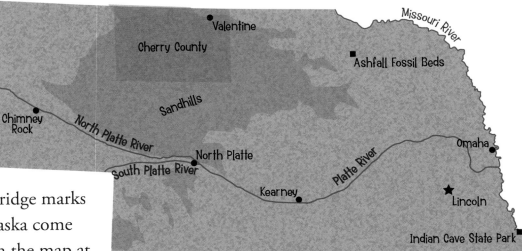

Bridge in Omaha

Indian Cave State Park

Do you like to draw animals? Long ago, in a cave in southeast Nebraska, people carved pictures of animals into the cave's stone walls. You can still see their carvings at **Indian Cave State Park**. The carvings are petroglyphs. One looks like a bison. Another resembles a horse. The people also carved squares marked with an X. What do you think they mean?

Petroglyph at Indian Cave

Capital: Lincoln

The Sower stands atop the Nebraska State Capitol in **Lincoln**. This bronze statue represents the importance of farming in Nebraska's story. *The Sower* has his shirt sleeves and pants rolled up, showing that he is ready for work. He is scattering seed by hand, which is a traditional way to plant fields. The sower is over 19 feet tall. He stands on a bronze bundle of corn, stacked on a bronze bundle of wheat.

The Sower

Sandhills and Sandhill Cranes

Miles of grass-covered sand dunes lie in the **Sandhills** of north-central Nebraska. This area is perfect for raising cattle. **Cherry County** in the sandhills has more head of cattle than any other county in the United States.

Sandhill cranes are named for this region of Nebraska. These magnificent birds can grow up to five feet tall. Their wingspan is sometimes seven feet wide.

Every year the city of **Kearney** is a resting spot for thousands of sandhill cranes as they migrate. The birds rest in the shallow waters of Nebraska's **Platte River**. Over 500,000 of these birds pass through Nebraska each year. Special viewing stations help people get an up-close look. The birds' calls create a magnificent chorus. As they rest, the cranes search for food in the wet meadows and farmlands near the river. After they have rested and eaten their fill, the sandhill cranes spread their wings. With a terrific whoosh they rise up, head back to the sky, and continue on their journey.

Sandhill cranes

Bailey Yard

Bailey Yard

Nebraska is in the middle of the country, so it is the perfect place for America's busiest train yard. Bailey Yard in the city of **North Platte** is actually the busiest train yard in the world. Trains heading north, south, east, and west pass through Bailey Yard. Up to 14,000 train cars pass through here every day! They carry grain, cars, steel, electronics, clothes, and other items you see every day. From the Golden Spike observation tower, visitors can look down and see this Union Pacific railroad yard in action. Bailey Yard never goes to sleep. It is open 24 hours a day, seven days a week.

Chimney Rock

As pioneers headed west in the 1800s, they wrote letters, journals, and books about what they experienced. They wrote about their joys and hardships. They wrote about landmarks they saw along the way. The landmark they mentioned most is **Chimney Rock**. This rock formation towers high above the Nebraska plains.

Chimney Rock

In the 1930s, the Frank Durnal family owned Chimney Rock. They realized how important the landmark is to the story of America. They didn't want anyone to clutter the landscape around it with modern buildings. The Durnal family donated Chimney Rock and eighty acres of land surrounding it to the Nebraska State Historical Society. Their generous gift preserved Chimney Rock for future generations.

Ashfall Fossil Beds

Land around Ashfall Fossil Beds

The spring rains of 1971 were heavy in Nebraska. In northeast Nebraska, the rainwater washed away part of a ravine. Later in the year, Michael Voorhies noticed part of an animal skull sticking out of the ground in the ravine. He dug a little deeper and found more than just a skull. He found the entire skeleton of a young rhinoceros! His discovery sparked a huge excavation of the site. An excavation is a careful dig in a certain area. Paleontologists are people who dig for fossils. The paleontologists in Antelope County found skeletons of deer, birds, turtles, horses, and camels. It appears that a volcanic eruption buried all of the animals in ash.

Today the fossil bed is safe inside **Ashfall Fossil Beds State Historical Park**. Workers constructed a building around part of the excavation site. The building protects the skeletons from the weather. Visitors can see the fossils still in place exactly as the paleontologists discovered them.

Fossil in Ashfall Fossil Bed

So let us know, let us press on to know the Lord. His going forth is as certain as the dawn;
And He will come to us like the rain, like the spring rain watering the earth.
Hosea 6:3

Activities

- Illustrate the geographic term for Nebraska in the *Atlas Workbook* (page 70).

- If you are using the *Lesson Review*, answer the questions for Nebraska (page 17).

- Read chapter 19 in *The Story of George Washington Carver*.

- Hands-On Idea: Pretend a couch or bed is your covered wagon as you travel west past Chimney Rock.

- Family Activity: Have a Fossil Dig (instructions on page 306).

Uncle Sam's Farm

During the mid-1800s, the United States government encouraged settlers to move west and establish farms. Jesse Hutchinson Jr. wrote these words at that time, celebrating the opportunity available in Nebraska and other states. (Track 34)

Of all the mighty nations in the East or in the West,
O, this glorious Yankee nation is the greatest and the best;
We have room for all creation, and our banner is unfurled,
Here's a general invitation to the people of the world.

Chorus:
O, come away! Come away! Come away, I say,
O, come away! Come away! Come right away.
O, come to this county, and have no fear of harm.
Our Uncle Sam is rich enough to give us all a farm.

St. Lawrence is our Northern line, far's her waters flow,
And the Rio Grande our Southern bound, way down in Mexico.
While from the Atlantic Ocean, where the sun begins to dawn,
We'll cross the Rocky Mountains far away to Oregon.

Chorus

The South may raise the cotton, and the West the corn and pork,
New England manufactories shall do up the finer work;
For the deep and flowing waterfalls that course along our hills,
Are just the thing for washing sheep, and driving cotton mills.

Chorus

Our Fathers gave us liberty, but little did they dream,
The grand results that flow along this mighty age of steam;
For our mountains, lakes and rivers, are all a blaze of fire,
And we send our news by lightning, on the telegraphic wire.

Valentine

Can you imagine heading out, getting some land, and starting a town? We don't think much about people doing that these days, but it used to happen often. David Mears worked for the Sioux City & Pacific Railroad. He acquired some land in Nebraska

Railroad bridge near Valentine

in 1882. Railroad workers were laying tracks and building bridges nearby, but there was no town. There were a few tents and a small number of simple buildings. A few soldiers lived nearby at Fort Niobrara, but there was no town.

When David Mears claimed his land in Nebraska, he hoped it would be the start of a town. Soon railroad workers built a depot, a livery stable, a restaurant, and a general store. Poof! A town was born. People named the town **Valentine**, the last name of a congressman from Nebraska. By 1886, just four years after David Mears dreamed of a town on his land, 750 people lived in Valentine. Valentine quickly became known as the toughest town in Nebraska.

Frances Fulton visited Nebraska in the 1880s when she was in her twenties. She described her travels in a book, *To and Through Nebraska by a Pennsylvania Girl*. People warned Frances not to visit Valentine. Frances wrote, "Valentine is considered one of the wicked places of Nebraska, on account of the cowboys of that neighborhood making it their headquarters." Frances visited the town anyway. She declared, "The Lord has always provided friends for me when I was in need of them, and I know He will not forsake me now."

Near Valentine

303

Frances observed that the land near Valentine "is one vast plain with here a house, and there a house, and here and there a house, and that's about all; very little farming done, no trees, no bushes, no nothing but prairie." As Frances traveled by train to Valentine, she met a minister. He was going to Valentine to spend his vacation preaching in the area. He was "the first minister bold enough to hold services" in Valentine. The minister traveled alone. He told Frances that Valentine was "too rough and bad to take his family there."

Frances was only in Valentine for a few hours. She mostly stayed in the safety of the depot while she waited for a ride to her next stop. Though the town was full of rough men, no one harmed Frances. She felt sorry for the lonely cowboys she saw in Valentine. "Poor boys!" she thought. "Where are your mothers, your sisters, your homes?" It made her sad to think of all the cowboys who lived in darkness, wasting their lives away.

The city of Valentine didn't stay rough forever. As more people moved in, Valentine calmed down and became a more peaceful place.

In 1941 Margarete Clare Phelps, the local postmaster, had an idea. She decided to promote the town of Valentine by taking advantage of the town's name. The town invited people from far and wide to put a valentine inside a second envelope and mail it to the Valentine post office. Workers there opened the outside envelope and stamped a special heart-shaped design on the valentine envelope that was inside. They put the heart-stamped valentine back in the mail so it could go to its final destination. People enjoyed receiving valentines postmarked from the town of Valentine.

Modern Valentine

After World War II, the postmaster's idea continued to grow. Local volunteers came to the post office to help stamp the huge piles of cards that arrived each year.

The town of Valentine still carries out Postmaster Phelps' idea. Thousands of cards still pour into the post office in January and February. Volunteers stamp the envelopes with a special Valentine stamp, then put the valentines back in the mail. This free service is one way the town shows its big heart.

Valentine takes advantage of its name in other ways, too. Heart-shaped decorations are everywhere. The street signs are red, and each one has a small white heart. You can even order a heart-shaped steak at a local restaurant.

Valentine has definitely turned around its reputation. It has gone from being "the toughest town in Nebraska" to being Heart City.

Above all, keep fervent in your love
for one another,
because love covers a multitude of sins.
1 Peter 4:8

Activities

- Complete the map activities for Nebraska in the *Atlas Workbook* (page 71).
- How would you describe your town to someone who has never been there? What special places can a person visit? What are some stores and other businesses in your town? Are there any parks? If you are keeping a creative writing notebook, write a description of your town.

Family Activity: Fossil Dig

Supplies:

- 2 cups flour (plus more for work surface)
- 1 cup salt
- 1 cup water
- parchment paper
- baking sheet
- sandbox (if you do not have a sandbox you can use a pile of clothes or stuffed animals to hide the fossils)

Directions:

- In a medium size bowl, stir flour, salt, and water together until it comes together into a dough ball.
- Turn the dough onto a lightly floured surface. Knead until smooth. Dough should be firm. Add flour to your surface if needed.
- Line a baking sheet with parchment paper.
- Form fossil shapes about ½" thick. Place your fossils onto the lined baking sheet.
- Bake at 325° for 30 minutes per ½" of thickness. (If your fossils are thinner, they will need less time; if they are thicker, they will need more time.)
- Let fossils cool completely before removing them from the baking sheet.

After your fossils are cool, have a family fossil dig contest. Take turns hiding the fossils in a sandbox (or a pile of clothes or stuffed animals) and letting one person find them. Time each person to see who can find all the fossils the fastest.

Be safe with the hot oven. Children must have adult supervision in the kitchen.

Prairie dogs in the Badlands of South Dakota

Unit 18
Midwest:
South Dakota and North Dakota

Both North Dakota and South Dakota were once part of Dakota Territory. In 1889 people divided the territory and formed the states of North and South Dakota. Find South Dakota on the map at the beginning of this book.

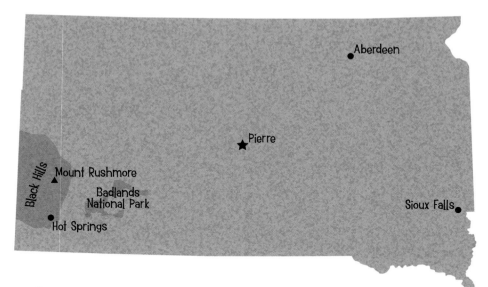

Courthouse made of Sioux quartzite

Sioux Falls

God placed a special kind of rock in the ground around Sioux Falls, South Dakota. Sioux quartzite is strong and durable. People in Sioux Falls have used it to build houses and government buildings. The rock commonly has a distinct pinkish hue, which gives the town a nice splash of color.

Sioux Falls is the largest city in South Dakota. Just a short walk from downtown, a waterfall tumbles over Sioux quartzite. After dark the city lights up the waterfall with changing colored lights.

Sioux Falls

Capital: Pierre

West of Sioux Falls is Pierre (pronounced *peer*), the capital of South Dakota. The waters of Capitol Lake reflect the state capitol building. An artesian well feeds this man-made lake. An artesian well has natural underground pressure. That means the well does not need a pump to bring water up to

South Dakota State Capitol and Capitol Lake

the surface. The well warms the water of the lake. Capitol Lake never completely freezes in the winter. This makes it a popular place for water birds when the weather is cold.

Badlands National Park

Badlands National Park lies in western South Dakota. Native people and early European settlers called these lands "bad." The rock formations made travel difficult and there wasn't much water available.

American bison

Pierre-Jean de Smet traveled through the Badlands in the mid-1800s. He wrote about the amazing rock formations God created here. The formations reminded him of large villages, ancient castles, majestic Gothic towers, and huge Egyptian pyramids.

Badlands National Park is home to many animals, from the small prairie dogs to the enormous American bison.

Badlands National Park

Needles Highway

Donkeys in the Black Hills

Black Hills

West of the Badlands lie the **Black Hills**. Granite pillars point to the sky on Needles Highway. Antelope, bison, and wild donkeys roam free. The wild donkeys aren't really very wild. If you put down your window to snap a picture, one of the donkeys will likely poke his head right inside your car!

Further into the Black Hills is **Mount Rushmore**. This monument honors four of our nation's presidents: George Washington, Thomas Jefferson, Theodore Roosevelt, and Abraham Lincoln. Around three million people from all over the world visit Mount Rushmore every year.

North of Mount Rushmore, Spearfish Canyon winds its way through the Black Hills. When many early pioneers headed west, they passed through this canyon. Imagine taking a wagon over the waterfall pictured below. The pioneers had to rough-lock their wheels when they crossed it so their wagons didn't run away from them. That's why the waterfall is called Roughlock Falls.

Mount Rushmore (caption under image below)

Gold!

In 1875 John B. Pearson discovered gold in the Black Hills. The U.S. government tried to keep his discovery a secret. The government had made a treaty with the Lakota-Sioux people. According to the treaty, the Black Hills belonged to the Lakota-Sioux.

Roughlock Falls

Sioux man in the Badlands

The government knew white men would invade the Black Hills if they knew about the gold. The secret got out, and sure enough, a flood of people rushed to the Black Hills.

Henri LeBeau was one of the many men who came to the Black Hills during the gold rush days. He created a line

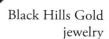

of Black Hills Gold jewelry featuring three colors of gold: rose, green, and yellow. He used the shapes of leaves and grapes in his designs. People in the Black Hills region still make and sell this style of jewelry today.

Black Hills Gold jewelry

Mammoths in South Dakota

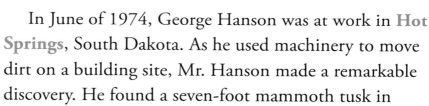
Mammoth

In June of 1974, George Hanson was at work in **Hot Springs**, South Dakota. As he used machinery to move dirt on a building site, Mr. Hanson made a remarkable discovery. He found a seven-foot mammoth tusk in the ground.

Mammoths are extinct, but apparently they once lived in South Dakota. Mammoths may have looked like the illustration above. The tusk and the many other bones discovered in the area became The Mammoth Site, a museum where visitors can see these wonders of God's creation.

Mammoth bones in South Dakota

Then God said, "Let the earth bring forth living creatures after their kind . . . " and it was so.
Genesis 1:24

Activities

- Illustrate the geographic term for South Dakota in the *Atlas Workbook* (page 72).

- If you are using the *Lesson Review*, answer the questions for South Dakota (page 18).

- Hands-On Idea: How many different colors can you find in rocks around your house?

Lesson 70: A Song and Story of South Dakota

South Dakota Song

This song appeared in a booklet about Roberts County, South Dakota, in 1893. (Track 35)

When the wheat is in the granary
  And the prices reach the sky,
And the roosters are a-crowing,
  And the chickens flying high;
When the city fellers squabble
  For the farmers' views and votes,
And the barn is full of timothy,
  And the bins are full of oats,
It's then that feller is a-feeling at his best,
  With the risin' sun to greet him
From a night of glorious rest;
  And the babies caper round him,
And the colts are kicking high,
  When the wheat is in the granary
And the prices reach the sky.

There's something kind o' hearty like
  About the sky and field,
With the stubble there a-laughing
  At a 30-bushel yield,
With the happy birds a-singing
  And the cattle in a doze,
And the hired man a-coming round
  To show his new store clothes.
A feller feels content
  And at peace with all the world,
When the golden flag of plenty
  Like a blessing is unfurled.
Oh, I tell you Nancy's happy,
  And the girls are flying high,
With the granary a-bustin'
  And the prices in the sky.

South Dakota farmland

312

Working Together

In the 1870s, the government sent surveyors to Dakota Territory to survey the land. These men took measurements to make maps and mark boundaries. One Dakota surveyor said, "As far as the eye can see, the land we are surveying is flat as a barn floor and tall grass covers a black soil that is 8 to 12 inches thick. There are no

James River in South Dakota

trees except along the James River. What a land for breaking plows!" To many people in the East, Dakota Territory sounded like the perfect place to start a new farm.

As new settlers moved to Dakota Territory, they organized communities. Many communities started out as wild and dangerous places. They were full of rowdy frontiersmen. **Aberdeen**, South Dakota, was different. Many refined, well-educated families settled here from the start. Some of the settlers were immigrants from Germany, England, and Scandinavia.

Aberdeen around 1910

Aberdeen depot around 1911

Towns that had a railroad often grew quickly. Railroads brought settlers. Railroads brought lumber and supplies. They made it easier to build towns. By 1886 Aberdeen had nine railroads leading into it. People called Aberdeen the Hub City of the Dakotas.

Gradually the settlers built stores, houses, offices, schools, and hotels. One year, the citizens of Aberdeen wanted a Christmas tree. The prairie did not have one to offer them. A railroad man shipped a tree to Aberdeen on a railroad car. The tree was small, but it would have to do. Residents set it up in a store and tied colorful decorations to the branches.

The people of Aberdeen elected officials to form the government of their little town. One of the first laws the town leaders passed set the speed limit on Main Street at 8 miles an hour.

As Aberdeen grew, the town's water supply ran low. The citizens voted to dig a town well. Workers dug for months. Finally, the water started flowing. Once it started, the people of Aberdeen didn't know how to stop it! The well was an artesian well, so it had natural pressure that sent the water to the surface. Suddenly Aberdeen had a stream of water shooting 60 feet into the sky. The water flooded Main Street. People went through town in rowboats! Workers dug a large ditch to make the water flow away from town. Local residents used at least 60 wagons to haul away the dirt dug out of the ditch. It was a huge project, but the people of Aberdeen worked together to get it done.

Courthouse in Aberdeen

Finally workers controlled the flow of water with a gate valve in the well. Visitors from far and wide came to Aberdeen to see the town's amazing well. Some thought it was the greatest well in the world.

Today Aberdeen is the third largest city in South Dakota. It is not only home to descendants of brave pioneers and immigrants who settled the area; it is also home to Goldilocks, Mary and her little lamb, and a cow jumping over the moon.

In the 1970s, the people of Aberdeen decided to build something special for their town. Local residents, businesses, clubs, and other organizations donated time and money to create Storybook Land. This park features statues and play structures from fairy tales and nursery rhymes. Visitors can climb Jack and Jill's hill, go inside the homes of the three little pigs, and ride Humpty Dumpty's Great Fall roller coaster.

Building Storybook Land was a big project. No one could have done it alone. The people of Aberdeen worked together to get it done.

Let us not lose heart in doing good,
for in due time we will reap
if we do not grow weary.
So then, while we have opportunity,
let us do good to all people,
and especially to those
who are of the household of the faith.
Galatians 6:9-10

Scenes in Storybook Land

Activities

- Complete the map activities for South Dakota in the *Atlas Workbook* (page 73).
- Imagine that you get to design a park for your town. What would be the theme? What would visitors be able to do there? If you are keeping a creative writing notebook, describe your park or draw a picture of it.

God put an abundant supply of oil below the ground in North Dakota. Above the ground, North Dakota farmers raise more dry beans, flaxseed, and spring wheat than any other state. North Dakota has about twice as many cows as people. Find North Dakota on the map at the beginning of this book.

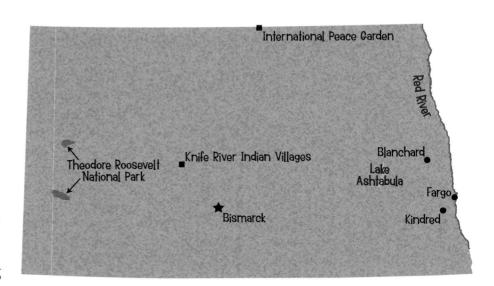

Bonanza

Imagine tens of thousands of acres of wheat, waving in the wind. Imagine 25 men sitting at a long table with benches down both sides. The men are hungry. They have been working for hours in the sun, harvesting wheat. Women have been bustling in the kitchen all morning to prepare the food. After the men finish a hearty meal, they leave the dining room and the next 25 men file in. The rotation continues until all the men on the farm have eaten. The men and the horses get back to work, harvesting row after row of golden wheat. Boats will carry the wheat down the **Red River** to market. It will be a bonanza crop for sure.

North Dakota wheat field

316

The word *bonanza* means something that creates sudden wealth. In the late 1800s and early 1900s, bonanza farms did just that in North Dakota. Wealthy men purchased thousands of acres and created huge wheat farms. They hired hard-working men to work their bonanza farm fields. The farms earned a great deal of money, but they didn't last very long. Some bonanza farms grew the same crop in the same soil year after year. This made the soil run out of important nutrients. Years of drought also discouraged bonanza farming. Before long, bonanza farm owners divided up their land and sold it off as smaller farms.

Harrowing a field on a bonanza farm

The Cass County Historical Society operates Bonanzaville in Fargo, North Dakota. The group works hard to preserve the pioneer history of the state. At Bonanzaville visitors step inside original bonanza farm buildings. They also tour other historic buildings, including a town hall, a creamery, and a harness shop.

KVLY-TV tower

It's Tall. Really Tall.

If you pass by the KVLY-TV tower in Blanchard, North Dakota, you have to look up . . . and up . . . and up 2,063 feet to see the top. When workers completed this tower in 1963, it was the tallest structure ever built anywhere in the world. A few towers have topped it since then, but this one is still the tallest tower in all of North and South America. The tower sends out a television signal that reaches hundreds of miles in all directions.

Ashtabula Wind Energy Centers

Around 1,500 wind turbines stand in North Dakota. Two hundred and fifty of them stand near Lake Ashtabula. The wind that sweeps across the prairie turns the blades on the turbines. The blades turn generators inside the turbines. The generators make electricity. The turbines of the Ashtabula Wind Energy Centers generate enough electricity to power 99,000 North Dakota homes. (Even though the turbines are tall, they don't come close to matching the KVLY-TV tower. You would have to stack up eight turbines to reach the height of the television tower!)

North Dakota wind turbine

Making snow angels on the capitol grounds in 2007

Capitol: Bismarck

In 2007 the people of North Dakota used the grounds of their state capitol in Bismarck to set a new world record. A huge crowd gathered there on a snowy February day. Together they created 8,962 snow angels—all at the same time.

Knife River Indian Villages

Knife River Indian Villages brings the cultures of the Mandan, Arikara, and Hidatsa people to life. These people once lived in earthlodge villages along the Knife and Missouri Rivers. Women built the lodges using logs, willow branches, dried grass, and sod. At Knife River Indian Villages you can see large circles in the ground where these lodges once stood. A reconstructed earthlodge helps visitors imagine what it must have been like to live in one.

Reconstructed earthlodge at Knife River

Theodore Roosevelt National Park

Theodore Roosevelt loved the rugged freedom of the North Dakota Badlands. He wanted to preserve beautiful places such as this for future generations. After Theodore Roosevelt became president in 1901, he set aside millions of acres of land in America. That land became some of the national parks and national monuments we enjoy today. Years later, President Harry Truman established **Theodore Roosevelt National Park** in North Dakota in his honor.

Near the park, visitors enjoy biking, riding horses, and hiking on the Maah Daah Hey Trail. The trail goes across rivers, through flat grasslands, and around badlands buttes. A butte is a steep rocky hill that is mostly flat on top. The trail gets its name from a Mandan phrase meaning "an area that will be around for a long time."

International Peace Garden

In 1928 Dr. Henry J. Moore of Canada dreamed of a garden where two countries could celebrate their friendship. The government of Manitoba in Canada, and the government of North Dakota liked Moore's idea. Both governments donated land to create a garden. People have lovingly planted and tended the flowerbeds at the Interntaional Peace Garden ever since.

International Peace Garden

Deceit is in the heart of those who devise evil,
But counselors of peace have joy.
Proverbs 12:20

Activities

- Illustrate the geographic term for North Dakota in the *Atlas Workbook* (page 74).

- If you are using the *Lesson Review*, answer the questions for North Dakota (page 18).

- Hands-On Idea: Pretend you work on a bonanza farm.

Red River Valley

Many people think of this folk song as a cowboy song about the Red River in Texas, but the original version is about the Red River that forms much of the border between North Dakota and Minnesota and flows into Canada. The words below are slightly different from the more common cowboy version, but they are closer to the original version of the song from the 1800s. In this version a girl sings the song to a soldier who is going away. Adieu is French for "goodbye." (Track 36)

It's a long time, you know, I've been waiting
For the words that you never did say,
But alas! All my fond hopes have vanished,
For they tell me you're going away.

Chorus:
O consider awhile ere you leave me,
Do not hasten to bid me adieu,
But remember the Red River Valley,
And the one that loved you so true.

From this valley they say you are going,
I shall miss your blue eyes and sweet smile,
And you take with you all of the sunshine
That has brightened my pathway a while.

Chorus

So remember the valley you're leaving,
How lonely and how dreary 'twill be
Remember the heart you are breaking,
And be true to your promise to me.

Chorus

As you go to your home by the ocean
May you never forget those sweet hours
That we spent in the Red River Valley
And the love we exchanged 'mid its bowers.

Chorus:
So consider awhile ere you leave me,
Do not hasten to bid me adieu,
But remember the Red River Valley,
And the one that loved you so true.

Red River

320

Keeping Bees

Honeybees gather nectar and pollen from flowers. They carry the nectar and pollen back to their hives. Inside their hives, bees turn the nectar into honey. The pollen provides the bees with protein. During the honey harvest, beekeepers extract (or take out) honey from the beehives.

North Dakota is rich with plants that honeybees love, such as sweet clover, alfalfa, canola, and sunflowers. Those plants are called honeybee forage. The summertime climate and the amount of daylight in North Dakota are just right for honeybees. North Dakota produces more honey than any other state.

Mark Sperry was born into a beekeeping family in Kansas in 1957. His grandfather kept a few hives in the backyard of his home. He harvested enough honey for his family and had a little left over to sell. Mark's dad enjoyed keeping bees like his grandfather. When Mark was young, his dad purchased a large beekeeping business and the family moved to North Dakota.

Mark Sperry's dad tending bees in 2011 at age 90

North Dakota sunflowers

As Mark grew up in North Dakota, his dad expected him to help with the bees. Mark wished he had more time to play with friends. He decided beekeeping was too much work for him. He went to college and became a wildlife biologist. After working for several years in Minnesota, he then decided to return to the family beekeeping business in North Dakota. He is glad he made that decision.

321

Mark Sperry finds honeybees fascinating. He enjoys spending his days with them. Of course there are days when he gets stung. He remembers getting stung right between the eyes when he was a little boy. Lifting heavy boxes full of honey in the hot weather is exhausting. Those things are part of keeping bees, though, and beekeeping is something Mark Sperry loves.

Mark's employee tending hives near a sunflower field

Mr. Sperry tends around 1,200 hives in and around **Kindred**, North Dakota. Each hive has up to 50,000 bees. Mr. Sperry has to spread out his hives so that there is enough forage to go around. Some of his hives are fifty miles away from his home. Mr. Sperry and his employee drive around and check on each hive regularly. They make sure the bees are healthy and have everything they need.

Mark Sperry tending a hive

Harvest time is in August and September. Mr. Sperry hires local homeschooled students to help extract the honey. They typically have enough honey to fill about two hundred 55-gallon containers.

Mark Sperry knows that every honey harvest is from the Lord. There are many ups and downs in the honey business. He never knows from one year to the next how much honeybee forage will be available. He has no control over the weather, but the weather affects how much honey his bees can make.

Mr. Sperry's faith in God gives him peace. He does his work for the Lord, and he knows the Lord will provide everything he needs.

Honeybees at work in a hive

Trust in the Lord
and do good;
Dwell in the land
and cultivate faithfulness.
Psalm 37:3

Activities

- Complete the map activities for North Dakota in the *Atlas Workbook* (page 75).
- What is a chore you have done that is exhausting, but rewarding? Think about how you felt while you were doing it and how you felt when the job was done. If you are keeping a creative writing notebook, write about that experience.
- Family Activity: Take an Agriculture Field Trip (instructions on page 324).
- If you are using the *Lesson Review*, take the Midwest (Part 2) Test (page 39).

Family Activity: Agriculture Field Trip

Arrange a time when you can visit a farming operation in your area. You might already live on a farm, but you can still find a place that is different from where you live. You might like to visit an agritourism business nearby, or you might like to just visit an older person from church who has fruit trees or who keeps cattle. Maybe there is a blueberry patch nearby or a farm that raises llamas or a person who owns a small flock of sheep. Bless someone in your area by giving them an opportunity to tell your family about their agriculture business or hobby.

Mountain goat in Glacier National Park in Montana

Unit 19
Rocky Mountain:
Montana and Idaho

Lesson 73: Montana

Montana has plenty of wide open spaces. That's why people call it Big Sky Country. The state holds the record for the largest snowflake ever to fall anywhere. Folks in Montana reported seeing a fifteen-inch snowflake in 1887. (It must have been an aggregate snowflake, which is made of several snow crystals clumped together.) Do you think you could have caught that one on your tongue? Find Montana on the map at the beginning of this book.

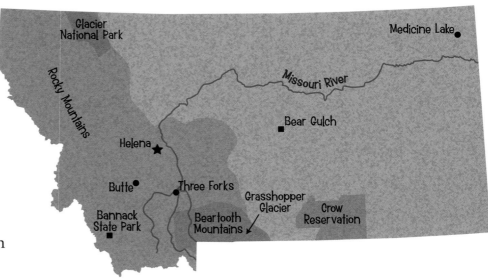

Glacier National Park

Rocky Mountains

Medicine Lake

Missouri River

Bear Gulch

Helena

Butte

Three Forks

Bannack State Park

Beartooth Mountains

Grasshopper Glacier

Crow Reservation

Huckleberries

How about some huckleberry fudge? Or pie? Or pancakes? Or maybe some chocolate-covered huckleberries? Montana has them all. Huckleberries grow wild in Montana and people there go wild over huckleberries. The berries are similar to blueberries. Berry pickers have to keep a lookout for bears—they love huckleberries, too.

Bear munching huckleberries

Yellowstone River

Missouri River

In the wilderness of the Rocky Mountains in Montana, near the city of **Three Forks**, three rivers meet. Where the three rivers meet, the **Missouri River** begins. This river flows across America for over 2,000 miles through deep canyons, around hills, and across broad valleys.

Near Three Forks

Painting of a Crow teepee from the 1830s

Crow Nation

Members of the Crow tribe live on the **Crow Reservation** in southern Montana. Just like native people on other reservations, the Crow live a modern lifestyle while working hard to keep the traditions of their people alive. Most of the people grow up speaking the Crow language, but they also learn English. A coal mine under the reservation brings in money for the tribe and provides jobs for some of the tribal members.

Grasshopper Glacier

Grasshopper Glacier lies in the rugged wilderness of the **Beartooth Mountains**. A glacier is a mass of ice on land. Inside Grasshopper Glacier are grasshoppers— millions of them—frozen in the ice. The grasshoppers were likely flying over the mountains many years ago when they were caught in a blizzard and froze to death. No one knows how long the grasshoppers have been in the ice, but at least one of the species there is now extinct.

Grasshopper Glacier in 1900

Bannack State Park

John White discovered gold in Montana on July 28, 1862. Soon many people rushed to Montana. The town of Bannack quickly sprang up near the site of John White's discovery. By the next year, the town had a population of over 3,000.

Bannack State Park

After a while, the value of gold went down and the gold around Bannack began to run out. People gradually moved away from Bannack and it became one of Montana's many ghost towns. A ghost town is a settlement from which most or all of the people who lived there have moved away.

Today at **Bannack State Park**, visitors can explore the empty buildings and imagine how life once was in the bustling town.

Butte

People once called **Butte**, Montana, the Richest Hill on Earth. The town's hill was full of silver, gold, and copper. In the late 1800s, the mining industry made the town grow quickly. By 1896 over 8,000 men worked in the mines. This one area produced over half of all the copper mined in the United States. People in Butte got rich. Word of the riches available in Butte spread around the world. Immigrants flocked to the area to work in the mines. Most of the immigrants came from Ireland. People also came from England, Lebanon, Canada, Finland, Austria, Italy, China, Montenegro, and Mexico. Some of the signs in the mines were written in sixteen languages to make sure all the miners could understand them.

Butte

Over the years, mining has greatly slowed down in Butte. The city is much smaller than it once was, but it is still thriving. Many residents love to celebrate their Irish heritage, especially around St. Patrick's Day. At one time more Irish people lived in Butte than in any other city in America.

Capital: Helena

Montana's capital is another Montana town that began as a mining camp. The gold in the area attracted many settlers. In the autumn of 1864 a group of the miners gathered to name their settlement. One person suggested Pumpkinville. Another thought of Squashtown. Not enough people at the meeting liked those suggestions, though. Several people suggested names from areas where they once lived. They settled on Helena, named after Helena Township in Minnesota. Sounds better than Squashtown, don't you think?

Montana State Capitol

Glacier National Park

Mountain goats, bighorn sheep, mountain lions, and elk are all at home in Glacier National Park. The park has mountains and valleys, forests and prairies, and 26 glaciers that show the majesty of God.

O Lord, our Lord,
How majestic is Your name
in all the earth.
Psalm 8:1

Glacier National Park

Activities

- Illustrate the geographic term for Montana in the *Atlas Workbook* (page 76).
- If you are using the *Lesson Review*, answer the questions for Montana (page 19).
- Read chapters 1 and 2 in *The Trumpet of the Swan*. (Parents, please refer to page 17 in the *Answer Key and Literature Guide* for comments about this book.)
- Hands-On Idea: Use building bricks or blocks to build an abandoned town.

Miners in Butte in 1939

Irish Miner's Song

Irish miners who came to Butte brought this Irish song with them to America. They sang it often on the streets of their Montana mining town. (Track 37)

There are six as fine a fellows, as e're your eyes behold,
They will turn the hardest rock into silver or bright gold.
There is two of them from Mizen Head, two more of them from Clare,
Two of them from Dingle town, the place of great renown.
Here's a health to every miner that works beneath the ground.

Oh, the farmer takes delight in the sowing of his corn,
T' huntsman takes delight in the sounding of his horn,
While the miner takes delight for to split the rock in two,
And to find out the treasure that lies beyond his view.

Butte copper mine in 1939

No Finer People Anywhere

Tribes of the Great Plains once hunted here. Circles of stone in the nearby hills show us where their teepees once stood. They gathered herbs and roots from the lakeshore to use as medicine. They believed the lake's waters brought healing. The Assiniboine people called the water *bda wauka*, which means "medicine water." European settlers named it Medicine Lake.

Medicine Lake lies in the remote northeastern corner of Montana. The lake welcomes thousands of migrating birds year after year. Around 2,000 pelicans hatch each year on a large island in the middle of the lake.

In 1906 European settlers established Flandrem near the lake. The new settlement thrived for a few years. C. J. Poe was the town's pharmacist. He was friends with an Assiniboine medicine man. Perhaps the two shared ideas about medicine. In 1910 a railroad company built a new rail line about two miles away from the town. The townspeople knew they were too far away from the railroad for it to serve their town well. Their solution was to move the town!

C. J. Poe with his friend (name unknown)

C. J. Poe

C. J. Poe put his house and his drug store on wheels and moved them along a railroad track to the new settlement of Medicine Lake. In addition to his work as a pharmacist, C. J. Poe assisted the local doctor and also worked as an optometrist (an eye doctor). He became the town's first mayor. The young town had many needs, such as a water system, smooth streets, sidewalks, and street lights. Through all the important decisions he had to make, C. J. Poe served his community well. He liked to say of his friends and neighbors in Medicine Lake, "There are no finer people anywhere."

Later in 1910, C. J. married his sweetheart, Marie. C. J.'s parents gave the couple a poplar tree as a wedding present, which they planted in their yard. Marie helped her husband run the drug store, which also sold jewelry, gifts, candy, and ice cream. C. J. and Marie had four children: Dorothy, Helen, John, and Virginia. According to the Poes' daughter Virginia, their home was full of faith, love, and happiness.

When the Poe children were young, they loved the snowy winters of Montana. The milkman gave the neighborhood children a special thrill. He let them tie their sleds in a line and attach the front sled to his horse-drawn sleigh. He pulled the children through town as he delivered milk to his customers.

Children of Medicine Lake in front of the town's first school bus (a horse-drawn wagon) in 1924

As a child, Virginia developed a love for music. Her older sisters helped her learn to play the piano. Virginia sang in school plays and played the trombone in a high school band.

Don and Virginia Carpenter

Virginia Poe married Don Carpenter and the couple continued to live in Medicine Lake. Long after her parents had died, Virginia Poe Carpenter loved to look at the poplar tree still growing in the yard of her childhood home. One hundred years after her parents' wedding, she saw the tree "as a symbol of their abiding love."

Don and Virginia Carpenter in 2007 celebrating their 60th wedding anniversary

For over 65 years, Virginia Carpenter played the organ for church services, funerals, weddings, and other occasions in Medicine Lake. After her husband entered a nursing home, she played the piano at church services for the residents there.

Virginia Carpenter always loved her hometown. She left it several times to take trips, but she always came back. In an interview when she was 84 years old, she said, "I won't leave until the good Lord tells me it's time to move, one way or the other."

Serve the Lord with gladness;
Come before Him with joyful singing.
Psalm 100:2

Activities

- Complete the map activities for Montana in the *Atlas Workbook* (page 77).
- Read chapters 3 and 4 in *The Trumpet of the Swan*.
- The tree C. J. and Marie Poe received as a wedding gift was special to their family. Do you have an extra special tree in your yard or a tree you especially like somewhere else? What makes it special? What do you like to do in it or under it? If you are keeping a creative writing notebook, write about that tree and why it is special to you.

Lesson 75: Idaho

Idaho Panhandle National Forest
Lapwai
Garnet
Opal
Agate
Rocky Mountains
Ketchum
Sun Valley
Boise
Craters of the Moon National Monument
Bruneau Dunes
Snake River
Shoshone Falls

God put 72 different kinds of gems, including garnet, opal, agate, and diamonds, under the ground in Idaho. That's how Idaho earned the nickname of the Gem State. Find Idaho on the map at the beginning of this book.

Idaho potato field

Idaho Potatoes

What would you like to order? Baked potatoes, mashed potatoes, potato soup, potato chips, or french fries? Idaho can satisfy all your potato cravings. More potatoes grow in Idaho than in any other state. Henry Spaulding is the first person we know of who grew potatoes here. The Spauldings moved to what is now **Lapwai** to share Jesus with the Nez Perce people in 1836.

Idaho potato harvest

Processing potatoes in Idaho

334

Craters of the Moon National Monument

Craters of the Moon National Monument

Only God knows when a volcanic eruption spewed lava across southern Idaho. It happened long, long ago. The lava created formations that resemble the surface of the moon, which is how the area got its name.

In 1969, soon after Neil Armstrong and Buzz Aldrin became the first men to walk on the moon, a group of other astronauts traveled to Idaho. The men studied and explored **Craters of the Moon National Monument** in Idaho to prepare for their own trip to the moon two years later.

Shoshone Falls

When pioneers traveled west on the Oregon Trail in the 1800s, many of them made a special stop to see **Shoshone Falls** on the **Snake River**. Shoshone Falls is 212 feet tall and 900 feet wide. The flow of the falls is greatest in the spring when melting snow fills the river as it crashes over the rocks.

Shoshone Falls

Sandboarding at Bruneau Dunes

Bruneau Dunes

Idaho's sand dunes are perfect for barefoot hiking, kite flying, and sandboarding. In most places in the world, the wind causes big changes to the shapes of sand dunes. The wind patterns at **Bruneau Dunes** keep the dunes there rather stable. When the wind blows the sand one way, winds from a different direction usually blow it back.

Capital: Boise

Many years ago, members of several different native tribes gathered in the Boise valley once a year for their annual Sheewoki fair. For weeks on end they traded and celebrated with one another.

Fur traders and missionaries began to settle in the Boise valley in the early 1800s. A few years later, many covered wagons began to pass through the area as people traveled west on the Oregon Trail. Most travelers were not interested in settling in the valley. The area was just a convenient place to pick up some supplies before they continued on their westward journey.

Miners poured into the region in 1862, hoping to strike it rich by finding gold. In 1863 a group of settlers worked with an Army officer to map out a new city: **Boise**. The people of Boise could see trees off in the distance, but their own town was pretty barren. Residents worked together to change that.

Native woman of Idaho in 1911

Boise in 1909

336

Boise

The local newspaper ran ads encouraging people to plant trees. The paper also praised people in the town by name who improved their property with new plantings. Seven years after the founding of Boise, the paper published this piece of news: "The Tree Mania prevails in this city. Almost every street is already ornamented with poplar, cottonwood and willow trees . . . . We flatter ourselves that we will be the premium or star city of the plains. . . . The trees already set out make a marked change in the appearance of our city." The residents' hard work payed off. Today people call Boise the City of Trees.

Northern Lights

Look at the shape of Idaho on page 334. The northern region of the state is called the panhandle. Idaho Panhandle National Forest is one of the best spots in America besides in Alaska to catch a glimpse of the northern lights.

The northern lights (or aurora borealis) are one of God's spectacular creations. When gases from storms on the sun meet the invisible magnetic field around the earth, the gasses create these beautiful lights. The northern lights dance across the sky in many colors, including green, red, blue, and purple. You can see the lights the best far away from big cities and other light pollution, which is why the Idaho panhandle is such a good place to see them.

The God said, "Let there be light"; and there was light.
Genesis 1:3

Northern lights in Idaho

Activities

- Illustrate the geographic term for Idaho in the *Atlas Workbook* (page 78).

- If you are using the *Lesson Review*, answer the questions for Idaho (page 19).

- Read chapters 5 and 6 in *The Trumpet of the Swan*.

- Hands-On Idea: Pretend you are training to be an astronaut at Craters of the Moon.

- Family Activity: Make Twice-Baked Potatoes (instructions on page 342).

It Happened in Sun Valley

This song appeared in a 1941 movie about Sun Valley. Inclusion of this song does not indicate endorsement of the movie.

(Track 38)

Howdy folks, let's go for a ride.
Get your favorite one to sit by your side.
Cuddle up in a sleigh,
Giddyap, Nellie Grey,
And away we go!

While you listen to the sleigh bells ring
You're yodeling to your baby.
You'll feel nice and warm
No matter how cold it may be.

Take a look at little Jack and Jill,
They ski down a hill that's a snowplow turn,
And look, there's a spill,
There's a spill on the hill.
When you're down it's a thrill to go up again!

Ev'rybody ought to learn to ski,
        for that is how we first met.
We were that Jack and Jill that came down a hill.
When I looked at you my heart took a spill,
Took a spill on a hill,
It's a thrill that I can't forget!

It Happened In Sun Valley not so very long ago.
There were sunbeams in the snow
And a twinkle in your eye.
I remember, oh so clearly,
That you nearly passed me by.
Then It Happened In Sun Valley
When you slipped and fell and so did I! *(repeat 4 lines)*

Now ev'ry year we go back,
And then we recall that fall and that moment
When we were there on a hill.
So we both take a spill and we're Jack and Jill again!

Sun Valley

Herd of sheep near Ketchum

Sheep and Skis

During the 1880s, Ketchum sprang up as a mining town in central Idaho. After mining slowed down in the area, many of the settlers who remained started ranches. A ranch is a large farm. Trains that once carried loads of minerals out of the area now carried load after load of sheep. In 1918 there were almost six times as many sheep in Idaho as there were people.

During the 1930s, Averell Harriman was in charge of the Union Pacific Railroad. He wanted to figure out a way to get more Americans to travel to the western part of the country. He hired a talented Austrian skier to explore the Rocky Mountains and look for the perfect place to build a ski resort.

After a long search, the Austrian man discovered Ketchum. It was a peaceful place that had a small population and the perfect slopes for skiing. "Among the many attractive spots I have visited," the Austrian wrote to Mr. Harriman, "this combines the more delightful features of any place I have seen in the United States, Switzerland, or Austria for a winter ski resort."

Sun Valley

After only seven months of planning and some quick but fancy construction work, the resort was ready for business. Now Averell Harriman had to figure out how to get people to come. He hired Steve Hannagan to promote the new attraction. Mr. Hannagan named the area Sun Valley. He invited popular movie stars to come experience the resort. When Americans learned that movie stars were going to Sun Valley, they wanted to visit for themselves. In addition to skiing, the resort offered ice skating, heated swimming pools, dog sledding, and horse-drawn sleigh rides.

Union Pacific postcards showing Sun Valley

340

Sun Valley prospered for a few years, but after the United States entered World War II, it shut down. It didn't stay closed for long, though. It reopened in 1942 for a different purpose.

The U.S. Navy brought wounded sailors to Sun Valley to recover. All the sporting options at Sun Valley were perfect for sailors who needed to regain their strength and build up their spirits after being wounded in the war. When the war ended in 1945, there were 1,603 sailors recovering at the resort. After the Navy didn't need the resort any more, Sun Valley reopened for visitors.

World War II Navy sailor

Though it is not as popular as it once was, sheep ranching is still a part of life around Ketchum. Each fall, the town hosts the Trailing of the Sheep Festival. During the festival, hundreds of sheep parade down Main Street on their way to winter pastures. An Episcopal priest stands in the middle of the street to bless the sheep as they pass by.

Trailing of the Sheep Festival in 2017

Ketchum and Sun Valley certainly display the majesty and splendor of our God and His creation.

For all the gods of the
peoples are idols,
But the Lord
made the heavens.
Splendor and majesty
are before Him,
Strength and beauty
are in His sanctuary.
Psalm 96:5-6

Activities

- Complete the map activities for Idaho in the *Atlas Workbook* (page 79).
- Read chapters 7 and 8 in *The Trumpet of the Swan*.
- If you were going to build a new attraction for tourists, what would it be? Would it be at the beach or in the mountains? In a desert or beside a river? What would people do there? If you are keeping a creative writing notebook, describe your attraction.

Family Activity: Twice-Baked Potatoes

Idaho grows more potatoes than any other state. Bake some for dinner—then bake them again!

Ingredients (6 servings):
- 4 large baking potatoes
- 1 tablespoon olive oil
- ½ teaspoon salt, plus more to taste
- 4 tablespoons unsalted butter
- ¼ cup sour cream
- 1 cup shredded cheddar cheese
- pepper to taste

Directions:
- Preheat the oven to 425°.
- Clean the potatoes. Pierce the potatoes 3-4 times each with a fork.
- Place the potatoes on a baking sheet, brush with olive oil, and sprinkle evenly with ½ teaspoon salt.
- Bake until a fork can be inserted and removed easily, 45 minutes to 1 hour.
- Remove from the oven and let cool.
- When the potatoes are cool enough to handle, cut each potato in half lengthwise.
- Scoop the inside of the potato out into a medium size bowl, leaving ⅛" of potato on the skin.
- Add the butter, sour cream, and ½ cup of cheddar cheese to the potato in the bowl. Add salt and pepper to taste.
- Using a potato masher or fork, mix together until smooth.
- Spoon the mixture back into the potato skins. Top with the remaining cheddar cheese.
- Return to the oven and bake until the cheese is melted and the potatoes are heated through, 20-25 minutes.

Be safe with knives and the hot oven. Children must have adult supervision in the kitchen.

Elk in the Rocky Mountains of Colorado

Unit 20
Rocky Mountain:
Wyoming and Colorado

343

Wyoming has a rugged landscape and harsh winters, fantastic mountains and amazing wildlife. Find Wyoming on the map at the beginning of this book.

Devil's Tower

In the northeastern corner of Wyoming, a huge stone tower rises out of the ground. Natural cracks running up and

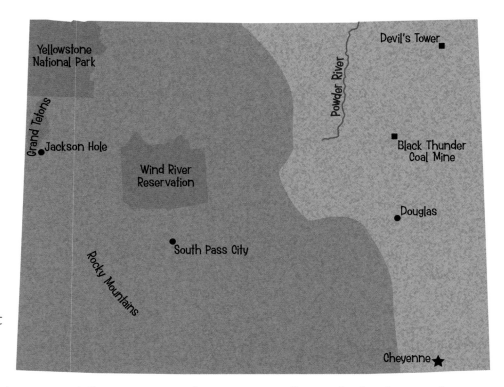

down the rock face cover the tower. The tower is a favorite spot for rock climbers, who use the cracks in the rock to help them get to the top.

The Arapahoe, Cheyenne, Crow, and Lakota people gave the tower names that mean "Bear's Teepee" and "Bear Lodge." To English speakers, the Lakota name sounded similar to the Lakota word for an evil spirit. The English speakers incorrectly began calling the tower Devil's Tower, and that name stuck. Many native people would like the name to be officially changed back to Bear Lodge.

Devil's Tower

344

Black Thunder Coal Mine

God placed an abundant amount of coal under the ground in Wyoming. The coal deposits around the **Powder River** are some of the largest in the world. Wyoming mines more coal than any other state.

At the **Black Thunder Coal Mine** in the Powder River Basin, workers can mine four tons of coal a second. They can fill a line of train cars that stretches three miles long with coal—every day. With all that coal going out, it's amazing to realize that this area still has enough coal to mine for another 200 years or more.

Jackalope

In Wyoming you might see a bighorn sheep on a high cliff, a herd of bison grazing in a valley, an elk or a moose standing in a meadow, an antelope bounding over a hillside, or . . . a jackalope!

In 1934 the Herrick brothers in **Douglas**, Wyoming, worked together as taxidermists. A taxidermist preserves animal bodies for display. One evening the Herrick brothers decided to have a little fun in their shop. They attached a pair of antlers to the body of a rabbit. The town liked their joke. So did tourists who visited Douglas. The Herricks kept on mounting and selling their "jackalopes," one after the other.

Douglas, Wyoming, became Jackalope City. An eight-foot concrete jackalope statue stands downtown. Signs beside the highway warn people to watch out for jackalopes crossing. The city issues jackalope hunting licenses (just for fun). The license allows hunters to shoot a jackalope on June 31 between midnight and 2:00 a.m. (If you check your calendar, you will see that there is no such thing as June 31.)

Jackalope

345

Capital: Cheyenne

Esther Hobart Morris statue

Inside the Wyoming State Capitol in **Cheyenne** stands a statue of Esther Hobart Morris. Esther Morris served as justice of the peace in South Pass City, Wyoming, in 1870. She was the first elected female official in the country.

Bucking bronco at Cheyenne Frontier Days

Each summer Cheyenne hosts the largest outdoor rodeo and western celebration in the world: Cheyenne Frontier Days. The event began in 1897. It was one day of pony races, steer roping, and bronco busting. The festival was a success and organizers decided to make it an annual tradition. Today around 200,000 people participate in Cheyenne Frontier Days, which lasts for ten days.

Wind River Reservation

The Northern Arapaho and the Eastern Shoshone tribes share the **Wind River Reservation** in the middle of Wyoming. These two tribes were once enemies, but in the late 1800s they set aside their differences to live peacefully together on this beautiful land. Under the reservation are valuable deposits of oil and natural gas.

Native dancer performs at Cheyenne Frontier Days

Wind River

Jackson Hole

The **Grand Tetons** are part of the **Rocky Mountains**. They tower above **Jackson Hole**, a valley in western Wyoming. Within Jackson Hole lies the National Elk Refuge, where thousands of elk come to spend the winter. Since 1910 people have been helping these majestic creatures survive the hard winters of Wyoming. With ranchers raising more and more cattle in the area, the elk were struggling to find enough to eat. That year the government of Wyoming set aside $5,000 to purchase hay to help the elk through the winter. The elk have been coming back ever since.

On the glorious splendor of Your majesty
And on Your wonderful works, I will meditate.
Psalm 145:5

National Elk Refuge

Activities

- Complete the map activities for Wyoming in the *Atlas Workbook* (page 81). (The geographic term illustration goes with the next lesson.)

- If you are using the *Lesson Review*, answer the questions for Wyoming (page 20).

- Read chapters 9 and 10 in *The Trumpet of the Swan*.

- Hands-On Idea: Combine different features of at least two animals and draw your own funny creature (like the jackalope). What is your creature called?

Lesson 78: A Song and Story of Wyoming

Git Along, Little Dogies

This cowboy song from the late 1800s talks about rounding up cattle and herding them to Wyoming. The term dogies *(DOUGH-gees) refers to calves who do not have a mother. The third verse mentions two weeds that grow in Texas and also two varieties of cactus plants the cattle ate. (Track 39)*

As I went a-walking one morning for pleasure,
I spied a cowpuncher come ridin' along;
His hat was throwed back, and his spurs were a-jinglin',
And as he approached he was singing this song.

Chorus:
Whoopee-ti-yi-yo, git along, little dogies,
It's your misfortune and none of my own;
Whoopee-ti-yi-yo, git along, little dogies,
You know that Wyoming will be your new home.

It's early in spring that we round up the dogies,
And mark 'em and brand 'em and bob off their tails;
We round up the horses, load up the chuckwagon,
And then throw them dogies out onto the trail.

Chorus

Your mother was raised away down in Texas,
Where the tall jimson weed and the sandburs grow.
We'll feed you up on prickly pear and cholla
Till you're ready for old Idaho.

Chorus

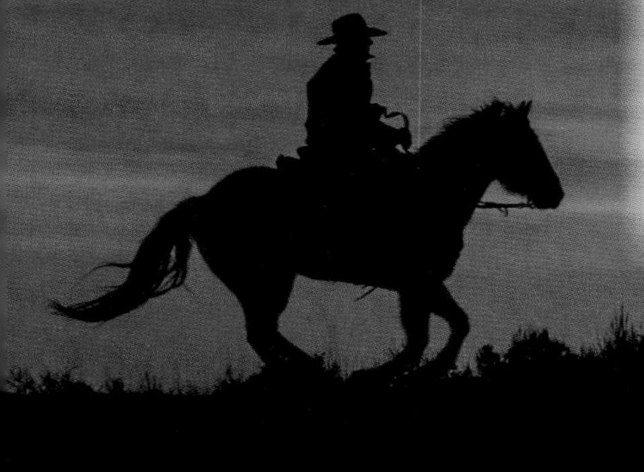

Wyoming cowboy

Marguerite's Backyard

In 1872 the United States government established our country's first national park: **Yellowstone**. The park spreads out across northwestern Wyoming and into Idaho and Montana. Yellowstone is filled with thousands of hydrothermal features. *Hydro* means water and *thermal* means heat. Hydrothermal features are places where hot water and steam come out of the earth. Hot springs under the ground in Yellowstone create pools of steaming water. Trillions of tiny living things called microorganisms live in these pools. A single microorganism is too small to see without a microscope. When trillions of them are all together, however, they turn the pools of water bright colors. Fumaroles in the park are like vents in the earth, releasing steam into the air. Several times a day Yellowstone's geysers shoot streams of hot water high into the air.

Yellowstone, the park with all these amazing features and more, was Marguerite Lindsley's backyard. Marguerite was born in Yellowstone in 1901 while her father was serving as the park superintendent. Marguerite's mother homeschooled her in their Yellowstone home until she was 14 when she attended Montana State College.

Grand Prismatic Spring in Yellowstone

During the summers while she was a college student, Marguerite worked as a part-time ranger at Yellowstone. At that time, many people thought only men should be park rangers. Marguerite was only the second female to work as a ranger. She proved that a woman could handle the work just fine.

After she graduated from college, Marguerite got a job in a science lab in Philadelphia, Pennsylvania. It was a long way from home. Her heart ached to be back in Yellowstone. Marguerite bought a motorcycle and left her job in Philadelphia. She set off on the motorcycle, bound for Yellowstone. A friend rode along in the sidecar. Neither hail nor sleet nor mud could stop these two determined women. They camped along the way. When they finally made it to Yellowstone, Marguerite was home.

In 1925 Marguerite became the first full-time female park ranger. The government did not have any park ranger uniforms for women, so Marguerite came up with her own design.

Marguerite loved Yellowstone. The park was a part of who she was. She loved to ride her horse Rex across the valleys. She loved to share stories and information about the park with visitors. Marguerite's work as a ranger included checking water gauges on the rivers, inspecting trails, watching for fires, and keeping track of animal populations in the park. The most thrilling trip she ever took was her 143-mile trip around Yellowstone, which she made one winter on skis.

Old Faithful Geyser in Yellowstone

Bison along Yellowstone's Firehole River

Marguerite was a skilled ranger, but she did have one close call. While leading a three-week tour through the park on horseback, Marguerite ended up standing in the wrong spot. Her leg suddenly sank into one of the hydrothermal features. Her leg was badly burned up to the knee, but she didn't let the accident go to waste. She used it to teach the guests on her tour about the dangers of hydrothermal features! The accident earned her the nickname Geyser Peg.

In 1928 Marguerite married another park ranger, Ben Arnold. After their marriage she resigned as a full-time park ranger, but she and her husband continued to enjoy experiencing Yellowstone together. Ben and Peg loved sharing the park with the many visitors who came to experience all the beauty God placed in this amazing corner of His creation.

Geyser Peg and Rex

Ah Lord God! Behold, You have made the heavens and the earth by Your great power and by Your outstretched arm! Nothing is too difficult for You.
Jeremiah 32:17

Activities

- Illustrate the geographic term for Wyoming in the *Atlas Workbook* (page 80).

- Read chapters 11 and 12 in *The Trumpet of the Swan*.

- If you were going to be a park ranger, where would you like to work? In Yellowstone? At a historic site? Near the ocean? If you are keeping a creative writing notebook, write about your imaginary park ranger job.

- Family Activity: Make Grand Prismatic Spring pictures (instructions on page 360).

Colorado is a wonderland for skiers and snowboarders. Millions of winter lovers visit the mountains of Colorado each year, where it tends to snow—a lot. **Wolf Creek Pass** usually receives over 400 inches of snow every winter. Bundle up and find Colorado on the map at the beginning of this book.

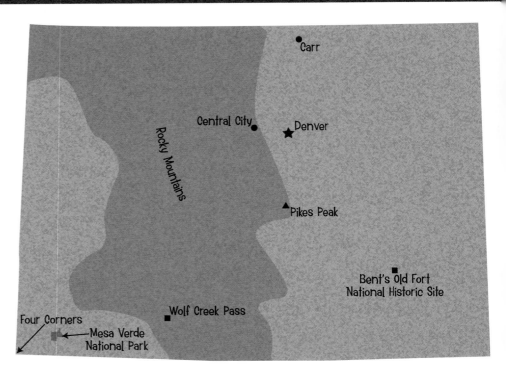

Winter in Colorado

Black-Footed Ferrets

Black-footed ferrets are the only ferrets native to the United States. When the last known black-footed ferret died in 1979, everyone thought the animal was extinct. Two years later, however, someone discovered a wild colony with 129 of these adorable creatures on a ranch in Wyoming. A sickness was quickly spreading through the colony and the ferrets were dying. A group of wildlife biologists rescued the last 18 ferrets.

Black-footed ferret

The U.S. Fish and Wildlife Service now operates the National Black-Footed Ferret Conservation Center near **Carr**, Colorado. Here the ferret population is growing. The ferrets learn how to survive in the wild in a safe environment, free from predators. Gradually the wildlife biologists are releasing black-footed ferrets back into the wild. The black-footed ferret is the most endangered mammal in North America, but it is making a comeback.

National Black-Footed Ferret Conservation Center

Denver Mint

Capital: Denver

In 1858 prospectors found gold near **Denver**. More miners came to the area, found gold, and then needed something to do with it. Traveling to and from Denver was difficult in those days, and shipping gold was expensive. A local company opened in 1860 that turned the miners' gold into coins. The United States government bought the coin operation two years later.

In 1906 the United States Mint at Denver produced 167 million pieces of gold and silver coin money. Today the mint can produce almost that many in a single week. The Denver Mint set a production record in the year 2000 when it produced 15.4 billion coins. If you see a tiny "D" on a coin, you know it came from Denver.

Coins marked with "D"

Bent's Old Fort National Historic Site

Southwestern Colorado was once a buffalo hunting ground for the Arapaho and Cheyenne people. In 1833 three fur traders built an adobe fort in the area to trade with the native people. Explorers, Hispanic traders, soldiers, and other travelers spent time at the fort as well. The fort was a good place to stock up on water, food, and other supplies. It also gave travelers a place to rest and to have their wagons repaired. The fort operated until 1849.

In 1976 workers built a reconstruction of the fort. Today reenactors at **Bent's Old Fort National Historic Site** dress in traditional costumes to demonstrate life at the fort in the 1800s.

Bent's Old Fort

Mesa Verde National Park

Hundreds of years ago, a canyon in southwest Colorado was home to Ancestral Puebloans. Spanish explorers named the area Mesa Verde, which means "Green Table" in Spanish. The name describes the fertile flat land at the top of the canyon.

Cliff Palace at Mesa Verde

The Ancestral Puebloans lived on top of the mesas and also built villages of stone in alcoves in the canyon walls. Most of their cliff dwellings had between one and five rooms, but some were larger. The largest cliff dwelling at **Mesa Verde National Park** is Cliff Palace, with over 150 rooms.

The Ancestral Puebloans created beautiful pottery and intricate baskets. They crafted tools using bones and stone. Archaeologists at Mesa Verde have found copper bells and macaw feathers. Ancestral Puebloans probably traded for these items with people from Mexico and Central America.

Four Corners

Colorado's southwestern corner meets the corners of New Mexico, Arizona, and Utah to form **Four Corners**. It is the only place in the country where four states come together at a single point. A monument stands at the site to show the boundary of each state. With each foot and each hand touching different spots on the monument, you can be in four states at the same time.

At the Four Corners Monument

Let all the earth fear the Lord;
Let all the inhabitants of the world stand in awe of Him.
Psalm 33:8

Activities

- Illustrate the geographic term for Colorado in the *Atlas Workbook* (page 82).

- If you are using the *Lesson Review*, answer the questions for Colorado (page 20).

- Read chapters 13 and 14 in *The Trumpet of the Swan*.

- Hands-On Idea: Look at some coins and see if you can find any that were made in Denver and are marked with "D."

America the Beautiful

*The **Rocky Mountains** pass through the middle of Colorado. One of the most famous mountains in this mountain range is **Pikes Peak**. Katherine Lee Bates visited Pikes Peak in 1893. She rode partway up the mountain in a horse-drawn wagon, then the rest of the way on a mule. After Miss Bates saw the view from the top of the mountain, she wrote this poem that Samuel A. Ward later set to music. (Track 40)*

O beautiful for spacious skies, for amber waves of grain,
For purple mountain majesties, above the fruited plain.
America, America, God shed His grace on thee
And crown thy good with brotherhood, from sea to shining sea.

O beautiful for Pilgrim feet, whose stern impassioned stress
A thoroughfare for freedom beat, across the wilderness.
America, America, God mend thine every flaw,
Confirm thy soul in self control, thy liberty in law.

O beautiful for heroes proved, in liberating strife
Who more than self their country loved, and mercy more than life.
America, America, may God they gold refine
Till all success be nobleness, and every gain divine.

O beautiful for patriot dream, that sees beyond the years
Thine alabaster cities gleam, undimmed by human tears.
America, America, God shed His grace on thee
And crown thy good with brotherhood, from sea to shining sea.

Pikes Peak

Angel of the Rockies

As a child, Clara Brown picked tobacco with her mother, day after day in the blistering sun. As an adult, she became one of the richest people in Colorado.

Clara was born into an enslaved family around 1800. When she was about 18 years old, she married Richard, who was also enslaved. Clara and Richard had four children. One of their daughters drowned when she was about eight. Not long after that, their master died and his slaves were sold off to pay his debts. Clara's family was torn apart. She, her husband, and all three of their children were sold in different directions.

Clara Brown

For the next 20 years, Clara served the family of George Brown in Kentucky. When George Brown died, his daughters helped their "Aunt Clara" become free. They helped her move to St. Louis where she worked as a washerwoman.

Aunt Clara (as many people called her) had a burning desire to find her family. She felt that her daughter Eliza Jane was the most likely family member still to be alive. She desperately hoped that one day she would find her.

Gold rush in Colorado

In 1859 Aunt Clara decided to head west, hoping she might find Eliza Jane. The Colorado gold rush was in full swing and Aunt Clara found a wagon train to join. On the journey, Aunt Clara cooked and did the laundry for 26 men. The journey was over 600 miles. Aunt Clara, who was around 59 years old, traveled most of it on foot.

Modern Central City

Aunt Clara settled in the mining town of **Central City**, Colorado. She continued to take in washing to earn money. Since the men spent their days mining, sometimes Aunt Clara found bits of gold in the wash water.

Even though she couldn't read or write, Aunt Clara became a good businesswoman. Sometimes a new miner arrived in the area with no tools. Aunt Clara gave him money to buy what he needed, in exchange for a portion of the money he earned through mining. She eventually saved enough money to buy land. She bought property in several different communities, including Denver.

Through the years, as black miners and pioneers came into the area, Aunt Clara asked one after another if they knew her daughter Eliza Jane. She couldn't find anyone who did.

Aunt Clara was a devoted Christian. She faithfully loved and served those around her, knowing that's what Jesus wanted her to do. She helped deliver babies and cared for the sick. She freely gave food and clothing to people in need, expecting nothing in return. If someone needed a place to stay, Aunt Clara let them stay in her home at no charge. She gave of her money generously, donating to several local churches. Before one church had a building of its own, Aunt Clara allowed them to hold services in her house. Her love and service to others earned her the affectionate title "Angel of the Rockies."

After the Civil War, Aunt Clara traveled back to the South to see if she could find her family. She didn't find her husband or any of her children, but she did find other relatives. She paid the way for family members, friends, and complete strangers to move to Colorado where she helped them establish new lives as free people.

Denver, Colorado, in 1898

When Aunt Clara was around 80 years old, most of her money was gone. She had used much of it to help others, and fires and a flood had brought destruction to her property. Still, Aunt Clara clung to her faith in God and her hope that she might one day find Eliza Jane. She published a notice in a newspaper asking if anyone could help her find her daughter.

In 1882 the help came in a letter. Someone informed Aunt Clara that a woman named Eliza Jane lived in Council Bluffs, Iowa, and was about the right age to be her daughter. As soon as she could, Aunt Clara set out on a train.

In Council Bluffs, Aunt Clara found Eliza Jane. As Aunt Clara finally wrapped her arms around her fifty-seven-year-old daughter, she wept. A local newspaper reported that at that moment the "joys and sorrows of a lifetime were forgotten, and only the present thought of."

Eliza Jane traveled back to Denver with her mother. They had three years together before Aunt Clara passed away in 1885. Many people came to Aunt Clara's funeral, including the mayor of Denver and the governor of Colorado. Today a stained glass window in the Colorado State Capitol honors the life of Clara Brown.

After Aunt Clara's death, the Colorado Pioneer Association declared, "We sincerely mourn the loss of this noble woman whose many acts of benevolence made her presence like an angel's visit."

Clara Brown stained glass window in the Colorado State Capitol

The greatest among you shall be your servant.
Whoever exalts himself shall be humbled; and whoever humbles himself shall be exalted.
Matthew 23:11-12

Activities

- Complete the map activities for Colorado in the *Atlas Workbook* (page 83).
- Read chapters 15 and 16 in *The Trumpet of the Swan*.
- The newspaper reporter who wrote about Clara and Eliza Jane Brown's reunion described a joyous occasion. Think of a joyous occasion you have seen. If you are keeping a creative writing notebook, write a description of that time.

Family Activity: Grand Prismatic Spring

Look back at the picture of the Grand Prismatic Spring on page 349. Make your own Grand Prismatic Spring on paper. Be careful as you work—food coloring stains hands and clothing!

Supplies:
- metal pan
- two small rocks
- white construction paper
- blue, green, and yellow food coloring
- spray bottle with water
- paper towels

Directions:
- Lay a piece of white construction paper on a metal pan outside in the sun. Place two small rocks in two corners to hold it in place.
- Gently squirt about 15 drops of blue food coloring spread out around the center of the paper.
- Gently squirt a ring of green drops of food coloring around the blue center.
- Gently squirt a ring of yellow drops of food coloring around the green.
- Slowly and carefully spray the food coloring dots with water. Don't spray too much. If your paper gets too wet the colors will run together too much.
- Use paper towels to dab any puddles of water. Your picture will be prettier if it dries without any puddles.
- If you still have any large white spots in your circle, you can add more squirts of food coloring and carefully spray them with water.
- Leave your picture in the sun to dry.

Arches National Park in Utah

Unit 21
Rocky Mountain:
Utah and Nevada

Jell-O, that wiggly jiggly sweet treat, is the official state snack food of Utah. On average the people of Utah eat more Jell-O than people in any other state. Find Utah on the map at the beginning of this book.

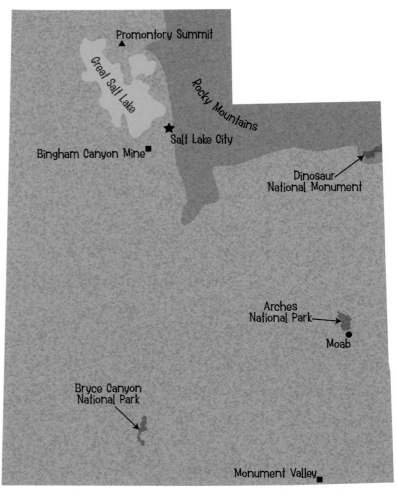

Dinosaur National Monument

In 1908 two fossil hunters found a huge dinosaur bone in the desert of eastern Utah. The bone was too large for them to move, but they hoped it meant there were more dinosaur bones nearby. The next year, one of the fossil hunters, Earl Douglass, returned to the area. After several days of digging, Mr. Douglass found just what he was looking for. He dug up one amazing bone after another. He thought he would only be digging in the desert for a few weeks. There were so many dinosaur bones, however, that his wife and son joined him and they stayed in the desert for 14 years!

In 1915 the government designated the area as **Dinosaur National Monument**. Visitors today can see approximately 1,500 dinosaur bones on display in the park's Quarry Exhibit Hall.

Dinosaur fossil at Dinosaur National Monument

Bingham Canyon Mine

Utah's **Bingham Canyon Mine** is so big, you can see it from outer space. The massive open-pit copper mine measures two-and-a-half miles wide. It operates continuously, day and night, all year long. The mine also produces other minerals, including gold and silver.

Bingham Canyon Mine

Great Salt Lake

The **Great Salt Lake** in northern Utah is one of the largest lakes in the country. Only the Great Lakes are bigger. The Great Salt Lake is important to the economy of Utah. Since the state owns the lake, companies pay the state to harvest salt out of the water. The salt from the lake is not pure enough to go in the salt shaker on your table, but people use it for other things, such as feeding animals, making fertilizer, and melting ice on roads in wintertime. Beside and beneath the lake are valuable deposits of oil.

The Great Salt Lake is so salty that not many animals can live there. Brine shrimp, brine flies, algae, and bacteria are four creatures that do live in the waters. People sell brine shrimp eggs from the lake to customers around the world for fish food. Many birds visit the marshes and wetlands around the lake, and other animals live on the shore.

One thing people who live near the Great Salt Lake have to get used to is the smell. Decaying plants and animals near the shore can cause quite a stink. Shewww-weee!

Great Salt Lake

Utah State Capitol

Capital: Salt Lake City

In 2002 Utah's capital city hosted the Winter Olympic Games. Over 2,000 athletes from around the world gathered in Salt Lake City to compete in winter sports such as skiing, figure skating, ice hockey, and snowboarding. President George W. Bush attended the elaborate opening ceremony, along with over 52,000 other people.

Golden Spike National Historic Site

On May 10, 1869, a crowd at Promontory Summit, Utah, celebrated an enormous accomplishment. Hardworking railroad employees had finished laying railroad lines that connected the East Coast and the West Coast of America. Travel across the United States would be easier than ever before.

At the Golden Spike Ceremony, the president of the Central Pacific Railroad and the vice president of the Union Pacific Railroad hammered in four special spikes made of gold and silver to "finish" the railroad. However, these spikes were only for the ceremony. A worker soon pulled them out so that four ordinary iron spikes could truly finish the line. The railroad president and vice president tried to hammer in the last iron spike, but they both missed! A regular railroad worker hammered the last spike in place and officially completed the first transcontinental railroad (a railroad that goes across a continent). You can see the spot at the Golden Spike National Historic Site.

Golden Spike Ceremony in 1869

Bryce Canyon National Park

Bryce Canyon National Park has the largest concentration of hoodoos found anywhere in the world. Do you know what a hoodoo is? The word is fun to say and hoodoos are fascinating to see. Hoodoos are irregular columns of rock and Bryce Canyon in Utah is full of them. God uses wind, water, snow, and ice to carve these rock features. The shapes of the hoodoos are still changing through erosion. Erosion is the process of something wearing away.

Hoodoos in Bryce Canyon

Monument Valley

Monument Valley sits on land in the **Navajo Reservation** of southern Utah. Sandstone rock formations tower up to 1,000 feet above the desert floor. In the 1930s a movie crew from Hollywood, California, came to Monument Valley. They used the rock features as a backdrop for a western movie. It was the first of several movies and television shows people have filmed in Monument Valley.

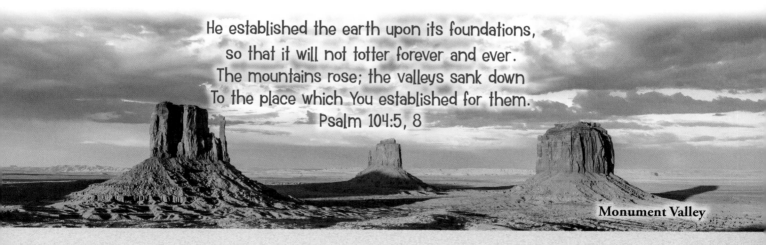

He established the earth upon its foundations,
so that it will not totter forever and ever.
The mountains rose; the valleys sank down
To the place which You established for them.
Psalm 104:5, 8

Monument Valley

Activities

- Illustrate the geographic term for Utah in the *Atlas Workbook* (page 84).
- If you are using the *Lesson Review*, answer the questions for Utah (page 21).
- Read chapters 17 and 18 in *The Trumpet of the Swan*.
- Hands-On Idea: Use play dough to make hoodoos.
- Family Activity: Make Salt Rainbows (instructions on page 378).

Lesson 82: A Song and Story of Utah

A Railroader for Me

As trains traveled back and forth across the United States, songs about the railroad did, too. This 1800s railroad song spread far and wide. (Track 41)

Chorus:
A railroader, a railroader,
A railroader for me;
If ever I marry in this wide world,
A railroader's bride I'll be.

Now I would not marry a blacksmith,
He's always in the black,
I'd rather marry an engineer
That throws the throttle back.

Chorus

I would not marry a farmer,
He's always in the dirt,
I'd rather marry an engineer
That wears a striped shirt.

Chorus:

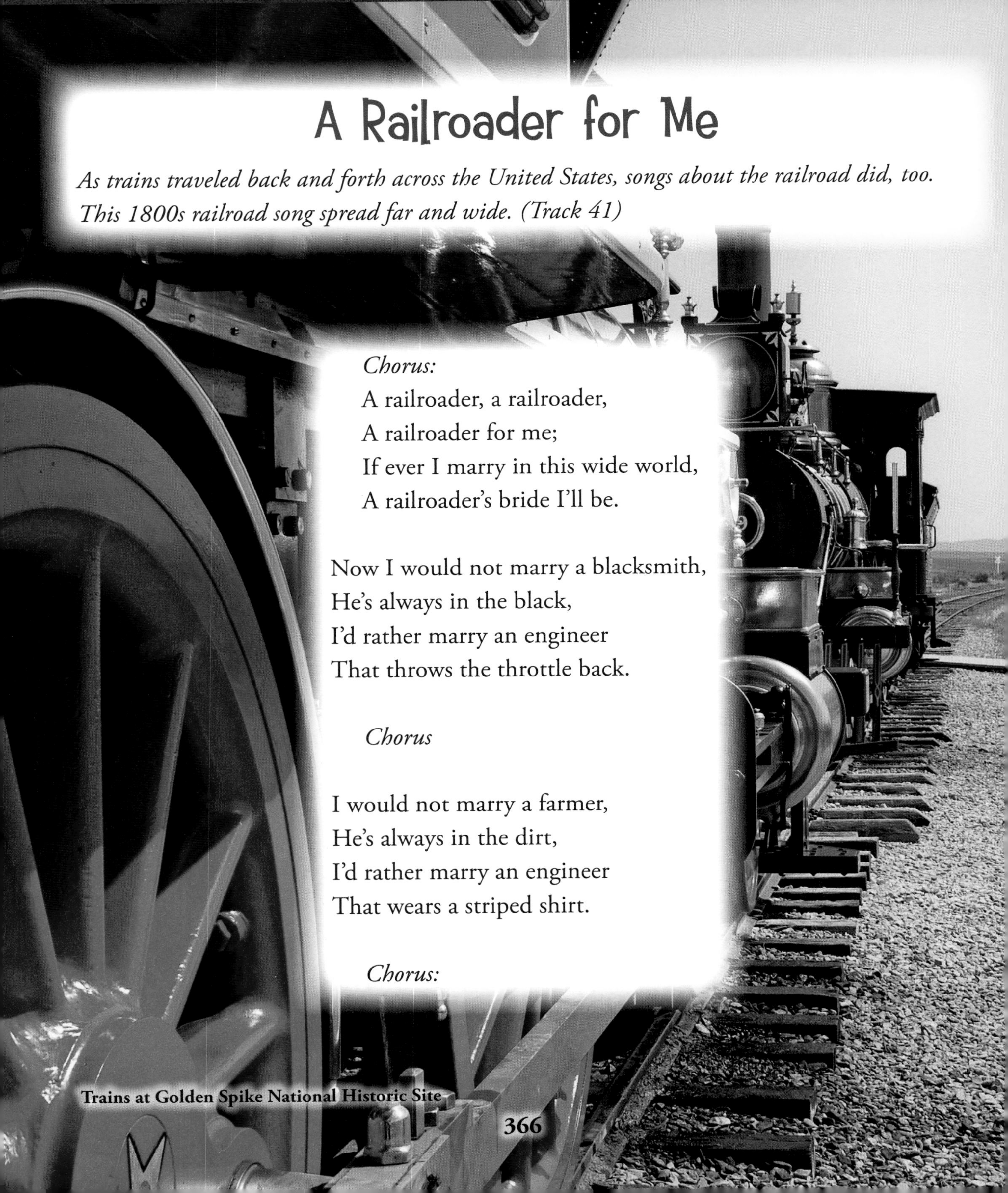

Trains at Golden Spike National Historic Site

Newspaper Men

Loren Taylor (called Bish by family and friends) had ten brothers and sisters. Their mother died in 1905 when Bish was thirteen. Bish was mostly on his own after that. He got a job transporting the mail from Moab, Utah, to other communities. Sometimes he carried the mail on a horse and sometimes he drove a stagecoach.

Buffalo Bill's Wild West Show poster from around 1899

While he was still a teenager, he began working with Buffalo Bill's Wild West Show. The show was a type of circus with a western theme that toured the country. Bish Taylor only stayed on for a week or two, when he decided he didn't want to spend his life cleaning out horse stalls. He tried working in a coal mine, but that job only lasted a day. When he was about 17, he got a job at a newspaper office.

When Bish was 18 years old, he went home to Moab for a visit. He thought the visit would be short, but a relative encouraged him to start working at a newspaper office in Moab. In no time, Bish found himself editor of the paper—at 18 years old. He became a popular figure in the community. People wanted him to run for the state legislature, but he wasn't old enough!

When he wasn't at the newspaper office, Bish Taylor loved to explore the beautiful scenery of southern Utah. He described the stone arches and other fantastic scenery in articles he wrote for his paper. His writings helped others in Moab and beyond appreciate the natural beauty around them.

Bish Taylor at work in 1914

Arches National Park

Through Bish Taylor's writings, word of the treasures in southern Utah spread. Eventually, word spread to the president of the United States. In 1929 President Herbert Hoover signed a proclamation to establish Arches National Monument (now called **Arches National Park**). The park protects land that includes over 2,000 stone arches.

Bish Taylor continued to edit and publish his newspaper in Moab for about fifty years. His paper had great influence in southern Utah. Members of the Utah State Press Association elected him to serve as the association's president. He also served Moab as town clerk and was a trustee of the local hospital, helping to make sure the hospital operated well.

Bish Taylor and his wife raised four daughters and one son. Their son Sam loved

Bish Taylor (left) at work around 1930

Sam Taylor at work in the 1990s

to explore the canyons and mountains around Moab, just like his dad. After he served in the military, Sam came home to Moab and continued to follow in his dad's footsteps through his public service and his work at the local newspaper. He worked as editor for even longer than his father had. Sam Taylor served as a state senator and in other government roles. He was also a deacon of the Community Church of Moab.

Bish and Sam Taylor had a lot in common: a drive to publish a great newspaper, a strong desire to serve their community, and great delight in the world God made.

For thus says the Lord, who created the heavens
(He is the God who formed the earth and made it, He established it and did not create it a waste place, but formed it to be inhabited), "I am the Lord, and there is none else."
Isaiah 45:18

Activities

- Complete the map activities for Utah in the *Atlas Workbook* (page 85).
- Read chapter 19 in *The Trumpet of the Swan*.
- If someone asked you to write a newspaper article, what would you write about? If you are keeping a creative writing notebook, write the article.

Lesson 83: Nevada

Nevada is the Silver State. The minerals mined in Nevada each year are worth more than the minerals mined in any other state. God put gold, silver, copper, magnesium, silica, and many other minerals under the ground here. There are over 100 mines scattered across the state. Find Nevada on the map at the beginning of this book.

Silver

Bristlecone Pine Trees

Have you ever tried to count the rings on a tree that someone has cut down? Most trees gain a ring each year, so by counting the rings people can discover the age of the tree.

Bristlecone pine trees live an amazingly long time. They grow slowly. Some years they do not even gain a ring in their trunk. These trees thrive in the harsh environment of Nevada's Great Basin.

Sheldon National Wildlife Refuge

Battle Mountain

Ruby Mountains

Lake Tahoe

Carson City

Great Basin National Park

Valley of Fire State Park

Hoover Dam

Colorado River

Bristlecone pine tree in Great Basin National Park

At the **Great Basin National Park** Visitor Center you can see a section from a bristlecone pine tree. It might take you a while, but if you stick with it you can count the rings—all 4,862 of them. Since bristlecone pines do not necessarily gain a ring each year, the tree could have grown for over 5,000 years. Sadly, a researcher cut down this ancient tree in 1964 to study its rings. How long might it have lived if he hadn't cut it down? Since 1964 people have discovered other bristlecone pines that are even older. Scientists believe that bristlecone pine trees are the oldest living trees in the world.

Ruby Mountains

Ruby Mountains

When miners found beautiful red stones in the mountains of Nevada, they called the peaks **Ruby Mountains**. It's a nice name, but the stones the miners found were actually garnets. Garnets are more common and less expensive than rubies. Still, the stones and the mountains from which they come are beautiful.

Sheldon National Wildlife Refuge

In 1931 the American pronghorn was in danger of becoming extinct. The government established the **Sheldon National Wildlife Refuge** in northern Nevada to help save them. Thousands of pronghorn now live on the refuge.

The pronghorn is the fastest land animal in North America and the second fastest in the world. Only the cheetah can outrun the pronghorn, which can speed across open fields at 60 miles per hour.

American pronghorn

Lake Tahoe

Lake Tahoe

Lake Tahoe, on the border of Nevada and California, is the largest alpine lake in the United States. An alpine lake is a lake that is at least 5,000 feet above sea level. The water of Lake Tahoe is a dazzling, sparkling blue. The lake is so clear that in some places you can see over 70 feet down into the water.

Capital: Carson City

Nevada's capital city is named after Kit Carson, a trapper, hunter, and guide who traveled throughout the West during the mid-1800s. Carson grew up speaking English, but through his travels he learned to speak Spanish, Navajo, Apache, Cheyenne, Arapaho, Paiute, Shoshone, and Ute. He helped maintain peace between the U.S. government and the Cheyenne and Arapaho people.

Kit Carson statue in Carson City

After people discovered gold and silver near **Carson City** in 1859, the community became a bustling place. Workers built a railroad to the city to transport people and goods, including the precious minerals mined nearby. During the 1870s, 36 trains came in and out of Carson City every day.

372

Valley of Fire State Park

God has carved fantastic shapes out of the sandstone in Nevada's **Valley of Fire State Park**. Minerals within the sandstone bring vivid patterns of yellow, red, purple, orange, and pink into the landscape. Bright flowers add even more color to the Valley of Fire. One of the park's highlights is Elephant Rock. It is easy to see why people call it that.

Elephant Rock

Hoover Dam

The enormous **Hoover Dam** stands in the **Colorado River** on the border between Nevada and Arizona. Workers building the dam poured the first load of concrete in 1933. They continued their backbreaking work day after day and poured the last load in 1935.

At its base, the dam is 660 feet thick. It is as tall as a 60-story building. Hoover Dam stores water that farmers use in Southern California. It generates electricity for over one million people. It provides water for several large cities and helps control flooding on the Colorado River.

As strong as Hoover Dam is, our God is so much stronger.

Hoover Dam

> The Lord is my rock and my fortress
> and my deliverer,
> My God, my rock, in whom I take refuge;
> My shield and the horn of my salvation,
> my stronghold.
> Psalm 18:2

Activities

- Illustrate the geographic term for Nevada in the *Atlas Workbook* (page 86).
- If you are using the *Lesson Review*, answer the questions for Nevada (page 21).
- Read chapter 20 in *The Trumpet of the Swan*.
- Hands-On Idea: Pretend you are a pronghorn. How fast can you run?

Lesson 84: A Song and Story of Nevada

Nevada, I Love You the Best

Karl R. Goetze wrote this song in 1914. He sang it at a banquet held for pioneers who had come to Nevada in the 1800s. (Track 42)

Way out in old Nevada, where the sagebrush grows,
Among the Rocky Mountains, where west winds blow,
You'll find contented people, of want no one knows;
It's the wonder State, the Sagebrush State of this old U.S.A.

Nevada, Nevada, you're known from east to west;
In Sagebrush State they all have faith, for you have stood the test.
Your mines are the greatest, your soil is the best;
Nevada, Nevada, I love you the best.

Sagebrush in Nevada

Pete and the Sheep

Pedro Barinaga grew up in the Basque region of Europe, between Spain and France. He was born there in 1892. Pedro's father was often away for work, so Pedro, his mother, and his siblings took care of the family farm. One day, as Pedro was mending a fence, his cousin stopped by to tell him that he planned to go to America. The cousin encouraged Pedro to do the same. The American West was full of opportunity. Many Basque were emigrating there to work in the mines and to herd sheep in the mountains. Pedro's cousin was ready for an adventure. He was sure Pedro should come along, too.

Pedro struggled. The promise of a new life in America sounded exciting, but he didn't want to leave his parents and his siblings. After pondering the question for three years, Pedro finally decided to go. He said goodbye to his family and boarded a ship bound for New York. Once there, he took a train to **Battle Mountain**, Nevada.

Pedro found a boarding house where other Basque immigrants lived. He bought new clothes and the supplies he would need to work as a sheepherder. He herded sheep for a while, then worked as a ranch-hand for several ranchers. In 1923 he married Elvira Pena, whose family was from Mexico. Pedro and Elvira had four children. Their oldest was Pete.

When Pete was a young boy, the Barinaga family moved from ranch to ranch, working for different ranchers. When he was old enough, Pete rode a horse three miles each way to go to school. When Pete was in sixth grade, his parents bought their own ranch at the foot of the Ruby Mountains.

Ruby Mountains

Pete Barinaga

Pete and his siblings grew up learning Basque, Spanish, and English. Pete went to school through eighth grade, then worked with his parents on their ranch. He also worked for some of their neighbors. When he was 18, he got a job as a sheepherder in southern Nevada.

Sheepherding in the Nevada mountains was lonely work, but Pete had a companion. He worked with John, an Italian sheepherder. Pete did most of the cooking for the pair out of their camping wagon.

One day in November, Pete was making bread when it started to snow. Pete was at their camp on one side of a mountain while John was with the sheep on the other side. By the time John got back to the wagon for dinner, the snow was piling up fast. John realized he should bring the sheep closer to camp. He went out into the snow and led them back over the mountain close to the camp wagon. Pete later recalled, "That night the wind blew and the camp wagon never stopped rocking all night."

In the morning, Pete jumped up and looked outside. "You can't see anything out there!" he called out to John. "The sheep must all be dead!" Pete and John both got dressed as quickly as they could and headed out to look for the sheep.

When they stepped outside, the snow came up to their waists. The juniper trees that grew on the mountain looked like mushrooms coming up out of the snow. Pete had little hope that the sheep could have survived such a snowstorm. Suddenly, though, he and John heard something. It was the sheep! The juniper trees, bent over with the weight of the snow, had made umbrella-like shelters. All the sheep were still alive.

Juniper tree

Through the 1960s, many Basque people continued to immigrate to Nevada and other western states to work as sheepherders. Today Americans with Basque heritage work hard to keep the traditions of their homeland alive. Basque festivals in Nevada, Idaho, and California showcase their traditional music and dances.

The Bible teaches that God will take care of His people, just as a shepherd takes care of his sheep.

Basque festival in Winnemucca, Nevada, in 2007

The Lord is my shepherd,
I shall not want.
He makes me lie down in green pastures;
He leads me beside quiet waters.
Psalm 23:1-2

Sheep

Activities

- Complete the map activities for Nevada in the *Atlas Workbook* (page 87).
- Read chapter 21 in *The Trumpet of the Swan*.
- Do you know of any other countries where some of your ancestors were born? Find those countries on a map. If you are keeping a creative writing notebook, write down the names of those countries.
- If you are using the *Lesson Review*, take the Rocky Mountain Test (page 41).

Family Activity: Salt Rainbows

Now that you have learned about Utah's Great Salt Lake, celebrate God's creation of salt with this beautiful craft. Handle yours carefully when you are finished so you don't end up with a scrambled rainbow!

Supplies:
- salt
- sidewalk chalk
- small clear bottles or jars with lids or stoppers
- paper (one sheet per chalk color)

Directions:
- Pour about 2 tablespoons of salt onto a sheet of paper. (You will need to use more if your bottle is not very small).
- Rub the salt with the side of a piece of chalk. The salt will begin to change color. Continue rubbing the salt with the chalk until you have the desired shade of color.
- Using the paper as a funnel, carefully pour the salt into your bottle or jar.
- Repeat this process with different colors and different amounts of salt until your bottle is full.
- Place the lid on tightly and keep your rainbow steady.

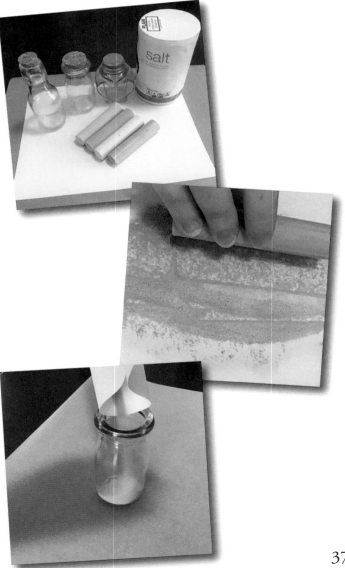

Big Bend National Park in Texas

Unit 22
Southwest:
Oklahoma and Texas

Lesson 85: Oklahoma

Great Salt Plains

Osage Reservation

Tulsa

Route 66

Clinton

Red Rock Canyon

Oklahoma City

Tuttle

Turner Falls

Oklahoma is home to more native people than any other state. In the early 1800s, at least five native nations lived in this part of the country. White settlers forced many native people from other parts of the country to move to Oklahoma. Today the population of Oklahoma includes native people from 39 different nations. Find Oklahoma on the map at the beginning of this book.

Council Oak Park

Tulsa

When the United States government forced the Lochapoka clan of the Creek tribe from their home in Alabama, the clan settled in northeast Oklahoma. The Creek held council meetings at their new home under an oak tree. Gradually the city of **Tulsa** built up in the area, but the Creek's Council Oak still stands in a Tulsa city park.

Eastern Collared Lizard

If you walk through a field in Oklahoma, you might spot an eastern collared lizard scurrying across the rocks. These lizards get their name from two bands of black on their necks that look like a collar. These lizards can run extremely fast on their hind legs. They are the state reptile of Oklahoma.

Eastern collared lizard

380

Turner Falls

Honey Creek flows through the Arbuckle Mountains in southern Oklahoma. The creek's water flows over **Turner Falls**, the highest waterfall in the state. The waterfall is named after Mazeppa Turner, a farmer from Virginia who moved to the area in 1878. He lived in a cabin on Honey Creek with his wife Laura, who was Chickasaw.

Turner Falls

Capital: Oklahoma City

On April 22, 1889, the United States government opened up land in central Oklahoma to any settlers who wanted to come and claim a piece of it. On that day, around 50,000 settlers rushed in to make their claim. Between four and six thousand of the settlers claimed lots in Oklahoma Station to establish homes and businesses there. Oklahoma Station later became **Oklahoma City**.

Oklahoma City became the state capital in 1910. Workers completed the capitol building in 1917, during World War I. Because of the war, there was not enough money to build a dome on top of the building. In 2001, 84 years later, the government of Oklahoma decided it was time for a dome. Workers finished the dome in 2002.

Oil well outside the Oklahoma State Capitol

The Oklahoma capitol is the only state capitol that has working oil wells around it. God put plenty of oil under the ground in Oklahoma. The oil wells draw the oil up out of the ground. Refineries turn the oil into products such as gasoline. Oklahoma has 77 counties. People operate oil wells in 72 them.

381

Braum's

The Braum family got into the dairy business in 1933 in Kansas. After a few years, they started producing ice cream. In 1968 the Braum family moved their dairy operation to Oklahoma.

Today the Braum's milking operation is one of the largest in the world. The company milks 800 cows every 32 minutes. Braum's has a special trolley system for the cows to ride to help them get from one part of the farm to another.

The Braum's processing facility in Tuttle, Oklahoma, is enormous. It produces 6,000 gallons and 3,600 half-gallons of milk every hour. They can also fill 3,000 cartons of ice cream an hour. Braum's makes their own milk jugs and ice cream cartons at their facility.

Sign for a Braum's Ice Cream & Dairy Store

Braum's sells their products at Braum's Ice Cream & Dairy Stores in Oklahoma, Kansas, Texas, Missouri, and Arkansas. They don't have any stores farther away than that because they want to make sure the dairy products their customers buy are fresh.

Red Rock Canyon

Red Rock Canyon

At Red Rock Canyon you can still see the ruts made by pioneer wagon wheels long ago. Thousands of people from the East traveled through Red Rock Canyon on their way to California in the mid-1800s. The canyon offered travelers fresh water and a good place for their animals to rest and graze. People still come to Red Rock Canyon to rest and enjoy the water (but these days they don't usually arrive in a covered wagon).

Route 66

Route 66 sign in Oklahoma

Clinton, Oklahoma, lies on Route 66. Construction crews completed this famous route in the 1920s. It connected Chicago, Illinois, with Los Angeles, California. The route passed all the way through Oklahoma. The Oklahoma Route 66 Museum in Clinton displays Route 66 souvenirs and helps visitors understand the importance of this road in the history of American travel.

Great Salt Plains

Oklahoma's **Great Salt Plains** are (as you might have guessed) very salty. This vast flat land is covered with a thin layer of salt that comes from salty water just below the surface of the ground. God forms selenite crystals within this wet, salty ground. Inside some of the crystals is an unusual hourglass shape made of sand and clay. No one has found any crystals like these anywhere else in the world. At Great Salt Lake Plains State Park, visitors are allowed to dig for these crystals and keep them. Some of the individual crystals are up to seven inches long. Sometimes the crystals grow in large clusters that weigh up to 38 pounds.

Selenite crystals

Worthy are You, our Lord and our God, to receive glory and honor and power;
for You created all things, and because of Your will they existed, and were created.
Revelation 4:11

Great Salt Plains

- Illustrate the geographic term for Oklahoma in the *Atlas Workbook* (page 88).

- If you are using the *Lesson Review*, answer the questions for Oklahoma (page 22).

- Read chapters 1 and 2 in *Philip of Texas*. (Parents, please refer to page 18 in the *Answer Key and Literature Guide* for comments about this book.)

- Hands-On Idea: The Creek held council meetings under a tree. Gather under a tree at your house for a family meeting or devotional.

Activities

The Boll Weevil Song

In the late 1800s, boll weevils entered the United States from Mexico. These little bugs caused enormous damage to America's cotton crop. Even though the boll weevils were terrible pests, an unknown author decided to have a little fun with the problem and write this song. (Track 43)

Now the boll weevil am a little black bug
Come from Mexico, they say.
Come all the way to Texas,
Looking for a place to stay,
Just a-looking for a home,
Just looking for a home.

Now the first time I seed the boll weevil,
He was sitting on the square.
The next time I seed the boll weevil,
He had all his family there,
Just a-looking for a home,
Just looking for a home.

Now the farmer took the boll weevil
And he throwed him on the ice.
The weevil said to the farmer,
"This sho' makes me feel nice!
Gonna be my home,
Gonna be my home."

So the farmer took the boll weevil
And he put him on the red hot sand
And the weevil said to the farmer,
"Gonna take this like a man,
It will be my home,
Gonna be my home."

Now the merchant got half the cotton
And the weevils got the rest.
It didn't leave the farmer's wife
But one old cotton dress,
And it's full of holes,
Plumb full of holes.

Well if anybody should ask you
Who it was who sang this song,
Say a guitar picker from a-Oklahoma city
With a pair of blue jeans on,
Just a-lookin' for a home,
Just a-lookin' for a home.

Oklahoma cotton field

Ballerinas in the Capitol

Elizabeth Marie and Marjorie Tall Chief shared a room on the second floor of their big house on a hill on the Osage Reservation of Oklahoma. Elizabeth Marie (whom the family called Betty Marie) was born in 1925 and Marjorie in 1926. The girls were best friends.

Alexander Joseph Tall Chief was their tall and handsome father. Alexander was a full-blooded member of the Osage tribe. He had shiny black hair and dark eyes. Betty Marie thought he looked like the native man on the heads side of a buffalo nickel. The girls' mother Ruth was a small Scots-Irish woman.

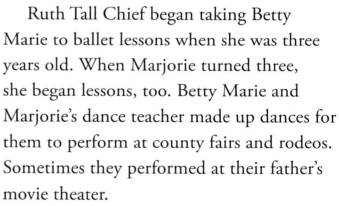

Buffalo nickel

People found oil beneath Osage ground when Alexander was a boy. The oil made the tribe wealthy. Alexander owned much property, including the local movie theater.

Ruth Tall Chief began taking Betty Marie to ballet lessons when she was three years old. When Marjorie turned three, she began lessons, too. Betty Marie and Marjorie's dance teacher made up dances for them to perform at county fairs and rodeos. Sometimes they performed at their father's movie theater.

The sisters loved to visit their Grandma Tall Chief who lived at the bottom of their hill. She wore her hair in one braid down her back and always had a tribal blanket across her shoulders. When the time came for the Osage tribe's traditional powwow, Mr. Tall Chief drove his girls and his mother to the far side of the reservation to participate.

Ballerina from the early 1900s

Traditional clothing of an Osage warrior

Betty Marie and Marjorie enjoyed seeing their people in traditional clothing. They liked the tom-tom music and the dancing. They watched the men dance in the middle of a circle of women who barely moved to the music.

When Betty Marie was eight years old, the family moved to California. Ruth enrolled the girls in an excellent ballet school. Both grew up to become famous professional ballerinas. Elizabeth Marie Tall Chief changed her name to Maria Tallchief.

While the Tall Chief sisters were taking ballet classes as children, three other native girls from Oklahoma were also learning ballet. Rosella Hightower was a Choctaw, born in 1920. Moscelyne Larkin was a Shawnee-Peoria, born in 1925. Yvonne Chouteau was a Shawnee, born in 1929. They also became famous professional ballerinas. These five ballerinas came to be called The Five Moons, or the Oklahoma Indian ballerinas, even though they never performed together.

In 1991, these five native women appeared in public together for the first time when they attended the unveiling ceremony for a mural at the Oklahoma State Capitol. Chickasaw artist Mike Larsen had painted *Flight of Spirit* to honor The Five Moons.

Flight of Spirit in the Oklahoma State Capitol

States choose works of art like *Flight of Spirit* to show what is important to the people in their state. On top of the Oklahoma State Capitol dome stands *The Guardian*. This statue of a native man stands seventeen feet tall. Enoch Kelly Haney, a Seminole-Creek man, created the statue. In addition to his work as an artist, Haney has served the people of his state as a minister, a member of the Oklahoma state legislature, and a councilman of his native Seminole Nation.

God gives each person special talents and abilities. It is up to each one of us to use those talents and abilities to honor our Maker.

The Guardian on the Oklahoma State Capitol

Maria Tallchief in 1954

Whatever you do, do your work heartily,
as for the Lord rather than for men,
knowing that from the Lord
you will receive the reward of the inheritance.
It is the Lord Christ whom you serve.
Colossians 3:23-24

Activities

- Complete the map activities for Oklahoma in the *Atlas Workbook* (page 89).
- Read chapters 3 and 4 in *Philip of Texas*.
- What is a special talent God has given someone in your family? If you are keeping a creative writing notebook, write about that person and the special talent you see in them.

Author's note: I would like to thank my mom, Charlene Notgrass, for writing "Ballerinas in the Capitol."

Texas is a big state. Only Alaska is bigger. Texas has more farms than any other state. The farms raise more cotton and more cattle than any other state. As the saying goes, "Everything is bigger in Texas." Find Texas on the map at the front of this book.

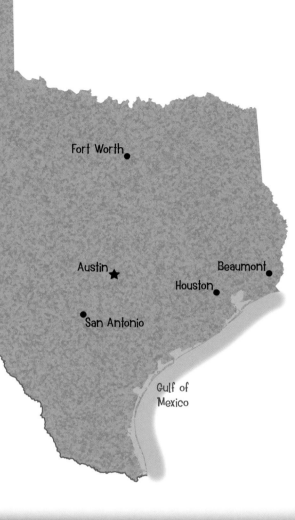

Cadillac Ranch

In 1974 three artists from California had an interesting idea. "Let's bury ten Cadillacs halfway in the ground in a field in Texas!" they said. That's just what they did. Visitors to Cadillac Ranch near Amarillo, Texas, are welcome to pick up a can of spray paint and add their own artistic touch to the cars. What color would you like to add?

Cadillac Ranch

El Paso

El Paso sits at the far western tip of Texas. Beside the city flows the Rio Grande, the river that forms the border between Texas and Mexico. Most of the people who live in El Paso or their ancestors came from Mexico or other Spanish-speaking countries. The city is full of Mexican traditions.

Mexican Folkloric Dancers perform in El Paso in 2010

Big Bend National Park

Big Bend National Park

Rio Grande is Spanish for Grand River. The Rio Grande flows south from El Paso for about 300 miles before it turns sharply to the north. The river then turns southward again and flows into the Gulf of Mexico. In the area where the river turns sharply lies **Big Bend National Park**. This rugged desert and mountain wilderness is home to an amazing variety of living things.

Some plants and animals that are common in Mexico only come as far north as this area. Other plants and animals that are common in the United States only come this far south. Big Bend has more types of birds, bats, butterflies, ants, scorpions, and cacti than any other national park in the United States.

Remember the Alamo!

The Alamo

Spain ruled Mexico for about 300 years. Mexico became an independent country in 1810. At that time, much of what is now part of the western United States belonged to Mexico. In the early 1800s, some people in Texas wanted to form their own country. They were called Texians. The Texians fought against the Mexicans in the Texas Revolution.

The most famous battle of the Texas Revolution was the Battle of the Alamo. The Alamo was a fort in **San Antonio**. The Mexican army defeated the Texians at the Alamo. When other Texians heard about the battle, it made them want to fight even harder for independence. "Remember the Alamo!" became their cry. A few weeks later, the Texians defeated the Mexicans and Texas became an independent country. The Republic of Texas lasted for nine years. In 1845 Texas became part of the United States.

Texas State Capitol

Capital: Austin

Remember how everything is bigger in Texas? Even the state capitol is bigger. The Texas State Capitol building in **Austin** is the largest state capitol in the United States.

Fort Worth Stockyards

Between 1866 and 1890, cowboys drove over four million head of cattle through **Fort Worth**, Texas. The city earned the nickname of Cowtown.

Fort Worth Stockyards

In 1887 a railroad company built a new rail line to Fort Worth. The city built a stockyard, which is a place to buy and sell livestock. Fort Worth became an even bigger Cowtown than before. In addition to cattle, ranchers bought and sold hogs, sheep, horses, and mules. During World War I, military officers came to Fort Worth to buy horses for soldiers to ride in battle.

Over time the stockyard became less popular, but people in Fort Worth wanted to keep their city's Cowtown image. Today people from all around the world come to Fort Worth to visit the Stockyards Museum. They watch cowboys drive cattle through the streets of the city twice a day, keeping an old Texas tradition alive.

Johnson Space Center

As astronauts ventured into outer space in the 1960s, the Johnson Space Center in **Houston** became our country's Mission Control Center. Workers there were responsible for communicating with astronauts while they were in space. They helped to make sure their missions were successful.

Today scientists and engineers at the center develop many things astronauts need in space, including electrical equipment, robotics, navigation tools, spacesuits, and spacewalking equipment. Astronauts at the space center train to go out and explore God's amazing universe.

Astronaut training at the Johnson Space Center

Behold, to the Lord your God belong heaven and the highest heavens,
the earth and all that is in it.
Deuteronomy 10:14

Activities

- Illustrate the geographic term for Texas in the *Atlas Workbook* (page 90).
- If you are using the *Lesson Review*, answer the questions for Texas (page 22).
- Read chapters 5 and 6 in *Philip of Texas*.
- Hands-On Idea: Make your own version of Cadillac Ranch by arranging toy cars in a pan of rice, a sandbox, the dirt, or whatever foundation your parents say is okay.
- Family Activity: Make a Prickly Pear Pillow (instructions on pages 396-398).

The Old Chisholm Trail

This classic western song tells of a cowboy's life driving cattle along the Chisholm Trail, which ran through Texas, Oklahoma, and Kansas. From 1867 until 1884, cowboys drove around five million cattle to market along the Chisholm Trail. (Track 44)

Come along boys and listen to my tale;
I'll tell you of my troubles on the old Chisholm trail.
Come-a ti yi yippy, yippy, yay, yippy yay!
Come-a ti yi yippy, yippy, yay!

I was born in Texas in the year '89,
I can ride anything this side the state line.
Come-a ti yi yippy, yippy, yay, yippy yay!
Come-a ti yi yippy, yippy, yay!

Foot in the stirrup, my seat in the saddle,
Best little cowboy that ever rode a-straddle.
Come-a ti yi yippy, yippy, yay, yippy yay!
Come-a ti yi yippy, yippy, yay!

I'm on my best horse and I am goin' on a run,
I'm the quickest-shootin' cowboy that ever pulled a gun.
Come-a ti yi yippy, yippy, yay, yippy yay!
Come-a ti yi yippy, yippy, yay!

With my blankets and my gun and a rawhide rope,
I'm a-slidin' down the trail in a long keep lope.
Come-a ti yi yippy, yippy, yay, yippy yay!
Come-a ti yi yippy, yippy, yay!

Texas longhorn

Near Beaumont, Texas

A Not-So-Crazy Idea

Pattillo Higgins was a wild young man. He only went to school through the fourth grade. He was a troublemaker who liked to play practical jokes. As a teenager, he was in a gun fight with some sheriff's deputies in his hometown of Beaumont, Texas. As a result of the fight, one man died and Pattillo lost an arm.

Even though he only had one arm, Pattillo was able to work as a logger at lumber camps along the Texas-Louisiana border. He continued his wild living until one night in 1885 when he was 21 years old. That night he attended a church revival and decided to let Jesus turn his life around. "I used to put my trust in pistols," Pattillo Higgins said. "Now my trust is in God."

Pattillo Higgins moved back to Beaumont and became a respectable real estate businessman. He also formed a company that manufactured bricks. He became part of a church and taught Sunday school classes.

Many factories in the late 1800s burned coal to provide the power they needed to run their machines. Mr. Higgins made a trip east to visit some modern factories that used oil and gas instead of coal. He liked what he saw. Producing oil and gas was becoming an important business. After he returned home to Beaumont, Mr. Higgins made plans to build an industrial city on nearby Spindletop Hill. He chose to call it Gladys City, named after one of the students in his Sunday School class. He believed there was natural oil and gas under the hill, and he wanted to find it. Many other businessmen thought he was crazy.

Pattillo Higgins

Mr. Higgins convinced two wealthy men to invest money in his project. In 1892 they formed the Gladys City Oil, Gas, and Manufacturing Company. They planned to drill deep into the ground, find oil, then build a city around Spindletop Hill. The company drilled . . . and drilled, but they didn't find what they were looking for. The hill was sandy, which made drilling difficult. Mr. Higgins still believed there was oil in the hill, he just didn't quite know how to get to it. He placed ads in magazines and newspapers, inviting geologists (scientists who study the earth) and engineers to come to Spindletop Hill and help develop the oil industry in Texas. Anthony Lucas saw one of the ads and decided to join the project.

Anthony Lucas was an engineer from Austria who now lived in America. During the 1890s he oversaw a salt mining operation on Avery Island, Louisiana (where Edmund McIllhenny invented TABASCO Sauce). Mr. Lucas joined Pattillo Higgins at Spindletop Hill. He began drilling for oil in June of 1900.

Anthony Lucas

Finally, months later, on January 10, 1901, everyone realized that maybe Pattillo Higgins wasn't so crazy after all. Mud began bubbling up from the hole were Anthony Lucas and his team were drilling. Suddenly six tons of four-inch drilling pipe shot up out of the hole. Everything went quiet until more mud, then gas, then finally oil gushed out of the ground. People called the stream of oil that shot over 100 feet into the air the Lucas Geyser. The oil flowed freely for nine days until Mr. Lucas and the other men could get it under control.

Drilling for oil

Lucas Geyser

The discovery of oil in Spindletop Hill began the Texas oil boom. It quickly changed the economy of Texas. Hundreds of companies began doing business in Beaumont. Texans began drilling for oil across the state. Cars were just beginning to become popular, and oil from Texas helped provide the gasoline needed to drive them.

In 2019 Texas produced more than 1.8 billion barrels of oil, more than any other state by far. Oil and gas production brings a great deal of money into the state. The industry provides jobs for hundreds of thousands of Texans.

Thank you, Pattillo Higgins. Your idea wasn't so crazy after all.

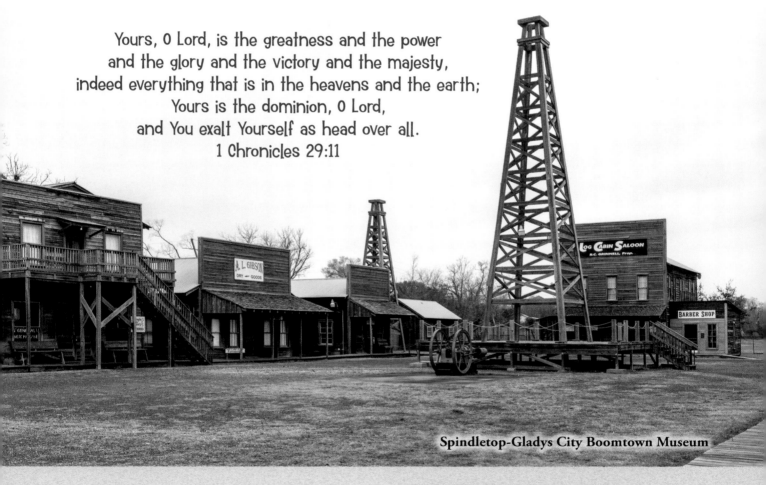

Yours, O Lord, is the greatness and the power
and the glory and the victory and the majesty,
indeed everything that is in the heavens and the earth;
Yours is the dominion, O Lord,
and You exalt Yourself as head over all.
1 Chronicles 29:11

Spindletop-Gladys City Boomtown Museum

Activities

- Complete the map activities for Texas in the *Atlas Workbook* (page 91).
- Read chapters 7 and 8 in *Philip of Texas*.
- What is something in creation you feel shows the "greatness and the power and the glory and the victory and the majesty" of God? If you are keeping a creative writing notebook, write about that part of God's creation and why you feel it is so amazing.

Family Activity: Prickly Pear Pillow

Celebrate the variety of cacti that grow in Big Bend National Park with this simple craft project. This Prickly Pear Pillow is a completely no-sew project (unless you decide to add the white yarn ties, which require just one simple stitch each). You can add red, yellow, or purple "flowers" to your pillow, just like a real prickly pear, or you can keep it plain with no flowers. It's up to you. Hopefully your pillow will be more comfortable than a real prickly pear would be.

Supplies:
- fiber fill
- green fleece (Decide on the size of pillow you would like to make and add 6" to allow for the knotted edge.)
- scissors
- ruler
- marker
- red, yellow, or light purple yarn for pompoms (optional)
- white yarn and large needle (optional)

Prickly pear cacti in Big Bend National Park

Be safe with scissors. Children must have adult supervision in the kitchen.

Directions:

- Fold the fleece so that the wrong side of the fleece is on the outside.

- Using a marker, draw the outline of a prickly pear cactus onto the fleece. Draw another outline 3" inside the first outline. The bottom of the cactus will be on the fold of the fleece (image 1).

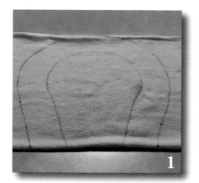

- Cut out the cactus shape along the outer line. You will be cutting through two pieces of fleece. Cut just to the inside of the outer line so that no black marks will show on the finished pillow. Do not cut across the fold on the bottom (image 2).

- Using a ruler and scissors, measure and cut small slits 1" apart all the way around the curved edge. Do not cut across the fold. Make sure you cut through both pieces of fleece (image 3).

- After you have made slits all around, go back around and continue cutting all the slits so that they reach the inner black line of the cactus shape (image 4).

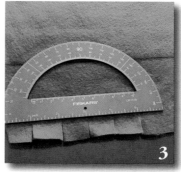

- If you would like to add white "spines" to the cactus, cut pieces of white yarn about 3" long. Use a needle to attach each spine to the front of the cactus. Make sure you do not sew through the back piece of fleece. Tie the two ends together with a double knot and trim the ends to the desired length (see image at left).

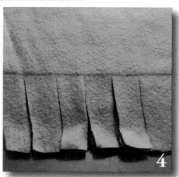

- Refold the fleece so that the right sides are facing out. You will no longer see the marker outline. The fold will still be across the bottom. Make sure to match up the slits on the front and back of the cactus (image 5).

Instructions continue on the next page.

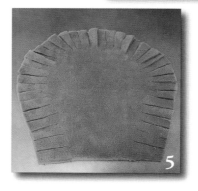

- Take hold of the lowest front and back strips on one edge of the cactus shape. Tie those strips together with a double knot. Continue tying the strips together with double knots on that side of the cactus. Tie the strips together along the other side. Leave the strips along the top untied (images 6 and 7).
- Stuff your pillow with fiber fill through the top opening. Put in one handful of fill at a time until the pillow is as fluffy as you want it to be (image 8).
- Tie the rest of the strips together with double knots around the top of the cactus.
- If you would like to add pompoms, look at the instructions for those below.

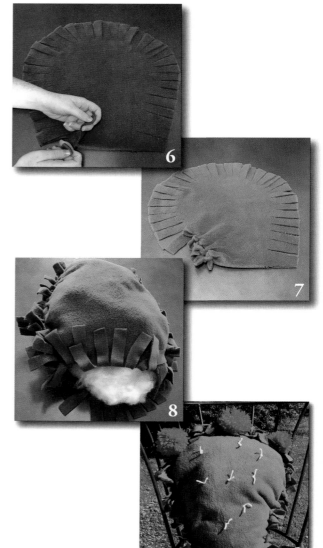

Pompom Instructions:
- If you would like to add pompom flowers, cut a piece of cardboard or fold a piece of paper to the size you would like your flower to be. This will be your pompom guide. A thicker guide that doesn't bend easily will work best.
- Wrap yarn around the paper guide approximately one hundred times for a pompom that is nice and full (image 10).
- Cut a piece of yarn twice the length of your paper guide. This piece of yarn will hold your pompom together.
- Carefully slide the wrapped yarn off the paper guide. Tie the single piece of yarn around the wrapped yarn with a tight double knot (image 11).

- Clip the ends of the yarn loops. Gently shake or fluff your pompom. You may need to shape up your pompom by trimming some of the ends.
- To attach your pompom flowers to your pillow, tie the long string that holds the pompom together under one of the knots on the top of the cactus with a double knot. Trim the ends of the yarn near the knot.

Saguaro Cacti in Arizona

Unit 23
Southwest:
New Mexico and Arizona

Lesson 89: New Mexico

Almost half of the people who live in New Mexico are Hispanic. Hispanic traditions and styles are an important part of the culture of the state. Find New Mexico on the map at the beginning of this book.

(Map labels: Shiprock, Navajo Nation, Bandelier National Monument, Santa Fe, Albuquerque, White Sands National Park, Lincoln National Forest, Hatch, Chihuahuan Desert, Chihuahuan Desert, Carlsbad Caverns)

Roadrunner

Roadrunners

New Mexico's state bird is not very good at flying, but it can run like the wind. Roadrunners can grow up to two feet long from beak to tail. They mostly eat small reptiles and rodents, but sometimes they munch on a scorpion or a rattlesnake. Watching the roadrunner speed through the desert at 20 miles an hour is quite a sight.

Carlsbad Caverns

Over one hundred caves lie below the **Chihuahuan Desert** in southern New Mexico. The most famous is **Carlsbad Caverns**. The U.S. government created Carlsbad Caverns National Monument in 1923. The first visitors entered the cave by stepping into a huge old mining bucket that workers lowered into the cave. Before long the government installed steps to make the entrance a little safer and easier.

Early visitors to Carlsbad Caverns

Brazilian free-tailed bats are popular residents of Carlsbad Caverns. Every summer, visitors love to watch as hundreds of thousands of these bats emerge from the desert caves in the evening to search for food. The bats migrate to Mexico to spend the winter in a warmer climate.

Carlsbad Caverns

White Sands National Park

Gypsum sand dunes stretch out as far as the eye can see in White Sands National Park. Gypsum is a mineral God created in the ground. White Sands has the largest gypsum dunefield in the world. The white dunes look like they are covered in snow. If you forgot to bring a sled, you can pick one up in the gift shop. They work great here!

The United States military oversees the White Sands Missile Range within the park. Every few weeks, the park closes to visitors for a few hours so the military can test missiles in the park's wide open space.

White Sands National Park

Chile Capital of the World

Spicy foods are popular in Hispanic cooking. Chile peppers add spice to salsa and many other dishes, such as soups and burritos. Hatch, New Mexico, is the Chile Capital of the World. Hatch chile pepper plants thrive in this valley. Most people in the small community have a connection with the chile pepper industry. They gather at the local airport every September to celebrate their famous crop at the Hatch Valley Chile Festival. Do you think you could win the chile pepper eating contest?

Harvesting chiles in Hatch

Albuquerque International Balloon Fiesta

Albuquerque International Balloon Fiesta

For nine days each October, colorful hot air balloons fill the skies above Albuquerque, New Mexico. Hundreds of balloon pilots and hundreds of thousands of guests from around the world gather for this International Balloon Fiesta. In the early morning, propane burners fill balloons of all shapes and colors with hot air as they prepare to launch. The climate and wind patterns common in Albuquerque make it a perfect place to enjoy a balloon ride.

Capital: Santa Fe

The Spanish established Santa Fe in 1607. *Santa Fe* means "Holy Faith" in Spanish. This community is older than the Pilgrims' settlement of Plymouth, Massachusetts. The Spanish built San Miguel Chapel around 1610. It is one of the oldest churches in the country. Santa Fe became the capital for the Spanish Kingdom of New Mexico. The area became a territory of the United States in 1848. New Mexico became a state in 1912 with Santa Fe as its capital.

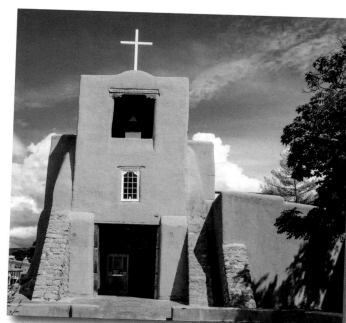
San Miguel Chapel

Between 1821 and 1880, American and Mexican traders used the Santa Fe Trail, an important trade route that ran from Santa Fe to Franklin, Missouri.

Bandelier National Monument

Hundreds of years ago, Ancestral Puebloans built homes against the stone walls of Frijoles Canyon. They carved more rooms into the soft canyon walls called cavates. Visitors to Bandelier National Monument can climb wooden ladders to explore the cavates and imagine the people who once lived in them.

Bandelier National Monument

Rock with Wings

New Mexico is home to 23 different native nations. The **Navajo Nation** lies in New Mexico, Arizona, and Utah. On Navajo land in northwest New Mexico, God has created a huge rock formation on the desert plain. The Navajo call it *Tsé Bit'a'í*, which means "Rock with Wings." According to a Navajo legend, an enormous bird carried the Navajo people to this land on its back. The bird landed in the desert and turned into this rock.

Americans later named the formation **Shiprock**. Geologists believe the rock was once part of a volcano. Six dikes (or walls of lava) stretch away from the formation, displaying the awesome power of our Creator God.

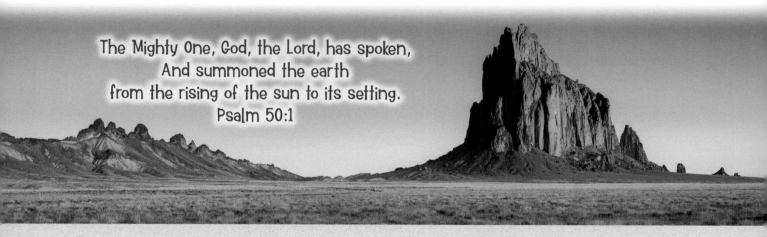

The Mighty One, God, the Lord, has spoken,
And summoned the earth
from the rising of the sun to its setting.
Psalm 50:1

Activities

- Illustrate the geographic term for New Mexico in the *Atlas Workbook* (page 92).

- If you are using the *Lesson Review*, answer the questions for New Mexico (page 23).

- Read chapters 9 and 10 in *Philip of Texas*.

- Hands-On Idea: Design a hot air balloon on paper or with play dough.

- Family Activity: Make Navajo Tacos (instructions on page 416).

Smokey Bear

A man stood at the top of a fire tower in the **Lincoln National Forest** of New Mexico, gazing out across the landscape. He often came here to check for signs of fire. As he looked out on this spring day in 1950, he spotted smoke in the distance. A wildfire was raging! He quickly called a nearby ranger station to let them know.

Crews quickly got to work to fight the blaze. Firefighters from Texas came to New Mexico to help. During the battle against the fire, about 30 firefighters found themselves caught in the path of the fire. They rushed to a nearby rockslide and lay face down for over an hour as the fire roared around them. Miraculously, they all survived.

Someone else was in trouble, too. A little bear cub, only two or three months old, wandered near the fire. He was alone, and he was scared. He scrambled up a tree as the fire continued to spread. Firefighters later found him in the charred tree. He was alive, but his paws and back legs were badly burned.

Forest fire

Ray Bell was a pilot who worked for the New Mexico Game Department. He tucked the bear in a shoebox and flew him to a vet in Santa Fe for treatment. The next day a local newspaper published a story about the bear and called him Hot Foot Teddy.

Ray Bell took the cub home with him. He and his family took care of Hot Foot Teddy for about two months. Don and Judy, the Bell children, were used to caring for the wild animals their father brought home. The family used one of Judy's bottles to feed the bear a mixture of honey, canned milk, and baby food. Hot Foot Teddy also snitched from the food bowl of the family's cocker spaniel.

Ray Bell with the rescued bear cub

A few years before the rescue of Hot Foot Teddy, the U.S. Forest Service had begun working to help Americans understand the importance of preventing forest fires. The Forest Service used the image of a cartoon bear named Smokey Bear on their posters. Hot Foot Teddy soon became known as Smokey Bear, the living mascot for the U.S. Forest Service.

News about Smokey Bear spread fast. Newspapers across the country printed his story. People wrote letters and called to check on the famous cub. After the Bell family nursed Smokey back to health, Smokey moved to Washington, D.C., where he lived at the National Zoo.

Judy Bell with Smokey Bear

405

Person in Smokey Bear costume sorting his mail

Smokey Bear continued to be the mascot for the U.S. Forest Service. He was one of the most famous animals the zoo had ever had. Thousands of children wrote letters to Smokey, assuring him they would help prevent forest fires. Some people even sent him gifts of honey. Smokey received so much mail that in 1964 the U.S. Postal Service created a new zip code just for him. The president of the United States is the only other U.S. resident who has his own personal zip code.

Smokey Bear lived at the zoo for 26 years. Even though he died in 1976, his image lives on in posters and advertisements that still remind Americans that "Only YOU can prevent forest fires."

God saw all that He had made,
and behold, it was very good. . . .
Genesis 1:31

Person in Smokey Bear costume
with children in Washington, D.C.

406

Smokey the Bear

In 1952, two years after firefighters rescued Smokey Bear, Steve Nelson and Jack Rollins wrote this song. They added "the" to the middle of Smokey's name to go with the rhythm of the song. The U.S. Forest Service wants everyone to know that the bear's real name is and always has been just plain Smokey Bear. (Track 45)

With a Ranger's hat and shovel
    and a pair of dungarees,
You will find him in the forest
    always sniffin' at the breeze.
People stop and pay attention
    when he tells 'em to beware,
'Cause everybody knows that he's the
    Fire Preventin' Bear.

Chorus:
Smokey the Bear!
Smokey the Bear!
Prowlin' and a growlin'
    and a sniffin' the air.
He can find a fire
    before it starts to flame,
That's why they call him Smokey,
    that was how he got his name.

You can take a tip from Smokey
    that there's nothin' like a tree,
Cause they're good for kids to climb on
    and they're beautiful to see.
You just have to look around you
    and you'll find it's not a joke
To see what you'd be missin' if
    they all went up in smoke.

Chorus
You can camp upon his doorstep
    and he'll make you feel at home.
You can run and hunt and ramble
    anywhere you care to roam.
He will let you take his honey
    and pretend he's not so smart,
But don't you harm his trees for he's
    a Ranger in his heart.

Chorus

If you've ever seen a forest
    when a fire is running wild
And you love the things within it
    like a mother loves her child,
Then you know why Smokey tells you
    when he sees you passing through,
"Remember . . . please be careful . . .
    it's the least that you can do!"

Chorus

Words and Music by STEVE NELSON and JACK ROLLINS
Copyright © 1952 (Renewed) CHAPPELL & CO., INC.
All Rights Reserved
Used By Permission of ALFRED MUSIC

Site of Smokey Bear's rescue in New Mexico

Activities

- Complete the map activities for New Mexico in the *Atlas Workbook* (page 93).
- Read chapters 11 and 12 in *Philip of Texas*.
- What do you think would be fun about being in a Smokey Bear costume at an event? If you are keeping a creative writing notebook, write about your thoughts.

Lesson 90: Arizona

Over fifty different kinds of cacti grow in Arizona. The largest is the saguaro, which can grow over 40 feet tall. A saguaro cactus (pictured on page 399) might be fifty years old before it grows its first arm. This plant has become a classic symbol of the American West. Find Arizona on the map at the beginning of this book.

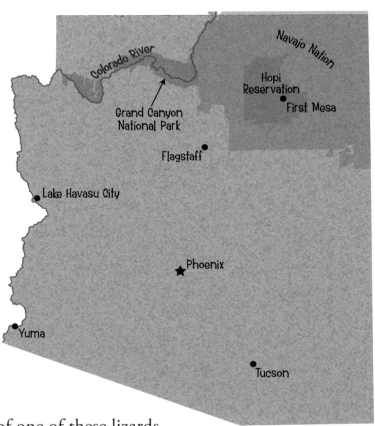

Gila Monsters

Gila monsters (pronounced HE-lah) live in deserts of the southwestern United States and northern Mexico. Catching a glimpse of one of these lizards can be hard since they spend almost all of their time in their homes underground. They can survive on as little as three meals a year.

Gila monsters are venomous, like poisonous snakes. When they bite, it hurts! These creatures can grow up to two feet long, which makes them the largest lizard native to the United States.

Gila monster and saguaro cacti in the Arizona desert

Flagstaff

Arizona's dry air, good weather, and large areas without any big city lights make it a stargazer's wonderland. Around thirty massive telescopes in Arizona open up the sky to those who want to see outer space up close.

Inside Lowell Observatory

Even in downtown **Flagstaff**, a city with around 70,000 people, the nighttime sky is gorgeous. Flagstaff has laws that limit the amount of light allowed to shine in the city at night. In 2001 the International Dark-Sky Association declared Flagstaff the first International Dark-Sky City. Residents and visitors love to gaze up and see the Milky Way galaxy stretching across the sky.

Flagstaff is home to the Lowell Observatory. An observatory is a place where people observe things God created. Lowell is an astronomical observatory where astronomers observe outer space. In 1930 an astronomer working at Lowell discovered Pluto.

Boneyard

You have probably seen a junkyard where piles of old cars and trucks and buses rust out in the weather. Have you ever wondered what happens to old planes? Some of them end up in boneyards.

At the Davis-Monthan Air Force Base aircraft boneyard in **Tucson**, row after row of retired military planes sit in the desert sun. The government chose this spot because the dry air helps preserve the aircraft. The hard earth can support the planes without needing any concrete runways.

Each year the military uses thousands of parts from the planes in the boneyard to repair other planes that are in use. This saves the military millions of dollars.

Aircraft boneyard in Tuscon

409

Winged Victory

Capital: Phoenix

The statue called *Winged Victory* stands on top of the Arizona State Capitol in **Phoenix**. The statue is actually a giant seventeen-foot-tall weather vane that turns depending on how the wind is blowing.

In the early 1900s, wild cowboys used to entertain themselves by trying to make the statue spin—by shooting her wing with bullets! These days cowboys find other ways to amuse themselves, and *Winged Victory* only turns when the wind changes.

Sunshine in Yuma

Yuma, Arizona, holds the record for the sunniest city in the world. The sun shines there 90% of the time, year round.

Every season is growing season for the fields and gardens in Yuma. The **Colorado River** provides water for the crops. During the winter, almost all of the U.S. lettuce crop grows in Yuma.

Harvesting lettuce in Yuma

London Bridge

London Bridge used to be falling down, falling down. Now it's standing firm in an Arizona desert. How on earth did that happen?

In 1967 the city of London, England, needed to replace a bridge in their city. They needed a new bridge that was larger and stronger.

The city government of London looked for someone who might be interested in buying the old bridge. Robert P. McCulloch Sr. offered to pay the most money for the bridge, so London sold it to him. Mr. McCulloch paid workers to move the bridge, piece by piece, from England to Arizona. He thought it would attract people to his new town in the desert.

Workers in London numbered each block of stone before they took the bridge apart. They shipped all the blocks across the Atlantic Ocean, through the Panama Canal in Central America, then up to California. From there the blocks traveled through the desert on trucks to **Lake Havasu City**. Workers reassembled the bridge, and it opened to the public in 1971.

Robert McCulloch was right. The bridge did encourage people to come to his town. London Bridge is now the second most popular tourist site in all of Arizona.

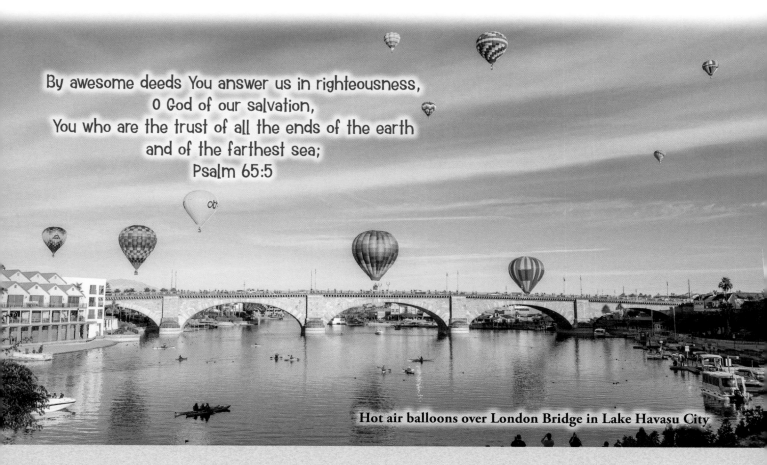

By awesome deeds You answer us in righteousness,
O God of our salvation,
You who are the trust of all the ends of the earth
and of the farthest sea;
Psalm 65:5

Hot air balloons over London Bridge in Lake Havasu City

Activities

- Illustrate the geographic term for Arizona in the *Atlas Workbook* (page 94).

- If you are using the *Lesson Review*, answer the questions for Arizona (page 23).

- Read chapters 13 and 14 in *Philip of Texas*.

- Hands-On Idea: If the sky is clear tonight, go out and look at the stars.

Cowboys' Gettin'-Up Holler

Cowboys on the trail had to wake up early. The cook had to wake up even earlier to get breakfast ready for all the hungry men. Once the coffee was ready and the hoecakes were done, the cook might wake up the cowboy crew with a "holler" like this. (A hoecake is similar to a pancake, but it is made with cornmeal instead of flour.) (Track 46)

Wake up, Jacob, day's a-breakin';
Fryin' pan's on an' hoecake bakin'.

Bacon in the pan, coffee in the pot;
Git up now and git it while it's hot.

Early in the morning, almost day,
Better come soon, gonna throw it all away.

Wake up, Jacob, day's a-breakin';
Fryin' pan's on an' hoecake bakin'.

Cowboys eating tomatoes around 1907

Nampeyo

First Mesa. Second Mesa. Third Mesa. For hundreds of years, three mesas in northeastern Arizona have been home to the peaceful Hopi people. A mesa is a flat-topped hill. The sides of a mesa are steep. On these mesas one generation

First Mesa in 1932

of the Hopi has shown the next how to weave baskets and create pottery. Older family members have taught the younger how to tend livestock and raise crops in the desert.

Cradleboard

In a village on **First Mesa** around the year 1860, a baby girl was born. According to custom, when the child arrived, the room was dark. Rabbit skins hung over the window and doorway to block the light. The baby's grandmother took care of the mother and baby in the dark room for 19 days. Then, early in the morning of the twentieth day, women from the village gathered to present their gifts to the mother and child. At sunrise the mother strapped the baby to a cradleboard and took the child outside for her first glimpse of the sun. The baby's grandmother gave her the name Nampeyo, which means "Snake Girl" or "Harmless Snake."

Nampeyo's mother and grandmother were skilled potters. Nampeyo watched them dig clay out of the ground. She learned to remove impurities from the clay. Nampeyo spent many hours watching, learning, and practicing until she became a skillful potter herself.

Nampeyo and her brother in 1875

In 1875, when Nampeyo was around 15, a newspaper reporter and a photographer from New York visited First Mesa. They noted Nampeyo's almond-shaped black eyes and her hair, done in the traditional Hopi style. The reporter wrote that her hair "was parted in the center, from the front all the way down behind, and put up at the sides in two large puffs, which, although odd to us, nevertheless seemed to enhance her beauty."

413

Grand Canyon

In the late 1800s, businessmen opened trading posts near the mesas where Hopi people could sell their traditional crafts. Nampeyo had perfected her process for preparing clay and making pottery. Her pieces were strong and beautiful and became popular. Many people traveling through the West wanted to own a piece of Nampeyo's pottery for themselves.

In 1901 the Santa Fe Railway established a new train route to take tourists to the Grand Canyon. The Grand Canyon stretches for 277 miles across northwestern Arizona. The Colorado River flows through the towering, multicolored canyon walls.

The Santa Fe Railway decided to build a shop at the Grand Canyon where visitors could purchase traditional tribal crafts. An architect designed the shop to look like a traditional Hopi home. The company invited native artists to live at Hopi House so visitors could watch them work.

Hopi House

Nampeyo was the first artist to live at Hopi House. She came in 1905 with her husband, two of their children, and other members of their family. They stayed for three months before returning home to First Mesa in time for the spring planting of corn. Nampeyo spent another three months at Hopi House in 1907.

Nampeyo and her family at Hopi House

414

In 1910 the Santa Fe Railway invited Nampeyo to travel to Chicago to demonstrate her pottery-making skills at a large event. An article in a Chicago newspaper described Nampeyo as "the greatest maker of Indian pottery alive." Nampeyo's husband traveled with her to Chicago, where he demonstrated traditional Hopi dancing. After the trip, Nampeyo and her husband returned home to the Hopi Reservation, which is surrounded by the Navajo Nation, in northeastern Arizona.

Nampeyo once said, "When I first began to paint, I used to go to the ancient village and pick up pieces of pottery and copy the designs. That is how I learned to paint. But now I just close my eyes and see designs and I paint them."

As Nampeyo grew older, her eyesight began to fail. She continued to create pottery, but was no longer able to paint the designs. She had taught her daughters well, however, and they carried on the family tradition. Today pieces of Nampeyo's pottery are on display in museums and in private collections around the world.

Nampeyo pottery

Just as Nampeyo molded clay into the shape she wanted it to be, so our Father in heaven molds each of us.

But now, O Lord, You are our Father,
We are the clay, and You our potter;
And all of us
are the work of Your hand.
Isaiah 64:8

Nampeyo

Activities

- Complete the map activities for Arizona in the *Atlas Workbook* (page 95).
- Read chapters 15 and 16 in *Philip of Texas*.
- What is a special bowl, platter, dish, or vase at your house? What is it made of? Where did it come from? What makes it special? If you are keeping a creative writing notebook, write a description of the item and why it is special.
- If you are using the *Lesson Review*, take the Southwest Test (page 43).

Family Activity: Navajo Tacos

Fry bread is popular among many native nations. Different regions and tribes have their own special recipes and cooking methods. Try your hand at this recipe. Add some toppings and turn your fry bread into Navajo tacos.

Fry Bread Ingredients:
- 3 cups all purpose flour
- ½ teaspoon salt
- 3 teaspoons baking powder, slightly rounded
- ¾ cups milk
- ¼ - ½ cup water
- vegetable shortening for frying

Topping Options:
- refried beans
- seasoned taco meat
- lettuce
- tomatoes
- black olives
- cheese
- sour cream
- salsa

Fry Bread Directions:
- In a medium bowl, stir together the flour, baking powder, and salt.
- Add the milk to the flour mixture and stir together with a fork.
- Add the water. Start by adding ¼ cup and then add more as needed to get the dough to come together. Don't overwork the dough.
- Cover the bowl with a light towel and let the dough rest for 45 minutes. (While your dough is resting, you can prepare your taco toppings.)
- Heat 1-2 inches of vegetable shortening in a large skillet over medium-high heat.
- Place the dough on a piece of parchment paper on the counter. Divide it evenly into 10 pieces.
- Using your fingertips, shape each piece into a circle. Do not overwork.
- Place as many circles as will easily fit into the hot oil. Be careful of splattering oil! Do not overcrowd the skillet.
- Fry on the first side until golden brown, about 1 minute.
- Using tongs, carefully turn over each circle and fry the second side until golden, about 45 seconds.
- Remove from the skillet to a dish covered with a paper towel to drain.
- While still warm, pile on your favorite taco toppings and enjoy.

Be safe with knives and the hot oil and stove. Children must have adult supervision in the kitchen.

Cannon Beach in Oregon

Unit 24
Pacific:
California and Oregon

417

Avenue of the Giants

Sacramento ★

San Francisco ●

Stanford ●

Central Valley

Yosemite National Park

▲ Half Dome

Death Valley National Park

Selma ●

Pacific Ocean

Sequoia and Kings Canyon National Park

During the spring and early summer, fields, hillsides, and gardens across California light up with the bright orange blooms of the California poppy. The native people of California once mixed the oil from poppy seeds with bear fat and used it on their hair. The California poppy is the state's official flower. Find California on the map at the beginning of this book.

California poppy

Death Valley

Death Valley sounds like a pretty miserable place. While it is one of the driest and hottest places in the world, God has created special plants and animals that can survive here and bring this desert to life. As the jackrabbit bounds across the desert floor, its large ears help it to stay cool. The desert's bighorn sheep can survive for several days without water. Kangaroo rats can survive their whole lives without drinking a drop of water.

Every once in a while, God paints a wildflower masterpiece in **Death Valley National Park** with a super bloom. Super blooms are rare, but when they happen every ten or fifteen years, the desert floor bursts into brilliant color. The flower seeds are always there, but it takes the right amount of rainfall at the right time for enough of the seeds to sprout and bring on a super bloom.

Death Valley super bloom

418

Sequoia Trees

General Sherman

God grows enormous trees in California. The General Sherman tree in **Sequoia and Kings Canyon National Park** is the largest known tree in the world. Giant sequoia trees can live for thousands of years because God made their bark resistant to rot, insects, and fire. Some of California's giant sequoia trees started growing before Jesus was born.

Central Valley

California grows more food than any other state. Farmers in the **Central Valley** raise more than 250 different crops that bring in around $17 billion each year.

About 2,000 growers around **Selma**, California, produce nearly 100% of the raisins sold in America. The growers let their grapes dry in the sun, either on the vine or on paper trays on the ground. California raisins travel to every state and to about 50 foreign countries.

Grapes growing in the Central Valley

Yosemite National Park

When the sun sets over **Yosemite National Park**, the granite mountains appear to be on fire. The rock formations light up with glowing red and orange light. The 14-mile hike up Half Dome is so popular that people enter a drawing for a chance to hike it. Only people whose names are drawn get to go up.

Sunset in Yosemite

Buffalo Soldiers in Yosemite in 1899

The first park rangers at Yosemite were Buffalo Soldiers. The Army sent these African American men to the West after the Civil War. Buffalo Soldiers built roads and trails. They worked to keep farmers from illegally grazing their animals on land the government owned. They also helped stop hunters from illegally killing the wildlife in Yosemite. Buffalo Soldiers helped Yosemite become the treasure it is today.

Silicon Valley

For many years, Stanford University in Stanford, California, has been a leader in science, engineering, and technology. Graduates of the school have started many successful tech companies in the area, which people once called Valley of Heart's Delight.

In the 1960s, this valley became the center for developing computers. Silicon is an element found in sand. People use it to make silicon chips. Computers use silicon chips to send, receive, and process information. Silicon chips are in many

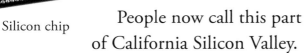
Silicon chip

items your family uses every day, including computers, tablets, smartphones, and automobiles.

People now call this part of California Silicon Valley. Silicon Valley is home to many of the world's largest technology companies, including Apple, Facebook, Google, and Netflix.

Apple campus in Silicon Valley

Capital: Sacramento

The gold ball on top of California's capitol dome in **Sacramento** represents a gold nugget. It stands as a symbol of the California Gold Rush that began in 1849. At that time, thousands of people rushed to California hoping to find gold and become rich.

California capitol dome

An 800-pound bronze statue of a bear stands inside the capitol, just outside the governor's office. Governor Arnold Schwarzenegger bought the statue in 2009. News reporters at the capitol soon nicknamed the bear "Mic" because it made a great place to set up microphones to interview the governor when he came out of his office. Highway Patrol officers named the statue "Bacteria Bear" because so many people rub their hands all over him.

Highway Patrol officer with "Mic" (or "Bacteria Bear")

Avenue of the Giants

In the early 1900s, logging companies came to northern California to cut down redwood trees. They wanted to use the lumber to make stakes for grapevines and shingles for houses. A group of people formed the Save the Redwoods League to stop the logging. They felt that logging the redwoods was like "chopping up a grandfather clock for kindling." Thanks to their efforts, people can drive down **Avenue of the Giants** and see many redwood trees still standing tall—very tall. The tallest redwood tree is over 379 feet tall.

Let the field exult,
and all that is in it.
Then all the trees of the
forest will sing for joy
Psalm 96:12

Avenue of the Giants

Activities

- Illustrate the geographic term for California in the *Atlas Workbook* (page 96).

- If you are using the *Lesson Review*, answer the questions for California (page 24).

- Read chapters I and II in *The Adventures of Paddy the Beaver*. (Parents, please refer to page 19 in the *Answer Key and Literature Guide* for comments about this book.)

- Hands-On Idea: Look at food items in your kitchen to see where they were grown.

Lesson 94: A Song and Story of California

Banks of the Sacramento

This song celebrates the days of the California Gold Rush, which began in 1849. Many hopeful gold miners traveled to California, some by land and others by sea. This song tells of miners who arrived by ship. (Track 47)

A bully ship and a bully crew,
Hoo-da! Hoo-da!
A bully mate and a captain, too,
Hoo-da! Hoo-da-day!

Chorus:
Blow, boys, blow,
For Californ-i-o!
There's plenty of gold, so I've been told,
On the banks of the Sacramento!

Oh, heave, my lads, oh heave and sing,
Hoo-da! Hoo-da!
Oh, heave and make those oak sticks sing.
Hoo-da! Hoo-da-day!

Chorus

It was in the year eighteen forty-nine,
Hoo-da! Hoo-da!
It was in the year eighteen forty-nine.
Hoo-da! Hoo-da-day!

Chorus

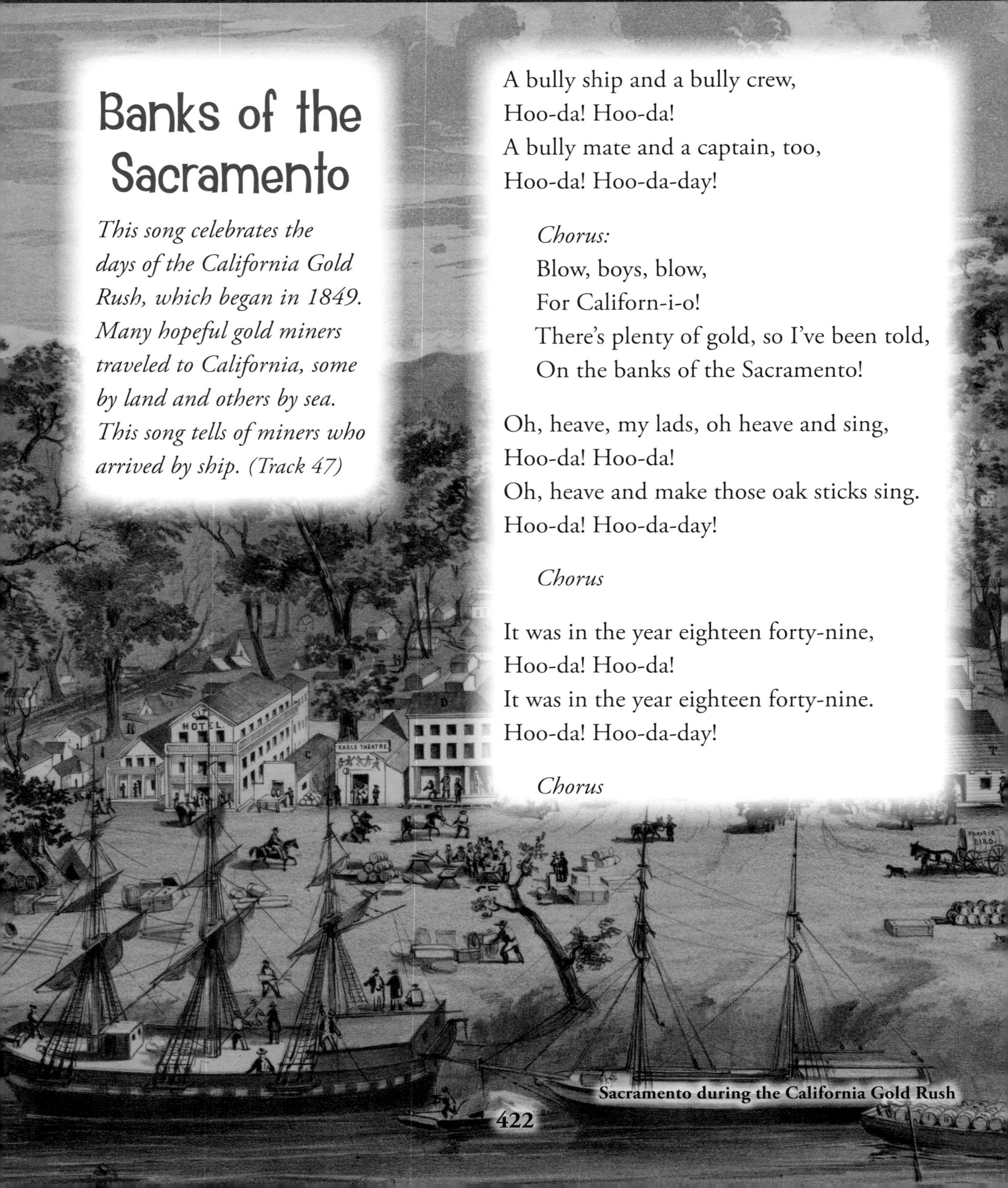

Sacramento during the California Gold Rush

Golden Gate Bridge in San Francisco

Cable Cars and Kindness

People in San Francisco have to keep their brakes working well. They have to be careful how they park. They have to make sure their groceries don't fall out of their cars as they unload them. If they aren't careful they might have to chase a cantaloupe a long way down the sidewalk.

The hills of San Francisco are steep. Don't you feel sorry for the mail carriers who have to walk them every day? Some streets have concrete steps instead of plain sidewalks to make getting up and down safer and easier.

San Francisco in 1866

Modern San Francisco

Since San Francisco's early days, the hills have made it hard to get around. In 1869 Andrew Hallidie watched a team of horses struggle to pull a heavy load up one of San Francisco's hills. The horses stumbled and fell. Mr. Hallidie watched in horror as the horses slid down the hill and died. It was a terrible accident. Mr. Hallidie decided he must figure out a better way for people to travel around his city.

Andrew Hallidie had come to America from England. He was born in London in 1836. His father was an engineer who developed cables made of wire and steel for cable railways. Young Andrew shared his father's love for inventing. When he was ten, he built a working electrical machine. At age 13 he began working in his brother's machine shop.

As a teenager, Andrew began to struggle with his health. When he was 15, his father decided to take him to California, hoping the change would improve his son's health. Andrew and his father set off in January of 1852. They traveled with hundreds of others who were also bound for California, hoping to get rich mining gold.

Andrew's father stayed with him in California for a time, but returned to England in 1853. Andrew, still a teenager, was on his own as he mined for gold in the California hills. Andrew wrote that he earned, "just enough to starve on, with beans, pork, and coffee, and pork, coffee, and beans for a change." During his mining years he survived one disaster after another. Once he was caught in the middle of a forest fire. Once he fell 25 feet from a suspension bridge. Another time he had a close call during an explosion in a mining tunnel.

Mining in California in 1866

At one of the mines where Andrew worked, miners used cars attached to a rope to transport rock down a hill. A rope pulled the empty cars back up. The rope wore out after only 75 days. Andrew suggested using a wire rope instead. The mine owners liked his idea. Andrew ordered supplies from San Francisco. He crafted a sturdy wire rope which lasted about ten times longer than the original one had.

Andrew Hallidie eventually gave up mining. He moved to San Francisco and started a business making and selling wire rope. Mr. Hallidie became famous for building suspension bridges that used his wire rope. In 1865 Mr. Hallidie decided to give up bridge building and focus on his wire rope business so that he could stay in San Francisco.

Andrew Hallidie

After watching the terrible horse accident in 1869, Mr. Hallidie invented a cable car system. Hidden wire cables inside cable car tracks pulled cable cars up and down the steep hills of San Francisco. The cables ran to powerhouses, where steam engines kept the cables turning and the cable cars moving. San Francisco's first cable car line opened in 1873. Mr. Hallidie's invention quickly spread to other big cities.

By 1906 over 600 cable cars ran through San Francisco. The city doesn't need cable cars as much today as it did in 1873, but San Francisco keeps the cable cars going anyway. They are an important part of the city's culture and are popular with tourists. On average between 15,000 and 20,000 people ride a San Francisco cable car every day.

Andrew Hallidie loved California. He gave much of his time to make his community a better place. He was a man of integrity, and his community respected and appreciated him. At his funeral in 1900, a minister said that Andrew Hallidie's kindness had fallen like gentle showers upon the thirsty earth.

He has told you, O man, what is good; and what does the Lord require of you but to do justice, to love kindness, and to walk humbly with your God?
Micah 6:8

Cable car in San Francisco

Activities

- Complete the map activities for California in the *Atlas Workbook* (page 97).
- Read chapters III and IV in *The Adventures of Paddy the Beaver*.
- How can you make kindness fall like gentle showers upon the thirsty earth? If you are keeping a creative writing notebook, write down some of your ideas.

Lesson 95: Oregon

Oregon is the Beaver State. The furry critter with the big paddle tail is featured on the back of the Oregon state flag. Oregon is the only state that has different images on the front and back of its flag. Find Oregon on the map at the beginning of this book.

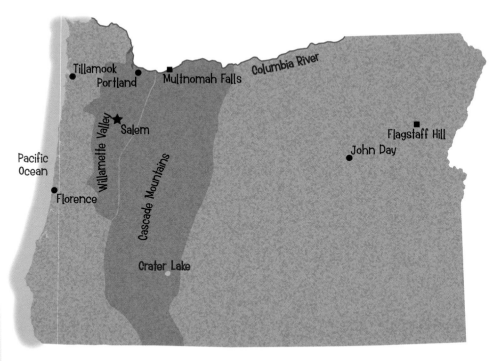

Beaver

Christmas Trees

Hundreds of Christmas tree farmers in Oregon plant and harvest millions of Christmas trees every year. Oregon grows more Christmas trees than any other state.

Christmas tree farm in Oregon

Crater Lake

Crater Lake

Many years ago, a volcano erupted in Oregon's **Cascade Mountains**. The volcano then collapsed, which created a caldera. A *caldera* is a bowl-shaped volcanic depression. As rain and snow fell on the caldera, it filled up and became **Crater Lake**. Crater Lake is the deepest lake in the United States and one of the clearest in the world.

Sea Lion Caves

The largest sea cave in the United States lies on Oregon's rocky coast near the city of **Florence**. A large sea lion colony spends the fall and winter inside the enormous cavern. The sea lions hunt for food outside the cave in the waters of the Pacific Ocean. During the spring and summer the mothers give birth to their young on the rocky ledges outside the cave.

Sea Lion Caves

427

Capital: Salem

The name of Oregon's capital city comes from *shalom*, the Hebrew word for "peace." Outside the Oregon state capitol in **Salem** stands a statue of a circuit rider minister on a horse. The words on the base of the statue read:

COMMEMORATING THE LABORS AND ACHIEVEMENTS OF THE MINISTERS OF THE GOSPEL WHO AS CIRCUIT RIDERS BECAME THE FRIENDS COUNSELORS AND EVANGELS TO THE PIONEERS ON EVERY AMERICAN FRONTIER

Circuit rider statue in Salem

Tillamook

Joseph Champion came to what is now Tillamook County in 1851. He lived in a hollow spruce tree, which he called his "castle." Neighbors were few and far between at first, but gradually the valleys around his "castle" filled up.

The settlers established the community of **Tillamook**. After they established their farms, the settlers needed a way to take their farm products to market. In 1854 they worked together to build the *Morning Star*. They frequently sailed this ship, loaded with fish, vegetables, and cheese, out of the Tillamook Bay, into the **Pacific Ocean**, then to the mouth of the **Columbia River**. They sailed up the Columbia River to **Portland**, where they sold their goods.

Tillamook County became famous for its delicious cheese. The settlers of Tillamook County operated several creameries in the area. In 1909 they joined together to create the Tillamook County Creamery Association. Grocery stores around the country now sell Tillamook cheese, ice cream, and other dairy products. A reproduction of the *Morning Star* stands outside the Tillamook Cheese factory.

Tillamook Cheese factory

Multnomah Falls

The mountains of Oregon are full of waterfalls. Multnomah Falls, which is fed by underground springs, is the tallest. The upper falls is 542 feet tall, while the lower falls is 69 feet. In the springtime, melting snow makes the roar of the falls even louder. From the trail at the top of the falls, hikers look out over the majestic Columbia River Gorge.

Oregon Trail

During the 1800s, thousands of pioneers from the East traveled in covered wagons to the West. Many followed the Oregon Trail, which led them through prairies, over mountains, across deserts, and finally to Oregon's lush Willamette Valley. When weary travelers finally reached Flagstaff Hill, they knew their journey was almost over. Today the National Historic Oregon Trail Interpretive Center stands on top of Flagstaff Hill.

[The Lord] sends forth
springs in the valleys;
They flow between
the mountains.
Psalm 104:10

Flagstaff Hill

Multnomah Falls

Activities

- Illustrate the geographic term for Oregon in the *Atlas Workbook* (page 98).

- If you are using the *Lesson Review,* answer the questions for Oregon (page 24).

- Read chapters V and VI in *The Adventures of Paddy the Beaver.*

- Hands-On Idea: Chew down a tree like a beaver. (Just kidding.) How about pretending that you are traveling west in a covered wagon instead?

- Family Activity: Make an Oregon Sunset picture (instructions on page 434).

Wait for the Wagon

George P. Knauff and R. Bishop Buckley published this song in 1851. It is one of many songs pioneers brought to Oregon on the Oregon Trail. (Track 48)

Will you come with me my Phillis, dear, to yon blue mountain free?
Where the blossoms smell the sweetest, come rove along with me.
It's ev'ry Sunday morning now when I am by your side,
So let's jump into the Wagon, and we shall take a ride.

Chorus:
Wait for the Wagon,
Wait for the Wagon,
Wait for the Wagon and we'll all take a ride. *(repeat)*

Where the river runs like silver, and the birds they sing so sweet,
There I have a cabin, Phillis, and something good to eat.
Come listen to my story, dear, it will relieve my heart,
So jump into the Wagon, and let's begin to start.

Chorus

Together, on life's journey, we'll travel till we stop,
And if we have no trouble, we'll reach the happy top.
Then come with me sweet Phillis, my dear, my lovely bride,
We'll jump into the Wagon, and all take a ride.

Chorus

Covered wagons

Kam Wah Chung

During the late 1800s, thousands of Chinese immigrants sailed across the Pacific Ocean to establish new lives in the American West. Many of the immigrants mined for gold and helped build railroads. Hundreds of Chinese people settled in the Oregon town of **John Day**. Ing Hay and

Town of John Day in 1909

Lung On were two of them. Together these men operated a successful business: Kam Wah Chung & Company. In Chinese the name means "Golden Flower of Prosperity." In the building they owned together, Lung On operated a store. Ing Hay worked as an herbalist (someone who treats and prevents illnesses using herbs).

Kam Wah Chung store

The Kam Wah Chung & Company building also served as a post office, a library, a temple, and a community center for the Chinese. At this time, many Americans were unkind to Chinese immigrants and made life hard for them. Some people were even violent toward the Chinese and wanted them to move away. Kam Wah Chung & Company was a safe place where the Chinese could relax and feel at home. The Chinese community in John Day was one of the largest Chinese communities in the country.

Kam Wah Chung & Company sold everyday items such as tools, clothing, flour, and sugar. The store also offered items imported from China, such as rice, soy sauce, and other items Chinese immigrants wanted.

Lung On

Lung On was a leader in the Chinese community. Both Chinese and non-Chinese people respected and admired him. He was smart and fun. He spoke English well, and often helped people in the Chinese community by being their interpreter so they could communicate with English speakers. In the early 1900s, many Chinese people moved away from John Day. Business slowed down at Kam Wah Chung & Company. One way Lung On kept the business going was by adding a car dealership and a gas station, which he operated with another local friend.

Ing Hay most likely learned about traditional Chinese medicine from family members in China before he came to America. After Ing Hay went into business with Lung On, he became known far and wide for his ability to help people get well. He knew just where to place his fingers on a person's arm to feel their pulse and determine what was wrong in his or her body. American doctors were amazed at his success.

Ing Hay

"Doc Hay" prepared medicinal remedies for his patients in the Kam Wah Chung kitchen. He used thousands of different herbs. Chinese people came from miles around to see him and receive his treatments. Sometimes Doc Hay made house calls, visiting sick people in their homes.

Over time, many non-Chinese people came to see Doc Hay as well. Patients who lived too far away to visit in person wrote Doc Hay letters describing their symptoms. Doc Hay mailed them remedies. Doc Hay was a kind and generous man toward his patients and his community.

Lung On passed away in 1940. Doc Hay continued to operate Kam Wah Chung & Company until 1948, when he entered a nursing home. He died in 1952.

Kam Wah Chung & Company

Ing Hay's nephew hoped the city of John Day would turn the Kam Wah Chung & Company building into a museum. Instead, people boarded it up and it sat mostly untouched for over ten years. In 1968, after Ing Hay's nephew had passed away, local volunteers finally opened up the building. They found Doc Hay's tools still on his table and food still in the kitchen. They also found a box full of uncashed checks worth over $23,000. Some think that perhaps Doc Hay did not cash the checks because he knew those patients did not have much money. Today the building and hundreds of original items inside it are part of the Kam Wah Chung State Heritage Site.

Lung On and Ing Hay did many things right. They were generous and cared about their neighbors. They were dedicated to making their community a better place. Sometimes, however, Lung On sold items in his store that were illegal. That was wrong. They also appear to have failed to send love and support back home to their families they left behind in China. We can learn from everyone in history—from the good things they did and from their mistakes. Only Jesus was perfect.

Even when we do not agree with a person's religion or convictions, we can still love that person as Jesus does. We can still learn from that person as long as we keep standing strong in Jesus, shining His light.

[God] desires all men to be saved and to come to the knowledge of the truth.
1 Timothy 2:4

Activities

- Complete the map activities for Oregon in the *Atlas Workbook* (page 99).
- Read chapters VII and VIII in *The Adventures of Paddy the Beaver*.
- If you moved to another country with different customs and traditions, what is something you would miss about America? If you are keeping a creative writing notebook, write about your thoughts.

Family Activity: Oregon Sunset

Supplies:

- scissors
- gluestick
- small circle to trace (such as a lid)
- pencil
- construction paper (including white, dark blue, black, and yellow)
- tissue paper in various sunset colors
- black and white crayons

Directions:

- Look at the picture on page 417 to help you visualize the Oregon coast as you make a picture of the sun setting there.
- Tear strips of tissue paper in a variety of widths and colors.
- Lay a piece of construction paper on the table for the background. Apply glue to an area of the paper and lay down some tissue paper strips. Continue this process until your sunset colors cover the page (except for about two inches across the bottom).
- Cut a strip of dark blue construction paper about two inches wide for the water. Glue it on the bottom of the construction paper under the sunset.
- Trace a circle onto a piece of yellow construction paper for the sun and cut it out. Glue it onto the sky near the water.
- Cut a few rock shapes out of black construction paper. Glue them onto the water.
- Use a black crayon to draw the shadows of the rocks on the water.
- Tear some tiny strips of yellow or orange tissue paper. Glue them onto the water under the sun to show the light reflecting on the water.
- Use a white crayon to draw ripples on the water.

Polar bear in Alaska

Unit 25
Pacific:
Washington and Alaska

435

Lesson 97: Washington

Imagine having so many apples that if you put them in a line they would circle the earth 29 times. That's how many apples grow in Washington State each year! Find Washington on the map at the beginning of this book. (Make sure you find the state and not Washington, D.C.!)

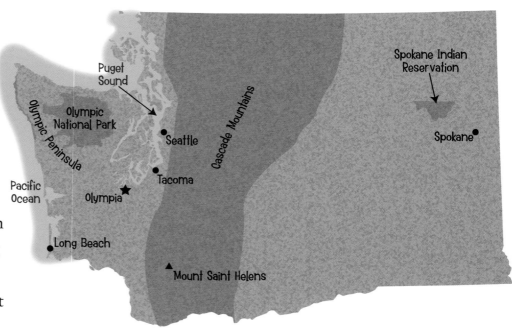

Washington apple orchard

Spokane woman around 1897

Spokane

Spokane means "Children of the Sun" in the Salish language of the Spokane people. The Spokane have lived in Washington, Idaho, and Montana for hundreds of years. Today many members of the tribe live on the **Spokane Indian Reservation** near the city of **Spokane**. The Spokane continue to pass down their history by telling their traditional stories from one generation to the next. The children learn to speak Salish in school. They also learn other customs of their people, such as how to cook using hot lava rocks.

436

Mount Saint Helens

The **Cascade Mountains** run across the state of Washington from the north to the south. The Cascades have five active volcanoes. The most recent eruption happened in 1980 on **Mount Saint Helens**.

In 1975 geologists predicted that Mount Saint Helens could possibly erupt sometime during the next 25 years. Five years later, in March of 1980, an earthquake signaled that the volcano was waking up. People noticed a large bulge growing on the north side of the

Eruption of Mount Saint Helens in 1980

mountain. The bulge grew as much as six and a half feet in a single day. The bulge was from magma, a hot liquid, building up inside the volcano. As the pressure continued to build, thousands of small earthquakes shook the mountain. A series of small eruptions let the world know that something big was about to happen.

On May 18, 1980, a massive earthquake hit. The quake caused a huge section of the mountain to break loose, creating an enormous landslide. The eruptions weren't small anymore. They were huge. Within minutes millions of tons of ash shot up 80,000 feet into the air. The wind picked up the ash and carried it east. Ash from Mount Saint Helens caused a blackout in Spokane 250 miles away. Ash fell from the sky as far away as the Midwest.

The Mount Saint Helens eruption caused a great deal of damage, but it also showed the mighty power of God over His creation. Scientists have been amazed at how fast the area has recovered from the volcano's damage.

Fog around Mount Saint Helens

Go Fly a Kite

Tens of thousands of people gather each year in **Long Beach** for the Washington State International Kite Festival. Some groups fly their kites together, creating figures and formations in the sky. A kite museum in Long Beach has over 1,500 kites from 26 countries around the world.

Washington State International Kite Festival in 2013

Capital: Olympia

Puget Sound is a large inlet (or arm) of the Pacific Ocean. It is named after Peter Puget, an English explorer who visited the area in 1792. At the southern end of Puget Sound lies Budd Inlet where many coastal tribes once gathered shellfish. Two American settlers moved to the area in 1846 and established a town. The town became **Olympia**. It is now the capital city of the state of Washington.

Puget Sound

Not long after the American settlers arrived at Budd Inlet, Chinese immigrants came to make a new home for themselves. They helped establish the city by pulling up stumps, building bridges, and smoothing streets. Many of their descendants still live in Olympia today.

In 1996 the people of Washington elected Gary Locke to serve as their governor. Locke's grandfather came to Olympia from China in 1890. Governor Locke was the first Chinese American governor in United States history.

Seattle

Seattle is Washington's largest city. In 1962 Seattle hosted a world's fair, a huge event where people from many different parts of the world displayed arts and accomplishments from their countries. The theme of the fair was "The Age of Space." Seattle built a huge tower for the fair called the Space Needle.

Space Needle

Olympic National Park

Stretching out from Washington toward the Pacific Ocean is the Olympic Peninsula. Olympic National Park lies on the peninsula. Within this park is an amazing assortment of ecosystems from coastline to glacier-capped mountains to rain forest. God makes a huge amount of rain fall on the Hoh Rain Forest each year, creating a lush green wonderland.

He who trusts in his riches will fall,
But the righteous will flourish like the green leaf.
Proverbs 11:28

Hoh Rain Forest

Activities

- Illustrate the geographic term for Washington in the *Atlas Workbook* (page 100).

- If you are using the *Lesson Review*, answer the questions for Washington (page 25).

- Read chapters IX and X in *The Adventures of Paddy the Beaver*.

- Hands-On Idea: With a parent, learn something about the governor of your state.

Kwanesum Jesus Hyas Skookum
(Always Jesus Is Very Strong)

The native people of the Northwest Coast spoke many different languages. In the 1800s, people developed Chinook jargon, a dialect that members of various tribes as well as traders and missionaries could use to communicate with each other. Myron Ells moved to Washington to share Jesus with the native people there. He and others who worked with him used traditional English tunes to create songs in Chinook jargon. (Track 49)

Kwanesum Jesus hyas skookum.	*(Always Jesus is very strong.)*
Kwanesum Jesus hyas skookum.	*(Always Jesus is very strong.)*
Kwanesum Jesus hyas skookum.	*(Always Jesus is very strong.)*
Kahkwa yaka papeh wawa.	*(So His paper [Bible] says.)*
Delate nawitka,	*(Truly so,)*
Delate nawitka,	*(Truly so,)*
Delate nawitka,	*(Truly so,)*
Kahkwa yaka papeh wawa.	*(So His paper says.)*

Washington Coast

Thea and Her Tugs

Thea Christiansen was a determined young woman who loved adventure. The idea of leaving her home in Norway, sailing to the United States, and marrying the man she loved was thrilling.

Thea was born in a small Norwegian village in 1857. When she was a teenager she met Andrew Oleson. The two decided to marry, but not until they were both in the United States. Andrew left Norway in 1878 to set up a home in America and earn enough money so that Thea could join him. Andrew found work as a carpenter in Minnesota.

Hammer

Andrew finally saved up enough money to pay for Thea's trip across the Atlantic Ocean. He sent the money back to Norway and waited for his bride to arrive. Instead, Andrew's brother showed up in America. Thea had given him the money instead! Andrew continued to work hard and again saved up enough money so that Thea could come to America. This time, Andrew's sister arrived in Minnesota. The determined young Thea had made up her mind that she was going to pay her own way to America. While her fiancé was working as a carpenter in Minnesota, she was working as a housekeeper in Norway. By 1881 she had saved enough money to join him.

There were many Norwegian immigrants in the United States with the last name of Oleson, so the couple changed their last name to Foss. After several years in Minnesota, the Foss family decided to move west to Washington. They traveled by train to Tacoma.

Andrew Foss built his family a houseboat made of driftwood and various pieces of lumber he found here and there. Thea had always been afraid of the water, so living on a houseboat with three young children was a challenge, but she was up to the task.

Tacoma sawmill in 1884

Thea Foss

Mr. Foss continued working as a carpenter in Tacoma. Soon after the family settled there, he left for a two-month job building a house in a nearby community. While he was gone, a fisherman sailed by the Foss houseboat. He asked Mrs. Foss if she was interested in buying his boat for $10. She offered him $5 instead. He agreed. Mrs. Foss painted the boat white and added green trim. She soon resold it at a profit and bought two more boats. She rented out her boats to fishermen for 50 cents a day. When Mr. Foss returned from his carpentry job, he showed his wife the $32 he had earned. She showed him the $41 she had earned while he was gone. Andrew Foss quickly put his carpentry skills to work and built more boats. Before long their new family business had over 200 boats.

The two eldest Foss children joined the family business early on. They dug worms and sold them for 2 cents a dozen to the fishermen who rented the boats. The Foss family also rented their rowboats to duck hunters and to people who just wanted to go out for a pleasure ride and have a picnic on the water. They used their boats to transport supplies to other larger ships in the waterways around Tacoma. Their slogan was "Always Ready."

Foss tugs and barges—"Always Ready"

Over the years, the Foss family added new types of boats to their business. After rowboats became less popular, they focused more on tugboats, which helped move logs up and down the water. Today the Foss Maritime Company operates in harbors, rivers, and oceans around the world. The company's tugs are still painted with the colors Thea Foss chose in 1889: white with green trim.

Thea Foss enjoyed managing a boarding house for their employees. Their son Henry remembered that his mother "never was more happy than when in her kitchen." She was always ready to enjoy a cup of coffee with anyone. Andrew and Thea helped many Norwegian immigrant families get started in America by offering them jobs and explaining American customs to them. They also helped them prepare for the exams they would take to become citizens of the United States.

Thea Foss died in 1927. Her funeral was one of the largest the people of Tacoma had ever seen. Foss tugboats sailed in a water parade with their flags at half mast in her honor. They sailed down Tacoma's City Waterway, which is now called the Thea Foss Waterway.

Thea Foss once wrote, "the law imprinted in all men's hearts is to love one another. I will look to the whole world as my Country and all men as my brothers."

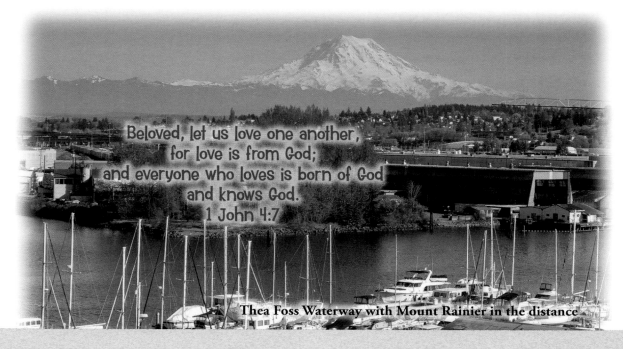

Beloved, let us love one another, for love is from God; and everyone who loves is born of God and knows God. 1 John 4:7

Thea Foss Waterway with Mount Rainier in the distance

Activities

- Complete the map activities for Washington in the *Atlas Workbook* (page 101).
- Read chapters XI and XII in *The Adventures of Paddy the Beaver*.
- What does it mean to look to the whole world as your country and all men as your brothers? If you are keeping a creative writing notebook, write your thoughts.

How about a mixture of fresh snow, seal oil, reindeer fat, and wild berries for dessert? Akutaq is a special treat the native people of Alaska have enjoyed for hundreds of years. The creamy frozen texture is like ice cream. Find Alaska on the map at the back of this book.

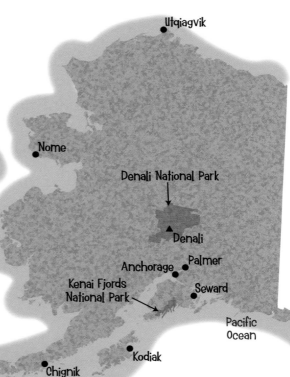

Alaska-Sized Produce

Because of Alaska's position near the North Pole, the daylight hours are especially short in the winter and especially long in the summer. With all those extra hours of sunlight in the summer, garden produce can grow big—really big. Each year at the Alaska State Fair in **Palmer**, gardeners enter their enormous produce, hoping to win a blue ribbon. The record carrot in 2017 was almost 6 feet long. The largest sunflower in 2015 measured two feet across. In 2012 the record cabbage was 138 pounds. The record giant pumpkin in 2019 weighed a whopping 2,051 pounds!

Winning entries at the Alaska State Fair

Totem Heritage Center

An impressive collection of totem poles stands at the Totem Heritage Center in **Ketchikan**. The Tlingit and Tongass people carved these poles during the 1800s. The totem poles honored important people from their communities and celebrated special events. Sometimes they illustrated a legend. People painted the poles with bright colors. Today some Alaska natives carry on the totem pole carving traditions of their ancestors.

Totem pole in Ketchikan

Capital: Juneau

The land of Alaska once belonged to Russia. The United States bought the land from Russia in 1867 and Alaska became a U.S. territory.

Juneau began as a gold mining town in 1880. On Christmas Day of that year, the community had a population of just 30 miners. The men feasted on clam soup and stuffed porcupine for their Christmas dinner. The next year, Juneau continued to grow and people built homes, stores, a bakery, a blacksmith shop, and a drugstore. Juneau became the capital of the U.S. territory of Alaska in 1906. It remained the capital when Alaska became a state in 1959.

Many Alaskan communities, including the capital of Juneau, do not have roads that connect them to the rest of the state. People reach them by boat and plane.

Juneau

Arriving in Juneau

445

Salmon

Anchorage is the largest city in Alaska by far. It is one of many places in the state that is popular with tourists—and salmon. Alaska's rivers and streams are teeming with salmon.

Salmon are born in freshwater streams. From there they swim to the ocean where they stay between eighteen months and eight years. God created each salmon to know exactly when the time is right to head back to the stream where it was born. The salmon fight against currents and jump up waterfalls to make it back to their home stream. Bears often wait above waterfalls to catch a salmon lunch as the fish head upstream. Once the salmon reach their home stream, they lay their eggs and die.

Humpback whale in front of a glacier at Kenai Fjords National Park

Kenai Fjords National Park

A fjord is a long, narrow inlet of the sea. The waters of a fjord are deep. High cliffs tower up beside the water. **Kenai Fjords National Park** has over 30 glaciers. The only glacier visitors can reach by road is Exit Glacier. When the road closes in winter, visitors can reach the glacier on a snowmobile, skis, snowshoes, an off-road bike, or a dogsled. Which one would you choose?

Denali National Park

The highest point in all of North America rises over 20,000 feet in **Denali National Park**. This mountain, **Denali**, has been an honored place for generations of Alaska natives.

Denali

446

Dogsled team racing across Alaska

Dogsleds

In the late 1800s and early 1900s, the only way to travel to certain parts of Alaska was by dogsled. The Iditarod Trail connected Anchorage to the town of **Nome**. Dogsleds carried people, mail, medicine, and other supplies. During the 1920s, airplanes became more common and dogsleds were not as necessary. Then came snowmobiles, and the Alaskan tradition of dogsleds began to fade away.

In the mid-1900s, people worked hard to make sure the dogsled tradition did not completely vanish. They established the Iditarod Trail Sled Dog Race. Around 65 teams compete in the race each year. It typically takes the teams between nine and twelve days to complete the course.

Utqiagvik

Utqiagvik is the northernmost city in the United States. It's so far north that for 79 days straight in the summer, the sun never sets. It's still daylight at midnight! During the winter, the sun does not rise for 61 days straight. Even with constant sunlight in the summer, it still might snow on the fourth of July.

> The heavens are Yours,
> the earth also is Yours . . .
> The north and the south,
> You have created them . . . .
> Psalm 89:11-12

Polar bears near Utqiagvik

Activities

- Illustrate the geographic term for Alaska in the *Atlas Workbook* (page 102).
- If you are using the *Lesson Review*, answer the questions for Alaska (page 25).
- Read chapters XIII and XIV in *The Adventures of Paddy the Beaver*.
- Hands-On Idea: Pretend some small stuffed animals are salmon. Have one person toss them "upstream" while another person is a "bear" and tries to catch them.

Just Back from Dawson

Sam Clarke Dunham lived in northern Alaska for about two years in the 1890s, working for the U.S. government. At that time Alaska was a U.S. territory. Dunham wrote several poems about life in Alaska, including this one. He hoped that his writings would help the government see their need to treat the people of Alaska fairly, like true American citizens. (Track 50)

I've just got back from Dawson, where the Arctic rainbow ends,
And the swiftly-rushing Klondike with the mighty Yukon blends;
Where the sun on Christmas morning in the act of rising sets,
So that just a minute's sunshine is all that region gets.

I've just got back from Dawson, where the large mosquitoes sing,
And soon as they forsake the camp, their small successors sting;
Where 'long about the last of June the sun again surprises
The new-arrived inhabitants, and while it's setting rises.

I've just escaped from Dawson, where the ice grows ten feet thick,
And dudes who like their baths served cold don't take 'em in a crick;
Where no one, be he rich or poor, is ever dubbed a "hero"
Till he has done his hundred miles at 60 less than zero.

Satellite image of the Yukon River

Benny's Flag

Chignik is a small village in southwest Alaska. Most people in the village depend on fishing to support their families. Benny Benson was born into this community in 1913. His father was Swedish. His mother was part Russian and part Aleut (an Alaska native). When Benny was just three years old, his mother died. The same year, the family's house burned. Benny's father was devastated. He sent Benny's older sister to a boarding school in Oregon. He sent Benny and his younger brother Carl to an orphanage in Unalaska on one of Alaska's Aleutian Islands. Benny and Carl traveled on a mail boat to reach their new home. In 1925 the children's home moved to Seward.

At this time, Alaska was still a territory. The territorial governor wanted Alaska to become a state. He decided that Alaska needed its own flag, just like each of the 48 existing states. He suggested a flag design contest open to school children in grades seven through twelve.

Chignik Harbor

Hundreds of schoolchildren took part, including Benny Benson. Benny created a design with gold stars on a blue background. The blue represented the Alaska sky and forget-me-not flowers. The large star on the flag represented the North Star. To Benny this star represented the future of the state of Alaska. The other stars on his design formed the shape of the Big Dipper constellation. The Big Dipper is part of a larger constellation of a bear. Benny said that the bear symbolized strength.

Local judges across Alaska chose the best designs from their students to send on to Juneau for the final judging. The judges in Juneau had to decide between 142 entries, including Benny's. The choice was obvious. All of the judges agreed on the one flag they thought was the best.

One day, as Benny sat with his class at school, their teacher's husband came into the room. He handed their teacher a telegram. As she read the message on the telegram, her students watched her mouth drop open. She was speechless. Everyone wondered what the message might be. They watched her hand the telegram back to her husband. He read the telegram out loud.

Benny nearly fell out of his seat. He had won the flag contest! Out of all the entries from all over Alaska, his design had won. Everyone at Benny's school was so excited they canceled classes for the rest of the day. It was time to celebrate.

At a ceremony in Seward, Benny received a gold watch with his flag design engraved on the back. He also received a $1,000 scholarship for his future education.

All over the territory, Benny's fellow Alaska natives were proud. They looked to Benny as a hero of their people, as his flag waved from all corners of the territory.

Benny Benson with his flag design

450

After Benny graduated from high school, he used his scholarship money to study diesel engineering. He later moved to Kodiak, Alaska, where he worked on airplanes.

When Alaska became a state in 1959, the government decided to keep Benny's design as the state flag. Ten years later, the United States sent Neil Armstrong, Buzz Aldrin, and Michael Collins into outer space. The astronauts carried small versions of all fifty state flags with them on their spacecraft. Benny Benson from Chignik, Alaska, was mighty proud that his flag design traveled all the way to the moon.

Be exalted, O God, above the heavens,
And Your glory above all the earth.
Psalm 108:5

Benny Benson Memorial in Seward

Activities

- Complete the map activities for Alaska in the *Atlas Workbook* (page 103).
- Read chapters XV and XVI in *The Adventures of Paddy the Beaver*.
- Imagine that it is your job to design a flag for your town or county. Draw a design and tell your family what the different colors and symbols stand for. If you are keeping a creative writing notebook, draw you design in there and write a description of the flag's meaning.
- Family Activity: Play State Flag Bingo (instructions on page 452).

Family Activity: State Flag Bingo

Supplies:
- State Flag Bingo boards and cards (available at notgrass.com/50links)
- scissors
- small items to use as markers (buttons, beans, coins, etc.)

Directions:
- Print the boards and cards. If possible, print them on cardstock. If not, you might want to glue them onto stiff paper.
- Cut apart the cards and lay them face down in the center of your playing area.
- Each player places a bingo board in front of her and places a marker in the center of her board on the FREE space.
- Take turns drawing a card from the center. If any player has the matching flag on his board, he places a marker on that space.
- Play continues until one player gets five markers in a row. That player calls out "Bingo!" and is the winner.

Sea turtle in Hawaii

Unit 26
Hawaii and the U.S. Territories

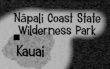

Nāpali Coast State Wilderness Park

Kauai

O'ahu

Pearl Harbor ★ Honolulu

Maui

Maluaka Beach

Pacific Ocean

Hawai'i

Mauna Loa

Kīlauea

Hawaii is the only state in our country that is made up entirely of islands. The Hawaiian islands lie in the Pacific Ocean approximately 2,500 miles from California.

King Kamehameha I united the Hawaiian islands into a single kingdom in 1810. The United States took over the islands in the late 1800s and Hawaii became a U.S. territory. It became our country's fiftieth state in 1959. Find Hawaii on the map at the back of this book.

Hawaiian Leis

Lei is the Hawaiian word for a garland or wreath. For hundreds of years, Hawaiians have strung together leaves, flowers, shells, feathers, and bones to wear around their necks. The royal families (and only the royal families) added kukui nuts to their leis.

Hawaiians still wear leis to celebrate everything from birthdays and graduations to friendship and weddings. They also love to share leis with the many tourists who come to their islands.

Lei

Animals of Hawaii

While bright and colorful birds flitter across the Hawaiian islands, manta rays and jellyfish swim in the waters around them. Hawaiian monk seals feed in Hawaiian waters and come ashore to sleep soundly on the beach. The ancient Hawaiian people called these animals *llio holo I ka uaua*, which means "dog that runs in rough water."

Hawaiian monk seal

Humpback whale in Hawaii

Humpback whales that live in Alaska during the spring and summer spend their winters in Hawaii. Humpbacks, sometimes nearly fifty feet long, make a big splash when they slap their tails on the surface of the water.

Spinner dolphins are a common sight in Hawaii. God created these dolphins to be amazing gymnasts. As a spinner dolphin heads toward the surface of the water to take a leap, he beats his tail rapidly. Once in the air, he spins once, twice, or perhaps even seven times before splashing back into the water.

Spinner dolphin

Volcanoes

Each Hawaiian island is made up of one or more volcanoes. Some of the volcanoes are still active, which means they could erupt at any time. The world's largest active volcano is **Mauna Loa** on the island of **Hawai'i**. The nearby volcano of **Kīlauea** erupted in 2018. Lava spewed from Kīlauea for about four months. The eruption changed the shape of the island, just as eruptions have for many years.

Lava running into the ocean off the island of Hawai'i

Hibiscus

455

Turtle Town

Sea turtles live in many places around the Hawaiian islands, but one of the best places to see them is at **Maluaka Beach** on the island of **Maui**. Grab your snorkeling gear and dive in. The water at "Turtle Town" is fine. An octopus or an angelfish might glide by as you look for a turtle. Don't get too close to the turtles, though. Since they are an endangered animal, it's against the law even to touch one!

Maluaka Beach

Iolani Palace

Capitol: Honolulu

Honolulu on the island of **O'ahu** is home to the only official royal residence in the United States. Iolani Palace was home to Hawaii's last king and queen from 1882 until 1893. The building then served as the capitol for the territory and then the state of Hawaii. Government offices moved to a new capitol building in 1969. In the 1970s workers restored Iolani Palace to its grand royal appearance.

Pearl Harbor

When people first came to Hawaii, they found a lagoon on the island of O'ahu. A lagoon is a shallow body of water. A coral reef separated the lagoon from the ocean. The lagoon was filled with pearl oysters. The people named the area *Wai Momi*, which means "Pearl Water." At first only small boats could enter the harbor. Eventually, islanders cut a channel into the reef so that larger ships could enter. The United States government later made the harbor deeper and widened the entrance more so they could use the harbor for Navy ships. The English name for the area is **Pearl Harbor**.

On December 7, 1941, while World War II was raging in other parts of the world, Japanese planes attacked Pearl Harbor to damage American ships and planes. After the attack, the United States joined in the fighting of World War II.

Today people from around the world come to visit the Pearl Harbor National Memorial. They come to honor the people who died in the attack, to remember World War II, and to celebrate the peace that came after it.

Nāpali Coast State Wilderness Park

Pearl Harbor

In the **Nāpali Coast State Wilderness Park** on the island of **Kauai**, waterfalls tumble down narrow, rugged valleys. Cliffs, called *pali* in Hawaiian, rise sharply from the ocean. Long ago Hawaiians built stone terraces among these valleys to grow taro. Taro is a vegetable similar to potatoes. Taro became an important part of the diet and culture of the Hawaiian people. Hawaiians enjoy mashed taro, taro pancakes, taro chips, and taro fries.

God is our refuge and strength,
A very present help in trouble.
Therefore we will not fear,
though the earth should change
And though the mountains slip
into the heart of the sea.
Psalm 46:1-2

Nāpali Coast State Wilderness Park

Activities

- Illustrate the geographic term for Hawaii in the *Atlas Workbook* (page 104).

- If you are using the *Lesson Review*, answer the questions for Hawaii (page 26).

- Read chapters XVII and XVIII in *The Adventures of Paddy the Beaver*.

- Hands-On Idea: Use building bricks or blocks to build Iolani Palace.

- Family Activity: Make Pineapple Pops (instructions on page 470).

Mele Kahuli
(Song of the Tree-shell)

This traditional Hawaiian song tells of the kahuli, a type of snail that lives in trees on the island of O'ahu. (Track 51)

Kāhuli aku, kāhuli mai   *(Little tree shell, little tree snail)*
Kāhuli lei 'ula, lei 'ākōlea   *(The shell of a red ornament)*
Kōlea, kōlea, ki'i ka wai   *(Kōlea bird, Kōlea bird, fetching the water)*
Wai 'ākōlea, wai ākōlea   *(Water from the 'ākōlea fern)*

Oo, o, o, o, o, o....o, o, o, o, o   *(sound of the Kōlea bird singing)*

Kahuli snail on O'ahu

458

Worldwide Voyage

Hawaii is part of Polynesia, an area that includes over 1,000 islands in the Pacific Ocean. The islands are spread out over about ten million square miles. People believe that long ago, before Jesus was born, men and women from Asia set out in canoes and discovered these islands. These people were skilled explorers who had an amazing understanding of how to use the stars, the wind, the waves, birds, and other signs in nature to help them navigate (or direct) their journeys. They discovered and settled one island after another in this huge expanse we call Polynesia.

In the 1970s, Hawaiian artist and historian Herb Kane (*KAH-ney*) dreamed of bringing back to life the ancient voyaging traditions of his people. After researching Polynesian canoes and voyaging, Mr. Kane organized a project to build the *Hokule'a,* a traditional Polynesian sailing canoe. He also helped to establish the Polynesian Voyaging Society. Herb Kane painted the Polynesian canoe below.

The Polynesian Voyaging Society could not find anyone in Hawaii who still knew how to sail in the traditional Polynesian way. The knowledge there was lost. The society invited Mau Piailug from Micronesia to come to Hawaii to teach them. Mau Piailug knew how to navigate the traditional way because people in Micronesia had passed down that knowledge from one generation to the next and finally to him.

Mau Piailug taught members of the society the art of wayfinding—the navigation method that uses the stars as a compass. They had to memorize the positions of more than 200 stars in the sky and watch where they rose and where they set. They learned to line up grooves in the canoe with certain stars near the horizon to make sure they were sailing in the right direction.

Hokulea II by Herb Kane

Mau Piailug helped his students understand how to read the shape, height, and color of clouds to help them understand the weather and give them clues about their direction. He also taught them how to watch seabirds for clues. Some birds leave their homes on land in the morning and return at night. The direction the birds are traveling help the navigators know how to find nearby land. Mau Piailug also explained how ocean swells (waves) help with navigation.

In 1976 the Polynesian Voyaging Society was ready for their first long journey. They sailed the *Hokule'a* to the island of Tahiti, a voyage of about 2,700 miles. They navigated their route using only traditional methods and did not use any modern navigation tools. After traveling for more than a month, they reached their destination. The people of Tahiti were so excited about the voyage that more than 17,000 people—over half of the population of the island—gathered on the shore to greet the *Hokule'a* when it arrived.

The successful journey by the Polynesian Voyaging Society prompted Hawaiians to work harder to preserve their culture. Schools began teaching the Hawaiian language again. They didn't want more of their history to be lost.

Sadly, the second journey of the *Hokule'a* ended in disaster. The canoe capsized and one crew member drowned. The Polynesian Voyaging Society could have given up their dreams, but they knew their lost crew member would want them to continue, so they did.

The *Hikianalia*

The Polynesian Voyaging Society completed a modern voyaging canoe in 2012: the *Hikianalia* (pictured at left). Both of the society's canoes combine traditional designs with modern inventions, such as canvas sails and fiberglass, to make them safer and stronger. The *Hikianalia* uses solar panels and wind energy to generate electricity onboard. Crew members on that canoe are able to keep in touch with the rest of the world.

In 2013 the Polynesian Voyaging Society launched a grand new adventure: a trip around the world. They sailed both the *Hokule'a* and the *Hikianalia*. On the Worldwide Voyage, the canoes stopped at over 150 ports in 23 different countries and territories. While in a port, local children and adults got to come on board and learn about the vessels. The local people also shared aspects of their own culture with the crew members through song and dance performances.

Each canoe had between 12 and 16 crew members at a time. Some crew members made the whole journey, while others took a turn for a few weeks. They joined the crew at one port and left it at another so someone else could take their place. In all, 245 crew members from around the world took part in the journey. Sometimes crew members ate food they brought onboard. Other times they caught fish to eat along the way.

The crew members on the Worldwide Voyage worked together as a team, monitoring the stars and clouds, enduring the cold and rain, and enjoying the glorious sunsets.

Through the Worldwide Voyage, the Polynesian Voyaging Society sought to share the Polynesian culture, to connect people around the world, and to encourage everyone everywhere to take better care of the earth.

Onboard the *Hokule'a*

If I take the wings of the dawn,
If I dwell in the remotest part of the sea,
Even there Your hand will lead me,
And Your right hand will lay hold of me.
Psalm 139:9-10

Activities

- Complete the map activities for Hawaii in the *Atlas Workbook* (page 105).
- Read chapters XIX and XX in *The Adventures of Paddy the Beaver*.
- What do you think it would be like to sail around the world? If you are keeping a creative writing notebook, write an imaginary journal entry about one day on your journey.

Lesson 103: The U.S. Territories

Several islands in the Caribbean Sea and in the Pacific Ocean are part of the United States, even though the islands themselves are not states. These islands are U.S. territories.

There are five U.S. territories where people live permanently. They are all tropical islands, which means they are near the equator. The islands offer shady palm trees, sunny beaches, rugged mountains, peaceful lagoons, and many other tropical delights. When you come to the section on each territory in this lesson, find it on the map at the back of this book. You will learn about the territory of Puerto Rico in the next lesson.

U.S. Virgin Islands

Between 1492 and 1502, Christopher Columbus made four trips across the Atlantic Ocean. Through his travels, people in Europe learned about the Caribbean Islands. Native people already lived on these islands, but many European countries wanted to rule the islands themselves. Some Europeans enslaved other people and forced them to work on sugar plantations they established on the islands.

In 1917 the United States bought a group of about 50 Caribbean islands from Denmark. They became the U.S. Virgin Islands, a territory of the United States.

Today Virgin Islands National Park on the island of St. John is the most popular tourist site on the islands. Visitors can hike to the ruins of a sugar plantation, see ancient petroglyphs carved into rock, and swim with sea stars, sea turtles, and maybe an octopus.

Trunk Bay in Virgin Islands National Park

Emerald tree skink, a reptile of the Mariana Islands

Northern Mariana Islands

The Mariana Archipelago is home to the Chamorro people. Some historians believe that the ancestors of the Chamorros came to these islands from Asia around 4,000 years ago. The Chamorros once built their houses on top of two-piece stone pillars called *lattes*. Many of these pillars are still visible on the islands. They stand as a reminder of the island's past and a tribute to the first people who lived there.

Spain took control of the Mariana Islands in the 1500s. Spain later sold the islands to Germany. Japan took over the islands in 1914. During World War II, the United States took the islands from Japan. The Northern Mariana Islands became an official territory of the United States in 1975. The flag of the Northern Mariana Islands features a latte stone in its design.

Latte on the Mariana island of Tinian

463

Banded anemone fish near the Mariana island of Rota

Guam

Guam is the largest island in the Mariana Archipelago. In 1898 the U.S. fought a war with Spain. As a result of the war, Guam became part of the United States.

The United States military keeps soldiers, sailors, and airmen stationed around the world to help keep peace and to be ready in case of war or other emergencies. Since Guam is close to Asia, the United States military decided it would be a good place for military bases. At Andersen Air Force Base and Naval Base Guam, military men and women train, drill, and prepare so they are ready to help others in need and to defend America's freedom.

Andersen Air Force Base on Guam

American Samoa

Historians believe the Samoan people have lived on the Samoan Islands for about three thousand years. An explorer from the Netherlands came upon the Samoan Islands in 1722. French explorers followed after him.

464

English missionary John Williams arrived in the Samoan Islands in 1830. The Samoan people were eager to hear the good news of Jesus. Christianity is still strong on the Samoan Islands today.

During the late 1800s, the United States, Germany, and Britain all wanted to use the Samoan Islands as a military base. The conflict could have resulted in a war, but a typhoon—a big storm in the ocean—hit the islands and most of the warships there sank.

In 1899 Britain decided to give up trying to control the islands. An official agreement divided the islands between Germany and the United States. The islands Germany once controlled are now an independent nation. The islands the United States received in the agreement are now the territory of American Samoa.

American Samoa is the southernmost land that is part of the United States. It is the only part of the United States that is south of the equator.

At one time, about half of the tuna Americans ate came from canning factories in American Samoa. Some tuna production has now moved to other countries, but tuna is still an important part of the economy of American Samoa.

Sing to the Lord a new song,
Sing His praise
from the end of the earth!
You who go down to the sea,
and all that is in it.
You islands, and those
who dwell on them.
Isaiah 42:10

Tuna boats in American Samoa

Activities

- Illustrate the geographic term for the U.S. Territories in the *Atlas Workbook* (page 106).

- If you are using the *Lesson Review*, answer the questions for the U.S. Territories (page 26).

- Read chapter XXI in *The Adventures of Paddy the Beaver*.

- Hands-On Idea: Use play dough to mold an emerald tree skink (see photo on page 463).

Lesson 104: A Song and Story of Puerto Rico

El Coquí (The Coquí)

The coquí *is a tiny frog that lives on the island of Puerto Rico. It makes a noise that sounds like its name. (Track 52)*

El coquí, el coquí siempre canta,
Es muy lindo el cantar del coquí,
Por las noches a veces me duermo
Con el dulce cantar del coquí.

Coquí, coquí, coquí, qui, qui, qui.
Coquí, coquí, coquí, qui, qui, qui.

(The coqui, the coqui's always singing,)
(The coqui's singing is very nice,)
(And sometimes, I go to sleep at night)
(With the sweet singing of the coqui.)

Coquí in Puerto Rico

San Juan, Puerto Rico

Giving All

On the Caribbean island of Puerto Rico, baseball is big. Islanders love to play the sport, and they love to watch the sport. For many people, baseball is an important part of being Puerto Rican. Find Puerto Rico on the map at the back of this book.

Puerto Rico became a territory of the United States as a result of the Spanish-American War of 1898. It is the largest U.S. territory. Over three million people live on the island of Puerto Rico, which is far more people than live in any other U.S. territory.

Over the years, many Puerto Rican men have joined baseball teams across the U.S. to play the game professionally. Puerto Ricans love to cheer them on. Many consider Roberto Clemente the greatest Puerto Rican baseball player of all time.

Roberto Clemente was born on August 18, 1934, in Carolina, Puerto Rico. He was the seventh child in his family. The family did not have much money. His father oversaw cutters at a nearby sugar plantation. His mother took in laundry and also helped in the sugarcane fields. Roberto helped the family by taking odd jobs to earn extra money. Even though times were hard, Roberto and his siblings never went hungry. Their parents always found a way to feed them.

While he was still a young boy, neighbors and family members noticed Roberto's skill in sports. Roberto loved baseball. The field where he played with other kids was muddy and had many trees in the way, but that didn't stop him from playing the game for hours, day after day. The kids used the branch of a guava tree for a bat and a tight knot of rags for a ball. With that equipment, Roberto's baseball skills continued to grow.

Sugarcane in Puerto Rico

Roberto felt like God wanted him to play baseball. When he was 18 years old, a professional Puerto Rican baseball team invited him to play for them.

Other professional baseball teams learned of Roberto's skill. In 1954 he played for a team in Montreal, Canada. In 1955 he joined the Pittsburgh Pirates, a Major League Baseball team. A baseball scout (someone who looks for players to play on baseball teams) once described Roberto Clemente by saying, "Nobody could throw any better than that, and nobody could run any better than that."

Statue of Roberto Clemente in Pittsburgh

Roberto was fun to watch on the baseball diamond. He excited fans as they watched his strong hitting, his terrific catches, and his amazing speed at running bases.

During the off-season, Roberto went home to Puerto Rico where he continued to play on a Puerto Rican team. He wanted to give the people of his homeland the opportunity to see him play. He was a national hero.

In 1964 Roberto married Vera Zabala, who was also Puerto Rican. It seemed the whole island celebrated their marriage. Thousands of people lined the streets to watch them drive by after their wedding.

Roberto Clemente's life was not only about baseball. He loved others and he found ways to serve and help and make a difference. He loved Jesus. His faith guided him in helping others. When he was home in Puerto Rico during the off-season, he held sports camps for Puerto Rican kids. He dreamed of one day building a sports center where children could learn about sports and also learn skills they would need in life. Mr. Clemente once said he wanted "to be remembered as a ballplayer who gave all he had to give." He also said, "Any time you have an opportunity to make a difference in this world and you don't, then you are wasting your time on earth."

Baseball

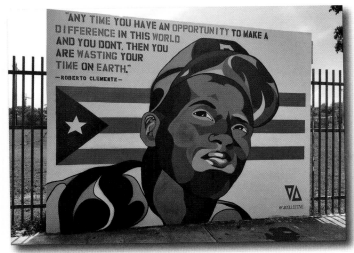

"ANY TIME YOU HAVE AN OPPORTUNITY TO MAKE A DIFFERENCE IN THIS WORLD AND YOU DONT, THEN YOU ARE WASTING YOUR TIME ON EARTH." —ROBERTO CLEMENTE—

Painting of Roberto Clemente in Miami, Florida

A friend of Roberto Clemente once commented, "With Roberto it was always faith and family first, everything else second."

Roberto Clemente played baseball hard and he it played well, even though he was often in pain from injuries. In 1971 he set a goal of making 3,000 hits in his Major League career. The next year, he met his goal. As the ball soared to the back of the baseball park and Roberto Clemente ran to second base, the Pittsburgh fans stood and cheered. His skill helped the Pittsburgh Pirates make it to the World Series—an annual baseball championship—two times.

Later that year, two days before Christmas, an earthquake hit the Central American country of Nicaragua. Roberto Clemente quickly organized an effort to raise money and gather medicine and food to help the Nicaraguans. On New Year's Eve, he and four others boarded a plane loaded with the donations. Soon after it took off, the plane crashed and everyone on board died.

Puerto Rico was shocked to learn of their baseball hero's sudden death. He and Vera had only been married eight years. They had three young sons.

Vera Clemente worked hard to honor her husband's legacy. On land donated by the government of Puerto Rico, she fulfilled his dream by building the Roberto Clemente Sports City. Over the years, hundreds of thousands of children have participated in events at the facility. The Roberto Clemente Foundation also carries on his legacy of faith, love, and service as it reaches out to people in need all around the world.

Sitting down, [Jesus] called the twelve and said to them,
"If anyone wants to be first, he shall be last of all and servant of all."
Mark 9:35

Activities

- Complete the flag activities for the U.S. Territories in the *Atlas Workbook* (page 107).

- Read chapters XXII in *The Adventures of Paddy the Beaver*.

- If you had enough money to build a place where kids in need could learn a certain skill, what would you want to help them learn? If you are keeping a creative writing notebook, write about the place you envision.

- If you are using the *Lesson Review*, take the Pacific and U.S. Territories Test (page 45).

Family Activity: Pineapple Pops

At one time, most of the world's canned pineapple came from Hawaii. Today most pineapple production has moved to other countries. Some Hawaiians still grow the tropical fruit, however, and it is still an important part of Hawaiian cooking.

Ingredients/Supplies:
- 1 can sliced pineapple rings (or fresh pineapple if you prefer)
- 1 ½ cups semi-sweet chocolate chips
- ¾ cup sweetened coconut
- 24 skewers

Be safe with knives and the microwave or stove. Children must have adult supervision in the kitchen.

Directions:
- Remove pineapple slices from the can and place on a paper towel to dry.
- Cut each pineapple slice into sections about 2" or 3" in length.
- Insert skewers into pineapple sections.
- Place pineapple pops on a parchment-lined baking sheet and place in the freezer for at least 30 minutes.
- Melt the chocolate chips in the microwave or with a double boiler on the stove. If using the microwave, use a microwave-safe container and melt for 20-30 seconds at a time, stirring between each time until the chips are melted.
- Allow melted chocolate to cool slightly.
- Place coconut into a dry skillet and toast on medium heat until golden brown. Be sure to watch the coconut and stir often—it will brown quickly.
- Remove the pineapple from the freezer. Dip each piece into the slightly cooled melted chocolate (a spoon may be helpful to spread chocolate evenly on pineapple pieces).
- Sprinkle the toasted coconut over each piece of chocolate-dipped pineapple. Place the pops back onto the lined baking sheet until the chocolate hardens.
- Enjoy immediately or place in a freezer-safe container and return to the freezer.

Sources

Special thanks to the individuals and families who provided information about their personal histories, their businesses and organizations, and their communities.

Historical and Cultural Organizations

Alabama State Council of the Arts
Alaska Historical Society
Alaska State Fair
Allegheny National Forest Visitors Bureau
American Samoa Historic Preservation Office
Anchorage Convention & Visitors Bureau
Appalachian Mountain Club
Arbor Day Foundation
Aroostook County Tourism
Ashtabula County Visitors Bureau
Atlantic City Free Public Library
Basque Museum and Cultural Center
Bear Gulch Pictographs
Belzoni-Humphreys Development Foundation
Capitol City Visitor (Springfield, IL)
Charleston Convention and Visitors Bureau
Chesapeake Bay Foundation
Cheyenne Frontier Days
City of Fountains Foundation
Civitan International
Colorado Virtual Library
Concord Historical Society
Connecticut History
Dalton Convention and Visitors Bureau
Delaware Museum of Natural History
Digital Atlas of Idaho
Dismals Canyon
Door County Visitor Bureau

Eastern Utah Human History Library
Eclectic Society of Little Rock
Encyclopedia of Alabama
Encyclopedia of Puerto Rico
Finger Lakes Tourism Alliance
Flagstaff Dark Skies Coalition
Florida Historical Society
Fort Worth Stockyards National Historic District
Freedom Trail Foundation
Friends of Idaho State Parks
Friends of Kam Wah Chung
Friends of Nevada Wilderness
Geographic Society of Chicago
Gilder Lehrman Center for the Study of Slavery, Resistance, and Abolition at Yale University
Golden Spike Tower and Visitor Center
Great Chillicothe Visitors Region
Greater Burlington Partnership
Green County Tourism
Harriet Tubman Historical Society
Haskell Free Library & Opera House
Hawaii Ocean Project
Historic Clarksburg, WV Historic Cemetery Alliance
Historical Association of Lewiston
HistoryLink.org
Hopi Cultural Center
Idaho Potato Museum
Iditarod Trail Committee
IFAS Extension - University of Florida
International Peace Garden
Iolani Palace
Kansas Historical Society
Kansas Wetlands Education Center

Kent Historical Society
La Junta Tourism
Lafayette Travel
Lake Havasu Tourism Bureau
Lake Pontchartrain Basin Foundation
League to Save Lake Tahoe
Lewes Historical Society
Lexington Visitor's Center
Life Leaders Institute
Louis Armstrong House Museum
Lowell Observatory
Maah Daah Hey Trail Association
Maine Historical Society
Mammoth Site of Hot Springs, South Dakota
Marblehead Lighthouse Historical Society
Marine Mammal Center
Milton Hershey School
Mining History Association
Minnesota Heritage Songbook
Minnesota Historical Society
Moab Museum
Montana Office of Tourism
Mount Washington Auto Road
Mount Washington Observatory
MuleDay.com
Museum of the City of San Francisco
Myrtle Beach Area Chamber of Commerce and CVB
Mystic Seaport Museum
Nashville Convention & Visitors Corp.
Natchez Pilgrimage Tours
National Museum of the American Indian
National Snow and Ice Data Center

National Wildlife Federation
Navajo Tourism Department
Nebraska State Historical Society
New England Historical Society
New England Ski Museum
New Hampshire State Council on
the Arts
North Carolina Sea Grant
North Carolina State University:
Moise A. Khayrallah Center for
Lebanese Diaspora Studies
Ocean City Life-Saving Station
Museum
Ohio History Central
Ohio History Connection
Ohio Memory
Okefenokee Swamp Park
Oklahoma Historical Society
Oregon Historical Society
OregonPioneers.com
PearlHarbor.org
Peoria Area Convention and
Visitors Bureau
Polynesian Voyaging Society
Preservation Society of Newport
County
Regional Office of Sustainable
Tourism/Lake Placid CVB
Rhode Island Red Centennial
Committee
Rhode Tour
Samuel Proctor Oral History
Program - University of Florida
Save the Bay
Silicon Valley Historical
Association
Sioux Falls Convention and
Visitors Bureau
Sleeping Giant Park Association
South Shore Convention and
Visitors Authority
Spearfish South Dakota Visitor
Center
Spokane Tribe Language and
Culture
St. Louis Community College
St. Paul Convention and Visitors
Bureau
State Historical Society of Iowa
State Historical Society of North
Dakota

Storm Heroes
Strataca: Kansas Underground Salt
Museum
Taylor House Museum
Texas State Historical Association
Tourism Santa Fe
Trailing of the Sheep
Turner Falls Park
U.S. Space and Rocket Center
United States Lighthouse Society
United States Lighthouse Society
University of Montana
University of Oslo Department of
Physics
University of Rhode Island
Upper Peninsula Travel and
Recreation Association
Vermont Historical Society
Virginia Wildfire Information and
Prevention
Virtual Nebraska / University of
Nebraska-Lincoln
Visit Albuquerque
Visit Austin
Visit Baton Rouge
Visit Carson City
Visit Salt Lake
Visit Savannah
Visit Sun Valley
Wausau/Central Wisconsin
Convention & Visitors Bureau
White House Historical
Association
White Mountain Attractions
Winterthur Museum, Garden &
Library
Wisconsin Historical Society
Wyoming State Historical Society
Wyoming's Wind River Country
Yale-New Haven Teachers Institute

Media

ABC7
American Missionary
Anchorage Daily News
Animal Frontiers
Arizona Daily Star
Arkansas Historical Quarterly
Associated Press
Astronomy Magazine

Baltimore Sun
BBC
Billings Gazette
Black Hills Visitor Magazine
C-SPAN
Cajun Country
CapeMay.com
CBS
Christian Advocate
CNN
Columbus Dispatch
Courier Post
Curbed San Francisco
Dallas County News
Deseret News
Distinctly Montana
Douglas County News-Press
Elko Daily Free Press
Expedition Magazine
Feast Magazine
First Things
Fodor's Travel
Forbes
Grand Forks Herald
Grand Strand Magazine
Great Plains Quarterly
Half-a-Hundred Acre Wood
Hawaii Magazine
Idaho Mountain Express
Idaho Statesman
Independent Record
Indianapolis Star
Daily Herald (Arlington Heights,
IL)
Inside Indiana Business
John Downer Productions
Kentucky Educational Television
Lincoln Journal Star
Lincoln Star Journal
Los Angeles Times
Mariner's Weather Log
McPherson Sentinel
Minnesota Public Radio
Missoulian
Music Magazine / Musical Courier
National Park Trips
National Public Radio (NPR)
Nevada Business Magazine
New Hampshire Public Radio
New Jersey Herald
New York Times

New York Times Magazine
News Journal
North Carolina Historical Review
Oregon Public Broadcasting
Our State Magazine
Oxford University Press Academic
    Journals
Pioneer Press
Popular Mechanics
Progressive Cattle
Public Broadcasting Service (PBS)
Rochester Post Bulletin
San Francisco Call
Scientific American
Smithsonian Magazine
Star Tribune
Sun-Sentinel (South Florida)
Telegraph (Macon, GA)
Texas Monthly
The Oklahoman
The State (Columbia, SC)
Times Daily (Florence, AL)
Times-Independent (Moab, UT)
Times-News (Twin Falls, ID)
USA Today
Washington Post
Western Folklore
Wisconsin State Farmer
WQAD News 8
WSIL-TV

Government Agencies

Alabama Department of
    Commerce
Alaska Public Land Information
    Center
Arkansas Secretary of State
Arkansas State Parks
Arlington National Cemetery
Bannack State Park
California Department of Parks
    and Recreation
California State Capitol Museum
Carson City, Nevada
Central Arkansas Library System
City and Borough of Juneau,
    Alaska
City and County of Butte-Silver
    Box, Montana
City of Aberdeen, South Dakota

City of Atlanta, Georgia
City of Burlington, Iowa
City of Deadwood, South Dakota
City of Douglas, Wyoming
City of Greensburg, Kansas
City of Greenville, South Carolina
City of Ketchikan, Alaska
City of Little Rock, Arkansas
City of Monticello, Minnesota
City of Olney, Illinois
City of Olympia, Washington
City of Pittsburgh, Pennsylvania
City of Santa Fe, New Mexico
City of Sun Valley, Idaho
City of Tillamook, Oregon
City of Twin Falls, Idaho
Colorado Parks & Wildlife
Colorado Virtual Library
Commonwealth of Kentucky
Commonwealth of Massachusetts
Connecticut State Library
Correspondence with Bob Dixson,
    former mayor of Greensburg,
    Kansas
Delaware Division of Historical and
    Cultural Affairs
Delaware River and Bay Authority
Delaware Tribe of Indians
Department of Energy and
    Environmental Protection
Department of Land and Natural
    Resources (Hawaii)
Eastern Arizona College
Florida Department of
    Environmental Protection
Florida Department of State
Franklin D. Roosevelt Library
Georgia Department of Natural
    Resources
Idaho Department of Commerce
Idaho Department of Health and
    Welfare
Illinois Department of Natural
    Resources
Indiana Department of Natural
    Resources
Iowa Department of Cultural
    Affairs
Iowa Department of Natural
    Resources

Kansas Geological Survey,
    University of Kansas
Kentucky Department of Tourism
Kentucky State Parks
Library of Congress
Maryland Department of Natural
    Resources
Michigan State Capitol
    Commission
Mississippi Department of
    Archives and History
Mississippi Department of
    Environmental Quality, Office of
    Geology
Mississippi Department of Marine
    Resources
Missouri Department of Natural
    Resources
Missouri House of Representatives
Missouri Secretary of State
Montana State Parks
Montana State University
NASA
National Archives
National Oceanic and Atmospheric
    Administration
National Park Service
National Weather Service
Navajo Nation Parks and
    Recreation
Nebraska Game and Parks
    Commission
Nebraska State Capitol
Nevada State Parks
New England Interstate Water
    Pollution Control Commission
New Jersey Office of Legislative
    Services
New Mexico Bureau of Geology
    and Mineral Resources
New York State Assembly
North Carolina Department of
    Agriculture and Consumer
    Services
North Carolina Department of
    Cultural Resources
North Dakota Office of
    Management and Budget
Office of Legislative Services,
    Office of Public Information
    (NJ)

Office of the Architect of the
  Capitol (Illinois)
Ohio Department of
  Transportation
Ohio Statehouse
Oklahoma Department of Wildlife
  Conservation
Oklahoma House of
  Representatives
Oregon Parks and Recreation
  Department
Oregon Secretary of State
Pennsylvania Capitol
Pennsylvania Department of
  Conservation and Natural
  Resources
Perkins Museum of Geology at the
  University of Vermont
Recreation.gov
Riley County, Kansas
Ronald Reagan Presidential
  Library and Museum
Smithsonian Institution
Spokane Tribe of Indians
State of Hawaii
State of Indiana
  State of Iowa
State of Montana
State of New Jersey
State of North Dakota
State of Wisconsin
Tennessee State Parks
Tennessee Valley Authority
Texas State Preservation Board
Tillamook Forest Center
U.S. Air Force
U.S. Army
U.S. Army Corps of Engineers
U.S. Census Bureau
U.S. Department of Agriculture
U.S. Department of Commerce
U.S. Department of the Interior
U.S. Fish and WIldlife Service
U.S. Forest Service
U.S. Geological Survey
United States Mint
University of Alaska
University of Arkansas
Utah Geological Survey
Voice of America

Washington Department of
  Natural Resources
West Virginia Department of Arts,
  Culture, and History
West Virginia General Services
West Virginia Legislature
White Earth Nation
White House

Companies, Associations, and Other Organizations

Ad Council
Albuquerque International Balloon
  Fiesta, Inc.
Alstede Farms
Amana Colonies
Answers in Genesis
Arch Coal, Inc.
Biltmore
Birthplace of Pepsi-Cola
Boeing Company
Braum's
Cabot Creamery
California Raisins
Cape Cod Select
Caterpillar
Center for Land Use Interpretation
Charleston Tea Garden
Chesapeake Bay Program
Dalton Paradise Carpets
Discipleship Ministries
Emerald Hollow Mine
Encyclopaedia Britannica
Food and Agricultural
  Organization of the United
  Nations
Foss Maritime Company
French Lick Resort
Goulding's
Hallmark Cards, Inc.
Hatch Chile Festival
Heinz History Center
Heritage Flower Farm
Hershey Company
Hocking Hills
Huntington Ingalls Industries, Inc.
Illinois Farm Bureau
Indianapolis Motor Speedway
Intel Corporation

Internet Corporation for Assigned
  Names and Numbers
Isle Royale Seaplanes
John Deere
Kansas Sampler Foundation
Kentucky Fried Chicken
Lost Sea
Louisville Mega Cavern
LSU Health New Orleans
Maine Lobster Festival
Maquoketa Chamber of
  Commerce
Matheson Real Estate Team
Mayo Clinic
McIlhenny Company
Michelin North America
Montana Connections Business
  Development Park
Monticello Chamber of
  Commerce and Industry
Mt. Olive Pickle Company
Mueller Water Products
Multnomah Falls Lodge
National Center for Atmospheric
  Research
National Geographic
New Orleans & Company
NextEra Energy Resources
North Carolina Sweet Potato
  Commission
Ohio Caverns
Old Town Trolley Tours
Pearls International
PepsiCo
PLAN Washington
Raccoon Forks Farms
Red Rock Canyon Adventure Park
Riceland
Roberto Clemente Foundation
Saint Lawrence Seaway
  Development Corporation
Sea Lion Caves
Smith Island Baking Company
Society for American Baseball
  Research
Space Needle
St. Lawrence Seaway Management
  Corporation
Standard Candy Company
Stanford University
Strasburg Rail Road Company

Stuttgart Chamber of Commerce
Swan Boats
Team USA
Tillamook Company
U.S. Kings
Vermont Maple Sugar Makers
Vermont Quarries Corporation
Vidalia Onion Festival
Walmart
Weather Channel
Weirton Chamber of Commerce
Wisconsin Dairymen's Association
Wolf Creek Ski Area

Books and Other Publications

America's Forgotten Constitutions - Robert L. Tsai, 2014.

Beyond Their Years: Stories of Sixteen Civil War Children - Scotti Cohn, 2016.

Biloxi Memories - Barbara Sillery, 2015.

Casper Jaggi: Master Swiss Cheese Maker - Jerry Apps, 2008.

Chronicles of the White Mountains - Frederick Wilkinson Kilbourne, 1916.

Creating the South Carolina State House - John Morrill Bryan, 1999.

Early History of Brown County, South Dakota - Territorial Pioneers and Descendants, 1965.

Falls of Niagara and Other Famous Cataracts - George W. Holley, 1882.

Fast Food and Junk Food: An Encyclopedia of What We Love to Eat, Volume 1 - Andrew F. Smith, 2012.

Folk Song of the American Negro - John Wesley Work, 1915.

Foss Maritime Company - Mike Stork, 2007.

Ghost Towns of North Mountain: Ricketts, Mountain Springs, and Stull - F. Charles Petrillo, 1991

Gilded Mansions - Wayne Craven, 2009.

Groton Avery Clan, Volume 1 - Elroy McKendree Avery and Catherine Hitchcock (Tilden) Avery, 1912.

Harriet, the Moses of her People - Sarah Hopkins Bradford, 1886.

History of Boise Sesquicentennial Brochure, 2013.

History of Cape May County, New Jersey: From the Aboriginal Times to the Present Day - Lewis Townsend Stevens, 1897.

History of Harrison County, West Virginia - Henry Hammond, 1910.

History of Vermont, Natural, Civil and Statistical, In Three Parts, with a New Map of the State, and 200 Engravings - Zadock Thompson, 1842.

History of West Virginia, Old and New, Volume 1 - James Morton Callahan, 1923.

Indiana: The Hoosier State - Richard Hantula, Kathleen Derzipilski, and Ruth Bjorklund, 2017.

It Happened in Yellowstone: Remarkable Events That Shaped History - Erin H. Turner, 2012.

Kite that Bridged Two Nations: Homan Walsh and the First Niagara Suspension Bridge - Alexis O'Neill, 2013.

Landmarks of Niagara County, New York - William Pool, 1897

Legends of the Seminoles - Betty M. Jumper, 1994.

Legends of the Skyline Drive and the Great Valley of Virginia - Carrie Hunter Willis and Etta Belle Walker, 1907.

Lenape Country: Delaware Valley Society Before William Penn - Jean R. Soderlund, 2015.

Light at the End of the Funnel: A Journey Through Disaster and Trauma - Jeffrey D. Blackburn, 2017.

McIlhenny's Gold: How a Louisiana Family Built the Tabasco Empire - Jeffrey Rothfeder, 2007.

Methodism in the Maryland and Delaware Peninsula, - Robert W. Todd, 1886.

Methodism of the Peninsula; or, Sketches of Notable Characters and Events in the History of Grand Canyon Women: Lives Shaped - Landscape - Betty Leavengood, 2004.

Montana Place Names from Alzada to Zortman - Rich Aarstad, Ellen Arguimbau, Ellen Baumler, Charlene L. Porsild, and Brian Shovers, 2009.

Mount Washington: A Handbook for Travellers - Frank Hunt Burt, 1906.

Mountain Biking in Boise - Stephen Stuebner, 2002.

National Parks and the Woman's Voice: A History - Polly Welts Kaufman, 2006.

Natural Bridge of Virginia and its Environs - Chester A Reeds, 1927.

New Song Book - Ezra Strong, 1836.

Newport and the Northeast Kingdom - Barbara Kaiser Malloy, 1999.

Pioneer Life in Illinois - F. M. Perryman, 1907.

Illinois Teacher: Devoted to Education, Science and Free Schools, Volume 5, 1859

Poets and Poetry of Springfield in Massachusetts from Early Times to the End of the Nineteenth Century - Charles Henry Barrows, 1907.

Records of the Governor and Council of the State of Vermont (Volumes V and VIII) - E. P. Walton, editor, 1877-1880.

Rehoboth Beach: A History of Surf and Sand - Michael Morgan, 2009.

Rock Climbing Virginia, West Virginia, and Maryland - Eric Horst and Stewart M. Green, 2013.

Sacred Places, North America: 108 Destinations - Brad Olsen, 2008.

Sheridan's Daybreak: A Story of Sheridan County and Its Pioneers Volume 1 - Magnus Aasheim, 1970.

Singers and their Songs: Sketches of Living Gospel Hymn Writers - Charles H. Gabriel, 1916.

Slave Narratives: A Folk History of Slavery in the United States - the Works Progress Administration, 1941.

To and Through Nebraska - a Pennsylvania Girl - Frances I. Sims Fulton, 1884.

Vermont School Journal, Volumes 5-6 - Hiram Orcutt, editor, 1863.

Vermont: The Green Mountain State, Volume 3 - Walter Hill Crockett, 1921.

'Werner Fecit': Christopher Werner and Nineteenth-Century Charleston Ironwork (Master's Thesis) - Kelly Ciociola, 2010.

West Virginia: A Guide to the Mountain State - Workers of the Writers' Program of the Works Progress Administration in the State of West Virginia, 1941.

Working at Play: A History of Vacations in the United States - Cindy S. Aron, 1999.

Image Credits

15 Work crew & road - New York Public Library; Granite - Phichai / Shutterstock.com

16 Library of Congress

17 Mountains - Natalie Rotman Cote / Shutterstock.com; Road - Jon Bilous / Shutterstock.com

18 Donna Ellenburg

19 Sean Pavone / Shutterstock.com

20 Maple tree - Ann Hull / Shutterstock.com; Cabot chees - Jeffrey B. Banke / Shutterstock.com; Cabot, VT - Green Mountain Drone / Shutterstock.com

21 meunierd / Shutterstock.com

22 Quarry - Vermont Quarries Corporation; Lake - Monika Salvan / Shutterstock.com

23 Jeffrey M. Frank / Shutterstock.com

24-25 James Kirkikis / Shutterstock.com

26 Tow rope - Marion Post Wolcott / Library of Congress; Chair lift - Cory Seamer / Shutterstock.com

27 DutchScenery / Shutterstock.com

28 Mount Greylock - abaiungo / Shutterstock.com; Bash Bish - Jennifer Yakey-Ault / Shutterstock.com

29 Statue - Carol M. Highsmith's America Project in the Carol M. Highsmith Archive, Library of Congress; Swan boats - Jose Gil / Shutterstock.com

30 Plimoth - Breck P. Kent / Shutterstock.com; Martha's Vineyard - melissamn / Shutterstock.com

31 flyben24 / Shutterstock.com

32 AN NGUYEN / Shutterstock.com

33 Cranberries - Daria A / Shutterstock.com

33-35 Rhodes Family

36 Wesley McCurdy

37 f11photo / Shutterstock.com

38 Carousel - Robellin / Wikimedia Commons / CC BY-SA 4.0; Coast - solepsizm / Shutterstock.com

39 Synagogue - National Park Service; Salt marsh - JonPeckham / Shutterstock.com

40 Roger Williams - New York Public Library; Lighthouse - Wangkun Jia / Shutterstock.com

41 Felix Lipov / Shutterstock.com

42 Library of Congress

43 Hens - Robynrg / Shutterstock.com; Harbor - Michael Sean OLeary / Shutterstock.com

44 Ariene Studio / Shutterstock.com

45 Crate - Eky Studio / Shutterstock.com; Monument - Swampyank / Wikimedia Commons / CC BY-SA 3.0

46 Sound - Joe Gowac / Shutterstock.com; Ship - jgorzynik / Shutterstock.com

47 Thimble Islands - phucTechnology / Shutterstock.com; Sleeping Giant - Julie Hulten

48 Mountain laurel - Jill Lang / Shutterstock.com; Footprints - Daderot / Wikimedia Commons / CC BY-SA 3.0

49 f11photo / Shutterstock.com

50 Barn - Joseph Sohm / Shutterstock.com; Peddler - Charles Green Bush / Library of Congress

51 Box - Ed Welter / Wikimedia Commons / CC BY-SA 3.0; River - Shanshan0312 / Shutterstock.com

52 Portrait - George Laurence Nelson / Kent Historical Society; Frame - Ruslan Ivantsov / Shutterstock.com

53 George Laurence Nelson / Kent Historical Society

54 Mev McCurdy

55 Jim Vallee / Shutterstock.com

56 Frederick Millett / Shutterstock.com

57 Hudson River - Scott Heaney / Shutterstock.com; Staircase - Nagel Photography / Shutterstock.com

58 Ski jump - Arteff.icient / Shutterstock.com; Dressing - Keith Homan / Shutterstock.com; Islands - Wangkun Jia / Shutterstock.com

59 Lake - antsdrone / Shutterstock.com; Niagara Falls - Linda Harms / Shutterstock.com

60 Ira Blount / Smithsonian

61 Ellet - New York Public Library; Rapids - Linda Harms / Shutterstock.com

62 Niagara Falls Heritage Foundation / Niagara Falls Public Library (Canada)

63 Walsh / The Strand Magazine; Bridge - Currier & Ives / Library of Congress

64 Fox - Harry Collins Photography / Shutterstock.com; Gorge - Nicholas A. Tonelli / Flickr / CC BY 2.0

65 Pittsburgh - photosounds / Shutterstock.com; Bridge - kallen1979 / Shutterstock.com

66 Capitol - Nagel Photography / Shutterstock.com; Factory - George Sheldon / Shutterstock.com

67 Buggy - Delmas Lehman / Shutterstock.com; Independence Hall - f11photo / Shutterstock.com

68 Harry Collins Photography / Shutterstock.com

69 Cannon - Alexis Catlett / Shutterstock.com; Captain Ricketts - Find A Grave; Sketch - Alfred R. Waud / Library of Congress

70 Kitchen Creek - Cvandyke / Shutterstock.com; Monuments - Nagel Photography / Shutterstock.com

71 Jon Bilous / Shutterstock.com

72 Cutting paper - Mev McCurdy; Mosaics - Pennsylvania State Capitol

73 George Sheldon / Shutterstock.com

74 Produce - Lester Majkowicz / Shutterstock.com; Rutan Hill - Lithium6ion / Wikimedia Commons

75 Lenape - Nikater / Wikimedia Commons; River - Tetyana Ohare / Shutterstock.com; Crabs - Jorge Moro / Shutterstock.com

76 Capitol - Steven Frame / Shutterstock.com; Sled - Seth Anderson / Wikimedia Commons / CC BY-SA 2.0; Barnegat - K.L. Kohn / Shutterstock.com

77 Taffy - EQRoy / Shutterstock.com; Boardwalk - Carol M. Highsmith's America Project / Library of Congress

78 Sahani Photography / Shutterstock.com

79 EQRoy / Shutterstock.com

80 Harrisons - National Portrait Gallery, Smithsonian; Fence - Kristina Wagner / Shutterstock.com

81 EQRoy / Shutterstock.com

82 Abeselom Zerit / Shutterstock.com

83 Fort - Noah Halstead / Wikimedia Commons / CC BY-SA 4.0 (cropped); Bridge - Mihai_Andritoiu / Shutterstock.com

84 du Pont - Everett Historical / Shutterstock.com; Winterthur - Carol M. Highsmith Archive / Library of Congress; Burris - Wikimedia Commons

85 Old State House & Courtroom - Nagel Photography / Shutterstock.com; Legislative Hall - Jon Bilous / Shutterstock.com

86 kathleen collins / Shutterstock.com

87 Sandpiper - Judy Gallagher / Wikimedia Commons / CC BY 2.0; Seagull - J Stubits / Shutterstock.com; Beach - Jon Bilous / Shutterstock.com

88 Tichnor Brothers Collection, Boston Public Library

89 Top - Tichnor Brothers Collection, Boston Public Library; Bottom - Ritu Manoj Jethani / Shutterstock.com

90 Anna Kucherova / Shutterstock.com

91 Sean Pavone / Shutterstock.com

92 Museum - refrina / Shutterstock.com; Horse - Mary Swift / Shutterstock.com

93 Horses - Assateauge - Brian Muck / Shutterstock.com; Fossils - Wilson44691 / Wikimedia Commons; Bay - Chesapeake Aerial Photo / Shutterstock.com

94 Traps - Leslie Billman / Shutterstock.com; Cake - Jane Thomas / Flickr / CC BY 2.0; Dome - Keri Delaney / Shutterstock.com; Quarter - Tom Grundy / Shutterstock.com

95 Baltimore - f11photo / Shutterstock.com; Submarine - Malachi Jacobs / Shutterstock.com; Falls - Jon Bilous / Shutterstock.com

96 Farm - Jon Bilous / Shutterstock.com; Tubman - National Park Service

97 Cabin - Steve Heap / Shutterstock.com; Shell - frank ungrad / Shutterstock.com; River - Elizabeth Reeves / Shutterstock.com

98 Night - sNike / Shutterstock.com; Lord's Prayer - New York Public Library; Marbles - Fæ / Wikimedia Commons / CC BY-SA 2.0; Corn - BestPix / Shutterstock.com

99 John Rose / Abby Aldrich Rockefeller Folk Art Museum

100 Lionel Pincus and Princess Firyal Map Division, New York Public Library

101 White House - dibrova / Shutterstock.com; Capitol - rorem / Shutterstock.com

102 Lincoln - Kevin Grant / Shutterstock.com; WWII - Pigprox / Shutterstock.com

103 Korea - Cristopher McRae / Shutterstock.com; Vietnam - Sean Pavone / Shutterstock.com

104 Bitkiz / Shutterstock.com

105 Fala - FDR Library; Rebecca - Library of Congress

106 Sheep - Library of Congress; Algonquin - Frances Benjamin Johnston / Library of Congress

107 East Room - T. W. Ingersoll / Library of Congress; Elephant - pandapaw / Shutterstock.com

108 Clara McCurdy

109 Steven Frame / Shutterstock.com

110 ship - Joseph Sohm / Shutterstock.com; Music - Bob Pool / Shutterstock.com; Carriage - Wangkun Jia / Shutterstock.com

111 Pig - Eric Isselee / Shutterstock.com; Tower - Smash the Iron Cage / Wikimedia Commons / CC BY-SA 4.0; Capitol - Rose-Marie Henriksson / Shutterstock.com

112 Arlington - TJ Brown / Shutterstock.com; Luray - Filipe Mesquita / Shutterstock.com

113 Jon Bilous / Shutterstock.com

114 Jon Bilous / Shutterstock.com

115 *Natural Bridge of Virginia and its Environs*

116 dmvphotos / Shutterstock.com

117 *Natural Bridge of Virginia and its Environs*

118 Spruce Knob - Jarek Tuszyński / Wikimedia Commons / CC BY-SA 3.0; Seneca Rocks (left) - Zack Frank / Shutterstock.com; (right) - MNDA / Shutterstock.com

119 Seneca Rocks - Harold Clagg Collection, West Virginia State Archives; Valley - Jon Bilous / Shutterstock.com

120 Capitol - Sean Pavone / Shutterstock.com; Miners - Everett Historical / Shutterstock.com; Statue - John M. Chase / Shutterstock.com

121 Bridge - Digital Relativity; Quarter - Jeff Cleveland / Shutterstock.com

122 Kristi Blokhin / Shutterstock.com

123 Malachi Jacobs / Shutterstock.com

124 School - Sherman Cahal / Shutterstock.com; Books - Alexlukin / Shutterstock.com

125 J. Norman Reid / Shutterstock.com

126 Donna Ellenburg

127 Alexey Stiop / Shutterstock.com

128 Farm - Anne Kitzman / Shutterstock.com; Churchill Downs - Thomas Kelley / Shutterstock.com

129 Louisville - f11photo / Shutterstock.com; Capitol - Alexey Stiop / Shutterstock.com

130 River - Brian Stansberry / Wikimedia Commons / CC BY-SA 4.0 (cropped); Cave - Wangkun Jia / Shutterstock.com; KFC - Jatuporn Chainiramitkul / Shutterstock.com

131 Jim Vallee / Shutterstock.com

132 Patrick Jennings / Shutterstock.com

133 Librarian - Goodman-Paxton Photographic Collection, Special Collections, University of Kentucky Libraries; Mountains - Jill Lang / Shutterstock.com

134-135 Goodman-Paxton Photographic Collection, Special Collections, University of Kentucky Libraries

136 Daniel Korzeniewski / Shutterstock.com

137 Carters - Wikimedia Commons; Lost Sea - gracious_tiger / Shutterstock.com; Nashville - f11photo / Shutterstock.com

138 Goo Goo - Keith Homan / Shutterstock.com; Mules - Andrew Watson / Flickr / CC BY-SA 2.0

139 Elvis - jdpphoto / Shutterstock.com; Memphis - Kevin Ruck / Shutterstock.com

140 Appealbydesign / Shutterstock.com

141 Zack Frank / Shutterstock.com

142 Cincinnati - New York Public Library; Fisk - KennStilger47 / Shutterstock.com; Piano - J. Helgason / Shutterstock.com

143 James Wallace / Black Library of Congress

144 Mev McCurdy

145 digidreamgrafix / Shutterstock.com

146 Thread - Dmitry Naumov / Shutterstock.com; Biltmore - ZakZeinert / Shutterstock.com

147 Alexander County and Hiddenite - Emerald Hollow Mine, LLC; Capitol - Steven Frame / Shutterstock.com

148 Sweet potatoes - Tanya_mtv / Shutterstock.com; Bottles - KLiK Photography / Shutterstock.com; Store - Grzegorz Czapski / Shutterstock.com

149 MarkVanDykePhotography / Shutterstock.com

150-151 Gingo Scott / Shutterstock.com

152 Cucumber - Kaiskynet Studio / Shutterstock.com; Pickles - Keith Homan / Shutterstock.com

153 Moise A. Khayrallah Center for Lebanese Diaspora Studies Archive, North Carolina State University

154 Quarter - Andrey Lobachev / Shutterstock.com; Greenville - Kevin Ruck / Shutterstock.com

155 Monument - Brian M. Powell / Wikimedia Commons / CC BY-SA 3.0; Trees - mogollon_1 / Flickr / CC BY 2.0

156 Myrtle Beach - MCphotoman / Shutterstock.com; Charleston - f11photo / Shutterstock.com; Tea - andysartworks / Shutterstock.com

157 Weaving - bddigitalimages / Shutterstock.com; Baskets - MSnider / Shutterstock.com

158 John Wollwerth / Shutterstock.com

159 Daise Family

159 St. Helena - Greg Thomas / Flickr / CC BY 2.0

160 Daise Family; St. Helena - Chris Lonsberry / Shutterstock.com

161 Daise Family

162 Left to right: Anton_Ivanov, REXI IMAGES, AJR_photo, pixelheadphoto digitalskillet, wong sze yuen / All from Shutterstock.com

163 Brian Lasenby / Shutterstock.com

164 Sean Pavone / Shutterstock.com

165 Okefenokee - Brian Lasenby / Shutterstock.com; Onion - Brian Zanchi / Shutterstock.com; Zipper - Brenda Rocha / Shutterstock.com

166 Atlanta - Kevin Ruck / Shutterstock.com; New Echota - Thomson200 / Wikimedia Commons

167 Dalton Convention & Visitors Bureau

168 Vyaseleva Elena / Shutterstock.com

169 Farm - Cromley Family; Peanuts - Alex Coan / Shutterstock.com

170-171 Cromley Family

171 Peanuts in shell - Ines Behrens-Kunkel / Shutterstock.com; Peanuts - Krailurk Warasup / Shutterstock.com

172 Snail - Jason Patrick Ross / Shutterstock.com; Dismals Canyon - LindaPerez / Shutterstock.com

173 Mussels - oksana2010 / Shutterstock.com; Dam and Rocket - George F. Landegger Collection of Alabama Photographs in Carol M. Highsmith's America Project, Library of Congress

174 Hydrant - Daderot / Wikimedia Commons; Capitol - Susanne Pommer / Shutterstock.com; Parks - Mccallk69 / Shutterstock.com

175 Heron - Darryl Vest / Shutterstock.com; Mailman - USPS

176 Altairisfar (Jeffrey Reed) / Wikimedia Commons / CC BY-SA 3.0

224 Portraits - McCurdy Family; Screwdriver - Andrii Spy_k / Shutterstock.com; Screws - Bobchoto / Shutterstock.com

225 McCurdy Family

226 Buckeyes - cvm / Shutterstock.com; Lighthouse - Doug Lemke / Shutterstock.com

227 Cleveland - Henryk Sadura / Shutterstock.com; Bridge - Kenneth Keifer / Shutterstock.com

228 Falls - Shriram Patki / Shutterstock.com; Capitol - Paul Brady Photography / Shutterstock.com

229 Steamboat - Bryan Busovicki / Shutterstock.com; Armstrong - NASA

230 Steven Russell Smith Ohio / Shutterstock.com

231 arthurgphotography / Shutterstock.com

232 Caverns - Rosamar / Shutterstock.com; Entrance - Tichnor Brothers Collection, Boston Public Library

233 Caverns (left) - Rosamar / Shutterstock.com; Crystal King - Rich Moffitt / Flickr / CC BY 2.0

234 Craft - Donna Ellenburg; Lighthouse - haveseen / Shutterstock.com

235 iyd39 / Shutterstock.com

236 Popcorn - Yeti studio / Shutterstock.com; Monument - Sean Pavone / Shutterstock.com

237 Monument - Library of Congress; Speedway - Grindstone Media Group / Shutterstock.com; Pinhook - National Park Service

238 Lieber - IN Dancing Light / Shutterstock.com; Creek - Kenneth Keifer / Shutterstock.com; Persimmons - pukao / Shutterstock.com

239 French Lick - Indiana State Library and Historical Bureau; West Baden Springs - Genevieve Borden / Shutterstock.com

240 MaxyM / Shutterstock.com

241 Outside - Serge Melki / Flickr / CC BY 2.0; Inside - MichelC+

242 People - Second Baptist Church, Bloomington, IN; Church - Elizabeth Mitchell

243 Renovations - Elizabeth Mitchell; Restored church - Dan Davis

244 Barge - Danita Delmont / Shutterstock.com; Camel rock - Tonya Kay / Shutterstock.com

245 Mound - Philip Rozenski / Shutterstock.com; Tablet - Herb Roe / Wikimedia Commons; Squirrel - Tony Campbell / Shutterstock.com

246 Truck - Wilson Hui / Flickr / CC BY 2.0; Artwork - RomanSlavik.com / Shutterstock.com

247 Lincoln - Joseph Sohm / Shutterstock.com; Bird - Danita Delmont / Shutterstock.com

248 Mark Baldwin / Shutterstock.com

249 F.M. Perryman - Public Domain; Hoe - Jamroen Jaiman / Shutterstock.com; Hogs - Nancy Gill / Shutterstock.com

250 Snake - fivespots / Shutterstock.com; Flower - Snowbelle / Shutterstock.com; Field - Tony Campbell / Shutterstock.com

251 steve52 / Shutterstock.com

252 Donna Ellenburg

253 Thyrymn2 / Shutterstock.com

254 Islands - Adam Haydock / Shutterstock.com (left); Jonah Anderson / Shutterstock.com

255 Globe - Lee Reitz / Shutterstock.com; Badger - critterbiz / Shutterstock.com; Statue - RAHurd / Wikimedia Commons / CC BY-SA 3.0; Madison - Ti / Shutterstock.com

256 Player - Mark Herreid / Shutterstock.com; Field - McDermott Images / Shutterstock.com; Orchard - Randy Kostichka / Shutterstock.com; Cherries - Hortimages / Shutterstock.com

257 Cow - Lyle E. Doberstein / Shutterstock.com; Cheese - azure1 / Shutterstock.com

258 Sea Wave / Shutterstock.com

259 Cowbell - mutation / Shutterstock.com; Farm - Ken Schulze / Shutterstock.com

260 Wisconsin Historical Society Image ID 33258 (top) and Image ID 33256 (bottom)

261 Can - Sagittarius Pro / Shutterstock.com; Wisconsin Historical Society Image ID 33251

262 Canoe - Wildnerdpix / Shutterstock.com; Capitol - IMG_191 / Shutterstock.com

263 Museum - Jeff Bukowski / Shutterstock.com; Flour - Sheila Fitzgerald / Shutterstock.com; Swan - Brian Kenney / Shutterstock.com

264 Swans - Brian Kenney / Shutterstock.com; Lighthouse - Jacob Clausnitzer / Shutterstock.com

265 Resort - Tony Webster / Flickr / CC BY-SA 2.0; Walleye - Dan Thornberg / Shutterstock.com; Rice - Michelle Lee Photography / Shutterstock.com

266-267 Jacob Boomsma / Shutterstock.com

268 House - Bobak Ha'Eri / Wikimedia Commons / CC BY 3.0; Stethoscope - Denis Gorlach / Shutterstock.com; Barrel - tristan tan / Shutterstock.com

269 Mayo family - Wellcome Collection / CC BY 4.0; Can - Keith Homan / Shutterstock.com

270 Donna Ellenburg

271 Felix Mizioznikov / Shutterstock.com

272 Shelly Hauschel / Shutterstock.com

273 Mural - Carol M. Highsmith Archive, Library of Congress; Outside - Grindstone Media Group /

Shutterstock.com; Inside - Nagel Photography / Shutterstock.com

274 Kitchen - New York Public Library; Cave - Glen Gardner / Shutterstock.com

275 House - kdotaylor / Shutterstock.com; Painting - Friends of American Art Collection, Art Institute of Chicago

276 Ken Schulze / Shutterstock.com

277 Snake Alley - Coalfather / Wikimedia Commons / CC BY-SA 4.0 (cropped); Bricks - formulanone / Flickr / CC BY-SA 2.0

278 Drawing - Morphart Creation / Shutterstock.com; Photograph - Digital Commonwealth

279 Travel Iowa

280 Americasroof / Wikimedia Commons / CC BY-SA 3.0

281 Arch - Joe Hendrickson / Shutterstock.com; Rocks - Charlene Notgrass; Cotton plant - Juris Sturainis / Shutterstock.com

282 Lake - Cheri Alguire / Shutterstock.com; Band - Branson's Famous Baldknobbers

283 Nagel Photography / Shutterstock.com

284 Marsh - LanaG / Shutterstock.com; Muskrat - Rick Grisolano / Shutterstock.com

285 Hallmark Archives, Hallmark Cards, Inc., Kansas City, Missouri, USA

286 Hallmark Archives

287 Fountain - Hallmark Crown Center; Hall - Hallmark Archives

288 Donna Ellenburg

289 ron99 / Shutterstock.com

290 Ricardo Reitmeyer / Shutterstock.com

291 Capitol - Steven Frame / Shutterstock.com; Prairie - Ricardo Reitmeyer / Shutterstock.com

292 Mine - Science History Institute; Rock - Robert D Brozek / Shutterstock.com

293 Rock City - Nationalparks / Wikimedia Commons / CC BY-SA 2.5; Monument Rocks - Lesleyanne Ryan / Shutterstock.com; Mount Sunflower - C. K. Hartman / Flickr / CC BY 2.0

294 FlanFoto / Shutterstock.com

295 Blackburn family - Jeffrey Blackburn; School - City of Greensburg, KS

296 Water tower - City of Greensburg, KS; Meeting - FEMA

297 Stairs - City of Greensburg, KS; Water tower - Kiowa County, KS Media Center

298 Bridge - EQRoy / Shutterstock.com; Girl - Mev McCurdy; Petroglyph - *Nebraskaland Magazine*, Nebraska Game and Parks Commission

299 Sower - Charles G. Haacker / Shutterstock.com; Cranes - William T Smith / Shutterstock.com

300 Yard - Janet Murrill / Shutterstock.com; Rock - Don Mammoser / Shutterstock.com

301 Fossil beds - Mawhamba / Wikimedia Commons / CC BY-SA 2.0; Fossils - Mawhamba / Wikimedia Commons / CC BY-SA 2.0

302 marekuliasz / Shutterstock.com

303 Bridge - marekuliasz / Shutterstock.com; Hills - Marshal Hedin / Flickr / CC BY-SA 2.0

304 Niobrara - marekuliasz / Shutterstock.com; Valentine - Ammodramus / Wikimedia Commons

305 Envelope - Notgrass Family; Valentines - tanyabosyk / Shutterstock.com; Street sign - Ammodramus / Wikimedia Commons

306 Donna Ellenburg

307 ESK Imagery / Shutterstock.com

308 Courthouse - AlexiusHoratius / Wikimedia Commons / CC BY-SA 3.0; Sioux Falls - Jacob Boomsma / Shutterstock.com

309 Capitol - Real Window Creative / Shutterstock.com; Bison - Holly Kuchera / Shutterstock.com; Badlands - Jason Patrick Ross / Shutterstock.com

310 Needles - trent mayer / Shutterstock.com; Donkeys - Tami Freed / Shutterstock.com; Mount Rushmore - Ozgur Coskun / Shutterstock.com; Falls - Brian A Wolf / Shutterstock.com

311 Sioux - New York Public Library; Gold - Charlene Notgrass; Mammoth - Warpaint / Shutterstock.com; Fossils - Rich Koele / Shutterstock.com

312 John Wollwerth / Shutterstock.com

313 River - Patrick Ziegler / Shutterstock.com; Aberdeen - Library of Congress

314 Depot - Library of Congress; Courthouse - Winkelvi / Wikimedia Commons / CC BY-SA 4.0

315 Lost_in_the_Midwest / Shutterstock.com

316 David Harmantas / Shutterstock.com

317 Harrowing - Internet Archives Book Images; Tower - FiledIMAGE / Shutterstock.com

318 Turbine - Greg Goebel / Flickr / CC BY-SA 2.0; Snow angels - North Dakota Media Library; Lodge - Traveller70 / Shutterstock.com

319 Park - Laurens Hoddenbagh / Shutterstock.com; Garden - Natalie Maynor / Flickr / CC BY 2.0

320 John Brueske / Shutterstock.com

321 Bees - Daniel Prudek / Shutterstock.com; Beekeeper - Mark Sperry; Sunflowers - Malgorzata Litkowska / Shutterstock.com

322 Mark Sperry (top); Thad Sperry (bottom)

323 Hive - BigBlueStudio / Shutterstock.com; Flower - Tsekhmister / Shutterstock.com

324 McCurdy Family; Apple - Ms. Abidika / Shutterstock.com; Bee - Protasov AN / Shutterstock.com

325 Danita Delmont / Shutterstock.com

326 Bear - Grey Mountain Photo / Shutterstock.com; River - welcomia / Shutterstock.com

327 River - Joseph Sohm / Shutterstock.com; Teepee - George Catlin / Smithsonian American Art Museum; Glacier - J.E. Haynes

328 Bannack - Rob Crandall / Shutterstock.com; Butte - Real Window Creative / Shutterstock.com

329 Capitol - Natalia Bratslavsky / Shutterstock.com; Park - Dan Breckwoldt / Shutterstock.com

330 Arthur Rothstein / Library of Congress

331 Poe and Medicine Man - Virginia Carpenter; Medicine Lake - Chris M Morris / Flickr / CC BY 2.0

332 Clinton Poe - Virginia Carpenter; Bus - *Rediscover Medicine Lake, Montana* 2010

333 Virginia Carpenter

334 Garnet - STUDIO492 / Shutterstock.com; Opal - Lensation photos / Shutterstock.com; Agate - Nastya22 / Shutterstock.com; Potato Images - B Brown / Shutterstock.com

335 Craters - Aneta Waberska / Shutterstock.com; Falls - Benny Marty / Shutterstock.com

336 Dunes - CSNafzger / Shutterstock.com; Woman - Milton Caldwell Helm / Library of Congress; Boise - George R Laurence Co / Library of Congress

337 Boise - Charles Knowles / Shutterstock.com; Northern lights - GMOutdoorPhotos / Shutterstock.com

338 CSNafzger / Shutterstock.com

339 Bob Pool / Shutterstock.com

340 Sun Valley - CSNafzger / Shutterstock.com; Postcards - Tichnor Brothers Collection, Boston Public Library

341 Sailor - Joe Haupt / Flickr / CC BY-SA 2.0; Festival - Terry Sanders

342 Donna Ellenburg

343 Nickolay Stanev / Shutterstock.com

344 Gary C. Tognoni / Shutterstock.com

345 Mine - Mary Evelyn McCurdy; Jackalope - Gates Frontiers Fund Wyoming Collection within the Carol M. Highsmith Archive, Library of Congress

346 Statue - Nathan Hughes Hamilton / Flickr / CC BY 2.0; Frontier Days - Lincoln Rogers / Shutterstock.com; River - Traveller70 / Shutterstock.com

347 Gary L Jones / Shutterstock.com

348 CD_Photography / Shutterstock.com

349 Lorcel / Shutterstock.com

350 Lorcel / Shutterstock.com

351 Bison - YegoroV / Shutterstock.com; Geyser Peg - Marguerite Lindsley - National Park Service

352 LanaG / Shutterstock.com

353 Ferret - Kerry Hargrove / Shutterstock.com; Conservation Center - Ryan Hagerty, USFWS / Flickr / CC BY 2.0; Mint - Jim Lambert / Shutterstock.com; Penny - T Cassidy / Shutterstock.com; Quarter - Fat Jackey / Shutterstock.com

354 Fort - Zack Frank / Shutterstock.com; Mesa Verde - Doug Meek / Shutterstock.com

355 Ken Lund / Flickr / CC BY-SA 2.0

356 John Hoffman / Shutterstock.com

357 Brown - Denver Public Library; Gold rush - Insomnia Cured Here / Flickr / CC BY-SA 2.0

358 Central City - robertzwinchell / Shutterstock.com; Denver - William Henry Jackson / Library of Congress

359 Morgan Speer

360 Mev McCurdy

361 anthony heflin / Shutterstock.com

362 Maciej Bledowski / Shutterstock.com

363 Mine - YegoroV / Shutterstock.com; Lake - Johnny Adolphson / Shutterstock.com

364 Capitol - f11photo / Shutterstock.com; Ceremony - Yale University Libraries

365 Canyon - Karel Triska / Shutterstock.com; Valley - Lucky-photographer / Shutterstock.com

366 Jerry Susoeff / Shutterstock.com

367 Poster - Library of Congress; Taylor - Zane Taylor

368 rayjunk / Shutterstock.com

369 *The Times-Independent* of Moab, Utah (top); Zane Taylor (bottom)

370 Silver - Vera NewSib / Shutterstock.com; Pine - Will Pedro / Shutterstock.com

371 Mountains - Neil Lockhart / Shutterstock.com; Pronghorn - Tom Reichner / Shutterstock.com

372 Lake Tahoe - topseller / Shutterstock.com; Carson - Naughtonkp / Flickr / CC BY-SA 4.0

373 Elephant Rock - Pierre Leclerc / Shutterstock.com; Dam - Tupungato / Shutterstock.com

374 Altrendo Images / Shutterstock.com

375 Amanda Davitt / Shutterstock.com

376 Barinaga - Basque Museum & Cultural Center; Tree - Neil Lockhart / Shutterstock.com

377 Festival - Ken Lund / Flickr / CC BY-SA 2.0; Sheep - Eric Isselee / Shutterstock.com

378 Donna Ellenburg

379 reisegraf.ch / Shutterstock.com

380 Oak - W. R. Oswald / Wikimedia Commons / CC BY-SA 3.0; Lizard - Kusska / Shutterstock.com

381 Falls - Charles Lemar Brown / Shutterstock.com; Capitol - Frank Romeo / Shutterstock.com

382 Braum's - Ken Wolter / Shutterstock.com; Canyon - Marelbu / Wikimedia Commons / CC BY 3.0

383 Sign - Mike Flippo / Shutterstock.com; Crystals - Cynthia Chotvacs / Shutterstock.com; Plains - Alyssa Stubblefield / Shutterstock.com

384 KylieP / Shutterstock.com

385 Nickel - Daniel D Malone / Shutterstock.com; Ballerina - Everett Collection / Shutterstock.com

386 Osage - George Catlin / Smithsonian American Art Museum; Mural - Charlene Notgrass

387 Statue - Joseph Sohm / Shutterstock.com; Tallchief - Wikimedia Commons

388 Steve Lagreca / Shutterstock.com

389 Dancers - Jeff Schultes / Shutterstock.com; Park - Zack Frank / Shutterstock.com

390 Alamo - Sean Pavone / Shutterstock.com; Capitol - Kushal Bose / Shutterstock.com

391 Stockyards - James Kirkikis / Shutterstock.com; Astronaut Bill Brassard (NBL) / NASA

392 Fotoluminate LLC / Shutterstock.com

393 IVAN KUZKIN / Shutterstock.com

394 Higgins and Lucas - Texas Energy Museum; Drilling - Library of Congress; Geyser - John Trost

395 Lyda Hill Texas Collection of Photographs in Carol M. Highsmith's America Project, Library of Congress

396 Pillow - Donna Ellenburg; Cacti - David ODell / Shutterstock.com

397-398 Donna Ellenburg

399 Anton Foltin / Shutterstock.com

400 Bird - Frank Fichtmueller / Shutterstock.com; Caverns - National Park Service

401 Caverns - Mariusz S. Jurgielewicz / Shutterstock.com; White Sands - sunsinger / Shutterstock.com; Harvest - Joseph Sorrentino / Shutterstock.com

402 Balloons - Kobby Dagan / Shutterstock.com; San Miguel - Andriy Blokhin / Shutterstock.com

403 Bandelier - Traveller70 / Shutterstock.com; Rock - Jon Manjeot / Shutterstock.com

404 yelantsevv / Shutterstock.com

405 Special Collections, USDA National Agricultural Library

406 Mail and DC - Special Collections, USDA National Agricultural Library; Sign - Jason Patrick Ross / Shutterstock.com

407 Joseph Sohm / Shutterstock.com

408 Evelyn D. Harrison / Shutterstock.com

409 Lowell - Lissandra Melo / Shutterstock.com; Boneyard - Mass Communication Specialist 3rd Class Amber Porter / U.S. Navy

410 Statue - Joseph Sohm / Shutterstock.com; Harvest - Berns Images / Shutterstock.com

411 London Bridge - Angel McNall Photography / Shutterstock.com

412 Library of Congress

413 First Mesa - National Park Service; Cradleboard - Barbara Ash / Shutterstock.com; Hopi - William Henry Jackson

414 Canyon - Fernando Tatay / Shutterstock.com; House - Ferenc Cegledi / Shutterstock.com; Nampeyo - National Park Service / Flickr / CC BY 2.0

415 Pottery - Jim Heaphy (Cullen328) / Wikimedia Commons / CC BY-SA 3.0; Nampeyo - Library of Congress

416 Donna Ellenburg

417 Chris Anson / Shutterstock.com

418 Poppy - Sodel Vladyslav / Shutterstock.com; Death Valley - Aperture Exposure Images / Shutterstock.com

419 Tree - Simon Dannhauer / Shutterstock.com; Grapes - Pia Benzer / Shutterstock.com; Yosemite - Mohamed Selim / Shutterstock.com

420 Soldiers - National Park Service; Chip - Tudor Voinea / Shutterstock.com; Apple - Uladzik Kryhin / Shutterstock.com; Dome - Sundry Photography / Shutterstock.com

421 Bear - Rober Couse-Baker / Flickr / CC BY 2.0; Trees - Lucky-photographer / Shutterstock.com

422 Library of Congress

423 Bridge - Lynn Yeh / Shutterstock.com; 1866 - Library of Congress; Modern - PixieMe / Shutterstock.com

424 Mining - Lawrence & Houseworth / Library of Congress; Hallidie - Internet Archive Book Images

425 Daily Travel Photos / Shutterstock.com

426 Beaver - Jay Ondreicka / Shutterstock.com; Trees - Jamie Hooper / Shutterstock.com

427 Lake - Wollertz / Shutterstock.com; Caves - B Norris / Shutterstock.com

428 Statue - Oregon Historical Quarterly; Tillamook - Rob Crandall / Shutterstock.com

429 Falls - Chris Harwood / Shutterstock.com; Center - TFoxFoto / Shutterstock.com

430 Samuel Colman / Smithsonian

431 John Day - Oregon Historical Society; Store - Ipoellet / Wikimedia Commons / CC BY-SA 3.0

432 Oregon Historical Society

433 Allen Woosley

434 Mev McCurdy

435 ArtphotoVideo / Shutterstock.com

436 Orchard - Khadija Ruby / Shutterstock.com;
Spokane - Frank La Roche Photographs, University
of Washington

437 Eruption - U.S. Geological Survey / Flickr; Fog -
Dene' Miles / Shutterstock.com

438 Festival - Bob Pool / Shutterstock.com; Sound
- Johnny Adolphson / Shutterstock.com; Space
Needle - cpaulfell / Shutterstock.com

439 Roman Khomlyak / Shutterstock.com

440 EB Adventure Photography / Shutterstock.com

441 Hammer - Olivier Le Queinec / Shutterstock.com;
Sawmill - Washington State Library / Flickr

442 Foss Waterway Seaport

443 Thye-Wee Gn / Shutterstock.com

444 Cabbage - Patrick Warber Photography; Pumpkins
- Nickolas warner / Shutterstock.com

445 Totem pole - lembi / Shutterstock.com; Arriving in
Juneau - FloridaStock / Shutterstock.com; Juneau -
Real Window Creative / Shutterstock.com

446 Bears - Laura Irlinger / Shutterstock.com; Kenai -
Nikki Gensert / Shutterstock.com; Denali - valiant.
skies / Shutterstock.com

447 Dogsled - Kirk Geisler / Shutterstock.com; Bears -
Hidden Ocean 2005 Expedition-NOAA Office of
Ocean Exploration / Flickr / CC BY 2.0

448 NASA Goddard Space Flight Center / Flickr / CC
BY 2.0

449 ALEUTIANEXPRESS / Wikimedia Commons /
CC BY-SA 4.0

450 Alaska State Library Historical Collection

451 Jimmy S Emerson, DVM

452 grebeshkovmaxim / Shutterstock.com

453 tropicdreams / Shutterstock.com

454 Lei - Mr Doomits / Shutterstock.com; Seal - Eddy
Galeotti / Shutterstock.com

455 Whale - Tyler Gray / Shutterstock.com; Hibiscus
- Videowokart / Shutterstock.com; Dolphin -
NOAA Office of National Marine Sanctuaries /
Flickr; Lava - U.S. Geological Survey / Flickr

456 Beach - Andy Konieczny / Shutterstock.com;
Palace - Richie Chan / Shutterstock.com

457 Pearl Harbor - Ppictures / Shutterstock.com; Coast
- Ingo70 / Shutterstock.com

458 Pacific Southwest Forest Service, USDA / Flickr /
CC BY 2.0

459 Copyright Herbert K. Kane, LLC

460 Papahānaumokuākea Marine National Monument
/ Flickr

461 Burt Lum / Flickr / CC BY 2.0

462 Trunk Bay - emperorcosar / Shutterstock.com

463 Skink - Leslie Ray Ware / Shutterstock.com; Latte -
RaksyBH / Shutterstock.com

464 Fish - Naima Niemand / Shutterstock.com; Base -
Senior Airman Gracie Lee - U.S. Air Force

465 Dr. Matt Kendall / NOAA, NOS, NCCOS,
CCMA, BGB / Flickr / CC BY 2.0

466 Falko Duesterhoeft / Shutterstock.com

467 San Juan - dimostudio / Shutterstock.com;
Sugarcane - Malachi Jacobs / Shutterstock.com

468 Statue - Eric Beato / Flickr / CC BY 2.0; Baseball -
Meng Luen / Shutterstock.com

469 Edgar Zuniga Jr. / Flickr / CC BY 2.0

470 Donna Ellenberg

Index

A

Acadia National Park, 2, 4
Agriculture, 3, 20, 33-35, 43-45, 76, 127-128, 132, 138-139, 148, 152, 156, 164-165, 169-171, 183, 191, 214, 229, 236, 240, 244, 246, 256-261, 263, 271-272, 274, 276, 299, 302, 312, 316-317, 324, 330, 339, 382, 384, 388, 419, 426, 428
Alabama, 172-179, 237, 380
Alamo, 390
Alaska, 101, 337, 388, 435, 444-451, 455
Albany, New York, 56-57
American Samoa, 464-465
Annapolis, Maryland, 92, 94
Arches National Park, 361-362, 368-369
Arizona, 21, 355, 373, 399, 403, 408-415
Arkansas, 190-197, 282, 382
Arlington National Cemetery, 112
Armstrong, Neil, 149, 229
Ashfall Fossil Beds State Historical Park, 298, 301
Assateague Island, 92-93
Atlanta, Georgia, 137, 164, 166, 171
Augusta, Maine, 2, 5
Austin, Texas, 388, 390
Avenue of the Giants, 418, 421

B

Badlands National Park, 308-309
Bandelier National Monument, 400, 403
Bannack State Park, 326, 328
Barinaga, Pete, 375-377
Bartlett, E. M. (Eugene Monroe), 194-197
Baton Rouge, Louisiana, 200, 202
Benson, Benny, 449-451

Bent's Old Fort National Historic Site, 352, 354
Big Bend National Park, 379, 388-389
Bismarck, North Dakota, 316, 318
Boise, Idaho, 334, 336-337
Boston, Massachusetts, 28-29, 44
Braum's, 381
Brown, Clara, 357-359
Bryce Canyon National Park, 362, 365
Buchanan, Dean, 223-225

C

Cabot Creamery, 20
Cadillac Ranch, 388
California, 101, 365, 372-373, 376, 382-383, 386, 388, 411, 418-425, 454
Cape Cod, 28, 31
Cape May, 78-81
Carlsbad Caverns National Monument, 400-401
Carson City, Nevada, 370, 372
Carson, Kit, 372
Carter family, 137, 140
Charleston, South Carolina, 154, 156
Charleston, West Virginia, 118, 120
Chesapeake Bay, 92-93, 95
Cheyenne (tribe), 344, 354, 372
Cheyenne, Wyoming, 344, 346
Civil War, 69-71, 83, 94, 102, 107, 112, 118, 124, 142, 159, 168, 184, 205, 236-237, 358, 420
Colorado River, 370, 373, 408, 410, 414
Colorado, 200, 343, 352-359
Columbia River, 426, 428-429
Columbia, South Carolina, 154-155
Columbia, Tennessee, 136,138
Columbus, Christopher, 100, 462

Columbus, Ohio, 226, 228
Concord, New Hampshire, 10, 12
Congaree National Park, 154-155
Connecticut, 37, 46-54
Crater of Diamonds State Park, 190, 193
Craters of the Moon National Monument, 335
Cumberland Falls, 128, 131
Cuyahoga Valley National Park, 226, 228

D

Daise, Ron, 158-161
Danbury Quarry, 22
Death Valley National Park, 418
Delaware Bay, 74-75, 82
Delaware River, 75
Delaware, 75, 82-90, 101
Denali National Park, 444, 446
Denver Mint, 353
Denver, Colorado, 352-353, 358-359
Des Moines, Iowa, 272-273
Dinosaur National Monument, 362
Dinosaur State Park, 46, 48
Dismals Canyon, 172
Dover, Delaware, 82, 84-85
Dr. Seuss, 29
Du Pont, E. I., 84

E

Elephant Rocks State Park, 280-281
Everglades National Park, 208, 210

F

Fireflies, 136
Fisk Jubilee Singers, 142-143
Florida, 157, 175, 208-216, 469
Fort Worth Stockyards, 390-391
Foss, Thea, 441-443
Four Corners, 352, 355
Frankfort, Kentucky, 128-129

G

Gateway Arch, 281
Georgia, 113, 157, 163-171
Glacier National Park, 325-326, 329
Golden Spike National Historic Site, 364, 366
Goo Goo Clusters, 138
Great Allegheny Passage, 64-65
Great Basin National Park, 370-371
Great Salt Lake, 362-363
Great Smoky Mountains National Park, 136
Green Giant Company, 269
Guam, 464
Gullah Geechee Culture, 157-162

H

Hallidie, Andrew, 423-425
Hallmark, 285-287
Harrisburg, Pennsylvania, 64, 66
Harrison, Benjamin, 79-81
Hartford, Arkansas, 190, 194-196
Hartford, Connecticut, 37, 46, 48-49
Hawaii, 453-461, 470
Helena, Montana, 326, 329
Hershey Company, 66
Higgins, Pattillo, 393-395
Honolulu, Hawaii, 454, 456
Hoover Dam, 370, 373
Hopi, 408, 413-415
Horseshoe crabs, 75

I

Idaho Panhandle National Forest, 334, 337
Idaho, 334-342, 348-349, 376, 436
Illinois, 244-251, 383
Immigrants/Immigration, 43, 56, 100, 152-
    153, 162, 212, 257, 274, 313, 328, 375-
    377, 431-433, 438, 441-443
Independence Hall, 67
Indian Cave State Park, 298
Indiana, 21, 235-243

Indianapolis, Indiana, 236-238
International Peace Garden, 316, 319
Iowa, 45, 271-279, 288, 359
Isle Royale National Park, 218-219

J

Jackson Hole, Wyoming, 344, 347
Jackson, Andrew, 81, 141
Jackson, Mississippi, 182-183
Jaggi, Casper, 259-261
Jamestown, Virginia, 110
Jefferson City, Missouri, 280, 283
Jefferson, Thomas, 67, 91, 111, 117, 310
Johnson Space Center, 391
Jumper, Betty, 213-215
Juneau, Alaska, 444-445, 450

K

Kam Wah Chung State Heritage Site, 431-433
Kansas, 290-297, 321, 382, 392
Kenai Fjords National Park, 444, 446
Kennedy Space Center, 208, 210
Kentucky Fried Chicken, 130
Kentucky, 127-135, 144, 357
Knife River Indian Villages, 316, 318
Korean War, 103

L

Lake Erie, 56, 64, 218, 226
Lake Huron, 218-219
Lake Michigan, 218, 220, 222, 236-237, 244, 246, 254, 256
Lake Ontario, 56
Lake Placid, New York, 56, 58
Lake Superior, 218-219, 254, 262, 264
Lansing, Michigan, 218, 221
Lighthouses, 7-9, 40, 42, 76, 149, 187-189, 203, 217, 226, 234, 262, 264
Lincoln National Forest, 400, 404

Lincoln, Abraham, 57, 102, 107, 142, 247, 310
Lincoln, Nebraska, 298-299
Lindsley, Marguerite, 349-351
Little Rock, Arkansas, 190, 192
London Bridge, 410-411
Long Island Sound, 46
Louisiana, 199-207, 393-394
Lowell Observatory, 409

M

Madison, Wisconsin, 254-255
Maine, 1-9, 18, 113
Manatee Springs State Park, 210
Maquoketa Caves State Park, 272, 274
Maryland, 92-100, 187
Massachusetts, 28-35, 402
Mayo, William, 268-269
McCurdy, Georgia, 223-225
McIlhenny family, 205-207
Menhaden (fish), 82
Mesa Verde National Park, 352, 354-355
Michigan, 217-225
Minnesota, 140, 262-269, 320-321, 329, 441
Mississippi River, 129-130, 136, 139, 182-184, 200, 202, 229, 244, 262-263, 280-281
Mississippi, 105, 181-189
Missouri River, 298, 318, 326-327
Missouri, 190, 280-287, 382, 402
Montana, 101, 325-333, 349, 436
Montgomery, Alabama, 172, 174
Montpelier, Vermont, 20-21
Morris, Esther Hobart, 346
Mount Rushmore, 308, 310
Mount Sunflower, 293
Mount Washington, 10, 13, 15-17
Mt. Olive Pickle Company, 152-153
Multnomah Falls, 426, 429
Mushroom Rock State Park, 292-293

N

Nampeyo, 413-415
Narragansett Bay, 38, 40
Nashville, Tennessee, 136-138, 141-143
National Mall, 100-103
Natural Bridge (Virginia), 110, 115-117
Nebraska, 289, 298-305
Nevada, 370-377
New Hampshire, 10-17
New Jersey, 73-83, 87
New Mexico, 355, 400-407
New York (state), 22, 46, 51, 55-63, 74, 131, 375, 413
New York City, 56-57, 137, 152, 238, 375
Niagara Falls, 56, 59, 61-63
North Carolina, 136, 146-153, 157, 214
North Dakota, 101, 308, 316-323
Northern Lights, 337
Northern Mariana Islands, 463-464
Nāpali Coast State Wilderness Park, 454, 457

O

Ohio River, 65, 118, 120, 226, 229, 244
Ohio, 142, 226-233
Oklahoma City, Oklahoma, 380-381, 384
Oklahoma, 166, 197, 214, 282, 380-387, 392
Olympia, Washington, 436, 438
Olympic National Park, 436, 439
Oregon Trail, 335-336
Oregon, 302, 417, 426-433, 439, 449
Outer Banks, 146, 149

P

Pearl Harbor, 454, 456
Pennsylvania, 64-71, 74, 84, 303, 350
Pepsi, 148
Phoenix, Arizona, 408, 410
Pierre, South Dakota, 308-309
Polynesian Voyaging Society, 459-461
Potomac River, 92, 95, 97-102, 112

Providence, Rhode Island, 38, 40, 44
Puerto Rico, 466-469

R

Raleigh, North Carolina, 146-147, 149
Raleigh, Walter, 149
Reagan, Ronald, 178-179
Rehoboth Beach, 87-89
Revolutionary War, 100, 265
Rhode Island Reds, 43-45
Rhode Island, 38-45
Richmond, Virginia, 110-111
Ricketts, Robert Bruce, 69-71
Roosevelt, Franklin, 105
Roosevelt, Theodore, 66, 310, 319, 106

S

Sacramento River, 422
Sacramento, California, 418, 420-422
Salem, Oregon, 426, 428
Salt Lake City, Utah, 362, 364
Salt water taffy, 77
Santa Fe, New Mexico, 400, 402, 405
Savannah, Georgia, 164
Seminole (tribe), 213-215, 387
Seneca Rocks, 118-119
Sequoia and Kings Canyon National Park, 418-419
Sheldon National Wildlife Refuge, 370-371
Shenandoah National Park, 110, 113
Sleeping Giant State Park, 46-47
Smith Island, 92, 94
South Carolina, 145, 154-161, 164, 169
South Dakota, 101, 307-315
Springfield, Illinois, 244, 247
Springfield, Massachusetts, 28-29, 32
St. Helena Island, South Carolina, 154, 158-161
St. Paul, Minnesota, 262
Statue of Liberty, 56
Strataca Underground Salt Museum, 292

T

TABASCO Sauce, 205-206
Tall Chief family, 385-387
Tallahassee, Florida, 208-209
Tallgrass Prairie National Preserve, 290-291
Taylor, Loren "Bish", 367-369
Tennessee River, 172-173
Tennessee, 130, 136-143, 152
Texas, 205-206, 348, 379, 382, 384, 388-395, 404
Theodore Roosevelt National Park, 316, 319
Thousand Islands / Thousand Island Dressing, 56, 58
Tiger family, 213-215
Tillamook Cheese, 428
Topeka, Kansas, 290-291
Totem Heritage Center, 445
Trenton, New Jersey, 74, 76
Tubman, Harriett, 96

U

U.S. Capitol, 100-101, 192
U.S. Space and Rocket Center, 173
Utah, 355, 361-369, 403

V

Valley of Fire State Park, 370, 373
Vermont, 19-27, 101
Vietnam War, 103
Virgin Islands, 462
Virginia, 92-93, 95, 97, 100, 107, 110-118, 124, 149, 381

W

Walton, Sam, 190-191
Washington (state), 436-443
Washington, D.C., 67, 79, 91, 95, 100-107, 112, 177-178, 192, 206, 238, 281, 405-406
Washington, George, 57, 117, 310
West Virginia, 109, 118-126
White House, 100-101, 105-107, 139, 178
White Sands National Park, 400-401
Williams, Roger, 38, 40
Williamsburg, Virginia, 110
Wisconsin, 253-261
Wood, Grant, 275
World War I, 106, 177, 381, 391
World War II, 95, 102, 119, 177-179, 185, 223, 304-305, 341, 456-457, 463
Wright Brothers, 229, 335, 451
Wyoming, 101, 344-352

Y

Yellowstone National Park, 344, 349-351
Yosemite National Park, 418-420

Also Available from Notgrass History

Experience the story of America as you learn about everyday people and the lives they lived. Hear their poems and songs, learn their dances and games, see pictures of them and their treasures. Meet the famous and not-so-famous Americans who shaped our country and created our story. Designed for children in grades 1-4, *Our Star-Spangled Story* is a one year U.S. history course. It features simple lessons with easy-to-follow instructions, full-color photographs and illustrations, and engaging supplemental activities. Journey into these pages to experience real-life American history! Visit notgrass.com to learn more.

Also Available from Notgrass History

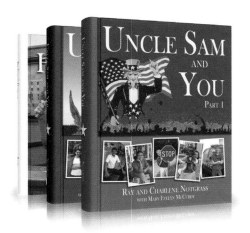

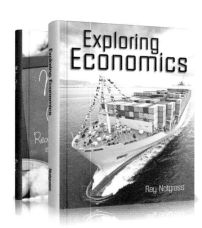

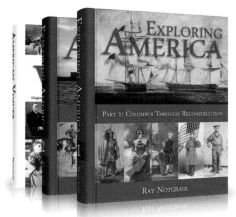

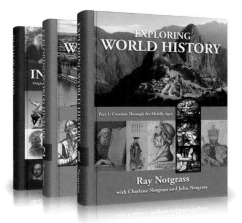

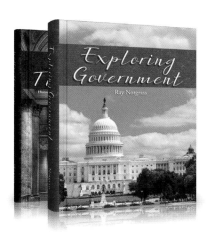

Visit notgrass.com to learn about these and other resources
for middle school and high school.

NOTGRASS
HISTORY

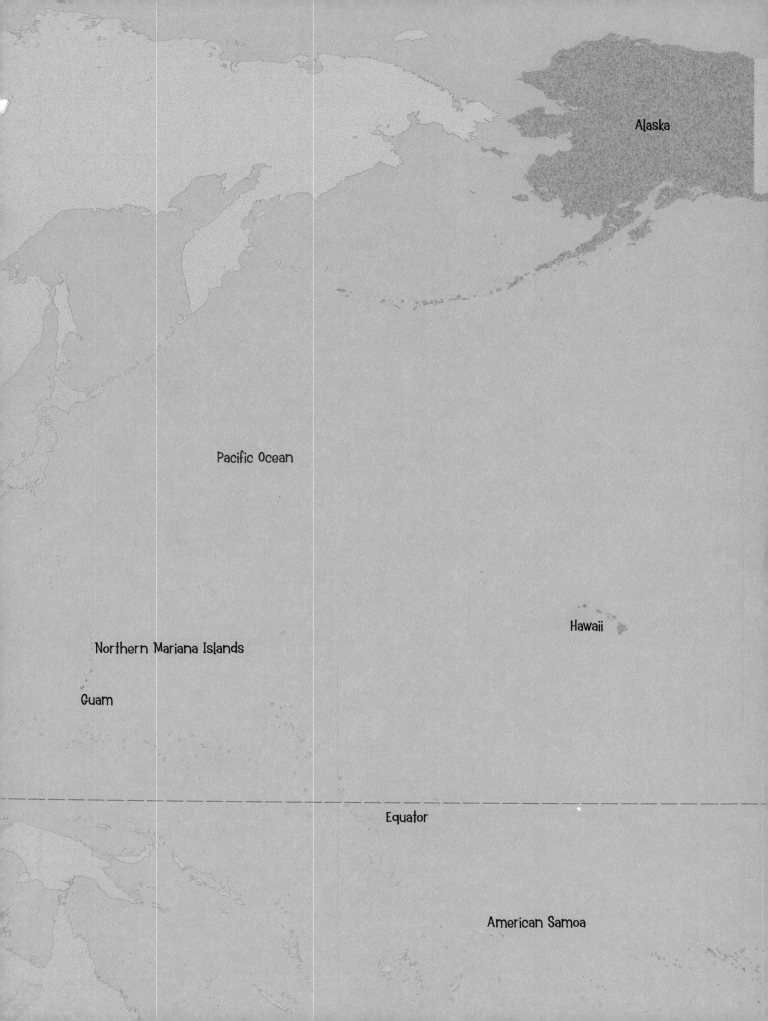